3

Women's Writing on the First World War

WOMEN'S WRITING
ON THE
FIRST WORLD WAR

Edited by
AGNÈS CARDINAL, DOROTHY GOLDMAN,
AND JUDITH HATTAWAY

OXFORD
UNIVERSITY PRESS

OXFORD

UNIVERSITY PRESS

Great Clarendon Street, Oxford OX2 6DP

Oxford University Press is a department of the University of Oxford.
It furthers the University's objective of excellence in research, scholarship,
and education by publishing worldwide in

Oxford New York

Athens Auckland Bangkok Bogotá Buenos Aires Calcutta
Cape Town Chennai Dar es Salaam Delhi Florence Hong Kong Istanbul
Karachi Kuala Lumpur Madrid Melbourne Mexico City Mumbai
Nairobi Paris São Paulo Singapore Taipei Tokyo Toronto Warsaw

and associated companies in Berlin Ibadan

Oxford is a registered trade mark of Oxford University Press
in the UK and certain other countries

Published in the United States
by Oxford University Press Inc., New York

British Library Cataloguing in Publication Data

Data available

Library of Congress Cataloging in Publication Data
Women's writing on the First World War / edited by Agnès Cardinal,
Dorothy Goldman, and Judith Hattaway.
1. World War, 1914–1918 Literary collections. 2. World War,
1914–1918—Women Literary collections. 3. Literature, Modern—20th
century. 4. Literature—Women authors. I. Cardinal, Agnès.
II. Goldman, Dorothy. III. Hattaway, Judith.
PN6071.E8W66 1999
808.8'0358—dc21 99–15282

ISBN 0–19–812280–2

1 3 5 7 9 10 8 6 4 2

Typeset in Bulmer
by Joyvee, Trivandrum, India
Printed in Great Britain
on acid-free paper by
Biddles Ltd.,
Guildford and King's Lynn

Acknowledgements

We are grateful to the many people who have helped us with suggestions
and advice during our compilation of this anthology. We would particularly
like to thank Marie Askham, Margaret Anderson, Mary Calthrop, Roger
Cardinal, Laura Dal Molin, Ruth and Rosmarie Meyer, John Norman,
Catherine O'Brien, Jerzy Strzetelski, Barbara Strzylewska, Claire Tylee,
Jenny Uglow. The staff of the London Library and the British Library
Reading Room offered invaluable help in finding biographical details of the
authors included.

We are indebted to the copyright holders for permission to reprint the
following:

Margot Asquith, from *The Autobiography of Margot Asquith*, reprinted by
permission of Eyre & Spottiswoode, publishers.

Enid Bagnold, *A Diary Without Dates*, reprinted by permission of William
Heinemann, publishers.

Vera Brittain, from *Testament of Youth*, reprinted by permission of Paul
Berry, her literary executor, and the Virago Press.

Mary Butts, 'Speed the Plough' from *With and Without Buttons*, reprinted
by permission of Camilla Bagg, daughter of Mary Butts.

Dorothy Canfield, 'La Pharmacienne' from *Home Fires in France*,
reprinted by permission of Henry Holt & Co, Inc.

Colette, three extracts from *Les heures longues,* Copyright Librairie
Arthème Fayard, 1917.

H.D. (Hilda Doolittle) *Asphodel* pp. 107–19, reprinted by permission from
Duke University Press, Copyright 1992.

Claire Goll, 'Die Wachshand' from *Der Gläserne Garten, Prosa von
1917–1939*, edited by Barbara Glauert-Hesse for the Fondation Yvan et
Claire Goll, Saint-Dié-des Voges. With permission from Wallstein
Verlag GmbH, D-37073 Göttingen. Copyright 1989 Argon Verlag
GmbH, Berlin.

Maude Gonne, from *The Gonne–Yeats 1893–1938*, ed. A. MacBride and A. Norman Jeffares. Reproduced by permission of A. M. Heath & Co., Ltd. on behalf of Anna MacBride White.

Augusta, Lady Gregory, from *Seventy Years,* reprinted with permission from The Lady Gregory Estate, Copyright 1994.

Radclyffe Hall, 'Fräulein Schwartz' and 'Miss Ogilvy Finds Herself', reprinted with permission from Copyright The Estate of Radclyffe Hall.

Constance Holme, 'Speeding Up, 1917' from *The Wisdom of the Simple and Other Stories* (World's Classics, 1937), reprinted by permission of Oxford University Press.

Sheila Kaye-Smith, from *Three Ways Home* (Cassell, 1937), reprinted with permission from Mrs B. M. Walthew, niece of Sheila Kaye-Smith.

Käthe Kollwitz, from *Tagebuchblätter und Briefe,* ed. Hans Kollwitz, reprinted with permission from Prof. Dr. Arne A. Kollwitz.

Berta Lask, 'Frauen gegen den Krieg', reprinted with permission from Professor Gisela Brinker-Gabler.

Ellen La Motte, 'A Belgian Civilian' and 'Women and Wives' from *The Backwash of War: the Human Wreckage of the Battlefield as Witnessed by an American Hospital Nurse,* reprinted with permission from G. P. Putnam's Sons, publishers.

Vernon Lee, from *Supernatural Tales,* reprinted with permission from Peter Owen, publishers.

Jo Mihaly, 'War Diary' from . . . *da gibt's ein Wiedersehn!* Reprinted with the permission of Frau Anja Ott, Schillerstr. 8, D-83209 Prien.

Katherine Mansfield, 'An Indiscreet Journey' from *The Short Stories of Katherine Mansfield,* Copyright 1924 by Alfred A. Knopf Inc and renewed 1952 by John Middleton Murry. Reprinted by permission of the publishers.

Zofia Nalkowska, 'Hrabia Emil', reprinted with permission from Irena Wroblewska-Kovsak, Warsaw.

E. Sylvia Pankhurst, 'Christmas 1914', from *The Home Front,* reprinted with permission from Professor Richard Pankhurst.

May Sinclair, from *A Journal of Impressions in Belgium,* reprinted by permission of Curtis Brown Ltd., London, on behalf of the Estate of May Sinclair, Copyright May Sinclair.

Helen Zenna Smith, from *Not So Quiet.* . . . Copyright Helen Zenna Smith.

Gertrude Stein, from *The Autobiography of Alice B. Toklas,* reprinted with permission of David Higham Associates, London.

Adrienne Thomas, from *Die Katrin wird Soldat,* Copyright 1989 Wilhelm Goldmann Verlag, München.

Helen Thomas, from *As It Was* (London, Faber and Faber), reprinted with permission of Myfanwy Thomas.

——*Time and Again*, reprinted with permission of Carcanet Press Ltd.

Sylvia Townsend Warner, 'My Mother Won the War' from *Scenes of Childhood*, reprinted by permission of Chatto & Windus, publishers, and the executors of the Sylvia Townsend Warner estate.

Antonia White, 'Surprise Visit' from *Strangers* (Virago Press), reprinted with permission from Little, Brown and Company (UK), London.

Rebecca West, 'The Cordite Makers' from *The Young Rebecca: Writings of Rebecca West*, reprinted with permission from the Peters Fraser & Dunlop Group Ltd.

Edith Wharton, 'Writing a War Story' from *The Collected Short Stories of Edith Wharton*, II, ed. R. W. B. Lewis (New York: Charles Scribner's Sons, 1969. Reprinted with permission of Scribner, a division of Simon & Schuster).

Virginia Woolf, from *The Diary of Virginia Woolf II: 1920–24*, reprinted with permission from the executors of the Virginia Woolf Estate and the Hogarth Press (publishers).

——*The Shooting Party*, reprinted with permission from the Society of Authors as the literary representative of the Estate of Virginia Woolf.

Although every effort has been made to secure permission prior to publication this has not been possible in some instances. If notified, the publisher will rectify any errors or omissions at the earliest opportunity.

Contents

PART III. THE WAR COMES HOME   121

Introduction

THE First World War inspired an outpouring of writing—both from Europe and from across the western world. The conflict has established itself in collective memory: in the eighty years since the armistice the long-term significance of the war has taken shape and the written records of the war have become part of the political and literary histories of the century. For much of this time the tradition of war writing was seen as belonging to men: but for many women also the war was the catalyst for creating a unique perspective and for developing a public voice. This anthology bears witness to the variety and scope of women's writing, and to the ways in which the war gave women of diverse conditions an opportunity to develop new means of self-expression. As a consequence, it asks us to reconsider what we should understand by 'war writing'. Unmediated reportage and narratives of scenes of war, central though they are to this corpus, constitute only one of its aspects. Some of the texts included here negotiate the actuality of war in modes other than simple realism and through experiments in style and form. It is through this range of writing that we can begin to recognize the significance of the First World War both for the modernist idiom and for the new developments in women's writing this century.

Above all, this anthology testifies to the variety of ways in which women on both sides participated in the conflict. Part of the significance of women's writing on the war lies in charting the new social roles which they found—a topic which has been explored thoroughly and is relatively well known.[1] Certainly, any anthology which omitted the literary realization of the experience of nursing, for example, would be justly criticized as incomplete. Of equal importance, however, are the accounts of women's struggle on the home front, their experiences of becoming autonomous, running a house or leaving it to do paid work, managing money, driving cars or

---

[1] For example, Arthur Marwick, *The Deluge: British Society and the First World War* (London: Macmillan, 1965); Françoise Thébaud, *La Femme au temps de la guerre de 14* (Paris: Éditions Stock, 1986).

travelling abroad to visit the front. The selection also reveals the ways in
which women took up positions in relation to the war. Predictably there is
great diversity: the ironic perspectives created in Marcelle Capy's 'The War
Got Him' or Rebecca West's 'The Cordite Makers'; direct commentary on
war's brutalizations in the pieces by Claire Goll, Vera Brittain, and Berta
Lask; the studied detachment that Virginia Woolf constructs when she
contemplates, for her diary, the political impact of peace. The anthology
has omitted, deliberately, to represent directly two important political
dimensions of the women's war: the international women's peace movement of the 1920s and the achievements of the suffragettes in Britain.[2] We
have, furthermore, made the conscious decision not to include those texts
of the 1930s in which the First World War figures against the backdrop of an
imminent further conflict.

The texts in this volume focus on the specific ways in which women saw
and narrated the war; they reveal the difference between women's experience and that of men and combatants; they illuminate their different perspectives on common experiences. What impresses is the commitment
with which women recorded their experience, painful or otherwise, their
self-awareness and confidence in being alert chroniclers of their part in the
conflict. Therefore narratives relating the excitement and exhilaration of
war are as indicative as those which speak of loneliness, anguish, and
bereavement.

Many pieces in the anthology are essentially reportage, either in its conventional form of diaries and journalism or in its subsequent mutations into
fiction. The intrinsic value of such writing lies in its immediacy and vivid-
ness and in the fact that it has the authoritativeness of the eyewitness. For
example, the diaries of May Sinclair, Margot Asquith, or some of Colette's
journalism, offer accounts of the war which can be dated precisely—day,
month, year. They are on-the-spot pieces, both in their awareness of time
and in the way that the writer's eye has been caught by detail. Writing like
this is not necessarily concerned with happenings of national importance
such as, for example, Louise Weiss's record of the moment of Armistice in
1918. Characteristic of women's reportage is the 'dailiness' which marks
their records, whether of life on the home front, in Mildred Aldrich's
village in occupied France, or the home economist's tale of the tragedy of

---

[2] The former has been well documented by, for example, Sybil Oldfield in *Women
Against the Iron Fist: Alternatives to Militarism, 1900–1989* (Oxford: Basil Blackwell, 1989);
Gisela Brinker-Gabler (ed.), *Frauen gegen den Krieg* (Frankfurt-on-Main: Fischer 2048,
1980).

melted butter:[3] writing which is aptly described as 'history deprived of generalisations'.[4]

Other pieces offer an unvarnished picture of attitudes at the time. Sylvia Pankhurst, for example, records conversations with working-class women in Scarborough after the 1914 bombardment and records first-hand that 'other home front [which] ran through the dingy terraces of working-class Britain':[5]

> People could not sleep now; many would not even go to bed. Everyone had a bundle made up in readiness for flight; but how little one could carry in a bundle! One could not afford to move one's home; and one's living was here in Scarborough. A widow she knew had her boarding house, her only means of livelihood, completely smashed and shattered. When would it be rebuilt? She shook her head. I asked her what was being done to relieve distress. Not much, she thought, and laughed ironically. They only think of asking women to knit socks for soldiers![6]

However, immediacy of reportage need not imply a naïve observer. Pankhurst here writes out of the experience of her pre-war years in the suffrage movement, her feminist solidarity, and her realization that the human costs of the war would be born unequally. The writing is at the same time immediate and self-aware: that 'Experience simulating Innocence' which makes for good reportage.[7]

For many women writers, on-the-spot experience, journals, and journalism were only the prelude to later, more sustained and reflective accounts. Like men, women assimilated and then reconstructed their experiences. Helen Zenna Smith's *Not So Quiet . . .* (1930), for example, exists both as a response to Remarque's *All Quiet on the Western Front* (1929) and also as a reconstruction, as fiction, of the lost diaries of a woman ambulance driver.[8] A decade after the war's end, the urge to revisit the war and to commemorate it in writing emerges in the work of both men and women and in the increasingly self-conscious literary and political uses made of the conflict. Women's accounts of the war which arise from the 1920s and later, were written with an awareness of the variety of stories to be told and the

---

[3] Dorothy Peel, 'Housekeeping in War Time', from *How We Lived Then, 1914–1918* (London: John Lane, 1929), 92.

[4] John Carey (ed.), *The Faber Book of Reportage* (London: Faber, 1987), p. xxxii.

[5] E. Sylvia Pankhurst, *The Home Front* (London: Hutchinson, 1987), p. xi.

[6] Ibid. 115–16.

[7] Carey (ed.), *The Faber Book of Reportage*, p. xxxiv.

[8] Helen Zenna Smith, *Not So Quiet . . . Stepdaughters of War* (London: Virago, 1988), introd. Barbara Hardy, 7.

knowledge that women writers were now contributing to the emergence of new literary and political sisterhoods.

For today's reader such 'second-wave' writing must have a different status and a different claim to value, not merely because it is often more overtly critical of the conflict. It raises issues, already familiar to feminist literary critique, of intertextuality and the problem of value. We might question, for example, the extent to which the interest and the merit of Smith's *Not So Quiet . . .* rests on its relationship to Remarque's novel, or whether it is appropriate to value Claire Goll's story 'The Wax Hand' as an example of German literary Expressionism. However, some of the texts in this anthology have merit quite simply because of the interesting and unusual ideas they develop and others are crucial as social and historical testimonies. All of them are important because they relate the war as an essentially female experience. In this they offer not only a complement to men's narratives of war but also a perspective which corrects and reshapes our understanding of war writing as a whole.

The notion that war is man's affair has been supported and reinforced by a literature of war which, traditionally, arises almost exclusively out of men's experiences. In this respect the First World War has been no exception. For example, in his definitive study on the memory and cultural influence of the war, Paul Fussell confirmed the soldier's experience in the trenches as central to the cultural development of our century.[9] Indeed, our understanding of the war has continued to be shaped by myths and images which have their origin in the poems, letters, and early jottings at the Western Front of a group of well-known soldiers such as Brooke, Sassoon, Graves, Apollinaire, Barbusse, Jünger or Trakl—young men who were able to transmute their sense of outrage into written form. Those who survived would, for the rest of their lives, continue to revisit, remember, reiterate, and assimilate that first raw confrontation with the actuality of war. In *The Penguin Book of First World War Prose* Jon Silkin echoes Fussell's observation when he writes of the 'energy and fascination each writer found in continually re-telling his story'.[10]

As part of the same process, the memory of war has acquired its distinctive imagery. Poppies and barbed wire, bayonets and figures caked in mud,

---

[9] Paul Fussell, *The Great War and Modern Memory* (London: Oxford University Press, 1975), chs. 2, 3, 4.

[10] J. Silkin and J. Glover (eds.), *The Penguin Book of First World War Prose* (Harmondsworth: Penguin, 1990), 13. Both critics (Silkin especially) are, however, careful to indicate the breadth and diversity of the writing, and the frequent conflicts and ambiguities within it.

trenches and vistas of the beauty of the dawn, are now firmly established as archetypal images of the First World War. Added to these comes an entire set of social and ideological perceptions: the recognition of the ineptitude of the General Staff; the civilians' inability to understand the soldier's experiences; the emergence of a new egalitarianism between the classes, as well as football games between enemy lines and intimations of homoeroticism—all of these have grasped the collective imagination as being determining for that 'lost generation', which belongs to a European history now turned mythology. Out of this obsession with the images and myths of the Great War our remembrance and its attendant literary canon has grown. It has been further confirmed and consolidated by critical accounts of the literature of the war and by reappraisal of the ways in which its dominant cultural values were created.[11] Few of these scholarly works, excellent though they are, have much to say on women's experience or on women's writing on the war.

In this context it may not be surprising that women writers were thought to have little to contribute to a set of predominantly masculine myths.[12] The male canon, while not directly inimical to women's writing about the war, often seems oblivious of its existence, let alone its claims to significance. Nevertheless some women's work has remained well known: Brittain's *Testament of Youth*, which recounts both what women lost in the war and their vicarious experience of the conflict, and Rebecca West's *The Return of the Soldier*, one of the first explorations of the effects of shell-shock on a soldier's family, are both works which have achieved something of the status of classics amongst women's war narratives. It is probable that readers have continued to find these works interesting as much for their depiction of women's roles as for their literary quality. However, in the last decade or so, the significance of such narratives of women's experience of the war has been revived both by academic work which has retrieved much forgotten or neglected writing by women and by the work of feminist historians and critics who have identified different contexts for it. Some early feminist work—for example Sandra Gilbert's ground-breaking essay 'Soldier's Heart'—may now in turn appear partial in its emphasis on confrontational

[11] For example, Bernard Bergonzi, in *Heroes' Twilight* (London: Constable, 1965), examines the changing ideas of the 'heroic' in and during the war years.

[12] In their recent anthology, *The Penguin Book of First World War Prose*, Silkin and Glover favour a more eclectic approach. Yet, even here, out of the eighty or so writers included only twelve are women, and the editors perpetuate women's marginalization by their narrow interpretation of a criterion for inclusion: nearly all of the authors they selected 'participated in the war in some way'.

gender politics. More recent feminist work has taken a less sharply opposi-tional position in, for example, its explorations of the complexity and moral ambiguity of women's responses to war or in the diverse accounts it has given of the ways in which women experienced the war, created their own cultural myths, and, during and after the conflict, assumed new roles in the national culture.[13]

This anthology does not seek to confirm, or deny, any of these critical positions. It attempts rather to reveal the range of different positions and voices—from the innocent to the complicit and their gradual politiciza-tion—which women writers adopted. Our selection strives to make avail-able to the reader a broad spectrum of writing which shows the concerns of women at the time and their particular ways of expressing them. Women participated in the war; felt its overwhelming impact on their lives; pro-duced their own literary representations of it—in short, they defined their own history. The diversity of their writing reveals, moreover, some unex-pected parallels and kinships. One of the rewards of compiling this anthol-ogy has been the discovery of the ways in which the war contextualizes writing which is, in different ways, essentially popular or 'of the moment'—Phyllis Campbell and Fanny Kemble Johnson, for example—with the pre-occupations and stylistic innovations of a developing modernism.

But women entered into the war with few literary models which were specific to their experience. Nor did they share the stock of motifs—literary or mythological—on which men drew when giving shape to their war experience. One way that women's writing signals this difference was through their own, unmediated perceptions of the sheer incongruity of the war, either in the way it erupted on to the home front or in the startling coex-istence of civilian and military regimes when they were in the war zone: 'we dined early in fur coats, skirts and shirts and all went to bed at 9.15 after an interesting general conversation upon the war and various other topics', Margot Asquith notes, reporting the arrangements for dining during her visit to Belgium in the winter of 1914. In parallel fashion they noted the remnants of pre-war life surviving into the conflict: May Sinclair remembers packing her commanding officer's copy of Freud during the fall of Ghent in 1914.[14]

Some writing extends the motif of the incongruous into a more sustained piece of notation, one which is capable of exploring the way that war changed houses, towns, and landscapes—the entire pre-war way of life.

---

[13] e.g. works by Elshtain; Tylee; Ouditt (see Bibliography).
[14] May Sinclair, *A Journal of Impressions in Belgium* (London: Hutchinson, 1915), 267.

Dorothy Canfield's 'La Pharmacienne', for example, uses the list of objects which constituted the 'past inventory' of her heroine's house—mahogany beds, copper cooking utensils, two hundred and twenty linen sheets—as a device to measure both the war's destructiveness and its potential for transforming the bourgeois past into a new order. Rebecca West inverts the motif when she notes that the regime in the munitions factory was strangely domestic—'it might be the precaution of a pernickety housewife concerned about her floors'.[15] Such writing, of course, also bears eloquent testimony to the way in which most women actually experienced the war, in roles which allowed them an acuity of observation which was inseparable from the sense of powerlessness of the onlooker confined to the edge of the conflict.

Recognition that these displacement devices might herald new modes of writing came slowly and patchily. Some writers registered the shift simply by reworking familiar genres such as the versions of the pastoral—some nostalgic, some ironic—found in Liesbeth Dill's 'Political Porcelain', Helen Thomas's *As It Was*, Mary Butts's 'Speed the Plough', or Mrs Henry Dudeney's 'Missing'. However Virginia Woolf is arguably more alert to the general issue than most other writers when she writes that her generation is doomed to partial vision: 'fragments—paragraphs—a page perhaps: but no more'.[16] If writers of the post-war generation could only register the shifts in perspective, 'a glimpse of a nose, a shoulder, something turning away, always in movement',[17] this was doubly true for those who tried to write about the war as it happened.

The section entitled 'Writing the War' represents the growth of reflective and self-conscious writing about the conflict. It demonstrates the different ways that women writers met the challenge of representing the war from where they stood, in trying to catch that which, during the next war, Elizabeth Bowen described as the 'flying particles of something enormous and inchoate'.[18] Snatching that experience was a survival mechanism in itself, just as, in Bowen's words, the survivors of the Blitz 'went to infinite lengths to assemble bits of themselves—broken ornaments, odd shoes, torn scraps of the curtains that has hung in a room—from the wreckage'.[19] But it

[15] Rebecca West, *The Young Rebecca: Writings of Rebecca West, 1911–1917*, ed. J. Marcus (London: Virago, 1983), 381.

[16] Virginia Woolf, *The Letters of Virginia Woolf, 1912–1922*, ed. Nigel Nicolson (London: Hogarth Press, 1916), 598.

[17] Ibid.

[18] Elizabeth Bowen, *The Demon Lover and Other Stories* (Harmondsworth: Penguin, 1966), 196.

[19] Ibid. 199.

also represents the attempts to reconstruct, out of the conflict, a new kind of identity and, with this, prototypes of expression which became seminal for women's writing this century. And this too has influenced our choice: 'Writing the War' illustrates how women contributed to those shifts in perception which contributed to both Expressionism and Modernism. At the same time, it is the special function of the later sections in this anthology to convey the sense of emergent ideas, changing modes of writing, and the process of revision and retrospection which had already commenced in the 1920s and which continues still today.

This book is the product of a collaborative effort between the three editors. While each of us undertook basic research for one or more geographical areas, there was, inevitably, much overlap. In the main Dorothy Goldman undertook the research and selection of material from the United States; Judith Hattaway selected those from Britain; Agnès Cardinal was responsible for texts from Europe as well as their translations.

I

THE WAR BEGINS

Sheila Kaye-Smith
(1887–1956)

A poet and novelist, Sheila Kaye-Smith was born in Sussex, where she lived most of her life writing and farming. Her first published novel was *The Tramping Methodist* (1908), after which she produced at least one book a year. Her fictional work, which may have been the butt of Stella Gibbons's parody, *Cold Comfort Farm*, is marked by its rural themes and excursions into melodrama: her novel *Sussex Gorse* (1916), to which she refers in this passage from her autobiography, is the story of a farmer whose ambition destroys his family. In this excerpt, however, Smith reveals not only the place which rural life had in her writing but also an awareness of the way it could be threatened by the war.

———

1   THREE WAYS HOME

FOR about a week before and a week after war was declared I think that most writers imagined their work was done for. It seemed impossible that anything so frail as one's imagination could survive in such a storm. Before long, however, the cry of other tradesmen—Business as Usual—proved to be no vain boast (or prayer). We found that writing and publishing would go on much the same; in fact the war seemed to give an urge to literature, especially to the more sensitive and imaginative kinds. Never in modern times had poetry such a vogue—poets were actually able to publish at their publishers' expense, and there is a rumour that some of them even received royalties. The great complex of violence, hate, lust, cunning, fear and other primitive emotions released by the explosion of war also dragged up from the bottom of our hearts the primitive urges of poetry and religion. Poets sang and people prayed—till the war ended, and poetry and prayer were bundled away and suppressed with uglier things.

At first I reacted to the war in much the same way as the War Office; that is to say I saw it in the terms of South Africa in 1899. Schoolgirl memories revived and asked naïvely to be repeated—Dolly Grey, Bluebell, the Absent-Minded Beggar and rows of patriotic buttons round my hat. It was an infantile reaction, but more harmless in me than at Whitehall.

I recovered from it fairly quickly. At first, of course, we all thought that peace was bound to come in a few months; and most civilians found an escape from the realities of Mons and the Marne in a dream of Russians pouring their countless hordes into France by way of every town and village in Britain. But when winter came and the tired armies settled down into the mud and the Principal Boys in all the pantomimes sang 'Tipperary', some of us began to wake up and feel ashamed. Personally I felt guilty till the end of the war.

Emotionally speaking, I had an uneasy time. After the first few months I could not join in the singing and hating, or believe in British propaganda or in the fact so obvious to the rest of the country that anyone with a German sounding name must be a spy. I could have smacked the distributors of white feathers, and such posters as 'Is your Best Boy in Khaki?' made me hot with shame. On the other hand I could not feel at ease with the definitely pacifist groups or with the Conscientious Objectors. In more than one case I suspected that conscience was only a rationalizing of a natural but unpopular objection to being maimed or killed, and I respected the few who were brave enough to state their objection in those terms. I also respected the large number who went, many of them already disillusioned, to suffer and die *with* humanity, though they could no longer feel they were dying *for* it—who refused to stand apart from the great woe either with or without a garment of righteousness.

I did a certain amount of war-work—I made swabs and bandages, I sold tea and doughnuts in a canteen, I added to the muddle of a War-Office department. But unlike so many writers at that period I was never really absorbed in the war or distracted by it—doubtless for the reason that I had been spared the fate of most of the women of England, and never had anyone I really and truly cared for out at the front. I was brotherless, my father was over seventy, and my best boy was not in khaki. So my attention was not forcibly dragged away from my literary work and fixed on some dark, imagined place overseas, held there by irregularly frequent buff envelopes, and then suddenly twisted out and knotted into a few hours of agonized happiness called leave. My heart was in England and available for the writing of *Sussex Gorse*.

I enjoyed writing it, for it was an escape from the turmoil and unhappiness round me, and once more I took a definite pride and pleasure in my work. I will not say that writing once more wore a gleam, for the days were passing when my interests must be like fairy queens in pantomime, with stars on their heads. But I enjoyed the ease and simplicity of my new technique—my imagination, unhampered by external difficulties, had a freer and deeper play than in any of the earlier books. Also, inspired by the novel's father, I thought less about the importance and glory of authorship and more about the fun and interest of ordinary human life.

Sheila Kaye-Smith, *Three Ways Home* (London: Cassell, 1937), 88–91

Radclyffe Hall
(1883–1943)

Radclyffe Hall wrote both novels and poetry and is best known for *The Well of Loneliness* (1928) in which the open discussion of lesbianism occasioned a trial for obscenity. Her concern with issues of gender and identity is clear even in this story of the first days of the war, 'Fräulein Schwartz'. Like Hall's later piece, 'Miss Ogilvy Finds Herself', the war is the starting-point for a story which concerns itself with women living in worlds which are essentially isolated and introspective.

2   FRÄULEIN SCHWARTZ

1

Mrs RAYMOND preferred that her boarding-house should be known as a private family hotel, thus: 'Raymond's Private Hotel' had been painted in brown on the peeling Corinthian columns, and again above the shabby front door in gilt letters across the fanlight. The house stood in a street that had seen better days; it was one of those endless Pimlico streets that meander dully towards the river. All its houses were fashioned precisely alike: tall fronts, sash windows, damp areas; moreover, they were large but without dignity, and solid while conveying no sense of comfort.

Mrs Raymond was the childless widow of a merchant who had had the misfortune to speculate in rubber; of that rash speculation nothing now remained but a starved rubber plant in the dining-room window. However, being a hard-headed woman and blessed by a lack of imagination, she had promptly opened a boarding-house which pretended to offer every home comfort.

'A home from home,' Mrs Raymond would say, 'that's what I aim at—a home from home.' And since it was cheap as such places went, her clients preferred not to contradict her.

Like every experienced landlady, Mrs Raymond had a very marked preference in boarders. She much preferred youthful and unattached men because, as a rule, they were docile and timid. At this time she had three such young men in her house: Mr Pitt, Mr Narayan Dutt and Mr Winter.

Mr Pitt belonged to the Y.M.C.A. He was secretary of some local branch, and he made a hobby of physical training. Mr Pitt spent much time running round Richmond Park in modest duck shorts and a drenched cotton singlet. When he ran his hands sawed the air helplessly, his chest heaved and his eyes bulged behind his glasses. Mr Narayan Dutt, who hailed from Bengal, was an earnest and a diligent medical student; he affected amazingly tight grey clothes and soft boots of a very unusual yellow. Mr Winter worked in a city office; his prospects were poor and so was his health—he suffered from chronic nervous dyspepsia.

Apart from a few occasional boarders, there were four other 'regulars', as they were called: Colonel Armstrong, of doubtful antecedents—he was said to be late of the Volunteers—two spinster sisters, the Misses Trevelyan, whose father had been a naval paymaster and who therefore despised the ambiguous Colonel, and an elderly person, by name Fräulein Schwartz, who gave German lessons at a couple of schools and eked out a living with private pupils.

Fräulein Schwartz was little and round and fifty, with neat greying hair and a very high bosom. She frequently sighed, and whenever this happened the plaid silk of her blouse creaked in sympathy—like many a German of her generation she displayed a mysterious preference for tartan. Gentle, and bewildered by life was Fräulein Schwartz; she had never been able to make up her mind about anything since the days of her childhood, and yet she had had to face grave decisions. She was incomplete, part of a philippine, the major portion of which was missing.

Her father had been a most learned professor—that is, learned in all save the getting of money. They had lived in a pleasant suburb of Dresden not far from the bridge called 'Der Blaue Wunder'. As a child she had frequently stood on that bridge and gazed down at the Elbe, feeling rather afraid, gripping her father's protective hand, so impressed had she been by the depth of the water. After his death, when she was past thirty, she had dutifully wished to support her mother by teaching English, God save the mark! She had failed, which was not in the least surprising, for among those problems that had always bewildered her most might be counted the English language. But indeed she had tried a number of things for nine years, until she had lost her mother: fine needlework; knitting thick, gaudy stockings for the muscular legs of those who climbed mountains; even serving in a shop had Fräulein Schwartz tried, but not one of her ventures had been successful. Yet now here she was giving German lessons in London, and actually making a living.

Fräulein Schwartz was the friend of all the world, a fact which naturally made her feel lonely, since the world had no time for Fräulein Schwartz, nor had it expressed the least wish for her friendship. She loved children and after them animals; but children had never found her amusing. Stray dogs liked her, and sparrows would feed from her hand—but this only if the weather were frosty. Her true romance never having been born, she must cherish the memory of her parents, of her childhood, of her distant Fatherland; her large Bible resembled a photograph album. And let no one presume to despise Fräulein Schwartz if her links with the past were connected with eating. Why not? The bread that is broken in love, in guileless enjoyment and simplicity, may sometimes become as manna from Heaven. And although her mouth watered a little, it is true—she had suffered long years of boarding-house cooking—her eyes watered still more for the innocent days that were gone past all earthly hope of recalling.

Zwieback and a glass of fine, creamy milk . . . a spring morning in a tidy suburban garden; the witch-ball supported on stiff iron legs, a large luminous sphere reflecting the world, itself as immense as the world in proportions. Two earthenware dwarfs with curly grey beards; friendly, affable dwarfs clasping circular bellies: 'Liebchen, do not make all those crumbs on the cloth; eat more carefully. What will the little men say? They are surely much grieved by untidy children!'

Apfelkuchen, always sweeter than sweet and tasting of the good, honest smell of ripe apples . . . the confectioner's shop in the Prager Strasse to which she had been taken on her sixth birthday. A smiling young salesman behind the counter who, when he had learned of the great occasion, had behaved as though she were really grown up and had actually called her: 'Gnädiges Fräulein.'

Schinkenbrot, crisp rolls stuffed with tender pink ham . . . picnics to Bastei with her parents in summer. The stout little steam-boat, so busy, so willing. The songs they would sing steaming home in the evening: 'Lorelei', because they were on the river, and sad old folk-songs because happy people will not infrequently sing about sadness.

Pumpernickel, the delectable sticky black bread . . . her mother cutting it into thin slices. Her mother's spreading and matronly hips, so reassuring beneath the check apron: 'Nein, Liebchen, you must wait for your Pumpernickel.'

Wiener Schnitzel, fried slices of juicy veal; a dish well beloved of her learned father. The dining-room of their suburban home ... a tiled stove of such aggressive dimensions that it all but ousted the dining-table. Her father, big, bearded and very blue-eyed, a kind of paternal and ageing Siegmund, bending over his plate of Wiener Schnitzel.

The hot spiced wine of All Hallowes E'en, and the childish games that would follow after. Flushed cheeks—that hot spiced wine was so strong— and a great deal of mirth when she and her friends must evoke ancient spells, each to get her a husband. Her father and mother holding hands, grown young again thanks to the hot spiced wine. They had been middle-aged just as she was now, and how strange that seemed—the kind father and mother.

And those little brown loaves of marzipan that invariably made their appearance at Christmas. Ach, du liebe Zeit, Christmas! The old market-place as fragrant and green as a miniature forest. Rich and poor alike buying Christmas trees and driving away with them then and there in old country carts or fine equipages. Snow and sunshine; the lake in the park frozen over, the band playing a waltz, the curvings and swayings of endless rosy-cheeked, bright-eyed skaters. Little ice sleighs, fashioned like gaudy birds. That fine pair of new skates with the curling fronts—what a lot they had cost. Ach, du liebe Zeit! she had surely possessed the most generous parents. Christmas day with its careful family presents; so much love had gone into each one with the making. Christmas night and the tree lighted up in the window just in case some poor creature outside should feel lonely: 'Töchterchen, raise the blind before we light up—ja, so! Töchterchen, we should always remember the sad people who cannot have Christmas trees...'

Remember! Fräulein Schwartz could hardly forget since now she herself was one of those people. Sentimental? Perhaps. But then Fräulein Schwartz had always been incurably sentimental.

2

Whether it was Providence who sent her a present, or Chance, is a very difficult question; but the fact remains that returning from a walk one Christmas Eve, Fräulein Schwartz found a kitten on the doorstep of Raymond's Private Hotel. It mewed; it looked at her with anxious blue eyes; it had draggled grey fur and a very pink nose; it was young, it was starving, and it needed protection.

Fräulein Schwartz's defrauded maternal heart leaped up at this sight: 'Armer Kerl!' she exclaimed. Then she gathered the kitten into her arms and proceeded to warm it under her jacket.

'You can't bring that thing in,' Mrs Raymond said firmly; 'I won't have a kitten messing up all my carpets.'

'Vhat you zay?' enquired Fräulein Schwartz. 'But he starve, he is young and he also needs me.'

'You can't bring him in,' Mrs Raymond repeated, 'it's a rule of this hotel not to take people's pets.'

'Dat is rubbish!' said Fräulein Schwartz, equally firm. And then: 'I inzist dat I bring him in.' And her pale Teuton eyes were so bright and so fierce, and her thick Teuton voice was so pregnant with battle that Mrs Raymond was completely nonplussed for a moment, and that moment gave her boarder the victory. 'I go buy him a tray and some nice zoft sand; he be clean, you vill see,' coaxed Fräulein Schwartz; for the beast's sake now bent on conciliation.

So the kitten was carried upstairs to her bedroom and was fed and caressed and generally tended. And its name, from that evening on, was Karl Heinrich, in memory of a very learned professor: 'For,' said Fräulein Schwartz, as she combed its thin fur, 'der liebe Vater vould never object, and you haf his blue eyes—so clear and so childish. Jawohl, I vill certainly giff you his name.' Then feeling a little doubtful she warned: 'But remember, dat name is a ferry great honour!'

This had been between five and six months ago, and now Karl Heinrich was growing up daily. He had changed his milk teeth; and had visited the vet for the purpose of sacrificing his manhood. He had learned that all carpets demanded respect and that Mrs Raymond would see that they got it. He had learned that sparrows were hatched to be fed and not necessarily to be eaten; whereas mice, could one catch them, were considered fair game—though Fräulein Schwartz never praised him for mousing. He was learning that Alice the parlourmaid, was one of those incomprehensible people who feel sick when a cat strolls into the room, and who consequently abhor the whole species. There was so much to learn with first this, then that, and yet life seemed wonderfully good to Karl Heinrich.

As for Fräulein Schwartz, it was really surprising what a difference his advent had brought about in her. She felt so much less lonely now at the thought that when she got home from work he would be waiting; that his food must be given, his coat brushed and combed, his ears looked to in case he be threatened with canker, his blue eyes watched for conjunctivitis, his temperature taken at least once a week, because being young he might get distemper—love, and a handbook on how to rear cats, had made her as crafty as any vet. Thus it must be conceded that Providence or Chance had been right in this choice of a Christmas present. For Fräulein Schwartz whose heart was so burdened with that large overload of maternal affection, Fräulein Schwartz the unwanted friend of all the world, was now wanted at last by a living creature. While Karl Heinrich, although, of course, as a cat who could trace his descent from a deity of Egypt, he could not quite sink to the level of a dog with lickings and wooffings and foolish tail-waggings; although he must stalk in the opposite direction, head in air, tail erect, when his owner called him—this just as a matter of etiquette—Karl Heinrich had grown to adore that owner, and his purr when he rubbed his sleek length against her skirt would be vibrant and long with controlled emotion.

'Ach, du viel geliebtes Ding . . .,' she must frequently murmur, kneeling down to stroke his grey comeliness. 'Ach, du mein Schatz', and other fond words she must speak to the cat in her guttural German.

And whether it was purely imagination—the imagination of a Fräulein Schwartz who was only too anxious to find compensations—or whether, as she sometimes assured Mr Winter, Karl Heinrich did really struggle to respond, making queer and very uncatlike sounds while blinking his eyes as though from great effort; whether all this was true mattered not in the least, since it gave such deep pleasure and consolation.

3

Between Alan Winter and Fräulein Schwartz there existed a kind of companionable liking. They met very seldom except at meals, but when they did meet they always felt friendly. He pitied her and she pitied him.

He would think: 'It's hard lines to be growing old and to have no real home—only this putrid place. I wonder what will happen when she's really old; her sort never manage to save much money.'

And she would be thinking how tired he looked, and how young he was to be so quiet and staid, and would long to teach him the student songs that she had been taught by her learned father, and would long to see him drink pints of beer, good iced beer—this in spite of his chronic dyspepsia. And though neither expressed sympathy for the other, since both of them were extremely shy people, yet they sometimes stopped if they passed on the stairs, stopped to talk for a little about Karl Heinrich. And Alan bought a ball on elastic which Karl Heinrich could make swing backwards and forwards, striking it deftly with soft, padded paws—a game that he found to be very amusing. And Fräulein Schwartz bought a bottle of tablets which the chemist assured her would cure indigestion, and she gave them to Alan who threw them away, but who, nevertheless, lied manfully when she asked him if he were not feeling better.

Thus the days drifted by. Fräulein Schwartz taught German and Alan

Winter slaved at his office; Mr Pitt ran round and round Richmond Park, and Mr Narayan Dutt went to lectures; and the Colonel was distant to the Misses Trevelyan, and the Misses Trevelyan were cold to the Colonel, and Mrs Raymond played bridge with her guests every evening, but methodically underfed them, and no one believed that a war could come, despite ominous hints that appeared in the Press.

'The world is now governed by high finance, the financiers would never permit such a thing,' said Mrs Raymond complacently . . . a view that was shared by even the Colonel.

4

The night after England's declaration of war Alan Winter returned from the City dead-beat. His head ached and he had a dull pain in his chest. All day the office had been in confusion, all day he had struggled to grasp the fact that this war, which seemed like an evil dream, might become for him a reality.

'But I cannot go out there and kill,' ran his thoughts. And then: 'Is it that, or am I a coward? Am I really afraid of being killed?' A question to which he had found no answer.

Raymond's Private Hotel was blazing with lights. He could hear the sound of excited voices as he vainly tried to escape to his room: 'Is that you, Mr Winter?' called Mrs Raymond. 'We've been waiting up for you. Well, what's the news? Come and tell us what they say in the City.'

Amazing the futilities that worried these people, he could scarcely credit his ears as he listened: what was likely to happen to trustee stocks, to consols and other gilt-edged investments? What was meant by national bankruptcy—did the City think it was likely to happen? And the income-tax; what did the City think?

Alan shrugged his thin shoulders, hating them all. 'I can't tell you because I don't know,' he snapped.

Colonel Armstrong eyed him malevolently: 'This,' said the Colonel, puffing out his chest, 'this, in my opinion, is Armageddon!'

And then it began. They argued, they disputed, they grew bitter towards the Kaiser and each other. Quiet people, hurled violently out of their ruts, their nerves had been jarred and their tempers suffered. It was natural enough, the whole thing was so strange—so terrifyingly sudden and strange; for the moment they buzzed like angry flies who were caught in the grip of some monstrous spider. Given time they would find their dignity again, but just for the moment they lost their tempers. Colonel Armstrong resented the Misses Trevelyan's irritating allusions to the senior service.

The Misses Trevelyan retaliated by asking impertinent, personal questions. Mr Pitt of the Y.M.C.A. called for vengeance upon every head wearing a Prussian helmet. Mr Narayan Dutt smiled enigmatically and remarked that such sentiments did not sound Christian; while Mrs Raymond, tired out and much worried, inveighed hotly against the food profiteers, declaring that she might have to put up her prices.

Some recent arrivals, a young couple from Norfolk, brought a stock of the most disconcerting rumours. The Germans had perfected Napoleon's idea and built rafts—they might shortly be landing at Dover; residents had been warned and were leaving the town which would be defended by an army of Russians. Food would soon become scarce; they might have to eat rats as the starving had done in the Siege of Paris—Mrs Wilson knew for a positive fact that the Government was going to commandeer chickens. Queer people had been met with all over the Broads, two such persons were drifting about in a wherry; spies of course, all England was riddled with spies and the police doing less than nothing about it. The Germans had bottled innumerable germs, anthrax and cholera germs among others, and these they would scatter in buses and tubes, spreading infection through-out the whole country. The navy was bristling with enemies, some of whom were flaunting their German names—Prince Louis of Battenberg, for instance; it was common knowledge that he would be shot, or at least arrested and put in the Tower—Mrs Wilson hoped it would be in a dungeon. Spies were everywhere, not a corner was safe; why, the great wire-less station quite near Llandudno had been run by a German man for years; he called himself Smith, but was really Schmidt. Mrs Wilson's uncle lived down in those parts and had long had his eye on this dangerous fellow. But the real peril lay much less in the men than in the vast, secret army of women; female spies masquerading as ladies' maids, private secretaries, and even as teachers. They had wormed their way into important houses where, of course, they had overheard conversations. And not to be out-done, Colonel Armstrong, Mrs Raymond, the Misses Trevelyan and Mr Pitt, must produce even more startling contributions, so that to hear them was to feel little doubt regarding the ultimate fate of the Empire.

Then Mr Pitt of the Y.M.C.A. stood forth as the champion of civiliza-tion; and his strong duplex spectacles catching the light, seemed to glow with the flames of his righteous wrath as he spoke of the brutal invasion of Belgium; of the broken treaty, the iron heel, the will to destroy a defenceless nation; of the Kaiser puffed up with arrogance like the blasphemous Beast of Revelation. Merciless they had been, those invading hordes, yes, and well prepared for their devilish work:

'God pity the women and children,' said he; 'this sort of thing isn't civilized. They'll stop at nothing, you mark my words. I'd like to exterminate the whole brood, yes, I would; they don't deserve anything else. What they need is total extermination!'

He was kind and extremely placid by nature, and on the whole quite a passable Christian. He had never handled a rifle in his life or done bodily ill to a living creature. He had certainly run round and round Richmond Park in a harmless desire for physical fitness, but prize-fights had always made him feel sick—he had said many times that they were degrading. But tonight something potent had gone to his head, something that was in the very air he was breathing, so that he demanded an eye for an eye, forgetting the crucified God of his Gospels. And although he did pity the women and children and sincerely believe in his own good intentions, although, Heaven knew, there was reason enough to cry out against this thing that had happened, Mr Pitt was not solely stirred by the wrongs and the agonies of an invaded Belgium. For side by side with his genuine pity and his quite justifiable indignation, lurked an instinct that was very unregenerate and old— mild Mr Pitt of the Y.M.C.A. was seeing red, as a long time ago some hairy-armed cave-man had done before him.

Alan said abruptly: 'I'm going upstairs.'

His head was now aching beyond endurance. He was weary unto death of Mr Pitt, of the Wilsons, of the Colonel, of them all, for that matter. He wanted to put the war out of his mind, if only for a few blessed hours during sleep. Without saying good-night he turned and left them.

And away in a corner of the drawing-room, alone, stupefied, for the moment forgotten; half convinced that her country had committed a crime, and yet yearning painfully over that country; credulous one minute, incredulous the next, as she clung to the memory of her parents, of the Germany that she had once known—diligent, placid, child-loving and simple; a land of fairy tales, Christmas trees, and artless toys fashioned for little children—away in a corner of the drawing-room sat Fräulein Schwartz, weeping large childish tears which dripped on to her tartan silk blouse unheeded.

5

England settled in to the grim stride of war. The Empire had swayed but had quickly recovered. Food rose sharply in price but nobody starved. A moratorium strengthened the banks which, despite Colonel Armstrong's fears, remained solvent; although after a time little, mean paper notes were to take the place of their weighty gold sovereigns.

Fellow clerks at Alan's office enlisted and their posts were soon filled by adventurous women, all anxious to do their bit for their country, all anxious to learn, yet impatient of learning. But Alan, the victim of his treacherous nerves, of his body that had failed him ever since childhood, of his horror of blood and of violent deeds, above all of his vivid imagination, Alan held back and did not respond to the loud bugle call of Kitchener's army.

Mr Pitt of the Y.M.C.A. was in khaki. He had twice been refused on account of bad eyesight, but had managed to get himself taken at last, and this was immediately made the excuse for a very unworthy campaign of baiting. Alan was a handy and obvious butt, sitting all day on a stool in safety. The Misses Trevelyan cut him dead when they met; Colonel Armstrong—himself much too old to serve—made frequent and barbed patriotic allusions. Even Mrs Raymond, try though she might to remember that Alan paid his bills promptly, that he seldom if ever complained of the food, the economy in fires or the tepid bath water, even Mrs Raymond now viewed him askance, and if she addressed him at all did so coldly.

It was true that he was not the only blot, there was Fräulein Schwartz to whom nobody spoke except Alan, who felt very pitiful of her. There was also Mr Narayan Dutt of Bengal—he had suddenly decided to leave the hotel, which the Misses Trevelyan thought highly suspicious. But then, as young Mrs Wilson remarked with more force than refinement: 'He's a yellow-belly!' Mr Wilson was being drilled down in Cornwall where his wife was daily expecting to join him. It was not very pleasant indeed, quite the reverse, but Alan would not let his thoughts dwell on these people; after all, he was fighting on the business front, and England's motto was: 'Business as usual!'

But if Alan's position was not very pleasant, Fräulein Schwartz's position was becoming desperate, for who in their senses would wish to learn German? Moreover, her very presence in the house was looked upon as a potential danger. Mrs Raymond had already asked her to leave, but Fräulein Schwartz had protested with tears that, alas, she could find nowhere else to go to. For Fräulein Schwartz had but to open her mouth to arouse an immediate antagonism. One woman had banged the door in her face: 'No, I 'aven't a room for the likes of you! Why don't yer go 'ome and stay with the Kaiser?' Yet cheap lodgings were an urgent necessity, since now she must live on her meagre savings.

Poor, ageing, inadequate Fräulein Schwartz, so anxious to be the friend of all the world yet so tactless in her methods of setting about it; for what must she suddenly try to do but perform little acts of unwelcome kindness, and this at a time when war-racked nerves would naturally lead to the worst interpretations. Mrs Wilson was convinced that she was a spy, hence those crafty offers to help with the housework; she wanted, of course, to get the run of the place, hoping to unearth some information. Mrs Wilson threatened to go to the police and was only dissuaded by Mrs Raymond who declared that this might ruin her hotel, especially if it got into the papers. In the end Mrs Wilson bought a miniature safe so that she could lock up her husband's letters.

Poor, ageing, inadequate Fräulein Schwartz; a more positive woman would have packed her trunks and tried to return to her native land. But the thought of that long and difficult journey, of passports, of frightening official delays punctuated by even more frightening questions, of a dwindling purse, and God knew what expense to be faced before she at last reached her country, had completely deprived her of her small stock of will, and so she had stayed on from week to week, innocent, blundering, bewildered and helpless.

Oh, but she was being crushed on the wheel, the fate of all those who are too tender-hearted. War, to her, seemed a great and most pitiful sin, even as it had to her learned father. It was said that her people did terrible things; it was also said that the English would starve them, two wrongs which could surely not make a right, and which left her more bewildered than ever. Each morning she prayed with great earnestness that God would bring peace to the warring nations; but at times God appeared to be very far off, so that she must seek a more present help in trouble. Getting up from her knees she would look at Karl Heinrich; then taking him on to her lap she would talk, for like most of her nation she dearly loved talking—indeed, she had suffered far more than they knew from the silence imposed by her fellow-boarders. And to all those deep problems which vexed her soul, Karl Heinrich would listen with infinite patience, though every recital would end much the same way: 'Aber, vhat has gone wrong mit de vorld, Karl Heinrich?'

Karl Heinrich would find himself at a loss, since not even the wisdom of Ancient Egypt, as he very well knew, could have answered that question. And so he would start to sway his sleek tail, conscious of a disagreeable sensation in the region of the fur along his spine, for cats hate to be placed at a disadvantage. Then all that frustrated love of long years, all that urge to serve, all that urge to succour, all that will to protect the helpless of the earth, would Fräulein Schwartz pour out on her rescue. And since those whom we speak of as lesser creatures have their own quiet ways of divining our emotions, Karl Heinrich would cease from swaying his tail and would try to sit very still on her lap, so fearful was he of hurting her feelings.

Passing the door on her way downstairs, the parlourmaid, Alice, would pause to listen. And that low guttural voice would fill her with rage; with a senseless rage that made her feel giddy, so that now Karl Heinrich must suffer as well—they must suffer together, he and his mistress. Not that he was a German; he could prove that his father who frequented the backyards of Pimlico, had been born in a coal-cellar here in London. He could prove that his mother who lived five doors away had come into the world *via* a cupboard in Chelsea; all the same he must suffer from the girl's hostile eyes that made him feel intensely uneasy. Then again, she refused to bring up his food, declaring that the cook would no longer prepare it; and once she had given him a surreptitious kick, an outrage which he bore with philosophy, reflecting that Alice did not like cats—it seemed a just possible explanation.

Fräulein Schwartz must go out and buy milk in a can from the dairy and a loaf of stale bread from the baker; and on this meagre diet Karl Heinrich must live, since no scraps were available from the kitchen. But one day, although money was growing so scarce, Fräulein Schwartz bought Karl Heinrich a fine red collar; and she scratched his name on the plate with a pin—she had feared that the shop might refuse to engrave it. Gentle she was, and bewildered by life, yet this collar was in the nature of a challenge.

'Can't abide the beast,' Alice confided to the cook, 'and 'im belonging to that German woman. Ought to kick the pair of 'em out of the 'ouse. *And* 'is name! If she 'asn't gone and scratched it on 'is collar. The impudence of it, but then that's 'er! Any'ow the beast turns me sick at me stomach.'

Ah, yes, Alice was very bitter these days; a little queer too and inclined to be spiteful, for her wide muslin apron hid more than her skirt. Much clasping in a thicket on Hampstead Heath had resulted in what she hid under her apron.

He had said: 'Oh, come on! Ain't I goin' to the front? Ain't I one of the 'eroes wot's about to protect yer? 'Course I'll marry yer when I gets 'ome on leave. But, Gawd, don't go keepin' me 'angin' about . . .' And one or two other things he had said; it had not been at all a romantic seduction. So possibly Alice was less to blame for her queerness than was 'Erb, and what he had called in his moments of spiritual insight: 'Nature.'

6

Incredible of course that Fräulein Schwartz should have suddenly longed for her fellow-boarders, yet so it was, and the evening arrived when she could not endure coventry any longer; when tucking Karl Heinrich under her arm, she went down to the gloomy drawing-room and, much daring, broke into the conversation. Alan Winter, who had not as yet gone upstairs, was filled with a sense of impending disaster. What a moment to select, the poor tactless old fool! Hadn't she looked at the evening papers? They would think she had come to gloat over the news. And why bring the cat? His name was enough—a nice beast, but such an unfortunate name! Fräulein Schwartz had not seen any papers for days, indeed, she now frequently feared to see them.

She was trembling, already regretting her impulse, already regretting that she had brought Karl Heinrich. He would not sit still, he wanted to play and the chair had some very alluring buttons.

'Sieh' mal, dat is naughty—you must be a goot boy. Do not do it! Be quiet a little, Karl Heinrich.'

She smiled awkwardly, glancing from face to face as a mother might do, half apologetic, half expecting a tolerant answering smile. But none came. Those animal-loving English could not find it in them to love Karl Heinrich—not just then, with the terrible lists of killed, of wounded and, more terrible still, of missing. Death and bereavement were every-where now; no one in that room was nearly affected, yet bereavement had entered into the house. There had been a great noise of sobbing in the kitchen and the housemaid had had to serve the dinner that night. The girl had explained that some very sad news had reached Alice, hence those sounds of sobbing in the kitchen. And this German woman sat and played with her cat! It was true that she had not come down to dinner, that her room being at the top of the house she could not have heard what went on in the basement, nevertheless, she should have more shame; her presence was little short of an insult. No, they could not smile at the playful Karl Heinrich.

And he ought to have known better. He, so wise a cat, was being nearly as tactless as his mistress. What imp had got under his glossy grey fur and made him behave like a wilful kitten? Fräulein Schwartz's round forehead began to shine as she sweated with worry and mortification. And she talked, how she talked! It was almost as though her long enforced silence had left her bursting, so that now she must let loose a torrent of words. Alan thought as he listened that never before had he heard Fräulein Schwartz being quite so foolish or speaking in such abominable English.

'If only I could manage to stop her,' he thought, glancing anxiously at their fellow-boarders.

They were doing their best. They were honestly trying to control their tongues and stifle their feelings; trying to answer her naturally, as though they were quite at their ease in her presence; trying in their unimaginative way to do the right thing, the dignified thing, on what to them was an odious occasion. But her thick Teuton voice jarred their every nerve, while her round Teuton face in their midst seemed an outrage when they thought of those wounded, missing, and dead. Quite suddenly they could not endure it and must start to castigate Fräulein Schwartz as if by so doing they struck at her country.

And now into the eyes of those quiet, dull people, crept a look that was unexpectedly cruel; the look of the hunter who corners his prey, watchful, alert with a sense of power—the power over life in the act of killing; while into Fräulein Schwartz's pale eyes came the puzzled, protesting look of the hunted. Then Fräulein Schwartz plunged, committing a blunder more grotesque than any that had gone before it. In her genuine will towards peace on earth, in her genuine conviction that all men are brothers, in her genuine distress at the miseries of war, she must try to make everyone there understand that she not only asked for, but offered friendship. But they did not understand; they mistook it for shame, since, alas, in this world it is seldom wise to show the cross hilt instead of the sword blade.

'Dere is someting I vant to zay,' she was stammering, 'it is dis. Mein Vater vas against all vars; he belonged to de Socialdemokraten, de people's party, de party for peace. He thought var vas a great und most pitiful zin . . . ach, ja, and I feel as did my dear Vater. But ve here, ve hafe not made de var, nicht wahr? It is not ve here who hafe vished to make it. I am Cherman and derefore I lofe my land; you are English and derefore you lofe dis England; and I tink dat ve all hafe zo much lofe in our hearts dat ve cannot help ourselves lofing one another . . .' She paused, gasping a little, but only for a moment, for now she was carried away by her creed. She was holding up the cross hilt of the sword and was strangely elated by what she was doing, so that her voice when next she spoke held in it the triumphant ring of the martyr: 'Because of my country I hafe wept many nights. It is said dat our zoldiers hafe killed little children—I do not know. It is alzo said dat your English navy is going to starve us; you cannot starve only vomen und men, and derefore you alzo vill kill little children—I do not know. I know only dis, dat ve all should unite to stop zo much zuffering. Ach, listen! I feel dat de spirit of my Vater is in me here,' and she struck her plump breast, 'dat my Vater vants me to say dese tings; dat my Vater zays he implores you to listen. He zays dat in our dear countries tonight, dere are many goot people who feel as ve do, and dat if dey could dey vould stretch out dere hands and vould zay: "Wir sind ja alle Brüder und Schwestern." ' Fräulein Schwartz stopped speaking; the light died from her eyes leaving them dull and curiously vacant.

Then a dreadful thing happened. Mrs Wilson laughed shrilly; she laughed peal upon peal, for she could not help it, was indeed scarcely conscious of what she did—she was very near an hysterical breakdown. Fräulein Schwartz's face became ashen, and from one of those dimly lit chasms of the mind in which lurk the abhorrent and forbidden thoughts that engender great hatreds and great disasters; in which lurk all the age-old cruelties that have stood to the races for self-preservation; in which lurk the hot angers of humbleness scorned, and the blinding resentments that urge to vengeance; from one of those dimly lit chasms of the mind there rushed up a mighty force fully armed, and it gripped Fräulein Schwartz and possessed her entirely, so that she who had been the friend of all the world was now shaken by gusts of primitive fury.

'Ach, accursed English, you vhat laugh at de dead; you who hafe not de heart vhat can feel compassion! May be it is lies vhat you zay of our men— yes—I tink it is you vhat kill vomen and children. I tell you all vhat my Vater vould hafe me, und you laugh, und you laugh at my dear dead Vater! But may be you laugh less one of dese days vhen our Uhlans ride through de streets of your London. May be you laugh much less vhen our ships blow up all of your cruel child-murdering navy. Gott! I tink ve vas right to make zuch a var; now I pray to Gott alvays dat He give us de victory!' And gathering Karl Heinrich into her arms she fled, while they sat stupefied and dumbfounded.

But someone was watching as she lumbered upstairs, clasping the cat to her heaving bosom. Alice stood aside to allow her to pass—she had heard that impassioned, tempestuous outburst.

'So,' she muttered, 'so you 'opes as your bloody Germans is comin' to ride through the streets of London; the devils as 'ave made my baby a bastard and me nothing but an 'ore all the rest of me days. So that's what you 'opes, you foul German bitch. Well, I'll teach yer; so now you can go on 'opin'!' And Alice shook her trembling fist in the air, half demented by the thought of her coming child, the bitter fruit of a brutal deflowering.

7

The next afternoon being Saturday, Alan Winter returned from the office early. It struck him that the parlourmaid looked rather queer when she opened the door, but the thought soon passed. Alice, as he knew, had received bad news which would doubtless account for her strained expression.

Then stumbling downstairs came Fräulein Schwartz, her eyes red, her grey hair grotesquely dishevelled; and she clung to his sleeve, peering up at his face as though not very certain of her reception. But for all that she clung with tenacity.

'Gott sei Dank it is you and not one of de others . . .' she panted. And then: 'Come quick up to Karl Heinrich!'

He stared at her, wondering if she had gone mad: 'Karl Heinrich!' he repeated stupidly. He was tired, and his head was still heavy with figures.

She nodded: 'Ach, Gott, he is terribly ill. If you vil not help me because I am Cherman, den help him, for he surely haf done notting wrong.'

Alan thought: 'And neither have you, you poor soul.' Aloud he said: 'I'll come up and see him.'

They climbed the interminable stairs side by side, and as they did so she tried to explain how it was that Karl Heinrich had been brought so low; tried hard to keep calm and tell Alan the symptoms. It seemed that she had gone out to look for a room, and that on her return she had found him in convulsions.

'I do not know much, but I run to my book on de cat, und I tink it vere surely convulsions. . . . And vhen I look round he hafe been very sick . . . ach, but sick, sick, sick hafe he been in my absence. Und vhen de convulsions vas past come de pain, de 'orrible pain. . . . Ach, my poor Karl Heinrich! Und now dere hafe come de very great weakness. And I cannot understand; I myself buy his milch, und his bread I also buy from de baker, und no meat hafe he eaten for many days; und vhen I leave him to go hunt a room, he was vell as never before hafe I seen him. Herr Gott! Vhat has happened? Vhat can hafe befallen?'

Alan tried to soothe her as best he could, but he felt a queer sinking in the pit of his stomach and a sudden tightening across his chest: 'Don't be frightened, it can't be serious,' he soothed, 'not if the cat was so fit when you left him . . .'

They had reached the top landing, he gasping for breath. The next moment she was pushing him into her bedroom. It was small and squalid, a despicable room, a disgrace to the house and to Mrs Raymond. He had never been in it until that moment, and he saw it for the unhappy thing that it was the sole refuge of a derelict human being. He supposed that there must be many such rooms in all cities, and many such derelict beings. Then his thoughts stopped abruptly—he had seen Karl Heinrich.

She had dragged the meagre pillow from her bed and had laid him upon it, just under the window. The beast seemed to have shrunk to half his size, and that was so queer—rather horrible even. And his glossy grey coat was now matted and dull. Some milk had stiffened the fur on his chest, spilt there when she had endeavoured to feed him. His whole body looked pitifully soiled but resigned, and Alan could feel its profound desolation. For seeing him thus, was to know that Karl Heinrich realized in some dim way that he was dying, and that he had not yet made friends with death—perhaps because he was still so young and had been very full of the joy of living.

Then Fräulein Schwartz sank on to her knees, not in prayer to God, but in love for His creature, and she slipped her arms under Karl Heinrich and rocked him as though she were rocking an ailing baby; and she murmured soft and consoling words, as though she herself were indeed a mother:

'Kleines Wörmchen, do not doubt und do not feel frightened. . . . Gott is kind, and all vill be vell, Karl Heinrich. He lofes you, for you are His little grey cat—tink of it dat vay, for Gott He made you. And I vill not leave you never, ach, nein, zo dat you shall not feel frightened und lonely. Can you hear me? Do you know I am mit you, Karl Heinrich? Ja, I tink dat you do, und dat it consoles you. Hafe great hope and fear notting at all, mein Schatz. . . . Zee, I shall alvays be very close.' She appeared to have forgotten Alan Winter.

'Look here, I'm going for a vet,' he said gruffly.

8

When he returned with the vet in half an hour, Fräulein Schwartz was sitting on the floor by the pillow. She was stroking Karl Heinrich methodically, and still talking—only now she was talking in German. For her mind had slipped back over many years to her mother and the days of her own young childhood, so that she was using little tricks of speech, half playful, half grave, and wholly consoling; so that she was telling of gnomes, but kind gnomes, and of other such folk who were all very kind; trying to lure Karl Heinrich away from the realms of pain into those of enchantment.

'Is she a German then?' whispered the vet.

Alan nodded: 'She is, but the poor beast isn't.'

The man flushed: 'I'm a healer, not an Empire!' he said sharply.

Turning, he went to Fräulein Schwartz: 'This gentleman has brought me to look at your cat. Do you mind if I make an examination? He's told me the symptoms. . . . I'm afraid they're pretty grave.'

Fräulein Schwartz got clumsily on to her feet and motioned to the vet to take her place. She gave him a searching look but said nothing. With gentle deftness he set about his task; lifting the eyelids, opening the mouth, pressing his ear to the beast's shrunken side, and listening again and again for the heartbeats. But Karl Heinrich was already a long way away; he had gone to the country that needs no frontiers, and where wars and the rumours of wars are forgotten.

The man shook his head: 'I'm too late,' he told them, 'but in any case I don't think I could have saved him. In my opinion this cat's been poisoned.'

'Poisoned? Oh, no, that's impossible! Who on earth would have done such a thing?' exclaimed Alan.

But Fräulein Schwartz spoke in an odd, hushed voice: 'If dat is de truth, den for me has he suffered, and for my nation, und for all de nations vhat zo cruelly go out to hurt vone another. Karl Heinrich vas only a little grey cat vhat I rescue vhen he was cold und starving; but now Karl Heinrich is very much more, he is zomething enormous und terrible: a reproach before Gott who vill not forget de zufferings of poor dumb beasts und of children. I hafe maybe lost him for a little vhile, ja. I hafe lent him to Gott, but only for a little; because Gott, who hates var, vill give him me back. He vill say: "Karl Heinrich hafe told Me about it; all de pain und de fear und de doubts vhat he felt before you come home in de end und find him, zo dat now he shall go again vhere he vould be, und dat is mit you—I gife back your Karl Heinrich." '

The vet glanced at Alan uneasily: 'I'd like to make an autopsy,' he murmured.

But Alan shook his head: 'Don't suggest it—no good—she's half crazy with grief, it would only distress her.'

'But she can't keep him here. I could take the body . . .'

Fräulein Schwartz swung round: 'Vhat is dat you are zaying? Aber nein; aber nein; I vill bury him myzelf.'

'Well—I'm sorry I couldn't save him, Fräulein.' The vet looked at his watch; there was nothing he could do, and moreover he had another appointment.

'If you'll come downstairs, I'll attend to your fee,' muttered Alan, and he almost ran from the room, conscious only of a wild desire to escape from the blemished beast and the grief-stricken woman.

Alone with her dead, Fräulein Schwartz spoke to God, and she told Him quite quietly about this great sorrow, and about the troubles that had gone before—her loneliness, her fears, her inadequacy, and the feeling that life had denied her fulfilment. She told Him of the wish she had always cherished to befriend the whole world, to be one great heart into which the whole world could creep for protection, and of how she had found that nobody came, that nobody wanted her heart but Karl Heinrich, who had thus in some strange way become the whole world, which was surely God's compassionate dispensation. Then she asked His forgiveness for all her transgressions; for her anger upon the previous evening and for all those terrible things she had said—none of which she had really meant, she assured Him. And for what she would now do she asked it also if, indeed, according to His wisdom it were sinful, which she could not believe since none other than He had sent her this very great love for Karl Heinrich.

'And I promise dat I vould not leave him, ach, nein, because he is only zo helpless a ding vhat I care for zince he vas a tiny kitten. Und he might feel strange, even mit You, mein Vater im Himmel, though I tell him of all Your kindness...'

For some reason she was praying in English, in the thick Teuton English that made people angry, that indeed, had nearly cost her her home—but perhaps God did not notice her accent. In any case she drew much comfort from her prayer and much courage; both excellent reasons for praying.

Presently, she was setting her bedroom in order, so that when they went in they should find it tidy; and this done she got money out of her trunk and left it on the table for Mrs Raymond.

'Zo! Und now I owe nobody notting,' she murmured, 'I am glad, for had it been otherwise, they vould all hafe zaid dat I paid not my rent because I vas vhat dey call: "A damn Cherman." ' And she actually smiled a little to herself, not unkindly, but rather with a vague toleration.

Finally, she pinned on her shabby black hat, then she slipped her arms into an old tweed ulster—it was ample, almost too big she remembered, and thus it could easily shelter them both. Lifting the stiffening body of the cat, she buttoned it gently under the ulster.

Poor, ageing, inadequate Fräulein Schwartz; even at this stupendous moment when for once in her life she had made up her mind, when for once she was filled with a great resolve, even now she must walk lop-sided through the streets, looking as though some abominable growth had laid its distorting hand upon her; indeed, more than one person turned to stare at the odd little woman who walked so quickly. Quickly, yes, for she had a long way to go before she would come to that quiet place where the trees bent forward over the river; where the river was dark and brooding with peace. By the time she had reached it she would be very tired and glad of her sleep, for the night would have fallen. Karl Heinrich was already fast asleep—she could feel him lying against her bosom.

Radclyffe Hall, 'Fräulein Schwartz', in *Miss Ogilvy Finds Herself*
(London: Hammond, 1959), 107–37

Margot Asquith
(1864–1945)

Margot Tennant was brought up without formal education yet developed a considerable literary talent. Her early life spanned several worlds: between 1886 and 1894 she made frequent visits to a factory of women workers in Whitechapel. 'I have derived as much interest and more benefit', she wrote, 'from visiting the poor than the rich, and I get on better with them.' She also moved in political and artistic circles: her friends included Gladstone, Balfour, Haldane, J. A. Symonds, and Virginia Woolf. Margot Asquith was the second wife of Herbert Henry Asquith, the Liberal politician. Although she was proud of his role as Prime Minister from 1908 to 1916, she took no part in the war effort after 1914. This extract from her autobiography, famous when published for its candour, reveals both her role as socialite and the sharpness of her observation.

———

3   WAR

I WILL end this chapter by quoting an account out of my diary of the only visit I paid to the Front in the Great War.

Henry and I went to Hackwood to stay with Lord Curzon to meet the Queen of the Belgians and her children.

After dinner when I told her I thought the war would certainly last over two years she was amazed and I could see she did not think it would be half as long.

She asked me to go and stay with her in Belgium and see the fighting Front.

There was a handsome Scotchman staying in the house, Major Gordon, secretary to the Duke of Wellington, with whom I made friends, and on hearing of Her Majesty's invitation he said he would accompany me; so on the 10th of December, 1914, we started off together.

I spent an uncomfortable night at the Lord Warden, and at 7 a.m. the next day Major Gordon and I crossed over to Dunkirk in the Admiralty ship, *Princess Victoria*. I was too sick to see anything on the journey; but the captain told me that floating mines and fear of German submarines accounted for our serpentine route and our arrival being delayed by over an hour.

It was Arctic cold when we arrived, but I wore sensible clothes: leather breeches and coat, a jersey over my blouse, a short serge skirt, a Belgian soldier's black forage-cap and a spotted fur overcoat. All very ugly but businesslike.

We took untold time to pass through the locks into Dunkirk Harbour. There we were met by a private chauffeur and the best Benz motor I have ever driven in, both smooth and powerful. Our Belgian drove us at a shattering pace on sheer and slippery roads.

Major Gordon was more than resourceful and kind: quite unfussy, and thinking of everything beforehand.

We drove straight from the Harbour to Milly Sutherland's Hospital.

There among the wounded I saw Arab, Indian and Moor soldiers lying in silence side by side. The distant expression of their mysterious eyes filled me with a profound pity, nor could they speak any understandable language to their nurses or their doctors.

After leaving the Hospital we went on to the Headquarters of the Belgian Army where we were met by General Tom Bridges, 'the heart and soul' as we were told of the Belgian Army and in many ways a remarkable man.

He gave us our passwords and passports for the next two days. 'Antoine' from 6 p.m. to 6 a.m., and 'Cassel' from 6 a.m. to 6 p.m.

We had a repelling meal in a dirty restaurant at Furnes before arriving at King Albert's Headquarters.

It was 4 o'clock and in drenching rain when we reached La Panne. The King's household received me with courtesy and cordiality in a brick and wooden house built on the sand dunes by the sea. The villa was like a lodging-house at Littlestone—pegs for hats and coats in a tiny hall, with a straight short wooden stair and no carpets. It was bald, and low and could only put up seven people—two men-servants, one housemaid, a cook and ourselves.

Comtesse Caraman-Chimay, the Queen's lady-in-waiting, is a delightful woman with fine manners and a great deal of nature and kindness. The Master of the Horse, M. Davreux—a cavalry officer in the Household— helped the servants to bring my things upstairs into a hideous bedroom, where I was glad enough to retire.

We messed in the kitchen. The only other sitting-room in the house was a warm, open-fired smoking-room where we sat after dinner. I was relieved not to have to walk in the rain 200 yards to dine with the King on the night of my arrival, as I was too tired to move.

We dined early in fur coats, skirts and shirts; and all went to bed at 9.15 after an interesting general conversation upon the war and various other topics.

My bald bedroom had neither curtains, blinds, nor shutters, and I put on a jersey over my nightgown. On one side the windows looked on to a sort of sand railway, covered with trucks and scattered villas, and the other on to the sea. Telephone and telegraph wires connected all the villas together and glass doors opened out on to brick paths; the whole place was sunny but bleak, and exposed to every gale.

Luckily for me it was a glorious day when I woke; and I shall not easily forget the beauty of the beach in the early morning. I saw nothing but stretches of yellow sand, and shallow ice-white lines of flat waves, so far out that no tide looked as if it could ever bring them any closer.

Detachments of mounted soldiers of every nationality and every colour were coming and going on the beach, and an occasional aeroplane floated like a gull upon the air. Troops of Moors (Goumiers, as they call them) rode past in twos and twos, mounted on white and grey arabs, tattooing odd instruments with long brown fingers. Though picturesque on the beach, they looked as if they might be ineffectual in battle.

At 1.30 on December the 12th, the Belgian Commander accompanied me across the brick paths through the sand dunes to the King's villa. My coat was taken off by two footmen in black, and I was shown into the sitting-room, where I found a tall fair man studying a map, and leaning over a low mantelpiece. He turned round and shook hands, and we sat down and began to talk. I thought to myself:

'You are extraordinarily like your King,' but I have often observed that Court people take on the look of their Kings and Queens, imitation being the sincerest form of flattery.

It was not till he congratulated me on having a remarkable husband, and alluded in touching terms to Henry's speech on him and the sorrows of Belgium that I suspected who he was. I instantly got up and curtsied to the ground, at which he smiled rather sadly, and, the Queen interrupting us, we all went into the dining-room.

We had an excellent lunch of soup, roast beef, potatoes, and a sweet flavoured with coffee.

I found the King easy and delightful; both wise, uncomplaining, and real. He has no swagger, and is keen and interested in many things. I told him I had bought several photographs of him to sign for me to take back to England, but they all had dark hair. He said it was clever of the photographer to give him any hair at all, as he was getting balder daily, and felt that everything about him was both dark and bald.

He told me, among other things, that the Germans had trained off to Germany all his wife's clothes and under-clothes, and all his own wine, adding:

'As I drink nothing, this is no loss to me, but it is strange for any soldier to steal a woman's clothes.'

After lunch M. Davreux, Major Gordon and I motored to the Belgian trenches and on to Pervyse Station. We passed a dead horse lying in a pool of blood and heard the first big guns I have ever heard in my life; the sound of which excited and moved me to the heart. Aeroplanes hovered like birds overhead in a pale and streaky sky.

We passed a convoy of men with straggling winter trees upon their bent backs going to hide the artillery. For miles round the country was inundated with sea-water; and the roads, where they were not *pavé*, were swamps of deep and clinging mud. The fields were full of holes, and looked like solitaire boards. The houses had been smashed and gutted and were without inhabitants; only a few soldiers could be seen smoking or cooking in the deserted doorways. Every church was littered with bits of bombs, and *débris* of stained glass, twisted ribbons of molten lead, and broken arms of the outstretched Christ.

Major Gordon had brought a wooden cross with him to put on the grave of the Duke of Richmond's son, and I had taken one out at the request of Lord and Lady Lansdowne to put on their boy's grave at Ypres, where we ultimately arrived.

The Ypres cemetery will haunt me for ever. No hospital of wounded or dying men could have given me a greater insight into the waste of War than that dripping, gaunt and crowded churchyard. There were broken bits of wood stuck in the grass at the head of hundreds of huddled graves, with English names scrawled upon them in pencil. Where the names had been washed off, forage-caps were hanging, and they were all placed one against the other as closely as possible. I saw a Tommy digging, and said:

'Who is that grave for?' He answered without stopping or looking at me: 'For the next . . .'

Two English officers, holding their caps in their hands, were standing talking by the side of an open grave, and single soldiers were dotted about all over the cemetery.

Major Gordon, who had borrowed a spade, asked me if I would help him by holding the cross upright, which I was only too glad to do till we had finished.

All the time I was standing in the high wet grass I thought of the Lansdownes and my heart went out to them.

Suddenly a fusillade of guns burst upon our ears. It seemed as if some of the shells might hit us at any moment, they were so near and loud. Aeroplanes circled over our heads, and every soldier in the cemetery put on his cap and rushed away.

An excited Belgian officer, with a few other men, ran up to me and pointing to a high mound, said would I not like to see the German guns, as one could only die *once*.

As Major Gordon had left me to go to a further cemetery, I was glad enough to accompany them.

Frightfully excited and almost deafened by the Crack! Crack!! Crack!!! Boom!! Boom!!! I tore up to the top of the hill with the officer holding my elbow.

Had it not been for a faint haze over the landscape I could have seen everything distinctly. Thin white lines of smoke, like poplars in a row, stood out against the horizon, and I saw the flash of every German gun. My companion said that if the shells had been coming our way they would have gone over our heads; the German troops, he explained, must have come on unknown to them in the night, and he added he did not think that either the Belgians, the British, or the French knew at all what they were up to.

A French officer, looking furious, arrived panting up the hill and coming up to me said I was to go down and remain under the shelter of the Hospital walls immediately. Two Belgian soldiers who had joined us asked me if I was not afraid to stand in the open, so close to the German guns. I said not more than they were, at which we all smiled and shrugged our shoulders; and the French officer took me down the hill to the Hospital quadrangle, where I waited for Major Gordon.

The clatter of the guns was making every pane in every window shiver and rattle till I thought they must all break, and sitting in our motor, writing my diary, I felt how much I should have hated fighting.

A French sentry after eyeing me for some time came up and presented me with his stomach-belt of blue cashmere. I thanked him warmly and gave him six boxes of Woodbine cigarettes, of which I had brought an enormous quantity. A Belgian Tommy, on seeing this, took off his white belt and presented it to me with a salute which moved me very much.

I began to think Major Gordon must be killed, as he had been away for over an hour. The sun was high and when he returned his face was bathed in perspiration. He told me he had put the Duke of Richmond's cross on his son's grave in a cemetery so close to the German lines he thought every moment would have been his last, and after munching a few biscuits we started off on our journey south.

On our way to Merville we stopped at Major Gordon's brother-in-law's house, a cottage at the side of the road. It was pitch dark and we had tea with him in the kitchen, lit by one dim oil lamp.

We had not been at the table more than a few minutes when a loud sound, like the hissing of an engine, made the whole cottage rock and sway.

I felt genuinely frightened and wondered what the children were doing at home.

An aide-de-camp dashed out of the room and came back scarlet in the face.

'If you please, sir,' he said, saluting: 'four Jack Johnsons have dropped thirty yards from the door.'

General Nicholson jumped up white as a sheet and said to his brother-in-law:

'Great God, what will the Prime Minister say? I've let you in, my dear Gordon! . . . but I assure you, Mrs Asquith, we've not had a shell or a shot here for weeks past. . . .'

I reassured him as to his fears of my personal safety and asked him why the Germans wasted ammunition on such a desolate, inundated spot, to which he replied:

'Pure accident! But let me tell you, if there had been no water, not a brick in this cottage would have remained above ground, and neither you nor I would have had an eyelash left! . . . Now, Dopp, give us the tea.'

After leaving our host we pursued our journey and arrived at Merville, where I was the only woman among 20 men who sat down to dinner that night with General Sir Henry Rawlinson.

It is always a surprise to an amateur why Generals and Ministers have such large staffs, and I have often wondered if they are kept for ornament, companionship, or use; but expect it is an unconscious form of vanity. All the time my husband was Prime Minister he never took a secretary away with him either at home or abroad, but in old days I have known idle and rich young men travel with a loader, a valet, a secretary, a coiffeur and a chiropodist.

Sir Henry and I knew each other hunting in Leicestershire and he received us with cordial hospitality. He not only gave us an excellent dinner—which was very welcome, as, except for tea and biscuits, we had had nothing to eat since the early morning—but he gave up his own bedroom and bath to me, an act of courtesy for which I shall ever be grateful.

I was glad to observe how popular my chaperon, Major Gordon, was wherever we went—nor was I surprised, as a better looking, better hearted, more capable and devoted person I have seldom met.

We left Merville on December the 14th, at 7.30 in the morning, and arrived at Havre that night.

On looking at the boisterous, choppy sea I made up my mind that nothing would induce me to spend twelve hours upon it, so after a peaceful night we motored back to Boulogne, starting at 7 a.m. and got back the same night to London.

Margot Asquith, 'War', from *The Autobiography of Margot Asquith* (London: Eyre and Spottiswood, 1962), 299–305

Lena Christ
(1881–1920)

Lena Christ is principally known for her many short stories of village life in Southern Germany and for her novel *Rumpelhanni* (1916) which was made into a successful film. The illegitimate daughter of a cook, she initially spent a happy childhood with her grandparents in rural Bavaria. Her troubles began when, at the age of 8, she had to go back to her mother who had married an innkeeper. After ten years of hard labour and domestic violence, she sought refuge in a convent where she remained until 1900. She subsequently married a local man and had three children but obtained a divorce in 1912. It was her second husband, Peter Jerusalem, who encouraged her to write. They were separated in 1919 when she became involved with another man. A year later she committed suicide by taking cyanide.

———

4　　　　　　SPIES!

HAVE you heard? . . . Spies!

A veil frames the coarse and wrinkly face. Large, chunky worker's hands hide in the wide sleeves.

Below the pleats of the dress two big feet stomp along in heavy boots.

With long strides the nun moves across the square; a little girl tries to greet her by holding out her hand. A gruff, almost masculine voice answers. The child turns and gazes after the nun who hurries on.

'Why are you staring so, little one?' a passing woman asks the girl.

'It's that nun; she looks just like a man!'

'A holy sister?' asks the old woman and just manages to catch a glimpse of a nun turning into a side street. As fast as her feet will carry her she runs after her.

'Oho! What's the rush, Frau Wimmer?'

'Can't stop. I've seen something: it's a man in a nun's habit!'

'Jesus and Mary! I've seen him too! I'll come with you!'

The two women hurry on until an acquaintance tries to stop them: 'Hey, not so fast my dears! There is surely no need for such a rush! . . .'

'Leave us be. Don't try and delay us, Herr Burger! We're in a hurry!'

'Yes, clearly, anyone can see that. Where's the fire?'

'We are following someone . . .'

'It's a man . . .'

'Yes—disguised as a holy sister . . . over there . . . see? . . .'

'What?—That sister?—Well, I'd better have a closer look at her!' And he too hurries after the nun.

In the meantime several bystanders have become curious; when they hear the word 'sister' they have made up their mind.

'What did you say? . . . A holy sister? . . . No doubt a Russian . . . or a spy! . . . Let's go and see!'

The nun is heading towards Rosenthal when, suddenly, she hears the noise of approaching feet. She turns and sees some people come rushing round a corner. They cross the road and, on the other side of the road, are keeping in step with her.

She touches her veil, checks her habit, shakes her head and walks on.

On the other side of the road the crowd is getting bigger. A little cobbler's apprentice shouts: 'Hey, Max come and see!—A spy!'

'A spy?'

Suddenly the crowd becomes agitated.

'Let's get the scoundrel before he can do any harm!' someone cries.

'Whack him one, the bastard,' another suggests.

'Arrest him!'—'Shoot him!'—'Let's get on with it.' The voices mingle wildly.

The nun begins to notice something.

She starts to run.

'Aha, now he's getting scared, the son of a bitch!' someone howls and everyone breaks into a trot.

'Sock him one!'—'Kill him!'—

The nun hurries along in flying haste. Suddenly she makes a dash into a yard, slams the wrought iron gate behind her, rushes into the house and up the staircase.

Just then a cook emerges from an apartment.

'In God's name, Miss, I beg you, protect me!'

A policeman comes running up the stairs followed by the Police Commissioner. Downstairs the crowd continues to howl and scream:

'Smash him to pieces! Make mincemeat out of him!—Cut him to ribbons!' The wild chorus continues.

Upstairs, an embarrassing investigation is taking place by the police, the owner of the house and the cook, in the course of which it emerges that the nun is indeed a woman and a nun.

The disconsolately sobbing sister is bundled into a car and, accompanied by the howls and jibes of the youths of the town, is taken back to her convent where for days, she lies in bed with a high fever.

Meanwhile the crowd is already busy sighting a new 'spy'.

Lena Christ, from 'Unsere Bayern' ('Bavarians Like Us'), trans. Agnès Cardinal, in *Erzählungen und kleine Prosa* (*Short Stories and Prose Pieces*), ed. Walter Schmitz (Munich: Süddeutscher Verlag, 1990), 46–8

Adrienne Thomas
(1897–1980)

AdrienneThomas was born into a wealthy family who owned a small department store in the bilingual city of Metz. When her family moved to Berlin during the war, she signed up as a Red Cross nurse. The extract below is taken from her semi-autobiographical anti-war novel *Die Katrin wird Soldat: Ein Roman aus Elsaß-Lothringen* (*Katrin Becomes a Soldier: A Novel from Alsace-Lorraine*) which was published in 1930. The book was a great popular success. It was translated into sixteen languages and earned her instant fame. When Hitler came to power in 1933 all her writings were banned and she had to go into exile. After a long odyssey through Austria, France, and the United States she eventually came to settle in Vienna in 1947. In two further novels she similarly draws on her personal experiences to describe life in fascist Germany and the problems of living in exile.

———

5   KATRIN BECOMES A SOLDIER

7 AUGUST 1914

THEY have arrested four hundred people here in Metz. They are all suspected of being spies. It appears that the initial meeting of the war tribunal took place yesterday. The first suspect is supposed to be a *fermier*, a local French farmer who allowed French officers to pose as farm hands on his farm.

Yesterday Belgium declared war...

Evening. 8.40 p.m. Our Metz Regiment, the 8th Rheinlanders, has stormed the town of Liège. Hurrah! Now the war will soon be over! In three weeks' time Paris will have fallen! The streets are full of jubilant people celebrating victory! Hurrah!

Evening. 11 p.m. Come to think of it: Paris in three weeks?—And to what purpose, I wonder? We can hear the thunder of cannons. The dreadful music of death reaches us from a great distance. While we listen, human beings are bleeding, are dying out there in the warm August night under a summer sky full of shooting stars.

9 AUGUST 1914

It seems that there has been some fighting in the countryside surrounding Metz. But it's all rumours. I had a glimpse of a group of wounded soldiers. One had a bandaged hand. Another carried an arm in a sling. All of them looked exhausted.

26 degrees in the shade today! Lieutenant Olbrich had orders to take part in a 'small military exercise' which took place from half past seven to one o'clock. After a nap he finally got up at four and joined me for tea. For a long time we sat over my atlas wondering how best to win the war quickly. I am sure Herr Olbrich too is in a hurry to get home. He is a university teacher in Berlin teaching—wait for it—maths! A Prussian and a maths teacher to boot!! And yet he is really nice. We never get the impression that he is a Prussian soldier imposed on us by the laws of war. Instead he lives with us like a well-liked guest. You can tell that he is used to dealing with young people. He is never patronizing and never laughs at me, not even secretly. Most people let a young girl know that she is really a child and does not belong in the adult world.

Just now he has again been called to the barracks. The maids are busy making jam and I have decided to contribute to the war effort by cleaning and tidying Herr Olbrich's room. It seems that war has broken out in our pink and white girls' bedroom. On the dressing table there is a cartridge-pouch, on one bed lies a leather belt and on the other the Litewka gun. The dainty marble bust of Pauline Buonaparte sports a Prussian helmet...

MONDAY, 10 AUGUST 1914

We are all terribly upset. The French have taken Mülhausen and are supposed to be on the advance towards us! Elsaß-Lothringen has become a battleground—shot to pieces—burnt out. They do not tell us where, two days ago, the thunder of cannons had come from. The newspapers are full of jubilations about Liège, nothing but Liège. Nothing is said about what is happening here. Papa says that we should all go to Berlin with Mama. I'd rather be cut to ribbons than leave here! This is where I belong—regardless what happens.

Later. At last I've found something to do. Thanks to Fräulein Stockmar. I met her in town and she sent me to Frau Dr Münz in Pinceletstraße who, with some hesitation (she seems to trust me as little as I trust myself) has engaged me for tomorrow morning, nine o'clock—to help with the jam making for the hospitals. At dinner I did a great deal of showing off with my new occupation: the number of tons of fruit to be processed increasing by the minute. 'If, one of these days, I am given fruit preserve with a strong burnt taste, I shall enjoy it all the more because it must be yours', says Herr Olbrich. 'I am making jam, not preserve,' I retort with dignity.

The day before yesterday I paid all the money I possess into the Red Cross account at the local paper, the *Metzer Zeitung*. Today my name figures in large letters in the paper, even though I thought I had paid it in anonymously. Someone in the office must have recognized me. Papa is very cross with me and tells me that one does not let oneself be mentioned in a newspaper for a measly ten Marks. Well, I didn't have any more, did I?

Tuesday, 11 August 1914

I have just seen the first red trousers on German soil! There was an almost impenetrable crowd at the station. But I am nimble and pushed my way through to the front row. And there stood the great monster for which half the town had turned out: a very small young man, no older than eighteen, flanked by two German soldiers. Blue coat, red trousers and cap. A good looking lad, bronzed by the sun who, I am sure, had never before been the focus of such interest of so many people. The crowd stared at him in silence but no one insulted the young prisoner who looked downcast as if he were a criminal.

Punctually at nine this morning I reported for 'duty'. I had no idea what exacting work jam making is! Frau Dr Münz has placed me in the building which used to be my old school which became a secondary school when we were moved to the new school in Montigny. So, after five years, I am back in the same house which had begun its career as a castle and later became a theatre and, during our difficult times, has been reduced to being a mere school. There we were now, sorting and stoning mirabelle plums in the small courtyard, separated from the Esplanade by a narrow street and a small vine-covered fence. And while I was working I thought that for six years of my life I had been labouring over multiplication tables, decimal points and endured the nightmare of algebra and higher maths in a house in which Napoleon III and the beautiful Empress Eugénie once watched a performance of *Madame sans Gêne*. And to think that rooms which once witnessed glittering balls and theatre performances, as well as children's pranks and laughter, would perhaps now be condemned to house the groans and fever dreams of the wounded and the last melting thoughts of dying men. And posterity will probably get nothing more out of the history of this old house than a handful of essay titles for school children.

It was a lovely summer's morning in the shady courtyard which was full of the scent of the famous mirabelle plums of Metz, donated by the village people of Lessy. Only the persistent wasps and our work reminded us of war. The flirting eyes of the passing young officers spoke of peace. But the real work came later. Lotte Cressin and I had to clean out the preserving jars. That may sound easy but it is really very difficult to get these enormous jars properly clean. Crash—and another one hit the floor. 'Don't worry—broken glass brings luck,' consoled Frau Dr Münz. Indeed later I was lucky enough to be delegated to the wash-house to clean the fruit with a hosepipe. Somehow I lost control over the pipe. It made itself independent and squirted water everywhere. Frau Dr Münz did not mention luck any more as she shook the water out of her hair and her dress and went to change her clothes. I however continued to work as 'Undine', as Lotte immediately christened me. Afterwards we had to pound half a ton of sugar to powder. There were only two alternatives: either I hit the sugar or I hit my hands. The sugar did get pulverized but afterwards my hands were covered in bleeding blisters. From one to three we were allowed to go home. Afterwards the jam was put on an open fire in the wash-house and it was my job to stir it all the time with a large wooden spoon while bits of hot jam kept spitting onto my face and neck. And it was boiling hot in there right next to the fire. Lotte came to the door, smirking and telling me that outside in the great courtyard the thermometer stood at 29 degrees Celsius. Had we been at school we would have been sent home because of the heat. I ignored her, pushed my sleeves further back and pretended to spit into my hands. I completed my war duty with full honours: the jam didn't burn.

At the dinner table I was proud to display a pair of hands which, I am sure, will never ever get clean again. In the service of the Fatherland they have been cut and burnt innumerable times. 'There is no doubt,' said Herr Olbrich, 'they will have to give you a war pension.'

It has been officially confirmed that the Seventh French Army Corps and a Division of Infantry from Belfort 'have been dislodged from their fortified position west of Mülhausen and pushed back towards the south. German losses are negligible while the French have many casualties.' Some say that the French, having been pushed south, are now on Swiss soil and hence will become inoperative. Others again say that the whole of Elsaß has become one big battle field and a sight of devastation.

We have no way of knowing the truth—we know nothing at all. I just think that no army should be allowed to speak of 'negligible losses'—'negligible'—how can the death of a man be 'negligible'—after all, he is dead for ever!

They say that somewhere near Metz twelve hundred French soldiers have surrendered without as much as firing a single shot. So soon?—Can the spirit of Napoleon really be so dead after just one hundred years?

Night-time. I'm so horrified, I can't sleep! Returning from the barracks, Lieutenant Olbrich has brought us details of the sack of Liège. It appears that the entire civilian population took part in the defence of the town. Women poured boiling water onto our men, wounded soldiers had their eyes gouged out, their noses and ears cut off. And this in Europe in the twentieth century! Blinded by hate and fury our contemporaries get carried away until the lowest beast on earth ranks higher than them.—Than them? Than all of us! Surely it is better to die than to bear witness to this kind of thing!

Adrienne Thomas, from Die Katrin wird Soldat: Ein Roman aus Elsaß-Lothringen, trans. Agnès Cardinal (Berlin: Propyläen Verlag, 1930), 148–54

Hilda M. Freeman
(born *c*.1890)

The following text is taken from *An Australian Girl in Germany: Through Peace to War, January–October, 1914*, a slim volume found in the Public Library in Victoria, Australia. The book appears to be the authentic travelogue of a young woman from Melbourne who, in 1914, found herself stranded in Germany, sick and at the mercy of strangers. The chief interest of this extract lies in the way the author gives voice to her struggle to define loyalties which, upon the outbreak of war, had been challenged, not just as a guest in Germany, but also by her dual status as a British citizen and as an Australian.

———

6   In Germany

I am not concerned with the argument as to which country has justice on its side. To me it is sufficient to know that my country is in danger. If I can help I am ready. If I can't, I am loyal. Right or wrong, we must stand by our own country and defend our race to the last man. Every Englishman, no matter in which dark corner of the globe he dwells, must do his best this day for his country. Anyone who does not is a traitor.

The men on the other side of the firing line can fight for England. Surely they will be delighted to have an opportunity of showing their love for their country. The people who are left in England can still be cheerful. Is there not that line of steel and fire between them and destruction? There is plenty of work to do in the Empire. The stream of patriotic feeling carries one on without individual effort. The feeling of the single person is generally identical with the feeling of the crowd. To be patriotic there is no heroic deed; it is the obvious thing to be.

But, oh, a different tale when one is alone in the enemy's land and the flood of public opinion is against one; when the general sympathy is not with the things beloved, but with the things abhorred. A different thing to be patriotic when the people around one are concentrating every thought, every atom of energy, every shilling, every man on the task of destroying one's own nation. There are no fellow sufferers (suffering is never so severe when shared); no comrades to cheer; no deeds to do. That is the hard part. There are no socks to knit for English soldiers, no fugitives to succour, no enemy to fight (they are only too near, but I am weaponless). Nothing but a dreadful inaction.

In England people can air their views of the Kaiser, of this dreadful organisation, of the hundred and one things which displease them in connection with the enemy. But here we are the helpless victims of that organisation. To speak disparagingly of the Kaiser means imprisonment or death. We may think or feel as we please, but on no account must we allow those feelings to be expressed in word, look or deed. In fact, in view of the dreadful things which might happen to us, we are compelled to be grateful for being graciously permitted to go our unobtrusive way unmolested.

I read hateful tales of the cruel deeds of the English, which *nothing, nothing* can induce me to believe. It is not pleasant to read such tales, but still all things have their compensations. I gain a clearer knowledge of the unreliability of the German reports, for no true Briton could believe for a moment the tales which we are told about our men.

I always knew that I loved Australia, but every day I realise more clearly that the love of the Empire is an integral part of my being. Every Briton who reads the German newspapers must feel intensely glad that his blood is British. After reading the tales of horror which are printed about us, I feel little thrills of superiority running through my veins, and I say to myself: 'In spite of it all I am proud of being a Briton. The Germans may think that Britons would do these things, but I *know* that they *would not.*'

We say in England that Prussians are arrogant and overbearing, and they say of us that we are conceited and self-satisfied; that we keep on imagining that we are the 'superior English', even in the face of overwhelming proofs to the contrary.

It is only in England that one can afford to be humble. To the foreigner one must always present the haughty side. The Germans tell me that we never fail to do so, and they are remarkable for their truthfulness—yes? They accuse us of being untruthful. They say of us:

> 'Silence is Golden,
> Speech is Silver,
> Lies are Britannia.'

I smile at that, for I have heard that the English accounts of the war differ very greatly from the German. Of course, when two descriptions of the same thing differ so widely from one another, 'someone has blundered', and that 'someone' is, naturally, the other chap.

I am suffering from a very bad attack of Suppressed Conversation. Of course, everyone knows that it is a dreadful thing for a woman to have a great deal to say and to be unable to say it. To me, here, speech is practically impossible. There is only one topic of conversation—the war—and on that subject I must be dumb. Happily, my friends—my friends, the enemy—recognise my absolute loyalty to Great Britain, and are kind enough to realise that discussion over the war must only bring suffering upon us all. I can think, even if I must not speak. If Germans were as clever at thought-reading as they are at many things, then I would have been put in prison long ago.

Tante and the children visited me one day. They brought my little Peterlie, the crow, to see me. Dorchen brought flowers. Tante said, 'Oh, you must get well quickly. We are all so sorry that you have been so ill. We want you to scold the English with us. They have done so many bad things. You will not own them any more.'

'Aren't you glad that you're an Australian?' said Ulric, with a smile at me. They spoke eagerly and meaningly, with quite a different feeling from that which the Baroness had last shown towards me.

'Yes, of course,' said Tante; 'Australians are quite different from the English. They are a different nation, and they are not fighting against us.'

I felt that if I chose to consider myself non-British I would be taken back into confidence. Something had happened evidently to the public feelings regarding Britain's Dominions. They seemed to be considered non-combatants.

'Now, we will see what Australia will do,' said Dorchen exultantly. 'She will not uphold England.'

'Australia is British, Dorchen,' I answered shortly. I felt that I was shutting myself out from their sympathy, but I couldn't help that.

A curious expression passed over Tante's face, and she pulled Dorchen's arm. She had evidently read my face aright. 'Of course, she is loyal, Dorchen.'

'Do you know what the English have done?' said Moritz. 'They have cut all the cables, and we can't even cable to Constantinople. England has destroyed all our communications with the outside world, and we can't let anyone, not America, not any of the neutral countries, know how things are with us. They learn everything through the British and French cables. Cutting the cables was quite against the rules.'

'They tell lies—such lies,' interrupted Ulric.

'Dreadful lies,' said Moritz; 'and they have captured Togo.'

'Another infringement of the laws,' said Tante quickly. 'They agreed beforehand not to touch each other's colonies.'

Moritz was eager to tell me all the news. 'They have captured some of our merchant vessels, and the captains didn't even know that war had been declared.'

'But we blew up one of their ships,' said Dorchen. 'Canada offered to give us 10,000 bags of flour, and England wouldn't allow it, because Canada belongs to her. That shows you that the Canadian sympathy is with us.'

'But Canada is British. Surely the Dominions will prove loyal,' I said sadly.

'Canada is the only one who is likely to prove loyal. Australia is going to declare her independence. New Zealand also, and Ireland must have Home Rule. The Empire has dissolved itself.'

So that was the reason for the renewed geniality. But, remembering Australia, I would not believe it. I knew that she would not be so heartless and selfish as to throw the Motherland over the moment that she was in trouble. 'I think that you are mistaken,' I said. 'I don't know about the other Dominions, but Australia will never desert England. Never!'

'I think she will, my dear. Why should she suffer under English rulership now that the opportunity is here for her to escape from it?'

I smiled. 'We don't want to escape from it. We are bound by love, not force.'

Tante looked steadily at me and smiled. I expect she thought I was being foolish. I felt that I was being my greatest enemy, but I could not help that.

Hilda M. Freeman, *An Australian Girl in Germany* (Melbourne: The Speciality Press, n.d.), 110–15

E. Sylvia Pankhurst
(1882–1960)

The daughter of the suffragette Emmeline Pankhurst, Sylvia Pankhurst took a leading part in the early stages of the militant campaign mounted by the Women's Social and Political Union, which had been founded by her mother; in 1906 she gave up her scholarship to the Royal College of Art and devoted herself to taking a leading part in the suffrage cause. She spent many periods in prison and on hunger strike. Unlike her mother and elder sister, however, Sylvia Pankhurst persisted in attempting to give the suffrage movement a broad social base by an involvement with working-class women in the East End of London. These differences grew into a disillusionment with militant policy, especially its abandonment of socialism. The war brought about a break with her mother and sister, Sylvia's pacifism contrasting with their support for the conflict—a rift which was completed when her mother, Emmeline, at the end of her life, decided to stand for parliament as a Conservative candidate. All these strands of her belief are visible in the excerpt from *The Home Front*. A prolific writer of articles and books, Sylvia Pankhurst retained her political commitment throughout her life.

---

7   CHRISTMAS 1914

IN the brief Christmas days, when the slackening of propaganda gave me a respite, I went with Smyth to see the havoc wrought by the Scarborough bombardment. Travelling by night we arrived in a cheerless dawn. The sky and sea were a leaden grey. The big amusement 'palaces' on the front were scarred and battered by shell-fire, iron columns twisted and broken, brick-work crumbling, windows gone. Yawning breaches disclosed the pictures and furnishings, riddled and rent by the firing, dimmed and discoloured by blustering winds and spray. The little steep streets, leading up from the foreshore, were barred by wire entanglements—the first I had ever seen—great stakes driven into the ground, with a mass of stout barbed wire threaded around and around them, and tangled about between. At many points were high barricades of sand-filled sacks, with a row of loopholes for the rifles.

We knocked at one of the sea-front boarding houses. The woman who opened to us was weary and dishevelled as though she had spent the night out in the storm. She gazed at us, startled and hostile, when we asked for a lodging. When we urged that we had come from London and understood she was accustomed to let, she hesitated suspiciously, then reluctantly explained that she had promised to hold herself in readiness to receive any shipwrecked seamen who might be saved from drowning. 'I've been up with them all night—some of 'em's gone, some of 'em's still here. We have to put 'em in hot blankets as soon as they're carried in.'

'But there won't be another wreck to-night!' we essayed, rather feebly, to rally her.

'There were three lots brought in here yesterday, and two the day before,' she answered mournfully, and pointed to the many craft out in the bay, telling us they were all minesweepers engaged in the perilous work of clear-ing away explosive mines laid by the German warships and daily causing the loss of many vessels.

This was an aspect of the German visit not recorded in the Press. In our ignorance of war, we heard her with shocked surprise.

She agreed at last that we should stay with her, on condition that we would leave at once if another party of shipwrecked mariners were brought in. Barely an hour had passed when her daughter flung open our door:

'Another boat's blown up! You'll have to go!'

Out we went to the blast. Groups of shawl-wrapped women were gazing seaward. 'They've landed some of them at that slip,' a woman told us, and pointed to a small dingy brown steamer with a cluster of people looking down at her from the quay. 'A motor-car's gone off with one of them—he was covered with a white sheet!' a shrill voice cried; and even as the words were uttered another car dashed away. A bent old crone ran by us wailing: 'He was a young man with black hair; with thick black hair; his head was all smashed in!'

Groups of people moved about us, awestruck, with a hand shading the eyes, gazing out to sea, or across to the little steamer at the end of the slip.

Someone advised us to enquire for lodgings at a near-by cottage, the front door of which opened directly on to the foreshore. A fisherman in his blue jersey was seated by the fire; his wife was too much troubled by the peril of the men out there in the bay, to consider whether or not she would give us a bed. She talked to us a long time before she could bring her mind to it. She spoke of the bombardment; it was terrible, the noise so loud, so fearfully loud, she thought she must go mad. Little children were killed; many people were injured. 'A lady who not five days before was singing in this Bethel' was helping a poor old woman down into her cellar, when she was struck dead by a piece of shell. No one knew when it might happen again; people could not settle down to ordinary life; all sense of security was destroyed. Her husband and the other fishermen were prohibited from following their calling because of the mines. Their means of support was stopped; yet he was best at home; yes, even if they should have to starve! She had a son in the Navy and a son-in-law on a mine-sweeper; that was enough!

It had been a hard year in Scarborough; the holiday-makers had cancelled their bookings when war broke out. If they had only paid a little for the rooms it would have helped poor people. The big hotels had compelled their clients to pay in full, but little lodging-house keepers could not enforce their contracts. She could not understand the War. She could not understand why Scarborough had been left without protection—why there were no guns. 'The War's nothing to us—we didn't want it! Cleverer people than us know what it's for!' So she ran on with bitterness, until at last, having grown used to us, she said that we might stay.

Later her daughter looked in to speak with us. She too must talk of the bombardment; it had terrified her inexpressibly and had seemed to last for years. People could not sleep now; many would not even go to bed. Everyone had a bundle made up in readiness for flight; but how little one could carry in a bundle! One could not afford to move one's home; and one's living was here in Scarborough. A widow she knew had her boarding-house, her only means of livelihood, completely smashed and shattered. When would it be rebuilt? She shook her head. I asked her what was being done to relieve distress. Not much, she thought, and laughed ironically. 'They only think of asking women to knit socks for soldiers!' A club had been started by philanthropic people for soldiers' wives. Some of her friends thought they would like to go there to see the War news; they could not afford to buy newspapers out of their miserable separation allowances; but when they read at the foot of the club's announcements: 'To keep you out of the public houses,' they would not go. She tossed her head. 'They only get bits of rubbish there!' Pleased to find listeners, she poured out her thoughts unprompted. 'Oh, it was terrible when war began; the streets full of soldiers jostling you, and trying to get you to speak to them—everyone could have got a young man! And they were making the girls drunk. I never thought before that we had crowds of girls in Scarborough who would behave so! But generally we have hardly any men here—they all have to go away to practise their trades. My brothers have gone—they all go. Perhaps it was because so many men wanted to make friends with them the girls' heads got turned—and so many of the girls were out of work! As for the men, I suppose they thought when they came to the seaside they ought to have a good time! They say there are 80 girls in the Workhouse maternity ward through it—and I know there are eleven from — —'s shop alone! People talked about it a lot, and they started women patrols; but it didn't do any good. As often as not the patrols scolded girls who were with their brothers or men they were engaged to. Some girls I know were waiting to meet their brothers at the Bar church. One of the patrols began to lecture them, and the clergyman joined in. The girls' soldier brothers and their friends arrived in the midst of it and made the clergyman and the patrol apologise. Interfering with the girls did no good, but now they don't seem to let the soldiers into the town after about nine at night; and anyway things are quite different now; the place is only too quiet. Nobody wants to come to the seaside any more!'

On Christmas morning, climbing by winding ways above the town, we saw the trenches recently dug by British soldiers along the cliffs; and higher still, great heaps of stone which fell from the old castle when its walls were shelled by the German ships.

Lodging among the cottages of the fisherfolk in these terraced streets of the old town seven years before, I had wandered often beneath those ancient walls, regarding them curiously as a relic of an age of barbarism long dead, confident in my faith in the sure advance of progress. To-day, in face of the evidence of present barbarism, my thoughts were sad.

Vainly seeking my old landlady, for she had left the town, I was accosted by some neighbours of hers who remembered me. It was the anniversary of their wedding, and hospitably they would have us enter, to celebrate it with tea and plum cake, in their warm kitchen. It was a Yorkshire custom, they said, to exchange visits on Christmas morning. The wife was a very pretty woman, turned forty, with the bluest of blue eyes, a little shy and diffident and pleased to let the rest of us talk. The husband was black-eyed and swarthy as a Spaniard, with great gold rings in his ears. He told us, as others in the town had done, that the German battleships came so close to the shore that the people (believing them British) feared they would run aground. He was at the window when the firing began, and he called to his wife: 'It's no good, lass, the Germans have come!'

Then he told her to go next door and help their neighbour to pacify her children. She was running to the back door, but he locked it and said: 'I'm an Englishman and a Yorkshireman, and they'll not make us go the back way!' He walked to the end of the terrace and stood facing the battleships. He was not hit, but he showed us a big bit of shell which had fallen beside him. Believing, like everyone else, that the Germans intended landing, he looked around for our soldiers. They were nowhere to be seen. After the bombardment ceased they got into their trenches and sang a hymn. 'They were no better than wooden soldiers!' he cried indignant. His wife reproved him, with a timid glance at us: 'What use would it have been for our British soldiers to come out to be killed?'

Turning to the new town, we found much damage, and especially in the neighbourhood of the wireless station. A shell had fallen and burst before a lofty building, boring a great hole in the ground; and almost to the roof, the walls were splashed with mud thrown up by the impact and scarred by shrapnel. In a small house with a side wall down, and two great holes in front, a mother and all her children had been killed—only her husband was left to mourn them. Three out of four rooms had been wrecked in a house near by, and within a stone's-throw the shattering of a classic portico had killed the postman and the housemaid at the front door. No street here had escaped; in some streets house after house was conspicuously battered; in others it seemed that only the windows had been broken—till from another angle one saw roofs broken in and walls with gaping holes.

Returning to our lodging we learnt that yet another boat had been blown up. It was bitterly cold; the wind howled fiercely. We huddled by the fire, saddened and chilled. A girl ran past the window sobbing and wailing. A few minutes later she passed again. As I heard her coming a third time I went out to her, and saw that she was about sixteen years of age, hatless and poorly dressed. In abandonment of grief, she flung herself now against the wall, now leaned her head for a moment upon a window-sill, crying: 'Dad! Dad! Oh, Dad!' As I came up with her two women met her. They knew her and understood what she muttered between her sobs better than I. They told me that her father was on one of the mine-sweepers out in the bay. She shrank into trembling reserve and, faltering nervously that she must go to her mother, fled from us in the dusk.

Next morning we called on our first landlady to learn the news of the night. As we came in sixteen lately shipwrecked mariners, who had recovered in her house, were leaving the door. She told us six others had been drowned, and a third vessel since our arrival blown up. Another, another, and yet another vessel was sacrificed during the morning. Again we had notice to quit our lodging to make way for the sea-drenched men. Scarborough was too sad for me. 'Let us get away to-night,' I said to Smyth.

As we stood on the breakwater before leaving we saw the lifeboat set forth again to the rescue, over the cold grey waves in the gathering dusk.

I was unnerved; the thought of death on the ocean—mankind in its courage, so small, so impotent on the vast waters—tugs at my heart more poignantly, I think, than death in any other guise. After the lapse of more than thirty years, I still can scarcely recall without tears the loss of the little Manx *Ben ma Chree* plying between Liverpool and Douglas, whose old hulk was lost in mid-winter storms, it was thought, by the sheer force of wild waters, battering on her hatches.

As the train carried us Londonward, away from the grey, sad sea, a revulsion of feeling seized me. How should one give one's mind to anything save the War?

'Let us go over to France,' I said to Smyth. 'One ought to know what one can.'

Passports and visas were obtained without difficulty. At Victoria Station we joined the long queue of people of many nationalities, lined up for examination in temporary wooden structures.

The formalities were brief: 'Vous êtes British?' from an interrogator unmistakably English, and our assurance that we were carrying no letters: that was all. The train and boat were crowded; soldiers and civilians crushed in together.

Boulogne was transformed: Cockney porters more numerous than French, grey-bodied motor cars for the British Army stacked on the quay, British motor-buses, painted even to the windows a dull mud colour, waiting in the road for British soldiers, British soldiers in khaki thronging the platform, a buffet announcing: 'Soldiers' Refreshments Here.'

The train went slowly. At every station women came in with collecting boxes for the French wounded.

We found Paris less brilliantly lighted than of old, but not in the grim pitch-darkness then shrouding London. None of the recruiting posters, we had grown accustomed to, glared from her walls; having Conscription, the French Government needed no such appeals for obtaining men. The replacing of men by women's labour, though more extensive, was less ostentatious than it was already becoming in Britain. The War was too near a reality for Paris to make a show of it as they did over here. Some of the large shops had been turned into relief workrooms for unemployed women; one saw them in their dark clothes sewing behind the plate glass windows, for a wage, we were told, of only 5d. per day. Some of the finest hotels were converted to military hospitals.

Dr Flora Murray and a staff of women were running a hospital under the French Government at Claridge's Hotel; for the British War Office was as yet unwilling to accept their aid.

We found Claridge's still as a sanctuary: in the entrance hall, no one; in the spacious inner hall, silence and lights shrouded in veils. A man in uniform sat at a high desk.

'Dr Murray,' we murmured.

He pointed beyond us and we saw her seated, far away and small, writing under a shaded lamp. She did not see us till we were close to her; and then she was so much the pitiful, small-voiced woman who had come to my bed-side in the days of the Cat and Mouse Act that at first I did not notice she was in khaki, a dull subdued tone of it, with a narrow, dark red piping: the uniform she had chosen for 'the women's hospital corps'. Flat-chested, hipless, emaciated, one might have judged her devoid of stamina; she was tireless in efficient activity; a characteristic example of the intelligent middle class woman, whom an earlier generation would have dismissed as an 'old maid'. With her almost excessive quietude and gentleness, she had over-borne many a seemingly cast-iron Army tradition. In defiance of all precedent, she gave equal treatment to officers and privates, placing them side by side in the same wards.

She led us into the great, brilliantly lighted wards. The soldiers had put up Christmas decorations: 'A Merry Christmas to our Doctors, Sisters and Nurses!' in letters of cotton wool. The unfinished hotel had lacked its heating apparatus when war broke out; no such work, even for hospital use, was undertaken now. Huge open braziers of glowing coke had been brought in. 'Highly unsatisfactory,' Dr Murray rightly called them, but to the casual observer cosy and picturesque. Convalescent soldiers gathered about them exchanging yarns. All turned in welcome to Dr Murray and her women orderlies. There was an atmosphere of friendliness and peace, wherein life seemed ordered well.

When we had taken tea, and the typical thin bread and butter and toasted bun of a modest English household, with Dr Murray and her orderlies, we returned to the wards, and were left alone to talk to the patients. They spoke of the hospital as the desert-worn traveller of the oasis; yet some murmured sadly: of what use to be healed thus speedily of one's wounds, to be sent back only the sooner, to death or worse? Dr Murray had often complained in the days of the Cat and Mouse Act that her work of restoring Suffragette prisoners, discharged in a state of collapse from the hunger and thirst strike, was futile. More hopeless indeed was her task to-day! Some of the lads now due for return to the Front looked enviously at those who had lost a limb; the cripples congratulated themselves on their mutilation; and yet thought ruefully of the years to come.

A sad little Frenchman, his right arm gone, told us in hopeless grief that he did not know what had happened to his wife and children; the invading Germans had swept over the country where they lived. A giant from Normandy, handsome and fair, with a knee which would not mend, complained that his wife had only 25 sous a day and his children 10 sous each. 'It is not much!' he said. 'My God! not much!' A Reservist from Sheffield, a serious fellow, older than most of them, with bitter complaint that he would never be well again, turned from us, resenting intrusion. Then he heard my name and eagerly begged for me to be brought to him, grasping at a talk with me as someone familiar, not merely one of the many sightseers, doing the round of the hospitals; for he had heard me speak at some time, and my sister Adela often when she was a Suffragette organiser in Sheffield. He unburdened himself: the horror of the War and its ugliness; the terrible misery of the first day under fire, the deafening noise of the shells bursting on all sides, and the dreadful sight of them flying overhead, the fear of being hit, the sight of other men killed, their bodies hideously mangled. At last the pressure of routine work at the gun, the sheer physical strain of hard toil, dulled the senses. He had served with thirty others in relays of ten, carrying ammunition to the guns. As one man was killed, another stepped out to replace him. When off duty they slept in a pit roofed with branches, but when firing was brisk only short sleeps of one or two hours were allowed. Toiling in all weathers, pains shot through him when he stooped to lift the heavy shells. At last he fell to the ground and could not rise. He was bundled off to hospital with rheumatism and heart strain.

Some convalescent soldiers were preparing to act a play. The stage was a large platform, with the bare white wall behind, and a little door in the centre, through which the players came and went. The drama was called 'The Deserter'; it was a grim satire on Army life, acted with ingenuous fidelity and received with the fervent sympathy of the ward. Deep-felt murmurs of assent and whispered reminiscences buzzed round us. We were shown first the recruiting office. In comes the new recruit, a gay and perky little fellow, ambitious to be in the Guards. Rejected as too short, he goes off in the sulks, refusing to join at all; but in a moment is back again, all enthusiasm: 'I say, Guv'nor, put me in one of them Specials!' He spreads out his papers obligingly: 'See, this is where I've worked.' Friendly, confident, brotherly, he feels himself a fellow worth having and is anxious to assist the Army to put his services to good use.

We pass to the barrack yard; a squad is being drilled by 'Ser'nt Brown', a ridiculous elderly figure with a red nose and abnormally prominent chest. The new recruit plays the fool to relieve his boredom, raising his feet abnormally high in contorted grotesquery, and looking round with a grin to receive the encouragement of his fellows. A young officer enters and exchanges absurdly exaggerated salutes with Sergeant Brown. He eyes the men in the ranks and curtly criticises each one's appearance, the sergeant slavishly emphasising his derision. The new recruit, impishly resentful, feigns stupidity. Coarsely reprimanded, he retorts and argues, determined to give as vehemently as he gets.

The privates in the audience rejoiced bitterly at his quips, whispering poignant personal recollections to each other: 'Aye, that's it! Do you remember when old Choker—'

'Is it like that in the Army?' I asked a young convalescent beside me.

He answered seriously: 'Oh yes; just like that.'

The scenes move quickly; the soldiers are discovered by officers playing cards in the barrack room. All scamper out save the new recruit, who remains, calmly shuffling the cards, and is arrested for 'gambling', to the evident satisfaction of Sergeant Brown. . . .

The privates are scrubbing the floors of the barracks, slovenly, surly, rated and browbeaten by the officers. The new recruit declares he is 'fed up', and will run away. We see him next marched on to relieve a sentry, made to repeat in stereotyped form the length of his beat and the position of an imaginary enemy. Left alone, he props up his gun, hangs his hat and coat on it, and absconds. . . .

Two officers sit gravely examining documents. The deserter is brought before them. Witnesses reel off the evidence in a style reminiscent of police courts: 'On the umph of the umph, umph, umph I arrested the prisoner on the steps of the umph, umph, umph. When I arrested 'im 'e became dis-ord'ly and in the barrack room 'e struck Ser'nt Brown a blow on the right cheek and Pri't Jones a blow in the left eye. . . .'

The deserter is committed to the Divisional Court Martial. The officers there take oath 'not to divulge anything which takes place within this Court until the sentence is promulgated'. The deserter questions the witnesses. Why, if he were drunk, did Sergeant Brown allow him to pay for drinks all round? Sergeant Brown and the other officer reply with a firm denial. 'Sergeant Brown never drinks!'

'Then why is his nose so red?'

The judges silence the prisoner with shouts of 'liar!' Asked whether he has anything to say for himself, he pleads that he ran away because he was 'fed up'. 'What is "fed up"?' asks the senior among the judges. A young offi-cer explains: 'Sick and tired of the life of the Army altogether.' The prisoner is condemned to death. He staggers a little and covers his eyes with his hand. They march him out.

'Are they sentenced to death for running away?' I asked the lad at my elbow.

'Oh yes, on active service; and then you have to dig your own grave.'

'Have you ever seen a Court Martial?'

'Yes,' he said gravely, and raked the red coals in the brazier uncomfort-ably with a bit of stick, hunching his shoulders away from me, to preclude further questions.

The stage is again a barrack room; the soldiers squat on the floor playing cards. They are surprised by Sergeant Brown and another officer, and attempt ineffectually to gather the cards under their coats. Affecting not to notice, Sergeant Brown orders them out on to the parade ground. The deserter is brought in and asked if he wishes to be tied up. He prefers to stand free. He asks Sergeant Brown if his conscience does not prick him. A firing party is called out. The deserter is shot. Sergeant Brown brings a squad of men to remove the body.

The soldiers in the audience had grown depressed and moody, the play was too real to them.

Not far from Claridge's was the great Hotel Majestic, now a war hospital

and, with two others, run at the cost of H. D. Harben, Fabian-Suffragist—
Daily Heraldite. The smell of ether met us as we entered. The air of the corridors reeked with it from the operations constantly taking place. Lovely
young women from London, with snow-white skin and rose-red cheeks,
serving as orderlies, dashed about, working tremendously hard, motoring
with Harben to the other hospitals, zealously demolishing French pastries,
as restoratives.

Harben himself received us gaily, effervescent with enthusiasm: such
wonderful cures they had, such marvellous operations! A great taciturn
French peasant had been brought in with a bullet imbedded in the nape of
his neck, completely paralysed in all four limbs; the bullet extracted, he
could move again; what an achievement! Marvellous! Harben enthused; the
lovely young orderlies beamed their pleasure.

There was a hopeless misery in the wards we had not felt at Claridge's. They
were more crowded; the cases were more serious. Bed after bed was occupied
by poor fellows one could not venture to disturb; figures heavily swathed in
bandages, racked in their torment, stilled in unconsciousness; Algerians,
Moors, Tunisians unable to speak to nurse or doctor, ghastly in pallor; an
English boy of nineteen, incurably injured, bandaged from head to foot, his
beautiful face half hidden by wrappings and his dark eyes drawn with pain.

A Yorkshire footballer had lost for ever the use of a foot and a hand.

'What will you do when you go home?' one of the doctors asked him.

'I don't know,' he answered, 'unless the Government have some idea of
setting me up in a little business.'

He turned to me as though he thought I had some power to intercede for
him, his eyes dumbly pleading for assurance that his case would not be
overlooked. I could not meet his gaze.

A Lancashire man, terribly wounded, who had undergone three operations and was awaiting a fourth, spoke to us with resentful suffering in his
voice and horror in his eyes.

Three young French officers in a private ward (there was no defiance of
Army standards here, officers and men were rigidly separated) had been
wounded together when experimenting with a hand grenade. One of them
had lost the sight of an eye and the use of an ear, but he spoke lightly of
returning to the War.

I wanted to see my mother; much as her war attitude grieved me, far apart as
our views had grown, I could not be in Paris, where her home was then,
without a visit to her.

We found her at her fireside with Sister Pine. She would speak of nothing but the War, talking fast and emphatically, obviously perceiving—though we did not gainsay her by a single word—the opposition in our hearts.

I listened unhappily, speechless, resolved to occasion no quarrel. When she demanded suddenly: 'What are *you* doing?' with a strain of contemptuous irony in her voice, which I well knew from childhood, I answered only: 'In the East End.'

When Norah Smyth added: 'We have been to Scarborough', Mrs Pankhurst turned on her a tirade, declaring it impossible to police a vast coast-line such as ours when every man and every ounce of ammunition was needed at the Front. Then she reverted to the bellicose thesis which Christabel, now her unchallenged mentor, was propounding at the time: The blockade! A war of attrition! Intern them all! She seemed a very Maenad of the War with her flashing eyes.

We were distant from each other as though a thousand leagues had intervened; an aching void, in truth; for we were near, so poignantly near in the memory of old efforts and old loves. My senses were bruised by each familiar mannerism employed to accentuate these unfamiliar themes. A sad anticlimax to a life's struggle—the thought knelled like a death bell in my brain. I was glad to get away, exhausted by sorrow.

At Senlis, we were told, we should most readily see the damage done by the German advance in the first weeks of the War. The destruction was more hideously complete than I had imagined possible. The buildings had been systematically demolished and reduced to mere heaps of debris. It was difficult to realise that these deserted ruins had so lately been inhabited. A solitary woman stood sorrowing beside the charred remains of her home.

On Christmas Eve Lily Macdonnell and other friends had gone carolling through the night to gather pennies for our distress work. In Covent Garden soldiers went with them to aid in the collection. In Westminster some passing soldiers, taking their last meal before departure for the Front, begged them to come into their hut to sing to them and share their frugal fare.

In the New Year we held great parties for the children in Bow, in Poplar, in Canning Town. In Bow Baths more than 1,500 children assembled. We had asked for a present for every child. Gifts poured in so lavishly that every child had an armful of toys and comfortable garments. Mrs Arncliffe Sennett provided an enormous Christmas tree magnificently decorated. Actresses, singers, musicians, provided entertainments for children and grown-ups with all the old brilliance of the Suffragette movement. Rosy-faced, smiling Mary Philips, wearing a red cap of liberty came knitting to represent Madame Lafarge; a gesture intended to remind us that Suffragette militancy was not dead. We were swept along in a whirl of loving enthusi-asm. To me our goal was the equalitarian society of mutual service—in each of our band, even the remotest, the most casually attached to us, some glamour stirred.

Sylvia Pankhurst, from *The Home Front* (London: Hutchinson, 1987), 114–26

Maude Gonne
(1866–1953)

Maude Gonne was born in Surrey to Anglo-Irish parents and grew up in England, France, and Ireland. Her mother having died early, Gonne was mainly educated by a French governess of strong Republican views. Encouraged by the patriotic French journalist Lucien Millevoie, by whom she had two children, she became a supporter of Irish Republicanism. She cam-paigned in France, Britain, and the United States, founded the group *Inghinidhe Na Eireann* (Daughters of Ireland) and was briefly the editor of *L'Irlande libre* in Paris. From 1903 to 1905 she was married to the Irish patriot John MacBride, who was to be executed in 1916 for his part in the Easter Rising. By 1917 she had returned to Dublin to join the struggle, her militant activities earning her repeated spells in prison. The following letter is one of many addressed to William Butler Yeats, who nurtured a lifelong passion for her.

———

8   LETTER TO WILLIAM BUTLER YEATS

Arrens
Pyrenees
26 August [1914]

My dear Willie

YOU seemed to have escaped the obsession of this war—I cannot; night & day I think about it *uselessly*. I cannot work, I cannot read, I cannot sleep—I am torn in two, my love of France on one side, my love of Ireland on

the other for I know what we should have done just the contrary apparently
from what we have done—Redmond seems to have wasted a glorious
opportunity & Ireland seems too confused & inarticulate to redeem his
mistake—

This war is an inconceivable madness which has taken hold of Europe—
It is unlike any other war that has ever been. It has no great idea behind it.
Even the leaders hardly know why they have entered into it, & certainly the
people do not—(I except England from this, she, as usual, is following her
commercial selfishness getting others to fight so her commerce of existence
shall be ensured by the weakening of Germany).

Is it the slave & Germanic race trouble? If so, what logically has France to
do with it?

If it goes on, it is race suicide for all the countries engaged in it who have
conscription, only the weaklings will be left to carry on the race; & their
whole intelectual & industrial life is already at a standstill. The victor will be
nearly as enfeebled as the vanquished. And who is to end it? In France, in
Germany, in Austria only the old men & children & women are left, these
are not necessary elements for a revolution which might bring peace.

Could the women, who are after all the guardians of the race, end it?
Soon they will be in a terrible majority, unless famine destroys them too. I
always felt the wave of the woman's power was rising, the men are destroying themselves & we are looking on—Will it be in our power to end this war
before European civilisation is swept away—The press is busily engaged
working up race hatred in the interest of war—to make the people who are
fighting confusedly fiercer. Every day in the French papers there is a column
of *German attrocities* most I should think invented, though in all war there
are attrocities enough, two days ago an official order from Viviani or the
minister of war not to treat German prisoners *too well* as they were barbar-
ians—! Before the war is over there will probably be atrocities on both sides
to make the Bulgarians envious—

The post takes a long time to distribute letters—about 7 to 10 days from
Ireland. Have you got Iseult's letter with the translations yet? She was very
slow sending them, as she & Mukerjea had both got a spell of idleness on
them. However, they were really sent off to you about a week ago—

Helen Molony practises voice production regularly & with very good
results on the edge of a mountain torrent. She is very well & in good spirits
& *quite strong* again. I think you will be quite safe in taking her back to the
Abby [*sic*]—she will not break down again—Let me know *when* she ought
to be back in Dublin—It may be difficult to get there just now—Are the channel steamers running regularly between France & England. I hear the mail

goes regularly once a day to & from Ireland, travelling in France is slow & difficult but *possible* now. Write to me often & send news. I want it *badly*. Also send me an Irish paper occasionally, those sent by friends seem to come through alright, with considerable delay, but *The Freeman* which I have subscribed to has ceased to arrive & want of Irish news makes me very restless.

Though we are in a such a quiet place, so far from the war, the weather is really *war weather* strange thunderstorms, & floods—a house was nearly swept away yesterday, the people say they have not seen things like that since 1870 during the war—We have all heard strange sounds in the hill, drums beating, bells ringing, hammering etc. I got up twice last night & opened my window I was so certain the church bell was ringing—but it was not.

Alwys your friend
Maud Gonne

Kathleen & I are very anxious about Toby who has voluntered & gone as despatch carrier with the English force to Belgium.

Maude Gonne, from *The Gonne–Yeats Letters, 1893–1938*, ed. Anna MacBride White and A. Norman Jeffares (London: Hutchinson, 1992), 348–9

II

THE WAR OBSERVED

Dorothy Canfield
(1879–1958)

Born in Kansas to an artistic and academic family, Dorothy Canfield gained one of the first Ph.D.s awarded to a woman from Columbia University; she was steeped in European culture and spoke French, Italian, Spanish, German, and Norwegian. She married in 1907 and, when her husband went to France in 1916 as an ambulance driver, she joined him with their son and daughter; the family remained there until 1919. She was a prolific and competent novelist and short story writer, and her war writings include *The Day of Glory* (1919) and *Home Fires in France* (1918) from which the following story is taken.

———

9   La Pharmacienne

When the war broke out, Madeleine Brismantier was the very type and epitome of all which up to that time had been considered 'normal' for a modern woman, a *nice*, modern woman. She had been put through the severe and excellent system of French public education in her native town of Amiens, and had done so well with her classes that when she was nineteen her family were thinking of feeding her into the hopper of the system of training for primary teachers. But just then, when on a visit in a smallish Seine-et-Marne town, she met the fine, upstanding young fellow who was to be her husband. He was young too, not then quite through the long formidable course of study for pharmacists, so that it was not until two years later, when Madeleine was twenty-one and he twenty-five, that they were married, and Madeleine left Amiens to live in Mandriné, the town where they had met.

Jules Brismantier's father had been the principal pharmacist there all his life, and Jules stepped comfortably into his father's shoes, his business, and the lodgings over the pharmacy. If this sounds common and 'working-class' to your American ears, disabuse yourself; the habitation over the pharmacy was as well ordered and well furnished a little apartment as ever existed in a 'strictly residential portion' of any American suburb. The beds were heirlooms, and were of mahogany, there were several bits of excellent furniture in the small, white-paneled salon, and three pretty, brocade-covered chairs which had come down from Madeleine's great-grandmother; there was a piano on which Madeleine, who had received a good substantial musical training, played the best music there is in the world, which is to say, German (Jules, like many modern young Frenchmen, had a special cult for Beethoven); and there was a kitchen—oh, you should have seen that kitchen, white tiles on the walls and red tiles on the floor and all around such an array of copper and enamel utensils as can only be found in well-kept kitchens in the French provinces where one of the main amusements and occupations of the excellent housewives is elaborate cooking. Furthermore, there was in the big oaken chests and tall cupboards a supply of bedding which would have made us open our eyes, used as we are to our (relatively speaking) hand-to-mouth American methods. Madeleine had no more than the usual number of sheets, partly laid aside for her, piece by piece, when the various inheritances from provincial aunts and cousins came in, partly left there in the house, in which her mother-in-law had died the year before Madeleine's marriage, partly bought for her (as if there were not already enough!) to make up the traditional wedding trousseau without which no daughter of a respectable bourgeois provincial family can be married. So that, taking them all together, she had two hundred and twenty sheets, every one linen, varying from the delightfully rough old homespun and home-woven ones, dating from nobody knew when, down to the smooth, fine, glossy ones with deep hemstitching on the top and bottom, and Madeleine's initials set in a delicately embroidered wreath. Of course she had pillowslips to go with them, and piles of woolen blankets, fluffy, soft and white, and a big puffy eiderdown covered with bright satin as the finishing touch for each well-furnished bed. Madeleine pretended to be modern sometimes, and to say it was absurd to have so many, but in her heart, inherited from long generations of passionately home-keeping women, she took immense satisfaction in all the ample furnishings of her pretty little home. What woman would not?

Now, although all this has a great deal to do with what happened to Madeleine, I am afraid you will think that I am making too long an inventory of her house, so I will not tell you about the shining silver in the buffet drawers, nor even about the beautiful old walled garden, full of flowers and vines and fruit-trees, which lay at the back of the pharmacy. The back windows of the new bride's habitation looked down into the treetops of this garden, and along its graveled walks her children were to run and play.

For very soon the new family began to grow: first, a little blue-eyed girl like Madeleine; then, two years later, a dark-eyed boy like Jules—all very suitable and as it should be, like everything else that happened to

Madeleine. She herself, happily absorbed in her happy life and in the care of all her treasures, reverted rapidly to type, forgot most of her modern education, and became a model wife and mother on the pattern of all the other innumerable model wives and mothers in the history of her provincial family. She lived well within their rather small income, and no year passed without their adding to the modest store of savings which had come down to them because all their grandmothers had lived well within *their* incomes. They kept the titles relative to this little fortune, together with what cash they had, and all their family papers, in a safe in the pharmacy, sunk in the wall and ingeniously hidden behind a set of false shelves. They never passed this hiding-place without the warm, *sheltered* feeling which a comfortable little fortune gives,—the feeling which poor people go all their lives without knowing.

You must not think, because I speak so much of the comfortableness of the life of this typical French provincial family, that there was the least suspicion of laziness about them. Indeed, such intelligent comfort as theirs is only to be had at the price of diligent and well-directed effort. Jules worked hard all day in the pharmacy, and made less money than would have contented an American ten years his junior. Madeleine planned her busy day the evening before, and was up early to begin it. The house was always immaculate, the meals always on time (this was difficult to manage with Madeleine cooking everything and only a rattle-headed young girl to help) and always delicious and varied. Jules mounted the stairs from the pharmacy at noon and in the evening, his mouth literally watering in anticipation. The children were always as exquisitely fresh and well-cared for as only French children of the better classes can be, with their hair curled in shining ringlets and their hands clean, as those of our children are only on Sunday mornings. Madeleine's religion was to keep them spotless and healthful and smiling; to keep Jules' mouth always watering in anticipation; to help him with his accounts in the evenings, and to be on hand during the day to take his place during occasional absences; to know all about the business end of their affairs and to have their success as much at heart as he; to keep her lovely old garden flowering and luxuriant; to keep her lovely old home dainty and well ordered; and, of course, to keep herself invariably neat with the miraculous neatness of French women, her pretty, soft chestnut hair carefully dressed, her hands white and all her attractive person as alluring as in her girlhood.

Madeleine saw nothing lacking in this religion. It seemed to her all that life could demand of one woman.

In the spring of 1914, when Raoul was five years old and Sylvie eight,

Madeleine was once more joyfully sorting over the tiny clothes left from their babyhood. All that summer her quick fingers were busy with fine white flannel and finer white nainsook, setting tiny stitches in small garments. Every detail of the great event was provided for in advance. As usual in French families, in all good families everywhere, the mother-to-be was lapped around with tenderness and indulgence. Madeleine was a little queen-regnant whose every whim was law. Of course she wanted her mother to be with her, as she had been for the arrival of Sylvie and Raoul, although her mother was not very well, and detested traveling in hot weather; and she wanted the same nurse she had had before, although that one had now moved away to a distant city. But Madeleine did not like the voice of the nurse who was available in Mandriné, and what French daughter could think of going through her great, dreadful hour without her mother by her to comfort and reassure her and to take the responsibility of everything! So of course the nurse was engaged and her railway fare paid in advance, and of course Madeleine's mother promised to come. She was to arrive considerably in advance of the date, somewhere about the middle of August. All this was not so unreasonable from a money point of view as it sounds, for when they made up the weekly accounts together they found that the business was doing unusually well.

All through the golden July heats Madeleine sewed and waited. Sometimes in the pharmacy near Jules, sometimes in the garden where Raoul and Sylvie, in white dresses, ran and played gently up and down the paths. They played together mostly and had few little friends, because there were not many 'nice' families living near them, and a good many that weren't nice. Of course Madeleine kept her children rigorously separated from these children, who were never in white but in the plainest of cheap gingham aprons, changed only once a week, and who never wore shapely, well-cut little shoes, but slumped about heavily in the wooden-soled, leather-topped 'galoches' which are the national footgear for poor French children. Like many good mothers in France (are there any like that elsewhere?) Madeleine looked at other people's children chiefly to see if they were or were not 'desirable' playmates for her own; and Sylvie and Raoul were not three years old before they had also learned the art of telling at a glance whether another child was a nice child or not, the question being settled of course by the kind of clothes he wore.

July was a beautiful month of glorious sun and ripening weather. For hours at a time in her lovely green nest, Madeleine sat happily, resting or embroidering, the peaches pleached against the high stone walls swelling and reddening visibly from one day to the next, the lilies opening flaming petals day by day, the children growing vigorously. Jules told his pretty wife fondly that she looked not a day older than on the day of their marriage, ten years before. This was quite true, but I am not so sure as Jules that it was the highest of compliments to Madeleine.

The last week of July came, the high-tide moment of lush growth. Madeleine was bathed in the golden, dreamy content which comes to happy, much-loved women in her condition. It was the best possible of worlds, she had the best possible of husbands and children, and she was sure that nobody could say that she had not cultivated her garden to be the best possible of its kind. The world seemed to stand still in a sunny haze, centered about their happiness.

Drenched in sunshine and peace, their little barque was carried rapidly along by the Niagara river of history over the last stretch of smooth, shining water which separated them from the abyss.

I dare not tell you a single word about those first four days in August, of the utter incredulity which swiftly, from one dreadful hour to the next, changed to black horror. Their barque had shot over the edge, and in a wild tumult of ravening waters they were all falling together down into the fathomless gulf. And there are not words to describe to you the day of mobilization, when Jules, in his wrinkled uniform, smelling of moth-balls, said good-bye to his young wife and little children and marched away to do his best to defend them.

There are many things in real life too horrible to be spoken of, and that farewell is one.

There was Madeleine in the empty house, heavy with her time of trial close upon her; with two little children depending on her for safety and care and cheer; with only a foolish little young maid to help her; with such a terrible anxiety about her husband that the mere thought of him sent her reeling against the nearest support.

Almost at once came the Mayor in person, venerable and white-bearded, to gather up the weapons in all the houses. To Madeleine, wondering at this, he explained that he did it, so that *if* the Germans came to Mandriné he could give his word of honor there were no concealed arms in the town.

It was as though thunder had burst there in the little room. Madeleine stared at him, deathly white. 'You don't think . . . you don't think it possible that the Germans will get as far as *this!*' The idea that she and the children might be in danger was inconceivable to her. Monsieur le Maire hastened to reassure her, remembering her condition, and annoyed that he should have spoken out. 'No, no, this is only a measure of precaution, to leave nothing undone.' He went away, after having taken Jules' shotgun, her little revolver, and even a lockless, flintless old musket which had belonged to some of the kin who had followed Napoleon to Russia. As he left, he said, 'Personally I have not the faintest idea they will penetrate as far as Mandriné—not the *faintest!*'

Of course when Jules left, *no* one had the faintest idea that his peaceful home town would see anything of the war. That horror, at least, was spared the young husband and father. But during the fortnight after his departure, although there were no newspapers, practically no trains, and no information except a brief, brief announcement, written by hand, in ink, posted every day on the door of the Town Hall, the air began to be unbreathable, because of rumors, sickening rumors, unbelievable ones . . . that Belgium was invaded, although not in the war at all, and that Belgian cities and villages were being sacked and burned; that the whole north country was one great bonfire of burning villages and farms; then that the Germans were near! Were nearer! And then all at once, quite definitely, that they were within two days' march.

Every one who could, got out of Mandriné, but the only conveyances left were big jolting farm-wagons piled high with household gear; wagons which went rumbling off, drawn by sweating horses lashed into a gallop by panic-stricken boys, wagons which took you, nobody knew where, away! away! which might break down and leave you anywhere, beside the road, in a barn, in a wood, in the hands of the Germans . . . for nobody knew where they were. The frightened neighbors, clutching their belongings into bundles, offered repeatedly to take Madeleine and the children with them. Should she go or not? There was nobody to help her decide. The little fluttering maid was worse than nothing, the children were only babies to be taken care of. After her charges were all in bed, that last night, Madeleine wrung her hands, walking up and down the room, literally sick with indecision. What ought she to do? It was the first great decision she had ever been forced to make alone.

The last of the fleeing carts went without her. During the night she had come to know that the first, the most vital of all the innumerable and tragic needs of the hour was the life of the unborn baby. She was forced to cling to the refuge she had. She did not dare fare forth into the unknown until she had her baby safely in her arms.

And perhaps the Germans would not come to Mandriné.

For two days the few people left in town lived in a sultry suspense, with no news, with every fear. M. le Curé had stayed with his church; M. le Maire stayed with the town records, and his white-haired old wife stayed to be with her husband (they had never been separated during the forty years of their marriage); good fresh-faced Sister Ste. Lucie, the old nun in charge of the little Hospice, stayed with some bed-ridden invalids who could not be moved; and there were poor people who had stayed for the reason which makes poor people do so many other things, because they could not help it, because they did not own a cart, nor a wheelbarrow, nor even a child's perambulator in which to take along the old grandfather or the sick mother who could not walk. Sœur Ste. Lucie promised to come to be with Madeleine whenever she should send the little maid with the summons.

Madeleine sickened and shivered and paled during these two endless days and sleepless nights of suspense. There were times when she felt she must die of sheer horror at the situation in which she found herself, that it was asking too much of her to make her go on living. At such moments she shook as though in a palsy and her voice trembled so that she could not speak aloud. There were other times when she was in an unnatural calm, because she was absolutely certain that she was dreaming and must soon wake up to find Jules beside her.

The children played in the garden. They discovered a toad there, during that time, and Madeleine often heard them shouting with laughter over its antics. The silly little maid came every few moments to tell her mistress a new rumor . . . she had heard the Germans were cannibals and ate little children, was that true? And was it true that they had a special technique for burning down whole towns at once, with kerosene pumps and dynamite petards? One story seemed as foolish as the other to Madeleine, who hushed her angrily and told her not to listen to such lies. Once the little maid began to tell her in a terrified whisper what she had heard the Germans did to women in Madeleine's condition . . . but the recital was cut short by a terrible attack of nausea which lasted for hours and left Madeleine so weak that she could not raise her head from the pillow. She lay there, tasting the bitterness of utter necessity. Weak as she was, she was the strongest of their little band. Presently she rose and resumed the occupations of the day, but she was stooped forward for very feebleness like an old woman.

She told herself that she did not believe a single word the terror-stricken little maid had told her; but the truth was that she was half dead with fear, age-old, terrible, physical fear, which had been as far from her life before as a desire to eat raw meat or to do murder. It was almost like a stroke of paralysis to this modern woman.

For two whole days the town lay silent and helpless, waiting the blow, in an eternity of dread. On the morning of the third day the sound of clumsily clattering hoofs in the deserted street brought Madeleine rushing down-stairs to the door of the pharmacy. An old farmer, mounted on a sweating plow horse, drew rein for an instant in the sun and, breathing hard, gave the news to the little cluster of white-faced women and old men who gathered about him. Madeleine pressed in beside her poorer neighbors, closer to them than at any time in her life, straining up to the messenger, like them, to hear the stroke of fate. Its menacing note boomed hollowly in their ears. The Germans were in the next town, Larot-en-Multien, only eight miles away. The vanguard had stopped there to drink and eat, but behind them was an antlike gray horde which pressed steadily forward with incredible haste and would be in Mandriné within two hours.

He gathered up his reins to go on, but paused to add a brief suggestion as to what they might expect. The Germans were too hurried to burn or to destroy houses; they were only taking everything which was easily portable. They had robbed the church, had taken all the flour from the mill, all the contents of all the shops, and when he left (the sight of the shining plate-glass windows of the pharmacy reminded him) they were just in the act of looting systematically the pharmacy of Larot, taking down all the contents of the shelves and packing them carefully into a big camion.

He rode on. The women dispersed, scurrying rapidly each to her dependents, children, or sick women, or old men. The Mayor hurried away to carry a few more of his priceless town records to the hiding-place. The priest went back to his church. For an instant Madeleine was left alone in the empty street, echoing to disaster impending. She looked at the pharmacy, shining, well ordered, well stocked, useful, *as Jules had left it*.

At the call to action her sickness vanished like a mere passing giddiness. Her knees stiffened in anger. They should not carry off everything from the Mandriné pharmacy! What could the town *do* without remedies for its sick? The mere first breath from the approaching tornado annihilating all in its path crashed through the wall which had sheltered her small, comfortably arranged life. Through the breach in the wall she had a passing glimpse of what the pharmacy was; not merely a convenient way for Jules to earn enough for her and the children to live agreeably, but one of the vital necessities of the community life, a very important trust which Jules held.

And now Jules was gone and could not defend it. But she was there.

She ran back into the shop, calling for her little maid, in a loud, clear voice such as had not issued from her throat since Jules had gone away. 'Simone! Simone!'

The maid came running down the stairs and at the first sight of her mistress expected to hear that her master had returned or that the French troops were there, so like herself did Madeleine seem, no longer stooping and shivering and paper-white, but upright, with hard, bright eyes. But it was no good news which she brought out in the new ringing voice. She said: 'The Germans will be here in two hours. Help me quickly hide the things in the cellar . . . you know, the further room . . . and we can put the hanging shelves over the door so they won't know there is another part to the cellar. Bring down the two big trays from the kitchen. We can carry more that way. Then light two or three candles up and down the cellar stairs. It won't do for me to fall, these last days.'

She was gathering the big jars together as she spoke, and taking out the innumerable big and little drawers.

In a moment the two women, one who had been hardly strong enough to walk, the other scarcely more than a child, were going slowly down the cellar stairs, their arms aching with the weight of the trays and then running back upstairs in feverish haste. Shelf after shelf was cleared of the precious remedies that meant health, that might mean life, in the days to come. The minutes slipped past. An hour had gone.

From her attic windows from where she could see the road leading to Lorat-en-Multien, a neighbor called down shrilly that dust was rising up in thick clouds at the lower end. And even as she called, silently, composedly, there pedaled into the long main street five or six men in gray uniforms on bicycles, quite calm and sure of themselves, evidently knowing very well that the place had no defenders. Madeleine saw the white hair of M. le Curé and the white beard of M. le Maire advance to meet the invaders.

'We can't do any more here,' she said. 'Down to the cellar now, to mask the door. No, I'll do it alone. Somebody must be here to warn us. We mustn't be caught down there.' She turned to go, and came back. 'But I can't move the hanging shelves alone!'

Simone ventured, 'Mlle. Sylvie? Could she watch and tell us?'

Madeleine hesitated a fraction. Sylvie, like her mother, had been asked to do very little with herself except to be a nice person.

Then, 'Sylvie! Sylvie!' called her mother with decision.

The little girl came running docilely, her clear eyes wide in candid wonder.

Madeleine bent on her a white, stern face of command. 'The Germans are almost here. Simone and I have been hiding papa's drugs in the cellar and we've not finished. Stay here . . . pretend to be playing . . . and call to us the moment you see the soldiers coming. *Do you understand?*'

Sylvie received her small baptism of fire with courage. Her chin began to tremble and she grew very white. This was not because she was afraid of the Germans. Madeleine had protected her from all the horrid stories which filled the town, and she had only the vaguest baby notions of what the Germans were. It was her mother's aspect, awful to the child, which terrified her. But it also braced her to effort. She folded her little white lips hard and nodded. Madeleine and the maid went down the cellar stairs for the last time.

When they came back, the troops were still not there, although one could see beyond the river the cloud of white dust raised by their myriad feet. The two women were covered with earth and cobwebs, and were breathing heavily. Their knees shook under them. Taking the child with them, they went up the stairs to the defenseless home. They found five-year-old Raoul just finishing the house-and-farmyard which he and Sylvie were beginning when she was called down. 'If only I had three more blocks to do this corner!' he lamented.

Twenty minutes from that time they heard heavy, rapid footsteps enter the shop below and storm up the stairs. There was a loud knocking, and the sound of men's voices in a strange language.

Madeleine went herself to open the door. This was not an act of bravery but of dire necessity. There was no one else to do it. She had already sent the children to the most remote of the rooms, and at the sound of those trampling feet and hoarse voices Simone had run away, screaming. Madeleine's fingers shook as she pushed back the bolt. A queer pulse began to beat very fast in the back of her dry throat.

The first Germans she had ever seen were there before her. Four or five tall, broad, red-faced men, very hot, very dusty, in gray, wrinkled uniforms and big boots, pushed into the room past her. One of them said to her in broken French: 'Eat! Eat! Drink! Very thirsty. Quick!' The others had already seized the bottles on the sideboard and were drinking from them.

Madeleine went into the kitchen and brought back on a big tray every-thing ready-cooked which was there: a dish of stew, cold and unappetizing in its congealed fat, a long loaf of bread, a big piece of cheese, a platter of cooked beans. . . . The men drinking at the sideboard cried aloud hoarsely and fell upon the contents of the tray, clutching, cramming food into their mouths, into their pockets, gulping down the cold stew in huge mouthfuls, shoveling the beans up in their dirty hands and plastering them into their mouths, already full. . . .

Some one called, warningly, from below. The men snatched up what bottles were at hand, thrust them into their pockets, and still tearing off huge mouthfuls from the cheese, the bread, the meat, they held, and masticating them with animal noises, turned and clattered down the stairs again, having paid no more attention to Madeleine than if she had been a piece of the furniture.

They had come and gone so rapidly that she had the impression of a vivid, passing hallucination. For an instant she continued to see them there still, in lightning flashes. Everywhere she looked, she saw yellow teeth, gnawing and tearing at food; bulging jaw-muscles straining; dirty foreheads streaked with perspiration, wrinkled like those of eating dogs; bloodshot eyes glaring in physical greed.

'Oh, les sales bêtes!' she cried out loud. 'The dirty beasts!'

Her fear left her, never to come back, swept away by a bitter contempt. She went, her lip curling, her knees quite strong under her, to reassure Simone and the children.

The house shook, the windows rattled, the glasses danced on the sideboard to the thunder of the innumerable marching feet outside, to the endless rumble of the camions and artillery. The volume of this wild din, and the hurried pulse of straining haste which was its rhythm, staggered the imagination. Madeleine scorned to look out of the window, although Simone and the children called to her from behind the curtains: 'There are millions and millions of them! They are like flies! You couldn't cross the street, not even running fast, they are so close together! And how they hurry!'

Madeleine heard some one come up the stairs and enter the hall without knocking. She found there a well-dressed man with slightly gray hair who informed her in correct French, pronounced with a strong accent, that he would return in one hour bringing with him four other officers and that he would expect to find food and drink ready for them. Having said this in the detached, casual tone of command of a man giving an order to a servant, he went away down the stairs, unfolding a map.

Madeleine had all but cried an angry refusal after him, but, as brutally as on a gag in her mouth, she choked on the sense of her absolute defenselessness in the face of physical force. This is a sensation which moderns have blessedly forgotten, like the old primitive fear of darkness or of thunder. To feel it again is to be bitterly shamed. Madeleine was all one crimson flame of humiliation as she called Simone and went into the kitchen.

They cooked the meal and served it an hour later to five excited, elated officers, spreading out maps as they ate, laughing, drinking prodigiously and eating, with inconceivable rapidity, such vast quantities of food that Simone was sure she was serving demons and not human beings and crossed herself repeatedly as she waited on table. In spite of all their haste they had not time to finish. Another officer came up the stairs, thrust his head in through the door, and called a summons to them. They sprang up, in high feather at what he had said, snatching at the fruit which Simone had just set on the table. Madeleine saw one of her guests crowd a whole peach, as big as an apple, into his mouth at once, and depart, choking and chewing, leaning over so that the stream of juice which ran from his mouth should not fall on his uniform.

Simone shrieked from the kitchen, 'Oh, madame! The garden! The garden!'

Madeleine ran to a window, looked down, and saw long rows of horses picketed in the garden. Two German soldiers were throwing down hay from the gable end of the Mandriné livery-stable which overlooked the wall. The horses ate with hungry zest, stamping vigorously in the flowerbeds to keep off the flies. When they had finished on the hay, they began on the vines, the little, carefully tended fruit-trees, the bushes, the flowers. A swarm of locusts could not have done the work more thoroughly.

As she stood there, gazing down on this, there was always in Madeleine's ears the incessant thundering rumble of the passing artillery. . . .

Through the din there reached her ears a summons roared out from below: 'Cellar! Cellar! Key!'

She was at white heat. She ran downstairs, forgetting all fear, and, raising her voice to make herself heard above the uproar outside, she shouted with a passionate wrath which knew no prudence: 'You low, vile thieves! I will not give you one thing more!'

Her puny defiance to the whirlwind passed unnoticed. The men did not even take the time to strike her, to curse her. With one movement they turned from her to the cellar door, and, all kicking at it together, burst it open, trooped downstairs, returning with their arms full of bottles and ran out into the street.

And all the time the very air shook, in almost visible waves, to the incessant thundering rumble of the artillery passing.

Madeleine went upstairs, gripping the railing hard, her head whirling. She had scarcely closed the door behind her when it was burst open and five soldiers stormed in, cocked revolvers in their fists. They did not give her a look, but tore through the apartment, searching in every corner, in every closet, pulling out the drawers of the bureaus, tumbling the contents on the floor, sweeping the cupboard shelves clear in one movement of their great hands, with the insane haste which characterized everything done that day. When they had finished they clattered out, chalking up something unintelligible on the door. Raoul and Sylvie began to cry wildly, their nerves undone, and to clutch at their mother's skirts.

Madeleine took them back into their own little room, undressed them and put them to bed, where she gave them each a bowl of bread and milk. All this she did with a quiet air of confidence which comforted the children. They had scarcely finished eating when they fell asleep, worn out. Madeleine heard Simone calling for her and went out in the hall. A German soldier, desperately drunk, held out a note which stated that four Herr-Lieutenants and a Herr-Captain would eat and sleep there that night, dinner to be sharp at seven, and the beds ready.

After delivering this he tried to put his arm around Simone and to drag her into the next room. Simone struggled and screamed, shriek after shriek, horribly. Madeleine screamed too, and snatching up the poker, flung herself on the man. He released his hold, too uncertain on his feet to resist. Both women threw themselves against him, pushing him to the door and shoving him out on the narrow landing, where he lost his balance and fell heavily, rolling over and over, down the stairs.

Madeleine bolted the door, took a long knife from the kitchen table, and waited, her ear at the keyhole, to see if he tried to come back.

This was the woman, you must remember, who less than a month before had been sitting in the garden sewing on fine linen, safe in an unfathomable security.

The man did not attempt to return. Madeleine relaxed her tense crouching attitude and laid the knife down on the table. The perspiration was streaming down her white cheeks. It came over her with piercing horror that their screams had not received the slightest response from the outside world. No one was responsible for their safety. No one cared what became of them. It made no difference to any one whether they had repelled that man, or whether he had triumphed over their resistance. . . .

And now she must command her shaking knees and trembling hands to prepare food for those who had sent him there. Of all the violent efforts Madeleine had been forced to make none was more racking than to stoop to the servility of this submission. She had an instant of frenzy when she thought of locking the door and defying them to enter, but the recollection of the assault on the thick oaken planks of the cellar door, and of its splintering collapse before those huge hobnailed boots, sent her to the kitchen, her teeth set in her lower lip. 'I never will forgive them this, never, never, never!' she said aloud passionately, more passionately than she had ever said anything in her life, and she knew as she spoke that it was not of the slightest consequence to any one whether she would or not.

At seven the meal was ready. At half-past seven the four officers entered, laughing, talking loudly, jubilant. One of them spoke in good French to Madeleine, complimenting her on her soup and on the wine. 'I told my friends I knew we would find good cheer and good beds with Madame Brismantier,' he told her affably.

Astonished to hear her name, Madeleine looked at him hard, and recognized, in spite of his uniform, a well-to-do man, reputed a Swiss, who had rented a house for the season, several summers back, on a hillside not far from Mandriné. He had professed a great interest in the geology of the region and was always taking long walks and collecting fossils. Jules had an amateur interest in fossils also, and this, together with the admirably trained voice of the Swiss, had afforded several occasions of social contact. The foreigner had spent an evening or two with them, singing to Madeleine's accompaniment. And once, having some valuable papers left on his hands, he had asked the use of the Brismantier safe for a night. He had been very fond of children, and had had always a jolly greeting for little Raoul, who was then only a baby of two. Madeleine looked at him now, too stupefied with wonder to open her lips. A phrase from 'An die ferne Geliebte', which he had sung very beautifully, rang in her ears, sounding faint and thin but clear, through the infernal din in the street.

She turned abruptly and went back into the kitchen. Standing there, before the stove, she said suddenly, as though she had but just known it, 'Why, he was a spy, all the time!' She had not thought there were such people as spies outside of cheap books.

She was just putting the roast on the table when some one called loudly from the street. The men at the table jumped up, went to the window, leaned out, exchanged noisy exultant words, cursed jovially, and turned back in haste to tighten the belts and fasten the buttons and hooks which they had loosened in anticipation of the feast. The spy said laughingly to Madeleine: 'Your French army runs away so fast, madame, that we cannot eat or sleep for chasing it! Our advance guard is always sending back word to hurry faster, faster!'

One of the others swept the roast from the table into a brown sack, all crammed their pockets full of bread and took a bottle under each arm. At the door the spy called over his shoulder: 'Sorry to be in such a hurry! I will drop you a card from Paris as soon as the mails begin again.'

They clattered down the stairs.

Madeleine bolted the door and sank down on a chair, her teeth chattering loudly. After a time during which she vainly strove to master a mounting tide of pain and sickness, she said: 'Simone, you must go for Sister Ste.

Lucie. My time has come. Go by our back door, through the alley, and knock at the side door of the Hospice . . . you needn't be gone more than three minutes.'

Simone went downstairs, terribly afraid to venture out, even more afraid to be left alone with her mistress. Madeleine managed to get into the spare bedroom, away from the children's room, and began to undress, in an anguish of mind and body such as she had not thought she could endure and live. But even now she did not know what was before her. In a short time Simone came back, crying and wringing her hands. A sentry guarded the street and another the alley. They had thrust her back into the house, their bayonets glittering, and one had said in French, 'Forbidden; no go out till daylight.' She had tried to insist, to explain, but he had struck her back with the butt end of his rifle. Oh, he had hurt her awfully! She cried and cried, looking over her shoulder, tearing at her apron. It was evident that if there had been any possibility for her to run away, she would have done it, any-where, anywhere . . .

Madeleine's little boy was born that night. She, who of course must needs have her mother to take all the responsibility, and the nurse whose voice was agreeable to her, went through her fiery trial alone, with no help but the fool-ish little Simone, shivering and gasping in hysteria. She was nothing but a pair of hands and feet to be animated by Madeleine's will-power and intelligence. In those dreadful hours Madeleine descended to the black depths of her agony but dared never abandon herself even to suffer. At every moment she needed to shock Simone out of her panic by a stern, well-considered command.

She needed, and found, strange, unguessed stores of strength and reso-lution. She felt herself alone, pitted against a malign universe which wished to injure her baby, to prevent her baby from having the right birth and care. But she felt herself to be stronger than all the malignity of the universe. Once, in a moment's lull during the fight, she remembered, seeing the words, zigzag like lightning on a black sky,—a sentence in the first little history-book she had studied as a child,—'The ancient Gauls said they feared nothing, not enemies, not tempest, not death. Until the skies fell upon their heads, they would never submit.' . . . 'They were my ancestors!' said the little Gaulish woman, fighting alone in the darkness. She clenched her teeth to repress a scream of pain and a moment later told Simone, quite clearly, in a quiet tone of authority, just what to do, again.

Outside, all night long, there thundered the rumbling passage of the artillery and camions.

In the morning, when Sylvie and Raoul awoke, they found Simone crouched in a corner of their mother's room, sobbing endlessly tears of sheer nervous exhaustion. But out from their mother's white, white face on the pillow looked triumphant eyes. She drew the covers down a little and lifted her arm. 'See, children, a little new brother.'

As she spoke she thrust out of her mind, with a violence like that with which she had expelled the ruffian from the door, the thought that the little brother would probably never see his father. It was no moment to allow herself the weakness of a personal sorrow. She must marshal her little forces. 'Come, Sylvie dear. Simone is all tired out; you must get us something to eat, and then you and Simone must bring in all you can of what is left in the kitchen and hide it here under mother's bed.' She had thought out her plan in the night.

During the next days Madeleine was wholly unable to stand on her feet. From her bed she gave her orders—desperate, last-resort orders to a defeated garrison. The apartment was constantly invaded by ravenously hungry and thirsty men, but her room was not entered. The first morning the door to her room had been opened brusquely, and a gray-haired under-officer entered hastily. He stopped short when he saw Madeleine's drawn white face on the pillow, with the little red, bald head beside her. He went out as abruptly as he had gone in and chalked something on the door. Thereafter no one came in; although not infrequently, as though to see if the chalked notice were true, the door was opened suddenly and a head with a spiked helmet thrust in. This inspection of a sick woman's room could and did continually happen without the slightest warning. Madeleine was buffeted by an angry shame which she put aside sternly, lest it make her unfit to nurse her baby.

They lived during this time on what happened to be left in the kitchen, after that first day of pillage, some packages of macaroni, tapioca, and corn-starch, part of a little cheese, some salt fish, two or three boxes of biscuits, a little sugar, a little flour. They did unsavory cooking over the open fire till their small supply of wood gave out. The children submitted docilely to this régime, cowed by their mother's fierce command not for an instant to go out of her sight. But the little maid, volatile and childish, could not endure life without bread. She begged to be allowed to go out, to slip along the alley to the Hospice and beg a loaf from Sister Ste. Lucie. There must be bread somewhere in town, she argued, unable to conceive of a world without bread. And in the daytime the sentries would let her pass.

Madeleine forbade her to leave the room, but on the third day when her mistress was occupied with the baby she slipped out and was gone. She did not come back that day or the next. They never saw or heard of her from that moment.

Madeleine and the children continued to live in that one room, shaken by the incessant rumble of the passing artillery wagons and by the hurrying tread of booted feet. They heard now and again incursions into the other rooms of their home, and as long as there were loud voices and trampling and clattering dishes, the children crept into bed beside Madeleine and the baby, cowering together under the poor protection of their mother's powerless arms. They never dared speak above a whisper during those days. They heard laughing, shouting, cursing, snoring in the rooms all around them. Once they heard pistol shots, followed by a great splintering crash of glass and shouts of wild mirth.

Madeleine lost all count of the days, of everything but the diminishing stock of food. She tried repeatedly to sit up, she tried to put her feet to the floor, but she felt her head swim and fell back in bed. She had little strength left to struggle now. The food was almost gone, and her courage was almost gone. As though the walls of the room were closing in on her, the approach of the spent, beaten desire to die began to close in on her. What was the use of struggling on? If she could only kill the children and herself . . . there was no hope.

One morning Sylvie said in a loud, startled whisper: 'Oh, *maman*, they are going the other way! Back towards Lorat . . . and yet they are still hurrying as fast as ever . . . faster!'

Madeleine felt her hair raise itself on her scalp. She sat up in bed. 'Sylvie, *are you sure?*'

And when the child answered, always in her strained whisper, 'Yes, yes, I am sure,' her mother sprang out of bed with a bound and ran to the window.

It was true. The dusty-gray tide had turned. They were raging past the house, the horses straining at the heavy artillery wagons, lashed into a clumsy canter by the drivers, leaning far forward, straining, urging; the haggard men, reeling in fatigue, stumbling under their heavy packs, pressing forward in a dog-trot; the officers with red angry faces, barking out incessant commands for more haste . . . and their backs were turned to Paris!

The Frenchwoman, looking down on them, threw her arms up over her head in a wild gesture of exultation. They were going back!

She felt as strong as ever she had in her life. She dressed herself, set the wretched room in some sort of order, and managed to prepare an edible dish out of soaked tapioca and sugar. The children ate it with relish, comforted by their mother's new aspect.

About two o'clock that night Madeleine awoke to an awful sense of impending calamity. Something had happened, some tremendous change had come over the world. She lay still for a long moment, hearing only the beating of her own heart. Then she realized that she heard nothing but that, that the thunder of the trampling feet had stopped. She got out of bed carefully, trying not to waken the children, but Sylvie, her nerves aquiver, heard and called out in a frightened whisper, '*Maman, maman!* What is it?' She caught her mother's arm, and the two went together to the window. They leaned out, looked to right and left, and fell to weeping in each other's arms. Under the quiet stars, the village street was perfectly empty.

The next morning Madeleine made the children swallow a little food before, all together, the baby in his mother's arms, they ventured out from their prison-room. They found their house gutted and sacked and sullied to the remotest corner. The old brocade on the chairs in the salon had been slit to ribbons by sword-slashes, the big plate-glass windows over the mantel-pieces had each been shattered into a million pieces, all the silver was gone from the drawers, every piece of linen had disappeared, the curtains had been torn down and carried away, and every bit of bedding had gone, every sheet, every blanket, every eiderdown quilt. The mattresses had been left, each having been cut open its entire length and sedulously filled with filth.

The kitchen, emptied of all its shining copper and enamel utensils, was one litter of splintered wood, remnants of furniture which had been cut up with the ax for fuel. Madeleine recognized pieces of her mahogany beds there. Through the kitchen window she looked down into the walled space which had been the garden and saw it a bare, trampled stable-yard, with heaps of manure at each end. She looked at all this in perfect silence, the children clinging to her skirts, the baby sleeping on her arm. She looked at it, but days passed before she really believed that what she saw was real.

A woman's voice called quaveringly from the landing: 'Madame Brismantier, are you there? Are you alive? The Germans have gone.' Madeleine stepped to the landing and saw old Sister Ste. Lucie, her face which had always been so rosy and fresh, as gray as ashes under her black-and-white coif. She leaned against the wall as she stood. At the sight of the sleeping baby in Madeleine's arms, the gray face smiled, the wonderful smile which women, even those vowed to childlessness, give to a new mother. 'Oh, your baby came,' she said. 'Boy or girl?'

'Yes,' said Madeleine, 'he came. A boy. A nice little boy.' For one instant the two women stood there in that abomination of desolation, with death all around them, looking down at the baby, and smiling.

Then Sœur Ste. Lucie said: 'There is nothing left in the pharmacy, I see. I thought maybe they might have left something, by chance, but I see everything is smashed to pieces. You don't happen to have any supplies up here, do you? We need bandages horribly at the Hospice, for the wounded. There are forty there.'

Madeleine knew the minute size of the little Hospice and exclaimed: '*Forty!* Where do you put them?'

'Oh, everywhere, on the floor, up and down the hall, in the kitchen. But we haven't a thing except hot water to use for them; all the sheets were torn up two days ago, what they hadn't stolen! If I only had a little iodine, or any sort of antiseptic. Their wounds are too awful, all infected, and nothing...'

Without knowing it Madeleine took a first step forward into a new life. 'There's plenty of everything,' she said. 'I hid them all in the far room of the cellar.'

'God grant "they" didn't find them!' breathed the nun.

Madeleine lighted a candle, left the sleeping baby in the charge of Sylvie, and went with Sœur Ste. Lucie down into the cellar. They found it littered and blocked with emptied and broken bottles. A strange hoarse breathing from a dark corner frightened them. Lifting her candle, Madeleine brought to view a German soldier, dead-drunk, snoring, his face swollen and red. The women let him lie as an object of no importance and turned to the hanging shelves. They heaved a long sigh; the blind was still there, untouched. Madeleine's device was successful.

As they looked among the heaped-up supplies from the pharmacy for bandages and antiseptics, Sœur Ste. Lucie told Madeleine very briefly what had been happening. Madeleine listened in a terrible silence. Neither she nor the nun had strength to spare for exclamations. Nor could any words of theirs have been adequate. The news needed no comment. M. le Maire was dead, shot in front of the Town Hall, on the ground that there had been weapons found in one of the houses. 'You know in the Bouvines' house they had some Malay creeses and a Japanese sword hanging up in M. Bouvines' study, things his sailor uncle brought back. The Mayor never thought to take those down, and they wouldn't give him time to explain. M. le Curé was dead, nobody knew or ever would know why—found dead of starvation, strapped to a bed in an attic room of a house occupied by some German officers. Perhaps he had been forgotten by the person who had tied him there. . . .' The nun's voice died away in sobs. She had been brought up under M. le Curé's protection all her life and loved him like a father.

Madeleine sorted bandages in silence, her throat very dry and harsh. Later Sœur Ste. Lucie went on, trying to speak more collectedly: 'The worst of trying to care for these wounded is not being able to understand what they say.'

'How so?' asked Madeleine, not understanding in the least.

'Why, I don't speak German.'

Madeleine stopped short, her hands full of bandages. 'Are they *German* wounded? Are we getting these things for *German soldiers?*'

Sœur Ste. Lucie nodded gravely. 'Yes, I felt just so, too, at first. But when I saw them wounded, bleeding, so sick, worn out. . . . How would you like German women to treat your husband if he should be wounded in Germany? We are all nothing but wretched sinners in the sight of God. And are we not taught to do good to our enemies?'

Of all this (which meant in reality simply that Sœur Ste. Lucie was a warm-hearted woman whose professional habit had been for forty years to succor the afflicted) Madeleine took in very little at the time, although it was to come back to her again and again. At the moment she thought that she did not believe a single word of it. She certainly did not at all think that we are the best of us but wretched sinners, and she had as remotely academic a belief as any other twentieth-century dweller in the desirability of doing good to your enemies. The idea of Jules wounded in Germany did indeed bring a flood of confused emotions into her mind. If Germany should be invaded, would Frenchmen be stamping into strangers' houses and taking the food out of the mouths of the owners, would they . . .?

'Well,' said Sœur Ste. Lucie, impatient of her trance-like stare.

It was none of what she had been thinking which now moved Madeleine to say automatically, 'Oh, of course we'll have to give them the bandages and the peroxide.' She could not have named the blind impulse which drove her to say this, beyond that a sort of angry self-respect was mixed with it. Her head ached furiously, whirling with fatigue and lack of food, her back ached as though it were being beaten with hammers. She renounced any attempt to think.

'Here,' said Sœur Ste. Lucie, staggering herself with exhaustion. 'The baby is only a few days old. You're not fit to be doing this.'

Madeleine, who had lain flat on her back for two weeks after the birth of the other two children, shook her head. 'No, no, I can do it as well as you. You look fearfully tired.'

'I haven't had my clothes off for ten days,' said the nun. 'And I'm sixty-two years old.'

In the street door, with her basket of bandages on her arm, Sœur Ste.

Lucie stood looking around her at the desolate filth-strewn shop, the million pieces of glass which had been its big windows covering the floor, its counter hacked and broken with axes. She said: 'We haven't any mayor and the priest is dead, and we haven't any pharmacy and the baker is mobilized, and there isn't one strong, well man left in town. How are we going to live?'

Madeleine took another step, hesitating, along the new road. She leaned against the counter to ease her aching body and put back her hair to look around her at the wreck and ruin of her husband's business. She said in a faint voice: 'I wonder if I could keep the pharmacy open. I used to help Jules with the accounts. I know a little about where he bought and how he kept his records. I wonder if I could—enough for the simpler things?'

'You have already,' said the nun, as she went away, 'and the first things you have given out are bandages for your enemies. God will not forget that.'

Madeleine received this with an impatient shrug. She was not at all glad that her first act had been to help the suffering among her enemies. She had hated doing it, had only done it because of some confused sense of decency. She heartily wished she had not had it to do. But if it had been necessary, she would have done it again . . . and yet to do it for those men who had murdered M. le Maire, so blameless and M. le Curé—so defenseless! . . . No, these were not the same men who lay bleeding to death in the Hospice to whom she had sent bandages. *They* had not murdered . . . as yet!

Her head throbbed feverishly. She renounced again the effort to think, and thrusting all this ferment down into her subconsciousness she turned to the urgent needs of the moment. It seemed to her that she could not breathe till she had set the pharmacy as far as possible in the order Jules had left it. This feeling, imperious and intense, was her only refuge against her certainty that Jules was killed, that she would never see him again. Without an attempt to set to rights even a corner of the desolated little home, upstairs, she began toiling up and down the cellar stairs carrying back the glass jars, the pots, the boxes, and bottles and drawers. It seemed to her, in her dazed confusion, that somehow she was doing something for Jules in saving his pharmacy which he had so much cared for, that she was almost keeping him from dying by working with all her might for him there. . . .

In the middle of the morning she went upstairs and found that Sylvie, working with Raoul, had cleared the kitchen of the worst of the rubbish. In a pot-closet under the sink there were two old saucepans which had not been stolen. Madeleine made a fire, stoically using her own broken-up furniture, and, putting a few potatoes (the last of their provisions) on to boil, sat down to nurse the hungry baby.

'*Maman* dear,' said Sylvie, still in the strained whisper of the days of terror. She could not speak aloud for weeks. '*Maman* dear,' she whispered, 'in the salon, in the dining-room I wanted to try to clean it, but it is all nasty, like where animals have been.'

'Hush!' said her mother firmly. 'Don't think about that. Don't look in there. It'll make you sick if you do. Stay here, tend the fire, watch the baby, and play with Raoul.' She outlined this program with decision and hurried back downstairs to go on with the execution of one conceived in the same spirit. If she could only get the pharmacy to look a little as it had when Jules had left it, it seemed to her that Jules would seem less lost to her.

She shoveled the incredible quantity of broken glass back through the shop into what had been her garden, hardening herself against a qualm of horror at the closer view of the wreckage there. The two big sycamore trees had been cut down and sawn into lengths to use for fuel in the open fire, the burned-out embers of which lay in a black ring where the arbor had stood.

She went back to her work hastily, knowing that if she stopped for an instant to look, she would be lost.

At noon she went upstairs, and with the children lunched on potatoes and salt.

She was putting the last of the innumerable drawers back in its place, after having tried it in all the other possible places, when a poorly dressed, rough-haired, scrawny little boy came into the shop. Madeleine knew him by sight, the six-year-old grandson of Madame Duguet, a bedridden, old, poor woman on Poulaine Street. The little boy said that he had come to get those powders for his grandmother's asthma. She hadn't slept any for two nights. As he spoke he wound the string about a top and prepared to spin it, nonchalantly. Looking at his cheerful, dirty little face, Madeleine felt herself a thousand years old, separated for always and always from youth which would never know what she had known.

'I don't know anything about your grandmother's asthma powders,' she said. The little boy insisted, astonished that a grown person did not know everything. '*He* always kept them. Grandmère used to send me twice a week to get them. Grandmère will scold me awfully if I don't take them back. She's scolding all the time now, because the Germans took our soup-kettle and our frying-pan. We haven't got anything left to cook with.'

The memory of her immensely greater losses rose burningly to Madeleine's mind. 'They took *all my sheets!*' she cried impulsively,— 'every one!'

'Oh,' said the little boy indifferently, 'we never had any sheets, anyhow.' This did not seem an important statement to him, apparently; but to Madeleine, her old world shattered, emerging into new horizons, beaten upon by a thousand new impressions, it rang loudly. The Germans, then, had only put her in the situation in which a woman, like herself, had always lived . . . and that within a stone's throw of these well-filled linen-closets of hers! There was something strange about that, something which she would like to ponder, if only her head did not ache so terribly. The little boy said, insistently, '*He* always gave me the powders, right away!'

Through obscure complicated mental processes, of which she had only the dimmest perceptions, *Jules* had always given the powders . . . how strange it was that precisely a bedridden woman who had most need of them should have owned no sheets . . . there came to her a great desire to send that old woman the medicine she needed. 'You go outside and spin your top for a while,' she said to the child; 'I'll call you when I'm ready.'

She went upstairs. Holding her skirts high to keep them out of the filth, she picked her way to the bookcase. Books were scattered all about the room, torn, cut, trampled on, defiled; but for the most part those with handsome bindings had been chosen for destruction. On the top shelf, sober in their drab, gray-linen binding, stood Jules' big record-books, intact. She carried down an armful of them to the pharmacy, and opened the latest one, the one which Jules had put away with his own hand the day he had left her.

The sight of the pages covered with Jules' neat, clear handwriting brought a rush of scalding tears to her eyes. Her bosom heaved in the beginning of sobs. She laid down the book, and, taking hold of the counter with all her strength, she forced herself to draw one long, regular breath after another, holding her head high.

When her heart was beating quietly again, quietly and heavily, in her breast, she opened the book and began studying the pages. Jules set everything down in writing, it being his idea that a pharmacist had no other defense against making those occasional mistakes inevitable to human nature, but which must not occur in his profession.

Madeleine read: 'March 10, sold 100 quinine pills to M. Augier. Stock low. Made 100 more, using quinine from the Cochard Company's laboratories. Filled prescription . . .' Madeleine's eyes leaped over the hieroglyphics of the pharmaceutical terms and ran up and down the pages, filled with such items, looking for the name Duguet. She had almost given up when she saw, dated July 30, 1914, the entry: 'Made up fresh supply Mme. Duguet asthma powders, prescription 457. Dr. Millier. Drawer No. 17.'

Madeleine ran behind the counter and pulled out No. 17. She found there a little pasteboard box marked, 'Duguet.'

'Oh, boy, little boy!' she called.

When the child came in she asked, 'Did your grandmother ever get any other medicine here?'

'No,' said the grandson of the bedridden woman, 'she hasn't got anything else the matter with her.'

'Well,' said the pharmacist's wife, 'here is her medicine.' She put the box in his hand.

'Oh, we never get more than four at a time,' he told her. 'She never has the money to pay for more. Here it is. Granny hid it in her hair so the Germans wouldn't get it. She hid all we have. She's got more than *five francs*, all safe.'

He put a small silver coin in her hand and departed.

The mention of the meager sum of hidden money made Madeleine think of her own dextrously concealed little fortune. She had noticed at once on entering the shop that the arrangement of false shelves which concealed the safe had not been detected, and was intact. She pushed the spring, the shelves swung back, and disclosed the door of the safe just as usual. She began to turn the knob of the combination lock. It worked smoothly and in a moment the heavy door swung open. The safe was entirely empty, swept clear of all the papers, titles, deeds, bonds which had covered its shelves.

As actually as though he stood there again, Madeleine saw the polite pseudo-Swiss geological gentleman, thanking Jules for the temporary use of his excellent safe.

She was petrified by this new blow, feeling the very ground give way under her feet. A cold, cold wind of necessity and stress blew upon her. The walled and sheltered refuge in which she had lived all her life was utterly cast down and in ruins. The realization came to her, like something intolerable, indecent, that *she*, Madeleine Brismantier, was now as poor as that old bedridden neighbor had been all her life . . . *all her life*. . . .

Somehow, that had something to do with those sheets which she had had and the other woman had not . . . her mind came back with a mortal sickness to the knowledge that she had now nothing, nothing to depend upon except her own strength and labor—just like a *poor* woman. She *was* a poor woman!

Somebody was weeping and tugging at her skirts. She looked down blindly. It was Raoul, her little son. He was sobbing and saying: 'Sylvie said not to come, but I couldn't stand it any more. I'm hungry! I'm hungry, and there isn't a thing left upstairs to eat! I'm hungry! I'm hungry!'

Madeleine put her hand to her head and thought. What had happened? Oh yes, all their money had been stolen, all . . . but Raoul was hungry, the children must have something to eat. 'Hush, my darling,' she said to the little boy, 'go back upstairs and tell Sylvie to come here and look out for the shop while I go out and find something to eat.'

She went down the silent, empty street, before the silent empty houses staring at her out of their shattered windows, and found not a soul abroad. At the farm, in the outskirts of town, she saw smoke rising from the chimney and went into the courtyard. The young farmer's wife was there, feeding a little cluster of hens, and weeping like a child. She stared at the newcomer for a moment without recognizing her. Madeleine looked ten years older than she had a fortnight ago.

'Oh, madame, we had three hundred hens, and they left us just these eight that they couldn't catch! And they killed all but two of our thirty cows; we'd raised them ourselves from calves up. They killed them there before the very door and cooked them over a fire in the courtyard, and they broke up everything of wood to burn in the fire, all our hoes and rake handles, and the farm-wagon and ... oh, what will my husband say when he knows!'

Madeleine had a passing glimpse of herself as though in a convex mirror, distorted but recognizable. She said, 'They didn't hurt you or your husband's mother, did they?'

'No, they were drunk all the time and they didn't know what they were doing mostly. We could hide from them.'

'Then your husband will not care at all about the cows and pigs and farm-wagons,' said Madeleine very firmly, as though she were speaking to Sylvie. The young farmer's wife responded automatically to the note of authority in Madeleine's voice. 'Don't you think he will?' she asked simply, reassured somewhat, wiping away her tears.

'No, and you are very lucky to have so much left,' said Madeleine. 'I have nothing, nothing at all for my children to eat, and no money to buy anything.' She heard herself saying this with astonishment as though it were the first time she had heard it.

The young wife was horrified, sympathetic, a little elated to have one whom she always considered her superior come asking her for aid; for Madeleine stood there, her empty basket on her arm, asking for aid, silently, helplessly.

'Oh, we have things left to *eat!*' she said. She put some eggs in Madeleine's basket, several pieces of veal left from the last animal killed which the Germans had not had time entirely to consume, and, priceless treasure, a long loaf of bread. 'Yes, the wife of the baker got up at two o'clock last night, when she heard the last of the Germans go by, and started to heat her oven. She had hidden some flour in barrels behind her rabbit hutches, and this morning she baked a batch of bread. It's not so good as the baker's of course, but she says she will do better as she learns.'

Madeleine turned back down the empty, silent street before the empty silent houses with their wrecked windows. A child came whistling along behind her, the little grandson of the bedridden Madame Duguet. Madeleine did what she had never done before in her life. She stopped him, made him take off his cap and put into it a part of her loaf of bread and one of the pieces of meat.

'Oh, meat!' cried the child. 'We never had meat before!'

He set off at a run and disappeared.

As she passed the butcher-shop, she saw an old man hobbling about on crutches, attempting to sweep up the last of the broken glass. It was the father of the butcher. She stepped in, and stooping, held the dustpan for him. He recognized her, after a moment's surprise at the alteration in her expression, and said, 'Merci, madame.' They worked together silently a moment, and then he said: 'I'm going to try to keep Louis' business open for him. I think I can till he gets back. The war *can't* be long. You, madame, will you be going back to your parents?'

Madeleine walked out without speaking. She could not have answered him if she had tried. In front of the Town Hall she saw a tall old woman in black toiling up the steps with a large package under each arm. She put down her basket and went to help. It was the white-haired wife of the old mayor, who turned a ghastly face on Madeleine to explain: 'I am bringing back the papers to put them in place as he always kept them. And then I shall stay here to guard them and to do his work till somebody else can come.' She laid the portfolios down on a desk and said in a low, strange voice, looking out of the window: 'It was before that wall. I heard the shots.'

Madeleine clasped her hands together tightly, convulsively, in a gesture of utter horror, of utter sympathy, and looked wildly at the older woman. The wife of the mayor said: 'I must go back to the house now and get more of the papers. Everything must be in order.' She added, as they went down the steps together: 'What will you do about going on with your husband's business? Will you go back to live with your mother? We need a pharmacy so much in town. There will be no doctor, you know. You would have to be everything in that way.'

This time Madeleine answered at once: 'Yes, oh yes, I shall keep the pharmacy open. I already know about the accounts and the simple things. And I have thought how I can study my husband's books on pharmacy, at night after the children are in bed. I can learn. Jules learned.'

She stooped to pick up her basket. The other woman went her way.

Madeleine stepped forward into a new and awful and wonderful world along a new and thorny and danger-beset path into a new and terrifying and pleasureless life.

A wave of something stern and mighty swelled within her. She put down her head and walked forward strongly, as though breasting and conquering a great wind.

Dorothy Canfield, Home Fires in France (New York:
Henry Holt and Co., 1918), 259–306

Rebecca West
(1892–1983)

Born Cicely Fairfield and educated in Scotland and London, Rebecca West embarked briefly on an acting career before taking up journalism in 1911. She joined the staff of the feminist publication *Freewoman* and, later, the *Clarion* where she was a political writer. West's reputation rests largely on her criticism and journalism but she also wrote fiction. Her short novel, *The Return of the Soldier* (1918), was one of the first accounts of the impact of shell-shock. This was followed by a steady output of fiction and criticism, much of which explored feminist questions, and also critical works and travel writing such as *Black Lamb and Grey Falcon* (1941). During the Second World War she worked as a journalist; she supervised BBC broadcasts to Yugoslavia and reported the Nuremberg trials at the end of the war.

---

10   THE CORDITE MAKERS

THE world was polished to brightness by an east wind when I visited the cordite factory, and shone with hard colours like a German toy-landscape. The marshes were very green and the scattered waters very blue, and little white clouds roamed one by one across the sky like grazing sheep on a meadow. On the hills around stood elms, and grey churches and red farms and yellow ricks, painted bright by the sharp sunshine. And very distinct on the marshes there lay the village which is always full of people, and yet is the home of nothing except death.

In the glare it showed that like so many institutions of the war it has the disordered and fantastic quality of a dream. It consists of a number of huts, some like the government-built cottages for Irish labourers, and some like the open-air shelters in a sanatorium, scattered over five hundred acres; they are connected by raised wooden gangways and interspersed with green mounds and rush ponds. It is of such vital importance to the State that it is ringed with barbed-wire entanglements and patrolled by sentries, and its products must have sent tens of thousands of our enemies to their death. And it is inhabited chiefly by pretty young girls clad in a Red-Riding-Hood fancy dress of khaki and scarlet.

Every morning at six, when the night mist still hangs over the marshes, 250 of these girls are fetched by a light railway from their barracks on a hill two miles away. When I visited the works they had already been at work for nine hours, and would work for three more. This twelve-hour shift is longer than one would wish, but it is not possible to introduce three shifts, since the girls would find an eight-hour day too light and would complain of being debarred from the opportunity of making more money; and it is not so bad as it sounds, for in these airy and isolated huts there is neither the orchestra of rattling machines nor the sense of a confined area crowded with tired people which make the ordinary factory such a fatiguing place. Indeed, these girls, working in teams of six or seven in those clean and tidy rooms, look as if they were practising a neat domestic craft rather than a deadly domestic process.

When one is made to put on rubber over-shoes before entering a hut it might be the precaution of a pernickety housewife concerned about her floors, although actually it is to prevent the grit on one's outdoor shoes igniting a stray scrap of cordite and sending oneself and the hut up to the skies in a column of flame. And there is something distinctly domestic in the character of almost every process. The girls who stand round the great drums in the hut with walls and floor awash look like millers in their caps and dresses of white waterproof, and the bags containing a white substance that lie in the dry ante-room might be sacks of flour. But, in fact, they are filling the drum with gun-cotton to be dried by hot air. And the next hut, where girls stand round great vats in which steel hands mix the gun-cotton with mineral jelly, might be part of a steam-bakery. The brown cordite paste itself looks as if it might turn into very pleasant honey-cakes; an inviting appearance that has brought gastritis to more than one unwise worker.

But how deceptive this semblance of normal life is; what extraordinary work this is for women and how extraordinarily they are doing it, is made manifest in a certain row of huts where the cordite is being pressed through wire mesh. This, in all the world, must be the place where war and grace are closest linked. Without, a strip of garden runs beside the huts, gay with shrubs and formal with a sundial. Within there is a group of girls that composes into so beautiful a picture that one remembers that the most glorious painting in the world, Velasquez's 'The Weavers', shows women working just like this.

One girl stands high on a platform against the wall, filling the cordite paste into one of the two great iron presses, and when she has finished with that she swings round the other one on a swivel with a fine free gesture. The other girls stand round the table laying out the golden cords in graduated sizes from the thickness of rope to the thinness of macaroni, the clear khaki and scarlet of their dresses shining back from the wet floor in a perpetually changing pattern as they move quickly about their work. They look very young in their pretty, childish dresses, and one thinks them good children for working so diligently. And it occurs to one as something incredible that they are now doing the last three hours of a twelve-hour shift.

If one asks the manager whether this zeal can possibly be normal, whether it is not perhaps the result of his presence, one is confronted by the awful phenomenon, beside which a waterspout or a volcano in eruption would be a little thing, of a manager talking about his employees with reverence. It seems that the girls work all day with a fury which mounts to a climax in the last three hours before the other 250 girls step into their places for the twelve-hour night shift. In these hours spies are sent out to walk along the verandah to see how the teams in the other huts are getting on, and their reports set the girls on to an orgy of competitive industry. Here again it was said that for attention, enthusiasm and discipline, there could not be better workmen than these girls.

There is matter connected with these huts, too, that showed the khaki and scarlet hoods to be no fancy dress, but a military uniform. They are a sign, for they have been dipped in a solution that makes them fireproof, that the girls are ready to face an emergency, which had arisen in those huts only a few days ago. There had been one of those incalculable happenings of which high explosives are so liable, an inflammatory mixture of air with acetone, and the cordite was ignited. Two huts were instantly gutted, and the girls had to walk out through the flame. In spite of the uniform one girl lost a hand. These, of course, are the everyday dangers of the high-explosives factory. There is very little to be feared from our enemies by land, and it is the sentries' grief and despair that their total bag for the eighteen months of their patrol of the marshes consists of one cow.

Surely, never before in modern history can women have lived a life so completely parallel to that of the regular Army. The girls who take up this work sacrifice almost as much as men who enlist; for although they make on an average 30s a week they are working much harder than most of them, particularly the large number who were formerly domestic servants, would ever have dreamed of working in peacetime. And, although their colony of wooden huts has been well planned by their employers, and is pleasantly administered by the Young Women's Christian Association, it is, so far as severance of home-ties goes, barrack life. For although they are allowed to go home for Sunday, travelling is difficult from this remote village, and the girls are so tired that most of them spend the day in bed.

And there are two things about the cordite village which the State ought never to forget, and which ought to be impressed upon the public mind by the bestowal of military rank upon the girls. First of all there is the cold fact that they face more danger every day than any soldier on home defence has seen since the beginning of the war. And secondly, there is the fact—and one wishes it could be expressed in terms of the saving of English and the losing of German life—that it is because of this army of cheerful and disciplined workers that this cordite factory has been able to increase its output since the beginning of the war by something over 1,500 per cent. It was all very well for the Army to demand high explosives, and for Mr Lloyd George to transmit the demand to industry; in the last resort the matter lay in the hands of the girls in the khaki and scarlet hoods, and the State owes them a very great debt for the way in which they have handled it.

Rebecca West, 'The Cordite Makers', from *The Young Rebecca: Writings of Rebecca West, 1911–1917*, ed. Jane Marcus (London: Virago, 1983), 380–3

M. A. St Clair Stobart
(?–1954)

In the Balkan War of 1912–13 Mrs St Clair Stobart founded the Women's Sick and Wounded Convoy Corps; in the First World War she organized hospitals in Belgium and France for the St John's Ambulance Association. Two books describe these experiences: *War and Women* (1913) and *The Flaming Sword: In Serbia and Elsewhere* (1916). Mrs Stobart was a resourceful, courageous, and formidably well-organized woman—qualities which are revealed in the extract. However, she was not completely feminist in her sympathies: she described men as 'the dominant race' and saw women's duty as saving life. In the latter part of the war she lectured for the British Ministry of Information, but later she became better known as an author and playwright. She became, also, a prominent figure in British spiritualism and, during the 1920s, wrote several books on this topic.

---

11 A WOMAN IN THE MIDST OF THE WAR

I AM neither a doctor nor a nurse, but I stand for the principle that all work connected with the sick and wounded is woman's work. As long as the honor of men is supposed to be concerned in destroying life, so long must the honor of women be concerned in the attempt to save life. No one disputes the right of men to protect the works—of art or of commerce— which they have themselves created. No one should dispute the right of women to protect the works—of human life—which they have at no less cost created.

But in the autumn of 1912, when the Balkan war cloud burst, and the hospitals in Bulgaria and Servia were overwhelmed with sick and wounded soldiers for whom locally there was no trained nursing and but little surgery available, the British Red Cross Society declared that there was no work fitted for women in the Balkans, and they dispatched to the front units composed of men only, to nurse the sick and wounded. Thus, apparently by the utterance of a few words, was the sphere of work which had been so hardly gained for women by Florence Nightingale to be taken from them.

But I had for years been training women to do all work which concerned the sick and wounded between the field and base hospitals, and I now determined to go out on my own account to the Balkans and see if it was true that there was indeed no work for women in those poorly equipped and impoverished countries. I found, as I had expected, that there was much work for women, and at the invitations of the Queen of Bulgaria, of the Bulgarian Red Cross, and of the Bulgarian Medical-Military authorities I cabled for my unit of women to follow me to Bulgaria.

The unit consisted of six trained nurses, ten orderlies, including cooks and others to carry on the general work of the hospital, myself as directress, and three women surgeons.

The Turks had cut the railway line near Adrianople, and from Jamboli we were forced to trek in open springless oxcarts, during seven days and nights, across the Rhodope Mountains and the plains of Thrace, to reach our destination, Kirk Kilisseh, the advanced headquarters of the Bulgarian army. Here we improvised and established during three months our hospital of war, under difficulties not likely to be surpassed in modern war-hospital work in Europe—with results which more than justified the enterprise and which upheld my principle that, in order to set men free for the fighting-line, women can safely be intrusted not only with the nursing but also with surgery and with the administration of a hospital of war in all its departments.

I returned to England, trusting that I might never again have to face the indescribable horrors which had made life during those three months one continuous nightmare. But in August the hounds of war were again unleashed, and the claims of women to be employed on active hospital service were once again shunted, and I realized reluctantly that to be permanently effective the Balkan object lesson must be reaffirmed. For, although woman nurses would probably be tolerated in the Belgian, French and English hospitals of war, the prejudice against woman surgeons still remained to be combated. I was told by an eminent man surgeon in London that soldiers objected strongly to being nursed by women, and that they would deeply resent being under the care of woman surgeons. I knew that against official statements of this sort argument by writing or by talking would be ineffective. The only way to prove that women can do this, that or the other with success is to go and do it.

I therefore once more found myself the organizer of a hospital unit of women ready to offer their services wherever they were needed. The unit comprised six woman doctors and surgeons, twelve trained nurses, and ten orderlies, including cooks, sanitary inspector, interpreter, secretary, and others to carry on the general work of a hospital of war, with myself as directress. We were provided, through the Women's National Service League and generous friends, with stores, clothing, X-ray apparatus and equipment for a hospital of one hundred and twenty beds. Promptly the Belgian Red Cross at Brussels invited us to establish a hospital in that town. I went in advance of the unit to make preparations, and the next day after my arrival I cabled, at the request of the Croix Rouge, to the unit to follow immediately.

The buildings of the large University were placed at my disposal, and I began the next morning (August 20) to transform lecture rooms and classrooms into wards and operating theater, etc., and everything was in train for the making of a successful hospital. But at 2 P.M. on that Thursday, as I was returning after luncheon to the hospital, to continue preparations, I saw the whole population of Brussels streaming from their houses to gaze at something. I followed, and saw the German army taking possession of Brussels. I knew then that my unit could not reach me, but as I was responsible for them and for the equipment, and thought that upon receipt of my cable they would have started and might now be in difficulties, I felt it my duty to try and reach them, traveling via Alost and Ostend. But the German General would grant a pass only to Venlo—in neutral territory in the Netherlands. This was better than nothing, as from there I could at least communicate with London, and I accordingly arranged to leave Brussels.

I had been accompanied by my husband and by the vicar of the Hampstead Garden Suburb, who had volunteered their services respectively as treasurer and as chaplain to my unit. Against my wishes they gallantly decided to come with me. We were told that we took our lives in our hands, as we should have to pass continuously through the German lines till we reached the Dutch frontier. But personally I knew that I should be much more uncomfortable if I stayed quietly in Brussels, as my friends and the Legations advised, than if I went through a few physical risks and discomforts in trying to do what any man in my position would have done without hesitation. We therefore secured the only taxicab we had seen in Brussels, and set forth from our hotel at 6 P.M., on Monday, August 24, with our be-Germanized passports.

After leaving the town behind, our road lay through dark avenues of overarching trees. We encountered all the time swarms of the gray German military automobiles, detachments of cavalry regiments in gray—infantry in gray, guns in gray, transport wagons in gray! Continually we were halted by soldiers who spread themselves across the road, but we showed our passports and were allowed to proceed.

We reached Louvain soon after eight that night, and drove through streets that seemed to belong to a city of the dead. Not a soul of all the inhabitants was to be seen—only the gray uniforms and bayoneted rifles dominating everything. We could not get food at the café hotel, but we were given beds. We left Louvain at five o'clock on the morning of the day the town was destroyed. We arrived at Hasselt at 8 A.M., and halted at a café in front of the station for some breakfast. We were about to continue our journey, when our chauffeur, a Belgian boy of eighteen, told us he could not get the taxi to start. Meanwhile, the soldiers guarding the station collected around us, an officer looked at our passports, was dissatisfied, said the stamped seal was worthless, that we were spies, and, shouting for six soldiers, who full-cocked their rifles ostentatiously and fixed their bayonets, told them to surround us.

'You are prisoners,' he said curtly. 'If you talk to each other, or if you move, you'll be shot immediately.'

We waited during an hour for orders from the Commandant, and were then marched as prisoners to the Hôtel de Ville. Here we were stripped and examined, our luggage was searched, and all papers and money were taken from us, and at 5 P.M. we were marched to the railway station, made to enter a coal truck attached to an engine, and were thus taken by our guard of six soldiers to Tongres. At Tongres we were again marched to the Hôtel de Ville. Here we were met by the Major in command, who was told that we had been arrested as spies.

'I suppose you know the fate of spies? Twenty-four hours!' he said.

This meant, of course, that we were to be shot.

We were taken upstairs, and spent the night lying upon straw upon the floor in an empty room, expecting at dawn to be called out and shot. But owing, as we believe, to the intervention of another officer who was, he told us, married to an Englishwoman, we were eventually sent by train as prisoners to Aachen. At Liège, on the way, all our papers were stolen from us, and we had to go on to Aachen without any of the papers which alone could prove that we were what we said we were.

At Aachen we were marched to the arrest cells in the military barracks. Here again we slept on verminous straw, and the next day once more went through the routine of being stripped and searched. Each of us was then separately brought before the judicial officer. At the end of the day we were marched off separately to prison. We were told that if, as a result of the trial, we were found guilty, we should be shot; if mercy was extended we should be imprisoned for three years in a German fortress; and, if found innocent, imprisoned till the end of the war.

It was midnight when I reached prison. Here again I was stripped and searched; all my possessions were removed, and I was taken by two wardresses to the cell I was to occupy. The door closed with a bang upon me, and the key turned mercilessly in the lock. Was that to be the end of my attempt to help the cause of women? I wished that they might at least have known that I had tried to reach them.

At the end of the next day, however, the miracle (which generally follows a critical situation, if you have faith enough) arrived. The officer who had conducted the last examination was of a different type from the other officers whom we had had the misfortune to meet, and had conducted the trial in an excellently just fashion. He was an officer of whom any nation might be proud, and I was thankful to have my previous impressions of German officers thus antidoted. He eventually, after various other vicissitudes of fortune, arranged for us to be liberated and escorted to the Dutch frontier. Thence we were free to go to London. There I found that my unit had never started, and we were therefore within a few days ready to accept an invitation from the British Consul-General, and from the Belgian Red Cross at Antwerp, to establish a hospital in that city.

We arrived in Antwerp by steamer from Tilbury on Tuesday, September twenty-second, and received an enthusiastic welcome from all the authorities. We were given as *locale* for our hospital the large summer concert hall of the Société de l'Harmonie in the Chaussée de Malines, surrounded by four or five acres of beautiful public gardens. Sleeping quarters for the staff were provided in a convent kept by a German sisterhood, just opposite the gate of the hospital in the Rue de l'Harmonie. A dark room for our X-ray apparatus in the hospital was fitted for us by the Croix Rouge, who also arranged, according to our requirements, the operating-room, provided baths, gas and water, and did all in their power to facilitate our work. Within a few hours the large concert hall, accustomed to reëcho the sounds of music created by the mind of man, was transformed into a ward.

The building itself was flimsy, for summer usage only, but the hall was lofty, and huge French windows, extending the whole breadth of the hall, opened on to the colonnade and gardens and gave us an ideal allowance of fresh air and sunshine. The coverlets of the comfortable iron beds were gayly striped in red, white and blue, or were in white, with a large red cross over the center, and responded finely to the efforts of the sunshine to make a cheery hospital. The atmosphere of hopefulness conveyed by these bright coverlets was, to my mind, a valuable contribution toward convalescence.

Within forty-eight hours from the time of our arrival the Croix Rouge and the military authorities showed their faith in our capacity by sending us forty wounded soldiers from the trenches at Lierre. In another couple of days ninety of our beds were filled, and before a week had passed one hundred and thirty-five wounded were under our care. For not only were our one hundred and twenty iron beds occupied, but also camp beds borrowed from another hospital were filled, and the wounded were also lying on straw mattresses on the tiers of the orchestral platform. The Medical-Military authorities, who came with the British Consul-General to visit us on our arrival, thus showed throughout their faith in the women's hospital, not only by keeping it filled, but also by sending us the severe cases directly from the trenches.

It is not a simple matter to deal on their first arrival with a batch of, say, fifty severely wounded soldiers coming directly from the front. The arrivals generally take place at night, and at Antwerp this added considerably to the difficulty, as no lights were allowed in the hospital after 8 P.M., and two or three tiny, smuggled nightlights, to illumine the whole big concert hall, were alone permissible. The routine of the arrival was as follows: The night silence of the hospital is suddenly broken by the loud ringing of the outer door bell. The door is hurriedly opened by the night watch, and immediately, from the depths of mysterious ambulance wagons, there streams into the dark corridor a procession of human remnants; some, who have received rough first-aid treatment upon the field, limping painfully, with the help of improvised crutches, scarcely knowing yet where their injuries lie; others, with head wounds and features blurred with blood and dirt; while others, the worst cases, strapped upon stretchers, uniforms indistinguishable, soaked in blood, are lying either silent with exhaustion or yelling with agony at every movement of the bearers, who help the nurses in the delicate task of transferring the broken burden from the stretcher to the bed.

The blood-sodden clothes can only, of course, be removed by the aid of knives and scissors. Immediate attention is then given by the doctors, some of whom are always on duty, and by the night staff of nurses and orderlies; and then, when the wounds have been dressed and the patient is quieted and comfortable, cups of hot soup, prepared by the night cook, round up the first treatment.

In theory the dirty and blood-stained clothes are not taken into the wards. The wounded man is undressed in a room set apart, bathed, and given clean garments, before he is put into the bed waiting, numbered, for him. His clothes are then collected in a bundle, and labeled ready to be sent next day to be disinfected; a disk noting the number of his bed is attached to his pyjamas or nightshirt, and an orderly and, if necessary, an interpreter collect, on a printed card, information as to identification number, name, address, parents, wife, age, etc. No easy job, when fifty, or possibly a hundred and fifty, arrive simultaneously. But in practice the men are too exhausted and too ill to answer elaborate catechisms when they first arrive; this sometimes has to be deferred, the number of the bed and the matricule, or identification number, alone being noted.

After a few days, washing the patients was made difficult because the water-works were destroyed by German shells, and all water subsequently had to be fetched in small quantities from the nearest wells and pumps, and boiled before being used. Of our patients, who were, with the exception of four

English Tommies, all Belgian, some spoke French in addition to Flemish, but others only Flemish, and for their benefit local interpreters very kindly attached themselves to us, and, until scared away by the bombardment, did good service to our unit.

But now, how about this dislike of man soldiers to be treated by woman nurses and woman surgeons? I can best reply to this by describing a little incident which took place four days after the establishment of our hospital, when ninety-four of our beds were occupied by Belgian soldiers.

I was returning into the ward after luncheon, when I saw a group of convalescent soldiers clustered in the center of the hall, around a table upon which stood, to my surprise, a plant and a huge bouquet of chrysanthemums. 'Go up to the soldiers; they are waiting for you,' I was told. I drew nearer, and a young soldier who had been wounded in the thigh with shrapnel hobbled, with the help of crutches, toward me, and, bowing politely, pointed at the flowers, and then handed me a small leather case containing two beautiful bronze medals. Upon each medal, on one side, was an impression of the Belgian King and Queen, and on the other side an inscription in French and Flemish. In excellent French the young soldier requested that my collaborators and I would accept these medals as a token of appreciation and gratitude on the part of himself and all his comrades for the care we had bestowed upon these our first Belgian patients.

I was taken completely by surprise, and it was difficult to remain unmoved, while these grateful soldiers made no effort to hide their emotions. But I made an impromptu reply in French for the benefit of the listening ward; the soldiers then cheered and shouted, and sang 'God Save the King,' followed by the Belgian national anthem and the Marseillaise. My only regret was that my friend, the eminent English surgeon, with his mid-Victorian notions as to the sphere of work of women, could not have been present at that little ceremony.

To my mind the episode was symptomatic of an atmosphere of faith, hope and love, which are of untold psychical value in hospital work—an atmosphere which only women can create. It was, I thought, well expressed one day by one of the wounded, who, sitting up in bed, looked around the large hall, and said to me: 'Ah, madame, it is like one great family here.' This same sentiment had been similarly voiced in the hospital at Kirk Kilisseh by a soldier who said: 'In other hospitals we are looked after by fathers—you are mothers, and that is much better.'

M. A. St Clair Stobart, 'A Woman in the Midst of the War', *The Ladies Home Journal*, 32:1 (Jan. 1915), 5–6

May Sinclair
(1863–1946)

A journalist and novelist, May Sinclair was a supporter of the suffrage movement and interested in psychoanalysis. Both concerns emerge in her writing about the war which includes novels such as *The Tree of Heaven* (1917), *The Romantic* (1920), and a range of journalistic writings. The extract below is from *A Journal of Impressions in Belgium* which records her experiences as secretary to a motor ambulance unit during the fall of Belgium in September–October 1914.

---

12   A JOURNAL OF IMPRESSIONS
IN BELGIUM

MADAME F. is very kind and very tired. She has been working here since early morning for weeks on end. They are short of volunteers for the service of the evening meals, and I am to work at the tables for three hours, from six to nine p.m. This is settled, and a young Red Cross volunteer takes me over the Palais. It is an immense building, rather like Olympia. It stands away from the town in open grounds like the Botanical Gardens, Regent's Park. It is where the great Annual Shows were held and the vast civic entertainments given. Miles of country round Ghent are given up to market-gardening. There are whole fields of begonias out here, brilliant and vivid in the sun. They will never be sold, never gathered, never shown in the Palais des Fêtes. It is the peasants, the men and women who tilled these fields, and their children that are being shown here, in the splendid and wonderful place where they never set foot before.

There are four thousand of them lying on straw in the outer hall, in a space larger than Olympia. They are laid out in rows all round the four walls, and on every foot of ground between; men, women and children together, packed so tight that there is barely standing-room between any two of them. Here and there a family huddles up close, trying to put a few inches between it and the rest; some have hollowed out a place in the straw or piled a barrier of straw between themselves and their neighbours, in a piteous attempt at privacy; some have dragged their own bedding with them and are lodged in comparative comfort. But these are the very few. The most part are utterly destitute, and utterly abandoned to their destitution. They are broken with fatigue. They have stumbled and dropped no matter where, no matter beside whom. None turns from his neighbour; none scorns or hates or loathes his fellow. The rigidly righteous *bourgeois* lies in the straw breast to breast with the harlot of the village slum, and her innocent daughter back to back with the parish drunkard. Nothing matters. Nothing will ever matter any more . . .

This place is terribly still. There is hardly any rustling of the straw. Only here and there the cry of a child fretting for sleep or for its mother's breast. These people do not speak to each other. Half of them are sound asleep, fixed in the posture they took when they dropped into the straw. The others are drowsed with weariness, stupefied with sorrow. On all these thousands of faces there is a mortal apathy. Their ruin is complete. They have been stripped bare of the means of life and of all likeness to living things. They do not speak. They do not think. They do not, for the moment, feel. In all the four thousand—except for the child crying yonder—there is not one tear.

And you who look at them cannot speak or think or feel either, and you have not one tear. A path has been cleared through the straw from the door down the middle of the immense hall, a narrower track goes all round it in front of the litters that are ranged under the walls, and you are taken through and round the Show. You are to see it all. The dear little Belgian lady, your guide, will not let you miss anything. '*Regardez, Mademoiselle, ces deux petites filles. Qu'elles sont jolies, les pauvres petites.*' '*Voici deux jeunes mariés, qui dorment. Regardez, l'homme; il tient encore la main de sa femme.*'

You look. Yes. They are asleep. He is really holding her hand. '*Et ces quatre petits enfants qui ont perdu leur père et leur mère. C'est triste, n'est-ce pas, Mademoiselle?*'

And you say, '*Oui, Mademoiselle. C'est bien triste.*'

But you don't mean it. You don't feel it. You don't know whether it is '*triste*' or not. You are not sure that '*triste*' is the word for it. There are no words for it, because there are no ideas for it . . .

Little things strike you though. Already you are forgetting the faces of the two little girls and of the young husband and wife holding each other's hands, and of the four little children who have lost their father and mother, but you notice the little dog, the yellow-brown mongrel terrier, that absurd little dog which belongs to all nations and all countries. He has obtained possession of the warm centre of a pile of straw and is curled up on it fast asleep. And the Flemish family who brought him, who carried him in turn for miles rather than leave him to the Germans, they cannot stretch themselves on the straw because of him. They have propped themselves up as best they may all round him, and they cannot sleep, they are too uncomfortable . . .

TUESDAY 29TH 5.30

It is my turn now at the Palais des Fêtes.

It took ages to get in. The dining-hall is narrower than the sleeping-hall, but it extends beyond it on one side where there is a large door opening on the garden. But this door is closed to the public. You can only reach the dining-hall by going through the straw among the sleepers . . .

From the door of the sleeping-hall to each auditorium, and from each auditorium down the line of the tables a gangway is roped off for the passage of the refugees.

They say there are ten thousand five hundred here to-night. Beyond the rope-line, along the inner hall, more straw has been laid down to bed the overflow from the outer hall. They come on in relays to be fed. They are marshalled first into the seats of each auditorium, where they sit like the spectators of some monstrous festival and wait for their turn at the tables.

This, the long procession of people streaming in without haste, in perfect order and submission, is heart-rending if you like. The immensity of the crowd no longer overpowers you. The barriers make it a steady procession, a credible spectacle. You can take it in. It is the thin end of the wedge in your heart. They come on so slowly that you can count them as they come. They have sorted themselves out. The fathers and the mothers are together, they lead their little children by the hand or push them gently before them. There is no anticipation in their eyes; no eagerness and no impatience in their bearing. They do not hustle each other or scramble for their places. It is their silence and submission that you cannot stand.

For you have a moment of dreadful inactivity after the setting of the tables for the *premier service*. You have filled your bowls with black coffee; somebody else has laid the slices of white bread on the bare tables. You have nothing to do but stand still and see them file in to the banquet. On the banners and standards from the roof and balustrades the Lion of Flanders ramps over their heads. And somewhere in the back of your brain a song sings itself to a tune that something in your brain wakes up:

> *Ils ne vont pas dompter*
> *Le vieux lion de Flandres,*
> *Tant que le lion a des dents,*
> *Tant que le lion peut griffer.*

It is the song the Belgian soldiers sang as they marched to battle in the first week of August. It is only the end of September now.

And somebody standing beside you says:

'*C'est triste, n'est-ce pas?*'

You cannot look any more.

At the canteen the men are pouring out coffee from enormous enamelled jugs into the small jugs that the waitresses bring. This wastes your time and cools the coffee. So you take a big jug from the men. It seems to you no heavier than an ordinary teapot. And you run with it. To carry the largest possible jug at the swiftest possible pace is your only chance of keeping sane. (It isn't till it is all over that you hear the whisper of '*Anglaise!*' and realise how very far from sane you must have looked running round with your enormous jug.) You can fill up the coffee bowls again—the little bowls full, the big bowls only half full; there is more than enough coffee to go round. But there is no milk except for the babies. And when they ask you for more bread there is not enough to go twice round. The ration is now two slices of dry bread and a bowl of black coffee three times a day. Till yesterday there was an allowance of meat for soup at the mid-day meal; today the army has commandeered all the meat.

But you needn't stand still any more. After the first service the bowls have to be cleared from the tables and washed and laid ready for the next. Round the great wooden tubs there is a frightful competition. It is who can wash and dry and carry back the quickest. You contend with brawny Flemish women for the first dip into the tub and the driest towel. Then you race round the tables with your pile of crockery, and then with your jug, and so on over and over again for three hours, till the last relay is fed and the tables are deserted. You wash up again and it is all over for you till six o'clock tomorrow evening.

You can go back to your mess-room and a ten o'clock supper of cold coffee and sandwiches and Belgian currant loaf eaten with butter. And in a nightmare afterwards Belgian refugees gather round you and pluck at your sleeve and cry to you for more bread: '*Une petite tranche de pain, s'il vous plaît, mademoiselle!*' . . .

[FRIDAY, OCTOBER 2ND] *EVENING, HÔTEL DE LA POSTE*

I dined in the crowded restaurant, avoiding the War Correspondents, choosing a table where I hoped I might be unobserved. Somewhere through a glass screen I caught a sight of Mr L.'s head. I was careful to avoid the glass screen and Mr L.'s head. He shall not say, if I can possibly help it, that I am an infernal nuisance. For I know I haven't any business to be here, and if Belgium had a Kitchener I shouldn't be here. However you look at me, I am here on false pretences. In the eyes of Mr L. I would have no more right to be a War Correspondent (if I were one) than I have to be on a field ambulance. It is with the game of war as it was with the game of football I used to play with my big brothers in the garden. The women may play it if they're fit enough, up to a certain point, very much as I played football in the garden. The big brothers let their little sister kick off; they let her run away with the ball; they stood back and let her make goal after goal; but when it came to the scrimmage they took hold of her and gently but firmly moved her to one side. If she persisted she became an infernal nuisance. And if those big brothers over there only knew what I was after they would make arrangements for my immediate removal from the seat of war . . .

SATURDAY, NOVEMBER 3RD

Mr L. asked me to breakfast. He has told me more about the Corps in five minutes than the Corps has been able to tell in as many days. He has seen it at Alost and Termonde. You gather that he has seen other heroic enterprises also and that he would perjure himself if he swore that they were indispensable. Every Correspondent is besieged by the leaders of heroic enterprises, and I image that Mr L. has been 'had' before now by amateurs of the Red Cross, and his heart must have sunk when he heard of an English Field Ambulance in Ghent. And he owns to positive terror when he *saw* it, with its girls in breeches, its Commandant in Norfolk jacket, grey knickerbockers, heather-mixture stockings and deer-stalker; its Chaplain in khaki, and its Surgeon a mark for bullets in his Belgian officer's cap. I suggest that this absence of uniform only proves our passionate eagerness to be off and get to work. But it is all right. *Our* ambulance is the real thing, and Mr L. is going to be an angel and help it all he can. He will write about it in the *Illustrated London News* and the *Westminster*. When he hears that I came out here to write about the War and make a little money for the Field Ambulance, and that I haven't seen anything of the War and that my invasion of his hotel is simply a last despairing effort to at least hear something, he is more angelic than ever. He causes a whole cinema of war-scenes to pass before my eyes. When I ask if there is anything left for me to 'do', he evokes a long procession of articles—pure, virgin copy on which no journalist has ever laid his hands—and assures me that it is mine, that the things that have been done are nothing to the things that are left to do. I tell him that I have no business on his pitch, and that I am horribly afraid of getting in the regular Correspondents' way and spoiling their game; as I am likely to play it, there isn't any pitch. Of course, I suppose, there is the 'scoop', but that's another matter. It is the War Correspondent's crown of cunning and valour, and nobody can take from him that crown . . .

May Sinclair, A Journal of Impressions in Belgium (London: Hutchinson, 1915), 60–5, 84–8, 121–2, 126–8

Claire de Pratz
(?–1916?)

A friend of Oscar Wilde and Maude Gonne, Claire de Pratz was working as a journalist in Paris in the years immediately preceding the war. She may have been bilingual since she contributed pieces to *La Petite Parisienne* as well as the *Daily News*. Her book *A French Woman's Notes on the War*, from which the extract below is taken, appeared in English in London in 1916. It contains reflections on patriotism and the nature of national identity as well as a series of evocative cameos picturing the reaction to the war of ordinary French people. The book seems to be genuinely autobiographical and describes how Pratz was poised to write a first novel when the war intervened and she felt obliged to devote herself to the war effort. A letter by Maude Gonne to W. B. Yeats written in April 1916 suggests that Claire de Pratz may have been one of the casualties on the ferry *Sussex* which was attacked by a German U-boat on 29 March 1916 on her way from Dieppe to Dover. However, she must have survived since she published at least one cookery book in the 1930s.

___

13   A FRENCHWOMAN'S NOTES ON THE WAR

BESIDES these new joys, what novelties have not been discovered since the beginning of the war by the weary and surfeited Parisians who formerly spent all their time in frivolities! Because economy is the order of the day on all sides, the more elementary forms of amusement are now being culti-vated, and one is discovering new sources of delight in the simpler pleasures. Just as the women of the jaded Court of Marie Antoinette found great charm in playing at butter-making, the neurasthenic ladies of 1914 have discovered a new enjoyment in cultivating the more unsophisticated pastimes.

There are even no dinner-parties now given in Paris, but occasionally a hostess invites a few of her old friends to a simple dinner—*le dîner de guerre*, she calls it—composed merely of two dishes. As the men-servants are all away at the war, the war-dinner is served by a simple handmaiden. Economy being severely practised in the household because of the necessary charities to be performed, it is taken quite as a matter of course that one's hostess should deprive herself of all unnecessary luxury, in order to come to the aid of some poor mother of a starving family.

The table therefore is not decorated with expensive flowers nor covered with a lace tablecloth. But the diners—not in evening-dress—gather around and chat together with greater intimacy and *abandon* than before. The suppression of all pomp and show has reduced the guests to their native simplicity, and they are all the better for it. At these informal gatherings, as well as at the knitting-parties, which have replaced the formal 'at home' calls in the afternoon, the conversation becomes more cordial, and people who formerly would have found time only to be mere acquaintances now become friends. The profounder qualities are allowed to become more apparent. One is not ashamed to show the true depths of one's heart, any more than one is ashamed to own one's poverty. It is no longer 'the thing' to be smart, but to be simple, real, and kindly.

Neither is there time or taste for talking scandal. No one even thinks of it. It is a curious fact that during war time, when everyone in the nation is in fear for the life of some loved one, no one wishes to speak unkindly of one's friends. Such habits may have been current last year—*avant la guerre*. But now *nous avons changé tout cela!* For the two periods are quite separate in the minds of all. There was the time *avant la guerre*, but now we are living in the time *pendant la guerre*. These terms will probably subsist for many generations on the lips of Parisians. *Avant la guerre* will signify all that is frivolous and meretricious, while *pendant la guerre* will signify all that is heroic.

Of course *la guerre* will now always mean for us this *particular* war, though until now *la guerre* to French people has meant the war of 1870. We now allude to that past war as *la guerre de '70*.

For the current expressions used by a generation typify that generation throughout history. . . .

I met a friend of mine, in the early months of hostilities, dressed in a dark serge gown originally made by one of the first dressmakers of Paris, and a long cloak of Breischwantz, from a celebrated fur emporium. With these she wore a very smart black velvet toque. These were the residue of her former luxury, but, having no money now even to buy kid gloves and black boots, she wore the white cotton gloves and pale yellow kid shoes of the preceding summer—and this without the slightest false shame! She is far from being an exception, however; for women thus attired are met in dozens every day in the *Métros* of Paris. But what do they care—so long as their men win in the end?

Claire de Pratz, *A Frenchwoman's Notes on the War*
(London: Constable, 1916), 154–7, 290

Cicely Mary Hamilton
(1872–1952)

As the daughter of an impoverished army officer, Cicely Hamilton always had to earn her own living. She first became an actress in a provincial theatre group and also worked as a teacher. She established herself as a playwright of note in 1908 with her play *Diana of Dobson's*. A great individualist and feminist, she passionately believed in women's right to autonomy and attracted fame and notoriety in equal measure with polemics such as *Marriage as a Trade* (1909) and her two suffragette plays *Just to Get Married* (1911) and *The Cutting of the Knot* (1916). She wrote several war novels of which the first, *William—An Englishman*, won the Femina Vie Heureuse prize in 1919. The extract below is taken from her book *Senlis* for which she had gathered material while working in a clerical capacity in a French military hospital.

—————

14   SENLIS

I NEVER saw Senlis before the coming of the German; he had ravaged and left it a full three months when I first tramped into the mutilated city—on a dripping day in December in the year the War began. Six miles we had trudged on the broad highway that leads from Creil, lying deep in its hollow, by uplands and woodlands to Senlis; six drizzling, straightforward, most lonely miles, with forest and field to the right and left and with hardly a soul on the road. We met five wayfarers between town and town; and of these (oddly enough, since we were in the French sphere of influence) not a single man was a native. One was a Belgian soldier and the other four hailed from Britain.

Normally, of course, though the time was winter, the road would have been less deserted; but it ran through the rear of the Zone of the Armies, and War Zone restrictions applied. War Zone restrictions—save on those thoroughfares where men and supplies went backwards and forwards to the front—meant a limit to traffic, awheel and afoot, unfrequented roads and a general suggestion of sleepiness. Behind the fighting in the trenches lay a backwater, a belt of calm—where authority discouraged the visitor and bade the inhabitant sit still. So much I had learned from some weeks in France when I set my face towards Senlis.

It was at the point where the road leaves the windy, unhedged upland for the shelter of the Forest of Halatte that we met the first travellers we had struck since Creil and saw the first batch of our countrymen. Pulling up the rise towards us came a lorry, protesting loudly as it pulled; its three occupants were all in uniform and two of the three wore khaki. That was in December 1914, before Belgium had taken to arraying her soldiers in dust-colour; so we hailed khaki (unseen for a month) with an Anglo-Saxon shout.

Khaki did not reply immediately; it had at the moment other business on hand, more enthralling than the greeting of strangers. Before the lorry came level with us its brakes went on and it halted; whereupon a lean brown figure leaped down from its seat and hurried to the rear with a rifle raised—unmistakably for business purposes. Our hearts beat fast with astonishment, perhaps anxiety; the trenches, we had good reason to believe, were twenty long miles and more away—yet the lorry had come to a sudden stop and khaki was out with a rifle. Gun and man vanished in a twinkling through a gate giving access to the forest; and as we drew level with the waiting car a shot cracked out close at hand. We thrilled and half-pictured an ambush of lurking Germans—an idea difficult to reconcile with the inertia and cheerfully expectant faces of our countryman seated at the driving-wheel and the stout blue Belgian beside him.

'A pheasant,' the driver enlightened—perhaps disappointed—us. 'My friend, he's a very good shot. He'll do us for supper . . . if he's got him.'

He hadn't; the pheasant was wily or swift and the very good shot had expended the taxpayers' ammunition in vain. He returned philosophically to confess failure and pass the time o' day with his countrywomen; whereafter the lorry—with the name of an Oxford Street shop yet distinguishable on its dirty side—rolled off in the direction of Creil and the north, while we plodded on our muddy way to Senlis.

We met khaki once again before we reached it; this time on an ambulance, bound southwards to Paris, whose driver and owner halted to speak to us 'because I saw you were English'. War-time, like its own code of morals, has its own code of manners which permits, amongst other deviations from the normal, of introductions offhand and self-made; we were ready enough both to talk and be talked to, and carried away from our brief acquaintanceship the knowledge that we should lunch and lunch well at the first hotel we came to. We were hungry enough by this time, and weary of the drizzle that stayed not—so right glad of the Hotel des Arènes and the *déjeuner* that timed with our coming.

Let me at once confess it, though I pass evermore for a Vandal: on my first visit to Senlis I troubled not to see the arena and sought not for the famous Roman wall. And on the whole, Vandal or not, I think I did wisely and well—since one clear impression to carry away is worth many half-blurred memories. Sight-seeing without motive for interest is purposeless staring, no more; and at the moment (it was in those first bewildering months of the War) I was not interested in the sports or defences of the Romans, in the doings or dwellings of the Gauls. What interested me was not the capital of the Silvanectes but Senlis, French Senlis, as its citizens had made, as the Germans had battered and left it. So I passed quite close to the Roman arena on the broad highroad from Creil; I took my lunch very heartily in its ancient and immediate neighbourhood—and I left it, without a pang of con-science for another and a later visit. . . . Thereby, as I say, I did wisely and well—for I got an impression unblurred.

It was an impression in its essence dramatic; far more dramatic, so it seems to me, than would have been obtained from the sight of a town com-pletely ravaged by the storm and brutality of war. There are towns and villages, not a few, over which battle and murder have swept to extinction, leaving in one scarce a stone in place, in the next but a misery of ruin. Senlis, on the other hand, was a study in violent contrast; the works of peace and the works of war stood cheek by jowl within its limits. A living town, an uninjured town—save for the one dead quarter. You walked one moment through orderly streets, provincially and pleasantly French; respectable, not too bustling, as became a Cathedral city; with here a wall and there a spire that had mellowed or crumbled through the centuries. You turned a corner: and side by side with prosperous order and ancient peace, with well-set shop-front and decorated spire lay a stretch of black desolation— of burned-out house after burned-out house, of ruin staring at ruin. So distinct and sudden was the cleavage between order and black desolation that it would have been possible—nay, easy—for a man to walk about the town and out of it without guessing that he had passed within a few short yards of streets for the most part in ashes.

The contrast, the sudden dramatic division, is due to the manner and nature of the havoc which the German wrought on the city. It was havoc deliberate and by fire, destruction at close quarters by the method of house to house. A bombardment from a distance may ruin more or less at haphazard; annihilate erratically and again erratically spare. Senlis was bombarded as the enemy neared it and the French fell back through the town; but the damage done was comparatively slight and fades into insignificance beside the wreckage wrought by fire. Houses in the Rue de la République and the streets adjacent were burned out systematically—by men who went steadily from door to door and worked on a definite plan. Senlis, says one who saw it, 'flamed methodically'; and thus you have a part of the town which is practically unscathed, and a part that is bare gaunt walls and heaps of rubble. . . . So, rumour has it, should Paris have burned had she fallen to the German sword; district by district and quarter by quarter, till France cried out for mercy and saved the remnant—on terms.

Cicely Hamilton, Senlis (London: Collins, 1917), 1–7

Annelise Rüegg
(1879–1934)

Annelise Rüegg was born near Zurich to working-class parents. While still in her teens she began travelling the world, working as a waitress and dedicating herself ardently, if naïvely, to the socialist cause. The extract below comes from her book *Im Kriege durch die Welt* (*Travels through a World at War*) of 1918, which gives an account of her experiences in Germany, France, and England, until her arrest and deportation from the United States. Nothing is known of her subsequent career.

15　　　Travels in Wartime

THE night train from London to Liverpool was packed. Sandwiched tightly between heroes of the air and heroes of the sea, I listened to the chat of British soldiers.

'Only the English fleet can bring us victory' ventured one of the sailors. It was not a view shared by the pilot who felt that the only sure way to destroy the enemy was from the air. Hearing them arguing, I could not remain silent. Victory, I told them, was going to come from below, from the awakening of the international proletariat.

It was past midnight when I finished my deliberations. The sailor who once nearly died of exposure on a life raft was ready to agree with me. But the pilot remained adamant that this kind of victory lacked British glamour and as such it was no victory at all.

Annelise Rüegg, Im Kriege durch die Welt, trans. Agnès Cardinal
(Zurich: Grütlibuchhandlung, 1918), 132

Mary Boyle O'Reilly
(1873–1937)

Mary Boyle O'Reilly's work extended to both journalism and writing novels as well as many philanthropic and social activities. She was a prison commissioner and was prominent in charitable organizations. She wrote for *Harper's Magazine* and for Boston newspapers: this short story was published first in the *Boston Daily Advertiser*.

---

16   IN BERLIN

THE train crawling out of Berlin was filled with women and children, hardly an able-bodied man. In one compartment a gray-haired Landsturm soldier sat beside an elderly woman who seemed weak and ill. Above the click-clack of the car wheels passengers could hear her counting: 'One, two, three,' evidently absorbed in her own thoughts. Sometimes she repeated the words at short intervals. Two girls tittered, thoughtlessly exchanging vapid remarks about such extraordinary behavior. An elderly man scowled reproval. Silence fell.

'One, two, three,' repeated the obviously unconscious woman. Again the girls giggled stupidly. The gray Landsturm leaned forward.

'Fräulein,' he said gravely, 'you will perhaps cease laughing when I tell you that this poor lady is my wife. We have just lost our three sons in battle. Before leaving for the front myself I must take their mother to an insane asylum.'

It became terribly quiet in the carriage.

Mary Boyle O'Reilly, 'In Berlin', *Boston Daily Advertiser*, 1915. Reprinted in
E. J. O'Brien (ed.), *Best Short Stories of 1915* (Boston: Houghton, 1915)

Käte Kestien

Nothing is known of Käte Kestien, the author of *Als die Männer im Graben lagen* (*When Our Men Lay in the Trenches*) of 1935. The following passage offers a representative sample of a book which recalls in evocative detail the many aspects of hardship endured by German women while their men were at the front.

―――――

17   A Night in a German Munitions Factory

I FOUND work in a factory one hour away from Cologne. When I entered the factory floor, the following day, heavy air enveloped me. For a moment I felt myself sway on my feet so that I had to sit down. 'It's the ether' said an elderly worker. 'You'll get used to it. Tomorrow you won't even notice it!' And indeed, I quickly got accustomed to the smell. They say that it makes you ill, but I was sure I could cope. Only sometimes, after midnight, I was seized by a paralysing weariness. My eyelids felt like lead and I began to see double. This was dangerous because, even though the work was less strenuous than what I'd been used to, here too I had to operate a machine which demanded accurate handling. I was working with gun powder which had to be filled into missiles. The machine cut it to the right shape. It was my job to reach past razor sharp blades, grab the neatly cut sticks of gun powder and push them across the table where four pairs of hands were putting them into bundles and packing them into cases. I had to operate the cutting machine at the right speed so that everyone working at the table was kept busy. And there was plenty of work! My machine was much bigger than the ones I had operated on previous jobs. It was imperative that one did not lose concentration for a single moment. Great speed was required when grabbing the sticks of powder and our working rhythm tended to get faster and faster. The nightshift was particularly dangerous. All of us had other duties at home. Indeed, many women took on night shifts so that, during the day, they could take care of their children. There was little time for sleep and sometimes there was none at all. It was at night that weariness crept into the limbs, especially around midnight, before the big break, when the air in the room had become dense and sticky.

I had been standing in my place at the table for about a week when it happened. A scream, as if from many mouths and yet just one single scream, rose through the room. A spirited young girl immediately rallied round and put a makeshift tourniquet on the arm of the injured woman. The machine had severed half her hand. Nobody could explain how it had happened but it must have been because she was overtired. She simply had not been quick enough. The accident had caused her to faint and she only came to after the men from the fire brigade had given her first aid.

'I don't want to go on a stretcher. Not on a stretcher!' she screamed. 'And, anyway, what's wrong with my hand?'

'Nothing to worry yourself about,' said one of the men. 'But you do have to go to hospital.'

'To hospital?' the woman repeated, horrified. 'I have four children at home! Is it not enough that my husband lies wounded in some hospital already? You won't get me there! No you won't.' She felt for her injured hand and a smile crossed her deathly pale face. 'Thank God, it's only the left.' Supported on both sides, she left the room. She absolutely refused to lie down on a stretcher and only agreed to being driven to the hospital so as to get a proper bandage for her hand.

For a brief moment the machines in the entire room had come to a halt. Now they began working again, just for another quarter of an hour, until it was time for the big midnight break. One minute before it started, the supervisor as usual called out: 'Now, begin to gather up all remaining bits of powder!' A woman, so pale in the face that it seemed that at any minute she too would need a stretcher, suddenly began to shout: 'I want that blood on the floor cleaned up during the break! I don't want to see it! I can't work properly while there remains a single speck of blood on the floor!' Some workers tried to calm her down.

When, after an hour's break in the canteen, we returned the floor had been scrubbed clean.

And again the machines began to work. Again our hands moved swiftly amongst the blades grabbing at the sticks while agile fingers neatly wound spiralling ribbons around the still moist and clammy powder. Soldiers without cockades on their caps were busy carrying the filled cases into the drying rooms. With bayonets at the ready the guards kept an eye on work-ing prisoners who whisperingly pleaded with us to slip them a cigarette. 'Let me go! Keep your hands off me!' a woman suddenly shouted. The officer in charge of the guards had been accusing her of having given a prisoner a cigarette. It was a charge she vehemently denied: 'I've got work to do here! It's a question of keeping one's eyes open so that one doesn't get one's fingers chopped off. Keep away from me, you Sir, with your fancy braids and so very far away from the fighting front!' The officer looked questioningly at the supervisor who shrugged his shoulders. No one knew how the cigarette got on the table.

'It's been one of those nights!' sighed the supervisor. 'But at least every-one keeps awake when things go crazy.'

Käte Kestien, from *Als die Männer im Graben lagen*, trans. Agnès Cardinal (Frankfurt-on-Main: Societäts-Verlag, 1935), 132–5

Mildred Aldrich
(1853–1928)

Born in Boston, Mildred Aldrich was an American journalist and friend of Gertrude Stein who 'retired' to a cottage on the banks of the Marne in June 1914, and stayed there throughout the war, which was, at times, perilously close. During that time Aldrich wrote letters home, probably to a fictive recipient; they were published first in American journals and then collected in four volumes entitled *A Hilltop on the Marne* (1915), *On the Edge of the War Zone* (1917), *The Peak of the Load* (1918), and *When Johnny Comes Marching Home* (1919); for this she received the Legion of Honour. The extract below comes from Letter XXIII (28 April 1916) from *On the Edge of the War Zone*.

---

18   ON THE EDGE OF THE WAR ZONE

LETTER XXIII

April 28, 1916.

I HAVE lived through such nerve-trying days lately that I rarely feel in the humour to write a letter.

Nothing happens here.

The spring has been as changeable as even that which New England knows. We had four fairly heavy snowstorms in the first fortnight of the awful fighting of Verdun. Then we had wet, and then unexpected heat—the sort of weather in which everyone takes cold. I get up in the morning and dress like a polar bear for a drive, and before I get back the sun is so hot I feel like stripping.

There is nothing for anyone to do but wait for news from the front. It is the same old story—they are see-sawing at Verdun, with the Germans much nearer than at the beginning—and still we have the firm faith that they will never get there. Doesn't it seem to prove that had Germany fought an honest war she could never have invaded France?

Now, in addition, we've all this strain of waiting for news from Dublin. The affairs of the whole world are in a mess.

There are many aspects of the war which would interest you if you were sitting down on my hilltop with me—conditions which may seem more significant than they are. For example, the Government has sent back from the front a certain number of men to aid in the farm work until the planting is done. Our *commune* does not get many of these. Our old men and boys and women do the work fairly well, with the aid of a few territorials, who guard the railway two hours each night and work in the fields in the daytime. The women here are used to doing field work, and don't mind doing more than their usual stunt.

I often wonder if some of the women are not better off than in the days before the war. They do about the same work, only they are not bothered by their men.

In the days before the war the men worked in the fields in the summer, and in the *carrière de plâtre*, at Mareuil-lès-Meaux, in the winter. It was a hard life, and most of them drank a little. It is never the kind of drunkenness you know in America, however. Most of them were radical Socialists in politics—which as a rule meant 'ag'in' the government'. Of course, being Socialists and French, they simply had to talk it all over. The café was the proper place to do that—the provincial café being the working man's club. Of course, the man never dreamed of quitting until legal closing hour, and when he got home, if wife objected, why he just hit her a clip,—it was, of course, for her good,—'a woman, a dog, and a walnut tree'—you know the adage.

Almost always in these provincial towns it is the woman who is thrifty, and often she sees but too little of her man's earnings. Still, she is, in her way, fond of him, tenacious in her possession of him, and Sundays and fête days they get on together very handsomely.

All the women here, married or not, have always worked, and worked hard. The habit has settled on them. Few of them actually expect their husbands to support them, and they do not feel degraded because their labour helps, and they are wonderfully saving. They spend almost nothing on their clothes, never wear a hat, and usually treasure, for years, one black dress to wear to funerals. The children go to school bareheaded, in black pinafores. It is rare that the humblest of these women has not money put aside.

You don't have to look very deep into the present situation to discover that, psychologically, it is queer. Marriage is, after all, in so many classes, a habit. Here are the women of the class to which I refer working very little harder than in the days before the war. Only, for nearly two years they have had no drinking man to come home at midnight either quarrelsome or sulky; no man's big appetite to cook for; no man to wash for or to mend for. They have lived in absolute peace, gone to bed early to a long, unbroken sleep, and get twenty-five cents a day government aid, plus ten cents for each child. As they all raise their own vegetables, keep chickens and rabbits, and often a goat, manage to have a little to take to market, and a little time every week to work for other people, and get war prices for their time,— well, I imagine you can work out the problem yourself.

Mind you, there is not one of these women, who, in her way, will not assure you that she loves her husband. She would be drawn and quartered before she would harm him. If anything happens to him she will weep bitterly. *But*, under my breath, I can assure you that there is many a woman of that class a widow to-day who is better off for it, and so are her children. The husband who died '*en héro*', the father dead for his country, is a finer figure in the family life than the living man ever was or could have been.

Of course, it is in the middle classes, where the wives have to be kept, where marriage is less a partnership than in the working classes and among the humbler commercial classes, that there is so much suffering. But that is the class which invariably suffers most in any disaster.

I do not know how characteristic of the race the qualities I find among these people are, nor can I, for lack of experience, be sure in what degree they are absolutely different from those of any class in the States. For example—this craving to own one's home. Almost no one here pays rent. There is a lad at the foot of the hill, in Voisins, who was married just before the war. He has a tiny house of two rooms and kitchen which he bought just before his marriage for the sum of one hundred and fifty francs—less than thirty dollars. He paid a small sum down, and the rest at the rate of twenty cents a week. There is a small piece of land with it, on which he does about as intensive farming as I ever saw. But it is his own.

The woman who works in my garden owns her place. She has been paying for it almost ever since she was married,—sixteen years ago,—and has still forty dollars to pay. She cultivates her own garden, raises her own chickens and rabbits, and always has some to sell. Her husband works in the fields for other people, or in the quarries, and she considers herself prosperous, as she has been able to keep her children in school, and owes no one a penny, except, of course, the sum due on her little place. She has worked since she was nine, but her children have not, and, when she dies, there will be something for them, if it is no more than the little place. In all probability, before that time comes, she will have bought more land— to own ground is the dream of these people, and they do it in such a strange way.

I remember in my girlhood, when I knew the Sandy River Valley country so well, that when a farmer wanted to buy more land he always tried, at no matter what sacrifice, to get a piece adjoining what he already owned, and put a fence around it. It is different here. People own a piece of land here, and a piece there, and another piece miles away, and there are no fences.

For example, around Père Abelard's house there is a fruit garden and a kitchen garden. The rest of his land is all over the place. He has a big piece of woodland at Pont aux Dames, where he was born, and another on the *route de Mareuil*. He has a field on the *route de Couilly*, and another on the side of the hill on the *route de Meaux*, and he has a small patch of fruit trees and a potato field on the *chemin Madame*, and another big piece of grass-land running down the hill from Huiry to Condé.

Almost nothing is fenced in. Grain fields, potato patches, beet fields belonging to different people touch each other without any other barrier than the white stones, almost level with the soil, put in by the surveyors.

Of course they are always in litigation, but, as I told you, a lawsuit is a *cachet* of respectability in France.

As for separating a French man or woman from the land—it is almost impossible. The piece of woodland that Abelard owns at Pont aux Dames is called 'Le Paradis'. It is a part of his mother's estate, and his sister, who lives across the Morin, owns the adjoining lot. It is of no use to anyone. They neither of them ever dream of cutting the wood. Now and then, when we drive, we go and look at it, and Père tells funny stories of the things he did there when he was a lad. It is full of game, and not long ago he had an offer for it. The sum was not big, but invested would have added five hundred francs a year to his income. But no one could make either him or his sister resolve to part with it. So there it lies idle, and the only thing it serves for is to add to the tax bill every year. But they would rather own land than have money in the bank. Land can't run away. They can go and look at it, press their feet on it, and realize that it is theirs.

I am afraid the next generation is going to be different, and the disturbing thing is that it is the women who are changing. So many of them, who never left the country before, are working in the ammunition factories and earning unheard-of money, *and spending it*, which is a radical and alarming feature of the situation.

You spoke in one of your recent letters of the awful cost of this war in money. But you must remember that the money is not lost. It is only redistributed. Whether or not the redistribution is a danger is something none of us can know yet; that is a thing only the future can show. One thing is certain, it has forcibly liberated women.

You ask how the cats are. They are remarkable. Khaki gets more savage every day, and less like what I imagined a house cat ought to be. He has thrashed every cat in the *commune* except Didine, and never got a scratch to show for it. But he has never scratched me. I slapped him the other day. He slapped back,—but with a velvet paw, never even showed a claw.

Didn't you always think a cat hated water? I am sure I did. He goes out in all weathers. Last winter he played in the snow like a child, and rolled in it, and no rainstorm can keep him in the house. The other day he insisted on going out in a pouring rain, and I got anxious about him. Finally I went to the door and called him, and, after a while, he walked out of the dog's kennel, gave me a reproachful look as if to say, 'Can't you leave a chap in peace?' and returned to the kennel. The one thing he really hates is to have me leave the house. He goes where his sweet will leads him, but he seems to think that I should be always on the spot.

Mildred Aldrich, *On the Edge of the War Zone* (Boston: Small,
Maynard and Company, 1917), 171–8

III

THE WAR COMES HOME

Käthe Kollwitz
(1867–1945)

Käthe Kollwitz is one of the most important graphic artists in Europe this century. She was the first woman to be elected a member of the Prussian Academy of the Arts but resigned her post in 1933 when Hitler came to power. She was born Käthe Schmidt in Königsberg (East Prussia) and studied art in Berlin and Munich. In 1891 she married Karl Kollwitz, a physician who chose to work in the slums of Berlin. Her encounter with the dispossessed was to remain the dominant theme in all her art. The extracts below bear witness to her relationship with her son Peter, a young painter, who was amongst the first victims of the war.

———

19   LETTERS AND DIARY ENTRIES

LETTER TO HER SONS PETER AND HANS, 11 JULY 1914

My dear boys,

. . . YES indeed, I'm afraid I do think that Peter is making a grave mistake. But you know that anyway, don't you Peter. I just wish that you'd embark on a proper course of study. As you say yourself, you cease to use your brain once you start using colours. I am really pleased about the way you grasp form and feel that you have a good way of seeing, as it were, 'organically'. But your way of using colours is sentimental. And one is only really entitled to the expression of sentiment after all the intellectual work has been done. If one prioritizes sentiment over thought one soon begins to feel queasy and ends up with a hangover. It's the experience of the dilettante. I'm sure this is a point on which we will continue to argue endlessly. But we do agree, do we not, that formal training is essential. If only we knew how and where. I did not see your self-portrait in its early stages; as it is it seems to me rather laboured. Maybe it would have been better if I had not so scrupulously averted my gaze every time I came to your studio.

DIARY ENTRY, 27 AUGUST 1914

Amid the heroic petrification that war has brought about, amid this almost unnatural ecstatic heightening of our emotional life, it touches me like music from heaven, like sobbings for peace, when I read that French soldiers are being kind to wounded Germans and even helping them. Or that German soldiers in the villages besieged by sharp shooters put up posters on houses with gentle warnings: 'Take care! Here lives an old woman who did me a kindness' or 'Old People Only' or 'Newborn Baby with Mother' and so on.

I see that Gabriele Reuter writes about the duty of women in *Der Tag*. She speaks of the orgasmic aspect of sacrifice. It is an expression which bothers me a great deal. How do all these women, who have spent their lives praying over the well-being of those they love, find the strength to send them off to face the cannons? I fear that after this great initial soaring of the spirit deepest despair and despondency must surely follow. This won't be a matter of just a few weeks; the task will be to endure for a very long time indeed, throughout the dreary days of November and into spring. Throughout March, the month of youth, meant for young men who wanted to live and who now lie dead. That's when the burden will be at its heaviest.

How lucky seem to me the people who now have small children, like Lise with Maria. For us whose sons are leaving the vital thread has snapped.

LETTER, NOVEMBER 1914

Dear Frau Schröder and dear Dore!
I'm afraid your beautiful scarf will no longer keep our boy warm. He is dead and buried. He fell near Dixmuiden, the first of his regiment. He did not suffer much.

They buried him at sunrise, his friends put him into the grave. Then they went away to do their terrible work. We thank God that he was taken so painlessly before the dreadful massacre even began.

Please do not come to see us. But we thank you for the sorrow which we know, you are feeling on our behalf.

Karl and Käthe Kollwitz and Hans

DIARY ENTRY, 8 JULY 1916

I am now 49 years old . . . And what did this last year bring me? And what did I contribute? . . . I feel myself getting older and weaker. When I look at my body, see my wilting face, my withered hands, I lose all courage. How am I to achieve all that still needs to be done? Sorrow and longing gnaw at my strength, and I do still need a lot of strength. I *pray* that I may be able to continue my work. Especially the sculpture for Peter, but all the other

projects too. Once I have completed them I shall be happy to die, but first I
need to get it all done.

Käthe Kollwitz, from *Tagebuchblätter und Briefe*, ed. Hans Kollwitz
(Berlin: Mann, 1948), 125–6, 56, 63

Augusta Isabella Gregory (née Persse)
(1852–1932)

Lady Gregory was the owner of Coole Park, centre of the Irish cultural renais-
sance of the 1890s and one of the founders of the Abbey Theatre whose principal aim was to promote Irish folk traditions. Of Anglo-Irish descent, she
taught herself Gaelic and translated many Irish sagas into English, and wrote
poems as well as over forty plays. The extent of her contribution to some of
the work of W. B. Yeats has only just begun to be acknowledged. When her
son was killed in action in 1918 the poet paid homage to him with the elegy 'In
Memory of Major Robert Gregory'. The following extract was written at the
beginning of the war and is included in her autobiography.

―――

20   THE FOLK-LORE OF THE WAR

12 AUGUST 1914. The war has been going on ten days.

The day before yesterday an old woman from Gort told me there would
soon not be a man left in Gort; they were being tracked for the reserve and
as out-soldiers. She said the war had begun in Mayo. 'There were guns in a
house, and information was given and they were brought away, and those
they were brought from began burning and scalding. That is the way the
fight began, and now there are five nations in it.'

A.W. writes from Galway, 'Three of O'Flaherty's best tram horses
have been taken and he finds it hard to manage with five. A tram accident
was caused by an untrained horse which ran off the line. Mary the cook
found it hard to get change for a note on Thursday, the shopkeepers seem
to have taken fright, and two near this charged 1/- and 1/6d. for changing
a note.

'P. is putting her servants on a lower diet, eggs only twice a week. A. is giving her servants potatoes only on alternate days for fear of famine, and thinks of lessening their weekly $\frac{1}{4}$ lb. of tea. I have only ordered the pullets to be kept for laying, and blackcurrants to be bottled so far.'

15 August.   Lady Gough writes that Hugo left for 'an unknown destination' on Wednesday with the Guards. The secret is wonderfuly well kept, not a word as to where the English force is. Mona Gough writes also that Guy has gone with his regiment. He telephoned good-bye to them at dinner. Hugo was splendid, making out little things for his mother to do, making her search the London shops for a revolver he thought was not to be had, being obsolete, but which unluckily she found. She writes. 'If he does not come back I shall love to remember all this and if he comes back its memory will increase the joy.' Very brave, as he is her only son!

A.W. writes from Galway. 'The Graces showed me a typewritten letter from the wholesale place which supplies his sugar, saying they could not execute his order as they hadn't an ounce of sugar on hand. One of the maids returned last night from the Bog of Allen where her home is near. Two men had been seen taking soundings and prowling about the bog for days saying they were going to make the peat into petrol and cloth. They were in treaty for a field with Mrs Butler. When arrested, plans, maps, etc., were found on them.' But I don't think the Bog of Allen would be of much use as an entrenchment!

16 August.   Slight Belgian victories reported at the Post Office and we had a special service and collection ('by request of the Prince of Wales'). The Gort Volunteers are said to have scattered for the most part on hearing of the war, but the Kiltartan ones are drilling well.

20 August.   An old man mending the sea wall at Burren says this was prophesied hundreds of years ago by Columcille, and it will not leave a man living in Ireland.

Marian has been to Gort to pay the books, and says only postal orders are given now to the old age pensioners, and when they went to do their shopping a publican refused to take them in exchange. So they went back to the Post Office, and Mrs Mitchell sent for the constable, and he sent for the publican and told him that if he did not take postal orders when offered his licence would be opposed at the next sessions.

To-day's news is that Brussels has been occupied by the Germans.

Namur taken, that is the great blow. Old Niland tells me that we shall be saved by the Russians. His cousin had been in the Crimean war and said,

'Three nations against them and they were the best of all. He'd frighten your heart talking of it. Where he was they had dykes dug, and to be waiting till the day came, and as many as sheep in a field you'd see the Russians firing.'

An aeroplane is said to have flown over Kinvara and turned its searchlight down on the streets.

The Abbey re-opened last night, we must try and make enough for wages.

Augusta, Lady Gregory, 'The Folk-Lore of the War', from *Seventy Years: Being the Autobiography of Lady Gregory*, ed. and with a foreword by Colin Smythe (Gerrards Cross: Colin Smythe Ltd., 1974), 509–10

Olive Schreiner
(1855–1920)

Olive Schreiner was born in South Africa. Her father was a Methodist missionary of German descent; her mother was English. After her early ambitions to study medicine or to become a nurse were thwarted by ill health, Schreiner became a governess. She wrote three novels, *Undine*, begun in the 1870s and published, posthumously, in 1928, *The Story of an African Farm* (1883), and *From Man to Man*, which remained unfinished and was also published after her death (1926). *The Story of an African Farm*, which anticipated much of the new woman fiction of the 1890s, made her reputation. It also brought her into contact with avant-garde circles and friendships with Eleanor Marx, Edward Carpenter, and Havelock Ellis—the last introduced her to Fabian socialism. From the 1890s Schreiner became a prominent voice in the women's movement: her *Women and Labour* (1911) is regarded as a seminal work.

---

21   LETTERS

To HAVELOCK ELLIS

London, *13th Oct.*

I AM going to-morrow to Durrants Hotel, Manchester Square. I hope I shall get better there as it's very dry. Do come and see me soon. I long to see you.

How scared people are about the Zeppelins? If you have lived through a war and had your house burnt and all you prized taken from you, you learn to take these things as all in the day's work. War *is* Hell. Though people like the English who have always made it in other peoples' countries have never realised [it]. It's when it comes to your own land that its full horror bursts on you. Did I tell you Oliver has joined his regiment and may be sent to the front any hour? And the diplomatists who for ten years have been bringing things into this state will live on. Our beautiful innocent ones, of all nations, must die. Goodbye, dear.

To Havelock Ellis

Kensington Palace Mansions, 16*th Oct.*

Yesterday at Durrants Hotel a boy brought a note. It ran: 'Madam, When Mrs Smith took the room for you she did not mention that your name was *Schreiner*. As we find that is either an Austrian or a German name you will please leave our Hotel at once.' Of course I took a taxi and my things and left at once. I have fortunately found this place. It's much more expensive. I can't stay but I must rest here as I'm worn out. [She stayed for ten months.] The great use of not being very poor is that it helps one to health.

To Edward Carpenter

London, *Oct.*

I think so much of your tired face as you went away. You know, Edward, we can live through all this, but it's simply crushing us, who had such hopes for the future 20 years ago. . . . I wish I could feel with you that this war is going to bring the Kingdom of Heaven. I feel it is the beginning of half a century of the most awful wars the world has seen. First this then another war probably of England and Germany against Russia, then as the years pass, with India, Japan and China and the Native Races of Africa. While the desire to dominate and rule and possess Empire is in the hearts of men, there will always be war.

To Miss E. Hobhouse

Maver Lake, Bude.

. . . Again and again when I tried to get rooms they wouldn't let me have them on account of my name. Just before I left I found very nice cheap rooms in Chelsea, there was a sweet refined looking little woman who let them; I told her I would take them, and come the next day. When I told her my name she turned and *glared* at me. I enquired what was the matter. She asked me if my name was not German. I said it was, but I was a British subject born in South Africa, that my husband was a British subject of pure British descent, and my mother was English, that my father who left Germany 80 years ago, was a naturalised British subject, and had been dead nearly 50 years. She turned round and stormed at me, all her seemingly gentle face contorted with rage and hate. She said that if my ancestors came from Germany 'three hundred years ago' it would make no difference, no one with a German name should come into her house, and poured forth a stream of abuse that was almost inconceivable. The worst was, that I was feeling so ill and worn out, that I dropped into a chair and burst out crying. It's the only time I've cried in two years. It seemed so contemptibly weak of me; but you know how you feel when you are utterly worn out mentally and physically! I could only say, 'It isn't because you are so unkind to me, it's because all the world's so wicked.'

Oh Emily the worst of war is not the death on the battle fields; it is the meanness, the cowardice, the hatred it awakens. Where is the free England of our dreams, in which every British subject, whether Dutch, English, French or German in extraction, had an equal right and freedom? I wouldn't have come here if I had not thought one would not be free here from these petty attacks. What this war has shown me is not so much the wickedness as the meanness of human nature. War draws out all that is basest in the human heart. Perhaps I shall be able to get up to London before you leave.

Olive Schreiner, from *The Letters of Olive Schreiner, 1876–1920*, ed. S. C. Cronwright-Schreiner (London: T. Fisher Unwin Ltd., 1924), 340–1

J. E. Buckrose (Annie Edith Jameson)
(?–1931)

J. E. Buckrose was a popular and prolific author: she was published by Mills & Boon and Hodder & Stoughton and she wrote for such magazines as *Good Housekeeping*. Her work comprised stories, essays, character sketches, and fiction. The last were described as 'north country novels'—many were set in Yorkshire—but they also included an early work entitled *The Art of Living: Social Problems Solved in a Novel Story* and a war novel, *The Silent Legion*

(1918), described by critics as offering 'the best picture of the home side of the war'. She published several series of stories about 'Our Street' in which, as in 'War Economy', social issues are woven into the narrative in a simple and accessible way.

---

22   WAR ECONOMY

IT was that bleak time about two o'clock p.m. when a barrel organ playing dance tunes in a grey street epitomises all the undignified woes—too small to mention—of humanity.

Miss Mildred Parkinson rose from the table to a waltz tune which wailed of indigestion, a servantless condition, and what she termed a fruitarian diet—meaning on the present occasion a cup of tea, a slice of margarine and bread, and an indifferent apple. Not that she was really poor, because her father, a small merchant in Flodmouth, had left her a sufficient fortune carefully invested, and her sharp, timid and pinched exterior hid a spirit which was generous to the point of recklessness.

A child with a flag to sell—a lady with a handbag and a subscription list— had the same fatal fascination for her that drink possesses for others, and when the war came, giving to this inclination the impetus of a perfectly blazing patriotism, only Miss Parkinson's inherited rectitude enabled her to keep out of the Bankruptcy Court.

But the child of Mr and Mrs Parkinson simply could not get into debt, though her spendthrift habits in the cause of charity were perhaps a sort of instinctive revolt against long years of saving. For every penny she owed represented something that Mr and Mrs Parkinson had done without. Her independence was a monument to the stern frugality which had governed two lives. And when her parents died one after the other in the great red bed, they were content because little Milly was all right.

Of course, she remained little Milly to them until the end—though her fair hair had then already turned grey at the roots, and her nose-end pink— and still she kept a secret feeling of being a bright young girl because she had always been that to them. So she tripped down the street in quite a sprightly fashion, entering the room where the working party was held with a flush and a slight giggle.

'So delightful of Mrs Montgomery-Brown to come and speak to us about War Economy,' she chirruped. 'She always wears such charming hats, doesn't she? Of course . . . lower down . . . equally no doubt . . . but in a carriage one only sees——'

Nobody listened to Miss Parkinson; they were distracted by the sound of wheels outside. Immediately a painted and gilded figure-head of immense local importance sailed breast foremost into this little backwater, and Miss Parkinson rejoiced to see that the limbs of the lady were appropriately clad in the best and most appropriate kind of war clothing—highly fashionable, of course, but with a hint of conscious reserve about the skirt.

The address which followed was a good one. We all felt impelled to try and make a penny do the work of twopence halfpenny, for we had already, even in pre-war times, obtained such excellent practice in making it do the work of twopence. It was when Mrs Montgomery-Brown urged us in moving accents not to throw away our bones that the atmosphere of the meeting changed a little. We—in our street—who read with avidity such articles in the weekly press as 'How to Make Mock Goose with a Vegetable Marrow and a Mutton Bone,' and fed our helpless families on the result!

But when she closed by saying that women could pay for this war by what they saved from the dustbins of England, if they only would, we felt our spirits respond to hers. We all thought, immediately, of somebody else's dustbin.

Before this moment of exultation had really died down, however, Miss Parkinson jumped up like a genteel jack-in-the-box and voiced the real feelings of the rest by stammering out:

'But how can you . . . if you *have* all you can . . . and you can't any more?'

The lady smiled vaguely, not knowing what Miss Parkinson meant; then she got under way again and moved out majestically with several ladies fluttering round her.

One evening about three weeks later Miss Parkinson went down our street with a step which she endeavoured to keep girlish and tripping, but which lagged when she forgot, like that of a tired, middle-aged woman.

It was a keen night, with a country freshness blowing from the fields of Holderness in the air, and she breathed deeply as she went along, greeting first one and then another.

'Off canteening!' she said, forcing herself to speak jauntily.

'I shall be there soon,' said the widow. 'I hope you got a proper meal yourself before starting,' she added, vaguely moved by some expression in Miss Parkinson's face to which she could give no name.

'Oh, yes, simple but nourishing. I am a great advocate of the single *plat*,' said Miss Parkinson, and with a gay giggle she continued her way.

When she reached the building in which the munition workers' canteen was held she was in quite a glow from the exercise and the sharp air. The place was at that moment almost deserted, and the one girl who stood by the stove watching the pans greeted Miss Parkinson with enthusiasm.

'Oh, here you are! I made sure you would be in good time. The others will come directly, but if you *could* look after these pans for a few minutes? I do so want to get away.'

Miss Parkinson assented, and in a minute or two she was left by herself before the great stove. At first she was only concerned to see that nothing burnt or boiled over, but soon the gentle, even simmering convinced her that she had only to leave well alone.

Then, gradually, as she stood there waiting, she became conscious of a most peculiar sensation inside. It seemed as if the appetising smell of the meat and vegetables were attached to invisible threads in her internal anatomy. Her mouth began to water. Her eyes shone.

A pot boiled over a little, and she was obliged to lift the lid. The rich fragrance of meat and vegetables became a taste which she could sense on her tongue. She held the lid in her hand, trembling, not knowing at all what was happening to her.

Suddenly, as she stood so over the pan, she was seized by passion for the first time in her restrained and ordered life—by the elemental passion of hunger.

With shaking hands she ladled a large helping of the stew into the saucepan lid, blew with a strange, incredible eagerness to cool it, and ate it in her fingers. She had never known such physical rapture as she experienced in gulping down those succulent morsels. The joy of a satisfied passion ran at last through her starved veins.

Then, after the final mouthful, reason awoke. Steps and voices sounded outside along the corridor. She stood staring at the saucepan lid in her hand in a sort of amazement—the dull wonder of satisfied passion.

As the first helper entered she turned and walked across the echoing floor to the sink, and held the saucepan lid under the tap.

All the evening as she ladled out portions and sped hither and thither, she seemed a stranger to herself. She was afraid to go home and to be alone with that stranger. In the end she was obliged to put on her coat and hat enduring an acute attack of indigestion after the hastily eaten stew, almost without being aware of it. The pain was so little compared with that cold sense of strangeness.

Just as she reached the door, however, there was a sudden hubbub at the other end of the room. An old woman with a bass voice and a beery eye, detected in the act of stealing a pork pie, was whining out huskily:

'I never did it afore. It came over me sudden as I must have the pie. I was going to pay to-morrow.'

Miss Parkinson paused at the door. Then, very slowly, she came back again and placed herself by the culprit's side.

'I'll pay,' she said. 'Please let her go.' The manageress, who only wanted to frighten the woman, gave Miss Parkinson a side look and replied sternly: 'Certainly not. Justice must be maintained.'

But Miss Parkinson was in no condition to observe meaning looks, and gazed round forlornly at these neighbours, whose good opinion she valued more than anything on earth, with a sense of saying farewell to them.

'Then I must tell you,' she replied. 'This woman has only done what I did. If you take her you must take me too.'

'Poor thing! Nervous breakdown! I said she was overdoing it,' murmured all the neighbours, greatly concerned.

The beery old woman leaned towards Miss Parkinson, urged by a great curiosity, and murmured: 'What was *your* fancy, me dear?'

'Stew,' said Miss Parkinson in a low tone. 'I had to have it. I meant to pay for it to-morrow.'

But when her associate in crime winked the eyelid nearest, and said jauntily, 'Same here!' poor Miss Parkinson's cup of humiliation was full indeed. In the silence which followed, the incorrigible old woman slipped out, still with the pork pie in her basket, undeterred by anybody. . . .

'Dear Miss Parkinson,' said the widow gently. 'You are under a delusion about the stew. I was here all the time. I served it out myself. You never had any.'

Miss Parkinson quailed a moment before the, to her, most terrible part of her confession, but in the end she flung out desperately:

'I ate it out of the saucepan lid!' Then she began to cry quietly. 'I know it was dreadfully vulgar. But no one can understand until they have been living rather simply for a time, how the smell of something good——'

There came another silence; and the pretty, emotional widow who broke it again by throwing her arms round Miss Parkinson's neck and murmuring with a break in her soft voice:

'Oh, you dear, dear Miss Parkinson!'

'Then. . . .' Miss Parkinson stared at the widow's hat feather tickling her nose, incredulous, 'then you wish to remain on visiting terms?'

And she never did understand what the widow meant by impulsively replying: 'I'll save every penny I can! I'll never buy any new clothes any more! I'll live entirely on herrings—I will, indeed!'

'Oh, I wouldn't do that,' replied Miss Parkinson, anxiously. 'Think of your digestion.'

J. E. Buckrose, 'War Economy', from *War Time in Our Street: The Story of Some Companies behind the Firing Line* (London: Hodder & Stoughton, 1917), 133–45

Sarah MacDonald

Sarah MacDonald was a writer on health and nursing; she was also the author of a novel, *Cavalcade of Endeavour* (1936). *Simple Health Talks with Women War Workers* is evidence both of the need for health education for those women entering munitions work—described by MacDonald as 'the battle of industrial life'—and also of the physical and emotional strains which such work imposed. The book is pre-eminently practical, for example in its advice that workers should not stand at their machines in high-heeled shoes. It is also frank in the way in which it deals with 'moral hygiene'—venereal disease and birth control. It is clearly intended for a mass readership and its style is suggestive of the way that the exigencies of wartime, when workers slept in shifts and shared beds, forced a departure from the standard approach and tone of health manuals. It is a strangely mixed piece of writing which, as it reflects on people's lives 'turned topsy-turvy' by three years of war, mingles patriotic reflection into a manual of homely advice.

---

23   SIMPLE HEALTH TALKS

A RETROSPECT

To you is given in these dark days
A vast responsibility.

John Oxenham

IN these little health talks I intend to speak simply and plainly, for, being one of you, as it were, no one can realize better than myself the difficulties and dangers of this new industrial life.

I say new, for although you have been doing this particular work for over three years, it is only now we see the fruits of the seeds of ill-health which have been sown from the very beginning.

If you will just think for a moment how differently we are built, both physically and mentally, from the majority of men, you will understand me when I say that women are indeed passing through a very critical period.

Amid the excitement arising from strange conditions of labour and the novelty of handling larger earnings, accompanied by the achievement of a once-forbidden independence, I think enthusiasm runs away with one, and women are apt to forget the extra strain, both on different parts of the body and of the nerves. The constant changing of working hours interferes with the usual habits of sleep, and the irregularity of meal-times interferes with the regular work of the stomach.

At the outset we must bear in mind that for us this war has been a series of 'phases'.

First there was the time when woman's share was to watch and wait, to see her husband off to the front, and to shoulder the responsibility of a dual parentage.

Next came 'the call of the King to his daughters', and—what a mighty response there has been! The fervour and determination which arose in woman can indeed be compared to the feelings of 'the boys' as they marched away to the strains of 'Tipperary'; the same love for country was implanted in each heart, and very soon not only bench and lathe, but almost all spheres of occupation hitherto closed to all but men were taken over by women and girls of all ages.

Feverish patriotism, if you like, reigned for the time with highly satisfactory results, and many who had lived sheltered lives were plunged along with their sister-women into a whirling Armageddon. Let those who would pass censorious judgment remember that women took up at a moment's notice trades for which men had been prepared by years of training.

Yet another phase, and a serious one, for work which demands long hours of toil in an unnatural atmosphere, with great physical and mental strain, will exact its toll.

The anxiety as to results which must be perfect is a constant strain on the highly-strung nervous system of most women, and, added to the trials of unusual toil, is the anxiety of the home, the ailments of the babies, and by no means least the troubles and burdens peculiar to our sex which, instead of becoming less, are increasing in number and intensity. So I contend that if women are sometimes blamed for lack of the concentration which is accredited to the opposite sex, well, they have ample excuse.

Feverish patriotism has gone, and in its place there has arisen a dogged determination with some, and with others a passive acceptance of things which must be endured.

Not, as a famous poet says, 'Seam and gusset and band', but 'Steel and shot and shell' have become the daily round and common task, and in the midst of it all we dream dreams and see visions, which, alas! are likely to become only too true—visions of 'damaged goods', and of ill-health from a multitude of causes, but, most deplorable of all, many ills which could be avoided or mitigated with a little knowledge and common sense. There is a well-known proverb which says, 'Prevention is better than cure', and this, I think, is very applicable to munition workers in particular, and the time to think of it is *now*, not in a morbid but in an intelligent manner.

We must remember that it is the *unusual* which does the damage, and our aim must be to make an effort to preserve nervous and moral health as well as physical fitness. It is natural that men and women should work, for nature requires an outlet for energy, and the girl who is occupied, interested, concentrated on some definite line of work, who uses her brain and muscles in moderation, is healthier and happier in consequence. But work should be tempered with reason and common sense.

Health demands that we should have air to breathe as pure as possible, water to drink as free from contamination as possible, food to eat in reasonable quantity and as wholesome as possible, clothing to wear reasonably adapted to circumstances, and a certain amount of exercise, recreation, and sleep.

We shall talk of these things together, remembering that they are necessary for the development of men and women who can do things and endure.

It is not the slightest use trying to tell you on scientific lines how to take care of your bodies; the whole system of living and eating has been turned topsy-turvy, and the only thing to do is to try to adapt ourselves to these altered conditions as best we can.

With that apology, therefore, for leaving the usual lines of health talks, we shall proceed.

Health and Hygiene

But words are things, and a small drop of ink,
Falling like dew, upon a thought, produces,
That which makes thousands, perhaps millions,
Think

Byron

We shall now have a little chat about HYGIENE. Do you know what that is? I will tell you.

HYGIENE is the science of cleanliness, the gospel of health; it is knowledge combined with common sense, and one of the high roads to perfect womanhood.

If we are healthy and strong we shall be able to do our work well and take pleasure in it, for we all know how different our work seems when we are feeling bright and well from what it seems when we hardly know how to drag through the day or night.

We hear a great deal these days about the *germs* of disease, and perhaps to some people it is rather a mysterious word which is not quite understood. A germ is like a tiny seed much too small to be seen without a strong microscope, and, like any other seed, must be planted in suitable soil if it is to grow.

The body is the soil, but the condition of the body which is best for the growth of these germs is an unhealthy one, while in a healthy body they will either not grow at all or grow very little.

That will explain to you why it is important to keep our bodies in a healthy state, and clean houses, clean air, and clean water all mean death to the germ. I shall tell you more about them as we proceed with our talks; for the moment we are only concerned with them in a general sort of way.

It is with some trepidation, I must confess, that I speak of the problem of hygiene in the home, or what in these times constitutes a home.

The question is a many-sided one, and certainly, so far as our own district is concerned, has been an acute one also, for houses have been filled to their utmost capacity.

Again, the prevailing custom of having beds fixed within the walls without free access of air is a great drawback to health, especially as, in times of pressure, workers of one shift have only left them in time for the workers of the other shift to enter. Think, think of the germs in those bedclothes and the poisoned air of those sleeping apartments!

It appears to me that the only satisfactory solution of this question would be to recruit the landladies and to infuse into their minds not only the great importance of germ-carrying, but the terrible quickness and consequences of germ-breeding; then, perhaps, we might see an energetic hustling of blankets and opening of windows between these day and night shifts. It is a terrible thought that one pair of heads should sleep on the pillows for perhaps seven to eight hours, to be succeeded by another pair for an equal length of time, with no guarantee as to the health of any of them.

Well, tackle the horror as best you can, you yourselves can at least see to it that the chimney is not blocked up with screens and air-plugs, and that your window is open whilst you are sleeping. If you are afraid of a draught it is a simple matter to open the window at the bottom, and fix a piece of brown paper over the opening, which means that the air will enter through the middle of the sash, and no draughts will be felt.

Why, fresh air is not only necessary for health but for life itself, and we need it, asleep or awake!

The air we breathe out is very different from the air we breathe in: it is warmer and damper, and contains a poisonous gas and very often disease germs.

So you see that when a number of people occupy one room, the risks are proportionately greater.

Again, the air is made impure by dust, and it *is* in your power to see that your rooms are at any rate clean and free from unnecessary accumulations. With those of you who are fortunate enough to be in your own homes a broader view can be taken, and with yourselves lies the whole responsibility of making clean healthy bedrooms where that wholesome rest may be obtained which is so necessary to satisfactorily 'carry on'.

If you are sleeping under such conditions as I have mentioned, you are not only running the risk of infection from others, but your general health is sure to suffer after a time, and you wake up every day feeling tired and heavy, with no appetite for food and no energy for work.

It is quite impossible for people to be healthy when for so many hours they are breathing air which has already been breathed over and over again until it is full of all sorts of impurities.

So it is *up* to you, girls, to keep an eye on your sleeping apartments, and to take a little interest in them. I feel I can say very little on this subject, but if by chance some of the landladies see this little volume, let me beg of them to mother the girls they take into their homes, to realize that the health of the future mothers of the race is, to a great extent, in their hands, and that these girls behind the firing line are somebody's daughters, just as much as the boys at the front are somebody's sons.

Night Work

Persevere, it is not thine to guess
The measure of thy worth and usefulness;
Though purposeless thy life may seem, yet still
'Tis only thou maybe that niche may fill.

H. M. B.

The popular cry is, 'Oh, how I hate the night-shift; it comes round far too quickly!'

So it does, but we must 'fall in' like good soldiers. Night work is one of the biggest trials of this industrial life; the atmosphere of the shops still laden with the breath of the day-shift just away, the artificial light for twelve long hours, the unnatural tension and apprehension, not of what actually happens but of what may happen, are all extremely trying to the temper and to the nerves.

The creepy-crawly feeling which only night can bring; the constant strain of the nerves in the wintry nights when aircraft is the danger; the tense moment when from a blaze of light the shops are suddenly plunged into darkness with just a glimmering lamp here and there; the fear of machinery, still running in the darkness; the awful silence, presently broken by a buzz of voices, with perhaps a groan from some poor exile who has already suffered much: these are trials never to be forgotten, and are bound to leave their mark on the general health and nervous system of those who pass through them.

What has become of the old notion that night air was injurious, I wonder? The simple fact is that there is not time to think of it, and thus, like many more notions of the kind, it has vanished into oblivion for ever, and thousands of human beings are working energetically through the dark hours of night and break of day with apparent unconcern.

Now you must understand that during every moment of your life your body is undergoing wear, tear, and repair, and that two low-tide points occur in the vitality every twenty-four hours, the one at about five in the afternoon, the other at about five in the morning, and these are partly due to exhaustion. The evening fall is accompanied by a rise of temperature, that of the morning by a fall of temperature, and as the night nears morning the atmospheric temperature is lowered also, with the result that the body is below par, as it were, at that time.

All this points to something being needed to help the condition and to the need of nourishment to support the lowered vitality. Those girls, therefore, are wise indeed who make a point of taking some refreshment during the early morning 'minutes'.

The chief consequences of night work are headaches and indigestion, the first arising from the deprivation of fresh air and sunlight and probably sleeplessness, for it is no small matter to grow accustomed to sleep night or day, especially with older people of settled habits.

Indigestion very naturally results as a consequence of warmed-up food, alteration of meal hours, and the habits of the bowels, and unfortunately one is just beginning to feel settled, when, heigh-ho! over we go again to the other shift; truly a remarkably trying life! It is scarcely one for which advice can be given, and I feel all I can say is, take sufficient rest, take walks in the sunshine, be careful in your choice of food, and above all, prepare yourself for the turn-over by taking an aperient during the end of the week.

I wonder shall I be forgiven if, for a few brief moments, I make a digression from the cold practical facts to speak of these nights in another fashion?

Clever pens, from time to time, give us descriptions of the doings of our men on the various fronts, stories which we read with great interest and treasure in our minds, but of the 'back of the front' little is said, and yet here, too, life has its pathos and its battles, fought by thousands who so short a time ago were sleeping as peaceful citizens in their beds instead of grimly working with death-dealing machines.

We have become rather used to war, have we not? and yet I know well what lies underneath that settled appearance, and that long trials smooth the surface only; the undercurrent is rippling, but ready to break forth once again into a rushing torrent at a moment's notice.

A glance through the window and the moon and stars tell us that the world should be asleep, but a glance into the various workshops tell us that the world is very much awake; the flapping of the countless belts, the roar of the furnace, and the constant buzz of machinery, all tell their own tale, as do the honest sweat pouring from the begrimed faces of the men folk and the earnest though tired looks of the girls.

Yet, in spite of our manifold tribulations, we are a fortunate country. I think so when at times my mind goes back to another arsenal in a foreign land, and I mingle again with a stream of people, old and young, each carrying a tiny lamp or candle—for it is dark and late and very dangerous to cross the narrow little bridge which spans the river.

I hear once more ringing out of the darkness the challenge: 'Stoy! Co-e-da?' and the password answered by each as they pass through the gates guarded by great fine fellows with bayonets fixed.

I see over and over again the sad faces of those little Serbian girls who stuck to their machines in spite of invasion, who were twice driven out by the Austrians, and yet returned a third time to their posts until finally driven out of their country.

What courage, what nobility, has been shown by the women of all lands! History will record it all in due time, but rest assured that individual effort, though seemingly unnoticed, will be recorded in that 'sometime, somewhere' of the future.

The long hours are wearisome and exacting, at times body and soul feel they can do no more, but remember, girls, just as the day follows the night, so there is reaction in the body, and there is pride in the knowledge that you are invaluable to your country if your work is done well.

Never in living memory will these night-shifts be forgotten; hands will be seared and scarred with wounds, shoulders will be bent and rounded, hearts will be broken, and yet—I will ask you a question, would you have missed them? would you? No! a thousand times no!

Sarah MacDonald, 'A Retrospect', 'Health and Hygiene', and 'Night Work'
from Simple Health Talks with Women War Workers (London:
Methuen, 1917), 1–12, 46–51

Monica Cosens

Monica Cosens produced several volumes of stories about Ireland as well as some plays. These exist as a marked contrast to her war writings: *Lloyd George's Munition Girls* (1916) and, during the Second World War, *Evacuation: A Social Revolution* (1940). Little biographical information exists, other than that which she records of her own experiences as a worker in a munitions factory. A prefatory note describes the book as a factual record—'the events as they happened'—and also indicates Cosens's affection for her co-workers and her admiration for the work which they undertook. These feelings emerge in the extract which follows, along with an account of the scale of munitions work and the industrial discipline which it imposed.

---

24   6676

NEW hands have to report themselves at the Main to be 'signed on' and given a factory number. I was allotted 6676, and from that moment I became a number. It was far more important I should remember 6676 than my own surname.

In order to keep the machinery running continuously day and night, the twenty-four hours is divided into three shifts, each of eight hours' duration.

I was enrolled on the afternoon shift, so it was about a quarter past two when I came out of the office adjoining the principal workshop, walked under the railway arch, along the side of the truck line embedded in mud, and crossed over the road to the enormous red brick shell-factory, which rumour said had been built in six weeks!

We were due to start work at 2.30, and the road was already black with 'hands' streaming towards the tall wooden gates. These were the Khaki girls, whose name originated from the khaki overalls they wear, and is now applied to the thousands of industrial hands engaged in different parts of the country upon munition work. They were coming from the station, they were getting off the trams coming from the one direction, and from off the trams coming from the opposite direction, while quite a number were hurrying down the hill where neither trams nor buses ran.

What an extraordinary number of girls! I had never seen so many together in my life before. Where had they come from? They were all so much of a type. All carried brown cardboard cases containing their overalls and their food. All laughed, pushed, giggled, jostled, screamed and shrieked. They all were shabbily dressed, but with aims at finery carried out in a cheap and tawdry manner.

The girl who walked in front of me with her arm tucked round the waist of her friend had her heavily-powdered face half hidden under a large black velvet hat trimmed with bright pink, from under which peeped numerous slides and combs studded with glass. She wore an orange-coloured golf coat, faded and dirty, whilst a black and white check skirt, tight and ill-fitting, dragged round her ankles and dipped on to the downtrodden heels of her shoes. She was one out of hundreds of others much like her among whom I had to work.

Frankly, I did not like the look of my companions. They were rough, loud-voiced, and gave me the impression of being ill-natured, and having sharp tongues under which I had no doubt I should smart.

These five hundred girls—for that is the number of hands engaged on each shift—impressed me, as they do most people at first sight, as being nothing but vulgar little hussies. I had not worked among them a week, though, before I had grown to like them, then to appreciate them, and finally to love them.

I followed them through the littered yard, picking my way in and out among rusty shell-bodies, and round piles of shavings, sometimes deep blue and sometimes copper-coloured, which afterwards I knew to be called 'swarf', the technical term for the cuttings from the shells as they are turned.

With a feeling of awe I followed the girls through the great wooden doors, and for the first time put my foot on the concrete flooring of a munition factory, crammed with row after row of engine-turned lathes.

Everything in the workshop seemed to be going at top speed. The wide leather belting was whizzing round at a tremendous pace. The machinists turned this key, cranked that wheel, jerked the wooden handles with astonishing celerity. Lines of men threw shells to one another, loading up a truck as quickly as peas are shelled into a basin. There was movement and bustle everywhere, and above all was that dull roar of machinery as ceaseless as waves breaking on the shore.

Like the others, I threaded my way in and out among the machines. The factory was different from what I had imagined, but perhaps I had drawn my picture from what the Grey Woman had told me. Where were the sparks of red-hot steel that I had expected to see clouding the atmosphere? I could not find them. There were many slight-looking girls at the lathes, and they seemed to have sufficient strength to carry out the work.

The cloakroom was small for the number who were in it, and it was difficult to find a corner in which I could hang up my coat and hat. Everywhere girls were changing into the khaki-coloured overalls bearing the brass initial letters of the firm for which they were working on the points of the collars. Round the one small mirror they pushed and shouted as they tried to get a square inch in which to see if their tight-fitting caps were arranged at a becoming angle. In another corner quite suddenly and unexpectedly something happened. It was a scrimmage of some sort. Everybody turned and ran to see what it was about. A heavy, dark-haired girl had taken hold of a sullen-looking woman with a mean pinched face and was shaking her by the shoulders.

Then there rose a voice shrill in accusation.

'It's my 'at, I tell yer! Give it back ter me. Yer stowl it three weeks back. Garn, yer knows yer did!'

'Yer dirty liar! It's mine, I tells yer! I bort it myself.'

'Dirty liar yerself! Yes, yer bort it cheap off one of them pegs 'ere. If yer don't 'and it over I'll scram it off yer lowsy 'ead!'

'Yer do it too, Rowse!' came from an admirer.

Then from someone else:

'I calls it a bit sorft when yer 'as yer 'at stowlen and the thief comes back a week liter with it pinned on to 'er own ugly fat 'ead.'

Lastly, from the outskirts of the crowd:

'Drag it orf!'

'Give 'er socks!'

'Ow—er—!'

'Gaw on!'

'I tell yer if yer don't 'and it over, and I means what I sye'—Rose was growing more impassioned. I saw her clench her hands and thrust her face close to that of the accused—'I'll pull it orf and yer 'air with it, strite I will.'

There was a pause.

Then in outraged tones:

'Yer won't give it to me? Blimme, then I'll tike it!'

Out flew her arms. Her hands trembled over that hat for one second and then descended upon it with a clutch-like grasp. The hat was tightly pinned. She dragged at it and tore at it.

The accused screamed with pain.

'Aw—aw! Yer devil! Yer devil! Let go er me! Let go er me! Yer're tearin' me 'air out, yer——'

Then 'Muvver' arrived.

Muvver is Mrs Brown, the cloakroom attendant—a fat, complaisant-looking woman with small kind eyes and large toothless mouth.

''Ere now! 'Ere now, what yer doin'? What's all this about?'

The crowd with one accord turned to explain to Muvver that 'Rowse 'ad 'ad 'er 'at stowlen three weeks agow and Flora 'ad come with it on 'er 'ead to throw it in Rowse's fice-like.'

Muvver sailed into the crowd to settle the quarrel, which had settled itself as far as the ownership of the hat was concerned, for all that remained of it was one shattered forget-me-not and a trampled half yard or so of faded pink straw.

Before we started work we had to attend to what is called 'clocking'.

I looked for my card, headed with my number 6676, on the rack, placed it in the slot beneath the clock, pushed down a handle, and when I took it out I saw printed on it 2.23, the exact minute at which I had clocked. This is to safeguard the hands being late, and if they are after time there is registered proof of what hour they do arrive, and they can be fined accordingly.

My next experience was of the machinery.

I was handed over by the day foreman—a fair and clean-looking man in a holland coat—to the care of a setter-up. He was close on seventy, but still vigorous looking, with a grey-white beard, smiling blue eyes and spectacles, and was known as 'Gran'pa'.

'So I've got to make a finish-turner of ye? That's what these machines are for—Finish-Turning, and it's very delicate work.'

Gran'pa was inclined to chat; and before he taught me anything he stood there with a shell tucked in the hollow of his arm telling me how an urgent order had come in for these particular shells and had to be executed within the week. He then explained how to put the plug in the shell, how to put the shell in the machine, how to crank it up and lock it, and how to start the lathe by pushing the control lever.

Now I have worked that lathe for several months it is easy, but at first it seemed so difficult. I had an absurd fear that I should break the machine—and it would take a giant to do that!

When Gran'pa had turned two or three shells he left me to experiment on the knowledge I had picked up from him.

I did not feel confident to manage that big machine. As long as the shell revolved and the tool continued to cut the rusty coating, leaving it bright and shining beneath, and I could stand and watch it, all was well. But what was going to happen when it came to the end and I had to do something?

The moment to act arrived. Nervously I stretched up my arm to push back the wooden lever.

The machine stopped. It was wonderful. And I had done it. I gained confidence. *Of course* I knew how to take out the shell! You uncranked that wheel and then it loosened and fell mechanically.

I tugged, I pulled, I tore at it. Nothing would move it.

I sighed and rested for a moment.

Then I tried again.

I pulled with all my strength till I was scarlet in the face.

I gave a sidelong glance at the machine next to mine. Whoever was working that had no trouble. My next-door neighbour took hold of the wheel and with both hands loosened it. Then she twiddled it round with one hand, holding the shell with the other.

Oh! how I envied her! Why had she such superhuman strength whilst I, apparently, was a weakling?

Again a vision of the Grey Woman rose up in my mind.

'You look very slight for such heavy work.'

Was it going to be too heavy for me? Oh! I hoped I was not failing!

In almost a frenzy I tugged at that wheel with every particle of strength in my body.

Then I heard a quiet voice behind me:

'You'll save yourself a lot of work if you first unlock the machine.'

Gran'pa turned a handle which I had forgotten all about.

'Now try,' he said.

I gave the cranking wheel a tug. It turned easily. I felt annoyed with myself for being so foolish, but I suppose I could not expect to learn everything in five minutes.

At half-past five we are given half an hour for tea.

By this time I was working the machine myself, slowly and laboriously, and with none of that accelerated speed which the others displayed, but with less of the fear that I had felt at first.

It was many hours since Rose and Flora had fought over the faded pink hat, for daylight had gone. Outside the trams whizzed past the long factory windows like glow-worms, and overhead through the glass roofing we could no longer see the fleecy white clouds hurrying and scurrying; instead, above the big electric globes all was black and dark.

I wished they would open one of those long windows in the roof, for the factory had suddenly become, to me, stuffy. My head ached, I had a feeling of nausea. A terror came over me that it might become unbearable. Suppose I had to leave my machine? What would the foreman say if he came and found it idle?

I no longer felt hot, but icy cold. I looked at my hands. They were as white as paper. I was faint, but I did not dare move from my post.

'Yer get along outside, the air'll pick y' up.'

The voice sounded far away, but really it was at my elbow. The Khaki girl on the machine next to mine was speaking to me, and for the first time I realized my next-door neighbour was Rose of the hat-incident.

'But will it matter if I do?'

'That'll be all right. They won't say nothin'. I'll put another shell in for yer.'

So I went and sat down on some planks in the yard, among the rusty shell-bodies and the piles of shavings. My head reeled. I could see nothing clearly.

''Ow y' feelin'? You looked proper sick in the shop.'

It was Rose. She had followed me out to see if she could do anything for me.

'Y'd better chuck it for t'night. Yer not fit for much. I'll come along with yer an' ask Ole Rabbit for a pass out.'

I could never have believed that the savage Rose—for that was the impression I had of her—could be so gentle and kind.

She took me by the arm and led me back to the factory. Then she put me to sit down on a barrow while she went to look for the foreman whom she called 'Ole Rabbit'.

I saw her coming back to me with a short man who wore a black suit, a turned-down collar and a bowler hat. His narrow jaw and elongated teeth gave him the appearance of a rabbit.

He spoke with a North Country accent.

'So you've been gassed too? That's what cooms of being an Industrial Soldier. Gassed the first time in action!' He smiled. 'That's hard luck!' It was the Rabbit's fancy to liken us to soldiers, and it was he who dubbed us the Miss Tommy Atkins' of Lloyd George's army.

'Gassed?'

'It's the fumes from the charcoal brazier that have upset you. Five or six have coom to me asking for passes out.'

He took from his pocket a tablet of printed forms.

'Noomber?' he queried.

'6676.'

'Reason for passing out,' he mumbled as he wrote it . . . 'Sickness.'

'There ye are! Coom back to-morrow well and ready for a hard day's work. There's plenty to be done, for we haven't killed the Kaiser yet.'

Monica Cosens, '6676', from *Lloyd George's Munition Girls*
(London: Hutchinson, 1916), 15–29

Dorothy Peel (Mrs C. S. Peel)
(1872–1934)

Dorothy Peel started her working life as a journalist and wrote a series of books on cookery and home economics, including *The New Home* (1899) and *How to Keep House* (1902). Her later career was extremely varied: in the words of *The Times*, when she died, 'her industry was astonishing, for she went down coalmines, inspected prisons, reformatories and factories, examined schools and studied diet for the young, in addition to regular journalism and four novels'. Dorothy Peel was the wartime director of Women's Services; she served on numerous committees from Town Planning to Labour Saving Houses; she produced a series of cookery books for the wartime economy: *Marriage on Small Means* (1914) and *The Eat-Less Cookery Book: War Ration Economy* (1917). She was best known, however, for her books of social and domestic history (*A Hundred Wonderful Years* (1926); *The Stream of Time* (1931); *Life's Enchanted Cup: An Autobiography* (1933)). When she looked back she saw the war as an interruption in which 'I, like other women, became absorbed in work other than that to which I had been accustomed'.

---

25   HOUSEKEEPING IN WAR TIME

So serious was the position of affairs in the spring of 1917, that it was thought wise to prepare for the time when, in order to secure the utmost economy in food and fuel, to free women to do the work of men and to ensure that the children should not suffer more from malnutrition than might be inevitable owing to scarcity, national kitchens would be required. The War Savings Committee had already been collecting information regarding such kitchens, and now the Food Controller authorized the organization of an experimental kitchen, for which premises in Westminster Bridge Road were secured. Eventually the National Kitchen Department of the Ministry became of considerable importance. Municipalities, associations and private persons also started kitchens.

These public or national kitchens filled a need, but owing to the failure of the German submarine campaign they fortunately never became a necessity.

The Queen opened the first Ministry of Food national kitchen, and, helped by Princess Mary, served a number of customers. Her Majesty seemed quite agitated by one minute child, who, reaching up to receive its purchase from the counter, seemed in imminent danger of spilling a plateful of scalding rice pudding on to the top of its head. In those days people had not learned the art of buying their dinners at public kitchens, and many of them omitted to bring any kind of receptacle, and, in order that they should not be too late to be served by the Queen, rushed madly home again to fetch a jug or basin. Cornflour and rhubarb jelly was one of the sweets of the day, and a supply of this dish had been put ready on a lower shelf of a serving-table. The enterprising and social yellow dog, which attends all functions from race to missionary meetings, naturally decided to attend the opening of the Westminster Bridge kitchen, and was discovered, having dodged through a mass of legs and squeezed himself behind the counter, sitting licking a pink mould with the greatest appreciation. Presently one of the servers came and shoo'd him away, but did not remove the pudding. One wondered who ate that pudding, because the yellow dog had licked it very neatly, and it still looked shapely and shining.

While the Queen was ladling out food a very old man shambled up and bought meat, vegetables and pudding, which he proceeded to place all together on a very dirty plate and cover them with a still dirtier piece of newspaper. He then shambled out, never having realized who it was who had served him. The fact that it was the Queen must have been pointed out to him by the crowd outside, for shortly afterwards he returned, edged his way back to the serving-counter and solemnly waved his hat three times at her.

It was thought by some of their promoters that national kitchens would endure and become a feature of the nation's life, but that opinion was not based on knowledge of the circumstances of the working people. A working family (like any other family) must have a home, they must have some means of warming that home and of procuring hot water, and the mother must spend most of her time in the house attending to her domestic duties. Therefore it cannot pay her to buy food to which must be added the cost of rent, wages, fuel and upkeep. The average working woman can provide food more cheaply than anyone else can provide it for her, and whilst she is able to do that and her income remains limited, working-class people in normal circumstances will cook their own food and eat it in their own homes.

Middle-class people are in a different position. By buying ready-to-eat food or by feeding at restaurants possibly they may economize in rent, in wages, in fuel and in the upkeep of service premises, and so, in spite of the greater cost of their actual food, achieve considerable saving in expenditure. Hence it is that the poor continue to live as they have been accustomed to live, but many of the younger middle-class people have adopted the bed-and-breakfast-house and motor-car style of living. The ready-to-eat food departments of the great caterers are their public kitchens.

It was in the spring of 1917 that, to save waste of fruit and vegetables, the Board of Agriculture arranged for teachers to travel about the country to demonstrate the art of bottling and canning. Owing to the continued high cost of living, bottling is much practised, but we have still to learn to make the fullest use of home produce. At present we buy an unnecessary quantity of foreign tinned goods.

It was also in this country a shock to many of us to learn how wasteful we had been of bread in the years of peace and plenty. It was calculated that about 9380 tons of bread were wasted each week in Great Britain, a statement which when made at food meetings caused a gasp of surprise and a murmur of 'I'm sure we don't waste bread in *our* house.' It was always in the houses of other people that waste took place.

Apropos of bread, it is worthy of note that when the price rose and continued to rise, and many complaints were made, the London County Council issued posters advising people to buy bread by weight, which is legal, and not by the loaf, as is customary except in poor districts, where it is usual to weigh the loaf and to add pieces to make up the correct weight. According to Press reports no notice was taken of this advice, but whether the bakers said this in the hope of discouraging the practice, or if it was true, who knows? During the most anxious months people were fined for feeding their poultry on bread.

This question of feeding animals became a serious one, and before the end of the war the miserable looks of the rationed horses caused many a heartache.

The scarcity of cereals gave rise to much controversy as to whether it paid better to invest food in pigs and poultry and eat it in its condensed form of bacon, ham or fowl, or to keep all grain suitable for human consumption and eat it as grain.

It was stated that eggs were a luxury food. A 2 oz. egg contains two-thirds of its weight in water, 11 per cent of shell and only 25 per cent of nutritive matter. There is less than 1 oz. of food in two average eggs. If the egg costs $2\frac{1}{2}d$. (in London and other towns it was unprocurable at that price in 1917, and rose to $4d$. and $5d$. and even $6d$.), its nourishment price is $6s.\ 8d.$ per lb. The hen eats far more in grain than she produces, we were assured, and 1 lb. of costly chicken is of less food value than $\frac{1}{2}$ lb. of grain.

The anxiety felt with regard to our food supplies was evinced by the questions put by members of food meeting audiences anent the food of pet dogs. Those who kept dogs and those who did not were almost as passionately opposed to each other as the drink controversialists. Fortunately the time never came which obliged us to eat our dog friends, as happened during the siege of Paris, when the price of dog was $2s.\ 8d.$ per lb. Then the animals in the Zoo were eaten and elephant flesh fetched $15s.$ per lb., a cabbage cost $6s.$, a cat $11s.\ 3d.$ and persons obtained 12 ozs. of very dry bread after waiting three hours in twelve degrees of frost.

An old account book shows that in the autumn of 1917 milk cost $9d.$ per quart, butter $2s.\ 6d.$ per lb., tea (controlled price) $2s.\ 6d.$ per lb., a cauliflower $1s.$, a fowl $12s.\ 6d.$, bananas $5d.$ each, a tin of peaches $4s.\ 6d.$ and a flat sponge sandwich cake the size of a tea plate $2s.\ 3d.$ It is noted 'Gay coming home on leave. Tried to get some preserved fruits for him, but none were obtainable.'

In Paris at that time the cost of living greatly exercised the French Government, and the following note appeared in *The Times:* 'The high price of living is being studied by the Ministry of Labour, and a table has just been published showing the increased cost of absolute essentials during the last four years. To feed four people in a working-man's home, for bread, meat, bacon, butter, eggs, milk, cheese, potatoes, dried vegetables, sugar, salad oil, paraffin and methylated spirit, the average cost per annum, according to prices in the third quarter of 1914, represented 1004 f. (£40). In 1917 it was 1845 f. (£73 16s.). By the end of June 1918 2331 f. (£93 4s.). No wonder it is hard to make both ends meet and that there is a cry for increased salaries.'

In Berlin the allowance of food per week for each person was $\frac{1}{2}$ lb. meat; $\frac{1}{2}$ lb. lard once a month allowed instead of meat; 5 lbs. potatoes or *kohlruben*—a kind of large, coarse turnip—which was substituted when potatoes were short; $4\frac{1}{2}$ lbs. bread; $\frac{1}{2}$ lb. oatmeal once a fortnight; $\frac{1}{2}$ lb. barley per fortnight; no tea or cocoa; coffee $\frac{1}{2}$ lb. of substitute once in six weeks; $\frac{1}{2}$ lb. jam (vegetable jam substitute) once in six weeks; no bacon or ham; no milk for adults. New milk was reserved for invalids and children below the age of six years. Families who had children over six but below ten years of age received one quart of skimmed milk once a week per household, irrespective of the number of children. $\frac{1}{4}$ lb. cheese at rare intervals if waited for in a two-hour queue; no fresh fruit or dried fruit; eggs sometimes one a week, sometimes one a fortnight; no green vegetables, biscuits, rice, sago, tapioca or semolina; butter less than 2 ozs.; margarine 1 oz.; fish an occasional half herring if the purchaser stood in a queue for it; $\frac{3}{4}$ lb. sugar once a fortnight. Treacle or golden syrup could be had only instead of sugar.

German women who had saved during their thrifty, hard-working lives were spending their capital on unrationed food, procurable only at fabulous prices. As they truly said, What was the use of money if they died of starvation in order to keep it? (This shifting of values at first greatly puzzled the uneducated in our own country. Before the war they could not buy because they had not the money. Now they had the money and still could not buy.) In Germany fuel was as scarce as food. Clothing also was rationed. The allowance to each woman was two dresses, two blouses, one coat, three of any undergarment, six handkerchiefs, two pairs of boots. In order to get a permit to buy an article of dress the purchaser had to declare on oath that she did not possess the above allowance of that article and surrender if called upon to do so her worn-out garments.

It was reported that the civilians in Berlin looked white and thin and were very irritable. The military governor of that city was obliged to issue a warning to shopkeepers that extreme rudeness to customers would be a punishable offence. A considerable number of complaints regarding the rudeness of shopkeepers were heard in this country: shopkeepers retaliated by complaining that their customers were utterly unreasonable and that the bother of coupons and orders of one kind and another drove them nearly crazy. Undoubtedly worries about food, the discomfort caused by shortage of fuel, and consequently of hot water, and by living in crowded quarters, the overwork from which many people suffered, added in many cases to torturing anxiety for the safety of husband, son or lover, did fray our nerves and make us irritable.

It added to the worries of patriotic housewives who were honourably observing the voluntary rations that, as they expressed it, they never knew where they were. One day they were begged to eat potatoes, and potato recipe leaflets flooded the country, and the next day they were begged not to eat potatoes, and indeed in many cases could not, because, owing to potato disease, the crop failed and only the recipes remained. In London at one time potatoes were so scarce that a rich man visiting friends to whom in pre-war days he would have brought expensive fruit, flowers or a box of chocolates, appeared with a bag of potatoes. At one moment rabbits could be procured—at a price—and the price made many would-be buyers so indignant that they demanded that rabbits should be 'controlled'. The Food Controller controlled rabbits, and promptly they disappeared from the market. 'Where *are* the rabbits?' cried indignant women at food meetings, the explanation being that when it was no longer possible to sell a rabbit at a high price its owner preferred to eat it himself, and did.

It became inadvisable for speakers and demonstrators to recommend the use of any one article, for whilst maize might be procurable here, it was unprocurable there, and wherever it happened to be, if everyone asked for it, the supply was soon exhausted. Although we learned to use maize and were thankful to have it, it never became well liked, but continued to be one of those foods which we admitted that people in that vague locality 'out there' might use, but which free-born Britishers would never condescend to in normal times. As for the varieties of dried beans with which we supplemented our lessening supplies of meat, those we frankly hated. When at a cookery demonstration a bean dish was suggested as a substitute for the meat which it was so difficult to obtain, a good lady laughed ironically. 'Give me 'usbin' that muck? Yes, I don't think!' Whilst another added, 'Give 'im beans, an' get a black eye for me pains!' Sometimes cheese was short and sometimes meat was short, and always fats were short, and mothers were terribly worried when milk was short and threatened to be shorter.

The different regulations which were made regarding meatless days annoyed us and drove the trade nearly frantic, and resulted in putting up the price of fish. Sole rose to 4s. per lb. and turbot to 3s., prices to which we were not unaccustomed later, but which horrified us then. There were many complaints that fish was destroyed to keep up the price, and a case of a fishmonger at Folkestone in whose refuse bin were found twenty-two mullet and five plaice gained considerable publicity. In the end it seemed best to leave the public to use what food they could buy to the best of their ability, and the meatless day order was rescinded.

In an Eat Less Meat appeal made by the War Savings Committee in the early winter of 1916, it was said that the civilian population was eating £500,000 worth of meat each day. It was at this time that some well-intentioned idiot suggested that everyone should send Christmas cards wishing their friends 'A Simple Fare Christmas', quite forgetting that owing to the scarcity of paper and of labour it was practically impossible to do any such thing. On the other hand, in order to save expenditure in printing, a Kentish Urban Council went to the other extreme and decided not to punctuate their official reports, which appeared without a single comma or full stop!

How thankful we were for 'offal', which was not rationed. Offal was the elegant term for liver, oxtails, sweetbread, kidneys, tripe. One begged the kind butcher to let one have a little bit, and sometimes he did and sometimes he did not. As a young married woman writing to a friend expressed it, 'We live mostly on entrails.' With scarcity, values changed, and a devoted youth home on leave from Ireland, where food was not controlled, visited his beloved bearing in his hand a pound of butter. Another traveller returning to London brought back some butter. He asked two or three ladies to luncheon, and whispered to the one of his choice that she should remain after the others had left, when he would give it to her. Alas! the other guests stayed late, and when the host departed to fetch the precious fat he found that, having put it on the window-sill in the early morning, the sun had reduced it to the state of melted butter. A still more tragic butter story is told of a lady who hurried home with her prize to find that an observation balloon was hanging in graceful folds from her roof and that its car was in the area. In the agitation of the moment she dropped the butter, and later returned to find that the puppy had eaten it and, with utter disregard for war-time economy, had been sick upon the drawing-room carpet.

Yet another matter which troubled the public during these trying months was the food waste which was stated to take place in military camps. However, when evidence was demanded it was seldom forthcoming. There may have been much waste during the earlier part of the war, but by 1917 it had ceased, and the soldier at home was certainly not over-fed. At a camp visited by a woman in an official position the day's dinner consisted of stew (what torrents of complaints there were about that Army stew!), potatoes and cabbage (of which Ambassador Page wrote 'the British have many vege-tables, and all of them cabbage'), custard-powder, custard and tinned fruit, which certainly did not seem either an excessive or a particularly well-chosen meal for young men taking hard exercise. This feast was genteelly served on tables covered with oilcloth adorned by aspidistras, their pots modestly draped in pink crinkly paper.

There was at that time in some camps a detestable habit of brewing tea in cauldrons in which the soup had been made. Tea is not improved by a layer of grease. This valuable commodity was undoubtedly matter in the wrong place: it would have been better to have added it to the fat collected from Army camps, which had produced sufficient tallow to provide soap for the Army, Navy and other Government departments with a surplus for public use and 18,000 tons of glycerine for ammunition.

Dorothy Peel, 'Housekeeping in War Time', from *How We Lived Then* (London: John Lane, 1929), 83–93

Blanche Wills Chandler

There is little biographical information on Blanche Wills Chandler, other than her authorship of the duologue *A Born Nurse* (1908) and *Tommies Two* (1917). The latter consists of fifty short sketches, originally published in newspapers and magazines such as the *Star*, *Punch*, the *Evening Standard*, and *Pearson's Weekly*. They are essentially comic sketches, a fact which gave the author both some misgivings and satisfaction: 'if these sketches win a smile from one man in the trenches, I am not ashamed to have written them.' The various pieces reveal how adept Chandler was at finding different narrative voices: the Oxford aesthete describing the decor of his dugout, or the farm labourer who recalls his attempts to explain the war to the local schoolmaster and squire.

---

26   A PATTERN OF PROPRIETY

IT was generally known that the Vicar had intentions with regard to Belinda Widdicombe. He was a fastidious man. He demanded an ideal propriety of conduct on the part of women. Belinda had fifty-six years of spotless behaviour to her credit. Then the war broke out and brought matters to a climax. Together they transformed the Sunday-school room into a canteen for soldiers and opened it with a sugar bun between them.

'Depend upon it they'll be engaged before peace is declared,' said the parishioners.

But Belinda wasn't sure. Of late she had felt herself developing a recklessness of demeanour in the presence of the military which made her tremble for her prospects. She had even found herself one day waving her handkerchief to a trainload of departing Tommies. She had talked to herself severely afterwards.

'Are you losing your senses, Belinda Widdicombe? Don't you know it is flying in the face of Providence with a man who considers modesty the brightest jewel in a woman's crown? Pray for the poor creatures at home in a ladylike manner. Don't make advances to them on a public railway platform. He may have been at the bookstall. Who knows?'

Belinda shivered. She was temporarily scared. But two days later she broke out again and found herself three-parts out of the window shouting 'Hip! Hip! Hip! Hurrah!' to a homecoming V.C. Her cook took her to task that time.

'I'd got ye by the legs all the time, miss, though ye didn't know it. Ye'd have pitched out on your head else, ye was that excited. And the Vicar raisin' his hat to ye at the time, and ye with your mouth open never takin' the ghost of a bit of notice of him, ye was so taken up with young Jimmy Bumpeter.'

Belinda's blood curdled. How often had she peeped between the curtains for a sight of that stately figure and drawn them close as he passed. It was vulgar to be seen looking out of the window. And now he had seen her head and shoulders over the sill bellowing at Jimmy Bumpeter—there was no other word for it, she had bellowed like a bull—with the cook holding her legs. Perhaps he had seen her legs too. . . . She wept tears of shame and repentance.

But that very same day there she was sneaking out of the barber's with her pockets bulging with Woodbines and boxes of matches. Then Miss Widdicombe took herself in hand.

'Look here,' she said, 'for fifty-six years you've been a well-conducted maiden lady. Out of the way of temptation before it's too late. Fly from the sight of khaki. You'll be kissing a corporal next.'

She addressed the canteen cake-cupboard key to the Vicar and tried a change at the sea.

It was a lone shore. There were no marching feet, no soul-stirring 'Tipperary', no bugles, nothing but hermit crabs and jellyfish. The Church was Perpendicular, the post-office two miles off. It was the very place to recover one's mental poise. Belinda made progress. Then one morning a postcard came from the Vicar. He hoped for her usual superintendence at the harvest decorations. Her heart leapt. He had overlooked the episode of Jimmy Bumpeter. There and then Belinda vowed never to disgrace herself with soldiers again.

She meant to keep her word. She didn't bargain for half a dozen Tommies tumbling into the second-class compartment which she occupied alone on her journey home. They were the merriest crew, and the sergeant was the merriest of the lot. He had them in hand though. When one of them fingered a stump of a cigarette he was on him in a moment. 'Where are yer manners, Bill Odgers? Carn't yer see there's a lady in the kerridge?'

Belinda sat stiff in her corner, her eyes on the *Church Times*, her lips pursed tight. She was trying to hold herself in. 'Be quiet, Belinda Widdicombe. It's not a smoking compartment, or you wouldn't have dreamt of getting into it. You hate smoke. You caught the parlourmaid's young man with a pipe in the scullery once and you gave her notice. The smell of it is enough for you. The train doesn't stop for an hour—and they're Tommies—and they're all dying to smoke. . . . What's that to you?'

Nothing—nothing at all. But Belinda found herself turning to the sergeant. 'Pray let them smoke. I don't object.'

The sergeant thanked her kindly, but he looked at her out of the tail of his eye, her grey hair, her gold-rimmed spectacles, her prim mouth, and he tipped a wink to the Tommies. They understood. She was a good old sort, but she wasn't the sort to stand baccy. Her kindheartedness was not to be imposed upon.

Belinda understood, too. Six Tommies dying for a smoke. Six knights of chivalry sacrificed for her. Something like a trumpet stirred her. What mattered what she suffered? If her eyes watered, if her head cracked—what of it? Who cared?

She was leaning to the sergeant again. But he shook his head. 'You don't know what you're askin', mum. It's temptin', as it's our last chance to-day; but our baccy's strong; we shouldn't like to incommode a lady.'

Then Belinda let herself go. It was to the devil, and she knew it. 'A fig for propriety, a fig for a husband! There's only one way. It'll kill me, but I'm going to take it. If there are two ends to the thing, pray Heaven I don't get the wrong end into my mouth.'

Then she put her hand in her pocket and drew out a Woodbine and a box of matches. Desperation gave her confidence. She got it alight first go. She flipped the match out of the window, crossed her legs, and puffed hard across the carriage.

'Mine's a bit strong, too,' she said; 'hope none of you mind?'

'Well, I'm blowed!' said a Tommy at the other window, whipping out a briar. Low but forcible remarks flew around.

'My mother wouldn't 'arf let her 'ave it!'

'Deceivin' old bird to look at.'

'Women are goin' it, no mistake!'

'Regler racin' card, you bet.'

They all lit up joyously with the exception of the sergeant. He kept his eye on Belinda.

The Vicar was at the station to meet her. She was clinging to the sergeant then. Her head was on his shoulder. She was sea green. They carried her out between them.

'Finest bit o' pluck I've seen out o' the trenches, sir,' said the sergeant. 'If ever a lady deserved the V.C. she do.' And he told what he knew.

The Vicar shuddered. 'A Woodbine, too!'—He was as fastidious in tobacco as in other things—'A heroine, indeed!'

He was very kind to Belinda on the way home. He knew she needed it. He remembered his first smoke in a hayloft. The parishioners think it may be before Christmas.

Blanche Wills Chandler, 'A Pattern of Propriety', from *Tommies Two* (London and Edinburgh: Sampson Low, Marston and Co. Ltd., 1917), 71–5

'A Little Nest Egg' describes, in comic vein, the hardships of bringing up babies in wartime. In an advertisement at the end of the volume, the publisher notes its popularity as a piece performed by 'our best platform elocutionists'.

———

27   A LITTLE NEST EGG

I'VE had two soldiers before. They give me a ornamental flower-pot when they left and they've sent me a picture postcard since, beginning 'Dear Mother.' That's their fun and Albert made no words about it. Very different behaviour to Mrs Dabtail's husband, who dragged her by the hair because he found her sewing on her billet's buttons.

These two are younger. Private Figgs is eighteen. Private Montague I should judge at twenty-two. I like Figgs, but I can't help taking more to Montague because he does take so to my Kitchener Jellicoe. I never see a young man go on with a baby like him, and the questions he does put to me.

'Now, Mrs Griddle, exactly how much of this woolly stuff does a nipper have on its head when it's born?'

'Don't you think a chunk of beef would make him grow more than all that sloppy stuff you shove into him?'

'I say, do you know, I've just counted, this kiddie's only got half a set of teeth.' My Kitchener having just cut his seventh.

'He's nuts on getting something cold on his gums, shall I give him a chew of my bayonet?'

Montague's clothes is very nice, nothing tawdry, and three sets of under things. Very different to poor Figgs, who had to go to bed at five the first Saturday night so as I could wash his shirt through for Sunday. Montague did stare. 'One shirt to his back! Poor beggar!' he said. And he went out and came back with such shirts as I could have cried over because they wasn't Albert's. I fancy he's paid into a slate club, and that accounts for his ready money.

He spends like water. He brings in things for tea that I can't bear to put a knife into, wicked wasteful things like meat pies with a holler instead of a meat inside to 'em, and tongues which is three parts jelly and tin; and when Albert happened to mention it was our wedding day, he brought in some fizzy stuff in a bottle that broke the centre vase on the parlour mantelpiece, father's present, when the cork went off, and Albert walked upstairs to bed in a manner which was a disgrace to a husband and a father and lost half a day's work at the foundry because his head didn't stop going round until twelve o'clock. Figgs was as bad. I pitied that boy from my heart when I see him staggering off to his shooting practice with his hand over his eyes. 'Pray 'Eaving, we don't 'ave any moving targets to-day,' he was groaning to himself.

This morning a telegram came for Montague. He went white as a table-cloth and asked me to open it. And what do you think I read? 'Fine girl. Mother and child doing well.' You might have knocked me down with a feather. I didn't spare him.

'Do you mean to say you've been spending money like a single man as you have,' I said to him, 'and you with a young wife and now a new-born baby dependin' on you? What's her beggarly separation allowance to keep the house goin' on and food the price it is? What you fritter away on cigarettes in the week would keep that child in Mellin's if so be as she's got to be brought up by hand, which God forbid, and, if not, there's the cradle and the pram to buy and the high chair. Have you got anything put by for a pram?'

'I fancy my mother's sending us a pram,' he said.

It made me mad the easy way he spoke.

'Poor old soul,' I said, 'and denyin' herself a bit o' meat to do it, I suppose.'

'No, the mater's a vegetarian,' he said, in a dreamy sort of way staring at Kitchener Jellicoe. Then he caught him up in his arms.

'I wish I could get a day off to see my little nipper,' he said. 'Do you think she's like this one?'

'Like as two peas, only a girl, and half the size,' I said; and then seeing how soft like he looked I put my hand on his shoulder and spoke persuasive to him. 'Now you turn over a new leaf,' I said, 'and give me half a crown of your pay every week and let me send it home to your poor wife. You won't miss it, and she won't have to pinch and screw as only those who've got a baby know how you have to. Soap alone is a item if she does her duty by the washin', and feeding-bottles is ruination. Now will you promise?'

'Done,' he said, and tossed me over the first two-and-six then and there. He gave me the address—grand sounding sort of name the house had, just the kind that attracts new married couples and they have to turn out at the end of the year or take a lodger—and I sent it in stamps with a little letter to Mrs Montague explaining how I'd wheedled it out of him, and of course I knew she wouldn't think of spending it when she was in clover with her separation money, but she'd put it by for a nest egg for the precious baby, and I said as how when her husband was off his appetite with his vaccin-ation—which I knew he would be by the others—I'd save a bit of his billeting money for her and the child.

I was as good as my word. I saved 3s. 4d. the week his arm took, and more when he was inoculated. Besides that I'm always getting twopences and threepences out of him, which I know he'd throw away in Woodbines if I didn't. Altogether I've sent her a nice tidy little sum.

This afternoon a motor-car drove up to our door. It was the grandest car I've ever seen, with fur rugs and flowers inside, and a lady as pretty as a picture, and a nurse in white and a baby. What that child's cloak must have cost made me hold my breath.

The next thing I knew was that Private Montague, who had just come in wet through and was having his puttees dried by the kitchen fire, was out in the road with his bare legs and his arms round the lady and the baby!

My knees went cold. I'd just posted her a P.O. for one and nine. I tried to explain, but I couldn't. I just broke down and pointed to the baby. 'I did it for her sake, my lady,' I said.

But her eyes were fixed on Kitchener Jellicoe. 'Yours is a boy,' she said; 'he'll fight for his country when he grows up. You've got all the luck, Mrs Griddle.'

And I think I have. For every shilling I had sent to her Private Montague turned into a sovereign there and then.

'A nest egg for Kitchener Jellicoe,' he said.

Blanche Wills Chandler, 'A Little Nest Egg', from Tommies Two (London and
Edinburgh: Sampson Low, Marston and Co. Ltd., 1917), 42–5

Ellen La Motte
(1873–1961)

Ellen La Motte was known for her writing, her nursing work, and for her determined opposition to the opium traffic in the 1920s. In her earlier career she specialized in anti-tuberculosis nursing—an experience which resulted in *The Tuberculosis Nurse* (1914). She was one of the first American nurses to arrive at French battlefields, having arrived in Paris in 1913. She was known to Gertrude Stein who described her as 'very heroic but gun shy' and she was an acquaintance also of Mary Borden (see no. 54). La Motte wrote about her war experience in *The Backwash of War: The Human Wreckage of the Battlefield as Witnessed by an American Hospital Nurse* (1916). She also wrote short stories, collected as *Civilization* (1919) and *Snuffs and Butters* (1925). In the 1920s her involvement with opium traffic resulted in *Peking Dust* (1919), *The*

Opium Monopoly (1920), and *The Ethics of Opium* (1924). She was also a contributor to major periodicals such as *Atlantic Monthly, Harpers*, and the *Nation*.

━━━━━━━

28   WOMEN AND WIVES

A BITTER wind swept in from the North Sea. It swept in over many miles of Flanders plains, driving gusts of rain before it. It was a biting gale by the time it reached the little cluster of wooden huts composing the field hospital, and rain and wind together dashed against the huts, blew under them, blew through them, crashed to pieces a swinging window down at the laundry, and loosened the roof of Salle I. at the other end of the enclosure. It was just ordinary winter weather, such as had lasted for months on end, and which the Belgians spoke of as vile weather, while the French called it vile Belgian weather. The drenching rain soaked into the long, green winter grass, and the sweeping wind was bitter cold, and the howling of the wind was louder than the guns, so that it was only when the wind paused for a moment, between blasts, that the rolling of the guns could be heard.

In Salle I. the stove had gone out. It was a good little stove, but somehow was unequal to struggling with the wind which blew down the long, rocking stove pipe, and blew the fire out. So the little stove grew cold, and the hot water jug on the stove grew cold, and all the patients at that end of the ward likewise grew cold, and demanded hot water bottles, and there wasn't any hot water with which to fill them. So the patients complained and shivered, and in the pauses of the wind, one heard the guns.

Then the roof of the ward lifted about an inch, and more wind beat down, and as it beat down, so the roof lifted. The orderly remarked that if this Belgian weather continued, by tomorrow the roof would be clean off—blown off into the German lines. So all laughed as Fouquet said this, and wondered how they could lie abed with the roof of Salle I., the Salle of the *Grands Blessés*, blown over into the German lines. The ward did not present a neat appearance, for all the beds were pushed about at queer angles, in from the wall, out from the wall, some touching each other, some very far apart, and all to avoid the little leaks of rain which streamed or dropped down from little holes in the roof. This weary, weary war! These long days of boredom in the hospital, these days of incessant wind and rain and cold.

Armand, the chief orderly, ordered Fouquet to rebuild the fire, and

Fouquet slipped on his *sabots* and clogged down the ward, away outdoors in the wind, and returned finally with a box of coal on his shoulders, which he dumped heavily on the floor. He was clumsy and sullen, and the coal was wet and mostly slate, and the patients laughed at his efforts to rebuild the fire. Finally, however, it was alight again, and radiated out a faint warmth, which served to bring out the smell of iodoform, and of draining wounds, and other smells which loaded the cold, close air. Then, no one knows who began it, one of the patients showed the nurse a photograph of his wife and child, and in a moment every man in the twenty beds was fishing back of his bed, in his *musette*, under his pillow, for photographs of his wife. They all had wives, it seems, for remember, these were the old troops, who had replaced the young Zouaves who had guarded this part of the Front all summer. One by one they came out, these photographs, from weather-beaten sacks, from shabby boxes, from under pillows, and the nurse must see them all. Pathetic little pictures they were, of common, working-class women, some fat and work-worn, some thin and work-worn, some with stodgy little children grouped about them, some without, but all were practically the same. They were the wives of these men in the beds here, the working-class wives of working-class men—the soldiers of the trenches. Ah yes, France is democratic. It is the Nation's war, and all the men of the Nation, regardless of rank, are serving. But some serve in better places than others. The trenches are mostly reserved for men of the working class, which is reasonable, as there are more of them.

The rain beat down, and the little stove glowed, and the afternoon drew to a close, and the photographs of the wives continued to pass from hand to hand. There was much talk of home, and much of it was longing, and much of it was pathetic, and much of it was resigned. And always the little, ugly wives, the stupid, ordinary wives, represented home. And the words home and wife were interchangeable and stood for the same thing. And the glories and heroisms of war seemed of less interest, as a factor in life, than these stupid little wives.

Then Armand, the chief orderly, showed them all the photograph of his wife. No one knew that he was married, but he said yes, and that he received a letter from her every day—sometimes it was a postcard. Also that he wrote to her every day. We all knew how nervous he used to get, about letter time, when the *vaguemestre* made his rounds, every morning, distributing letters to all the wards. We all knew how impatient he used to get, when the *vaguemestre* laid his letter upon the table, and there it lay, on the table, while he was forced to make rounds with the surgeon, and could not claim it until long afterwards. So it was from his wife, that daily letter, so anxiously, so nervously awaited!

Simon had a wife too. Simon, the young surgeon, German-looking in appearance, six feet of blond brute. But not blond brute really. Whatever his appearance, there was in him something finer, something tenderer, something nobler, to distinguish him from the brute. About three times a week he walked into the ward with his fountain pen between his teeth—he did not smoke, but he chewed his fountain pen—and when the dressings were over, he would tell the nurse, shyly, accidentally, as it were, some little news about his home. Some little incident concerning his wife, some affectionate anecdote about his three young children. Once when one of the staff went over to London on vacation, Simon asked her to buy for his wife a leather coat, such as English women wear, for motoring. Always he thought of his wife, spoke of his wife, planned some thoughtful little surprise or gift for her.

You know, they won't let wives come to the Front. Women can come into the War Zone, on various pretexts, but wives cannot. Wives, it appears, are bad for the morale of the Army. They come with their troubles, to talk of how business is failing, of how things are going to the bad at home, because of the war; of how great the struggle, how bitter the trials and the poverty and hardship. They establish the connecting link between the soldier and his life at home, his life that he is compelled to resign. Letters can be censored and all disturbing items cut out, but if a wife is permitted to come to the War Zone, to see her husband, there is no censoring the things she may tell him. The disquieting, disturbing things. So she herself must be censored, not permitted to come. So for long weary months men must remain at the Front, on active inactivity, and their wives cannot come to see them. Only other people's wives may come. It is not the woman but the wife that is objected to. There is a difference. In war, it is very great.

There are many women at the Front. How do they get there, to the Zone of the Armies? On various pretexts—to see sick relatives, in such and such hospitals, or to see other relatives, brothers, uncles, cousins, other people's husbands—oh, there are many reasons which make it possible for them to come. And always there are the Belgian women, who live in the War Zone, for at present there is a little strip of Belgium left, and all the civilians have not been evacuated from the Army Zone. So there are plenty of women, first and last. Better ones for the officers, naturally, just as the officers' mess is of better quality than that of the common soldiers. But always there are plenty of women. Never wives, who mean responsibility, but just women, who only mean distraction and amusement, just as food and wine. So wives are forbidden, because lowering to the morale, but women are winked at, because they cheer and refresh the troops. After the war, it is hoped that all unmarried soldiers will marry, but doubtless they will not marry these women who have served and cheered them in the War Zone. That, again, would be depressing to the country's morale. It is rather paradoxical, but there are those who can explain it perfectly.

No, no, I don't understand. It's because everything has two sides. You would be surprised to pick up a franc, and find Liberty, Equality, and Fraternity on one side, and on the other, the image of the Sower smoothed out. A rose is a fine rose because of the manure you put at its roots. You don't get a medal for sustained nobility. You get it for the impetuous action of the moment, an action quite out of keeping with the trend of one's daily life. You speak of the young aviator who was decorated for destroying a Zeppelin single-handed, and in the next breath you add, and he killed himself, a few days later, by attempting to fly when he was drunk. So it goes. There is a dirty sediment at the bottom of most souls. War, superb as it is, is not necessarily a filtering process, by which men and nations may be purified. Well, there are many people to write you of the noble side, the heroic side, the exalted side of war. I must write you of what I have seen, the other side, the backwash. They are both true. In Spain, they bang their silver coins upon a marble slab, accepting the stamp upon both sides, and then decide whether as a whole they ring true.

Every now and then, Armand, the orderly, goes to the village to get a bath. He comes back with very clean hands and nails, and says that it has greatly solaced him, the warm water. Then later, that same evening, he gets permission to be absent from the hospital, and he goes to our village to a girl. But he is always as eager, as nervous for his wife's letter as ever. It is the same with Simon, the young surgeon. Only Simon keeps himself pretty clean at all times, as he has an orderly to bring him pitchers of hot water every morning, as many as he wants. But Simon has a girl in the village, to whom he goes every week. Only, why does he talk so incessantly about his wife, and show her pictures to me, to everyone about the place? Why should we all be bored with tales of Simon's stupid wife, when that's all she means to him? Only perhaps she means more. I told you I did not understand.

Then the *Gestionnaire*, the little fat man in khaki, who is purveyor to the hospital. Every night he commandeers an ambulance, and drives back into the country, to a village twelve miles away, to sleep with a woman. And the old doctor—he is sixty-four and has grandchildren—he goes down to our village for a little girl of fourteen. He was decorated with the Legion of Honour the other day. It seems incongruous.

Oh yes, of course these were decent girls at the start, at the beginning of the war. But you know women, how they run after men, especially when the men wear uniforms, all gilt buttons and braid. It's not the men's fault that most of the women in the War Zone are ruined. Have you ever watched the village girls when a regiment comes through, or stops for a night or two, *en repos*, on its way to the Front? Have you seen the girls make fools of themselves over the men? Well, that's why there are so many accessible for the troops. Of course the professional prostitutes from Paris aren't admitted to the War Zone, but the Belgian girls made such fools of themselves, the others weren't needed.

Across the lines, back of the German lines, in the invaded districts, it is different. The conquering armies just ruined all the women they could get hold of. Any one will tell you that. *Ces sales Bosches!* For it is inconceivable how any decent girl, even a Belgian, could give herself up voluntarily to a Hun! They used force, those brutes! That is the difference. It's all the difference in the world. No, the women over there didn't make fools of themselves over those men—how could they! No, no. Over there, in the invaded districts, the Germans forced those girls. Here, on this side, the girls cajoled the men till they gave in. Can't you see? You must be pro-German! Any way, they are all ruined and not fit for any decent man to mate with, after the war.

They are pretty dangerous, too, some of these women. No, I don't mean in that way. But they act as spies for the Germans and get a lot of information out of the men, and send it back, somehow, into the German lines. The Germans stop at nothing, nothing is too dastardly, too low, for them to attempt. There were two Belgian girls once, who lived together in a room, in a little village back of our lines. They were natives, and had always lived there, so of course they were not turned out, and when the village was shelled from time to time, they did not seem to mind and altogether they made a lot of money. They only received officers. The common soldiers were just dirt to them, and they refused to see them. Certain women get known in a place, as those who receive soldiers and those who receive officers. These girls were intelligent, too, and always asked a lot of intelligent, interested questions, and you know a man when he is excited will answer unsuspectingly any question put to him. The Germans took advantage of that. It is easy to be a spy. Just know what questions you must ask, and it is surprising how much information you can get. The thing is, to know upon what point information is wanted. These girls knew that, it seems, and so they asked a lot of intelligent questions, and as they received only officers, they got a good lot of valuable information, for as I say, when a man is excited he will answer many questions. Besides, who could have suspected at first that these two girls were spies? But they were, as they found out finally, after several months. Their rooms were one day searched, and a mass of incriminating papers were discovered. It seems the Germans had taken these girls from their families—held their families as hostages—and had sent them across into the English lines, with threats of vile reprisals upon their families if they did not produce information of value. Wasn't it beastly! Making these girls prostitutes and spies, upon pain of reprisals upon their families. The Germans knew they were so attractive that they would receive only officers. That they would receive many clients, of high rank, of much information, who would readily fall victims to their wiles. They are very vile themselves, these Germans. The curious thing is, how well they understand how to bait a trap for their enemies. In spite of having nothing in common with them, how well they understand the nature of those who are fighting in the name of Justice, of Liberty and Civilization.

Ellen La Motte, 'Women and Wives', from *The Backwash of War: The Human Wreckage of the Battlefield as Witnessed by an American Hospital Nurse* (New York and London: G. P. Putnam's Sons, 1916), 95–111

Lucie Delarue-Mardrus
(1880–?)

Lucie Delarue-Mardrus was a well-known member of the French aristocratic élite, and friend of Proust, Gide, and Rodin. Her poems, plays, and novels were considered exemplary and tended to feature in school readers, especially in France's secondary schools for girls. 'The Godmother' is a good example of the way that, unlike in Britain and the United States, the war in France put into question the drive towards female emancipation which had been well on the way during the *Belle Époque*.

---

29   THE GODMOTHER

WITH a sigh Géo loosened the package of letters which the Bureau of Good Works was in the habit of sending her each week. Too delicate for hospital work, she had tried many other things since 1914 before deciding upon her true function in the Great War. At last she had discovered her proper rôle. It was to be herself a correspondent and to find other correspondents for soldiers who wish to have godmothers, longing for the little blue postage stamp which so brightens the sombre life of the trenches.

Patiently Géo began to read the letters. About her the dismantled condition of her studio showed that she had painted little or nothing in the last three years. A cushion fell to the floor; the cat moved over on the divan closer to her mistress. Then the old serving woman entered to carry away the tea tray—the little solitary tea which the young woman had taken while continuing to read the soldiers' missives—a task which she always found extremely interesting.

Those who have never been able to have children often care for orphans in order to appease their heart emptiness. Géo wrote to the poilus so as to feel that she had some one at the front.

To have some one at the front, some one for whom to tremble, some one to grow tender over or to take pride in—that is today a prime necessity for the feminine heart. A woman of our time suffers if she is not on an equality in this respect with all the others. To be like the others—that is also a form of Sacred Union. Our feelings are the same, whether death is concerned or glory. Joy and grief are shared equally. That is why the sorrows of war, despite its horror, are perhaps lighter to bear than the sorrows of peace. No woman today feels isolated, whatever may be her misfortune or her happiness. There is among women a new mental war mood, which has all the authority of an established fashion.

Géo, alone in her class, suffered in solitude. All those letters to which she wrote answers were tinged with a sense of unreality. Twenty godsons were not worth one husband.

Wearily she let fall into her lap the letter which she was reading. Her big grey eyes stared at vacancy; her hand brushed back from her brow a tangle of henna-coloured curls.

'What in the world has become of him?'

She reviewed her short life. She was now a little more than twenty-eight years old. She could have been, like the others, a wife and a mother. Married before she was twenty to a good and attractive man, who chose her because he loved her, she had not then truly understood her destiny.

It was an epoch—that before the war—when people talked much about 'living their lives'. That formula meant a good many things to a good many persons. It covered exploits even more venturesome than those of a little personage like Géo.

Géo was called at that time Mme. Charles Bouvier, and one can well believe that that simple designation and status hardly satisfied her ambitions. Having married in order to obtain her freedom (for she was, after all, too honest and too conventional to quit her family and live all alone), she had opposed to the loyal tenderness of her good fellow of a husband the bold laugh—the Nietzschean laugh—of the epoch.

Sentiment? Husband? Children? Home?

The young wife had genius, so she thought. A year after her marriage, she rented a studio. And because she was entering her twentieth year, like all other young girls of that age her conception of the future was precise and unalterable. That age has no soul, just as a new house has none. It still smells of the plaster.

The little wife, like so many others, constructed her life according to her own ideas, as if one could fabricate it out of hand. Her only thought was to break, to slash and to turn things upside down. At twenty-three she was divorced. Her husband, wearied and broken, had disappeared completely from her life.

She was free! She dropped her married name and even her family name. She became Géo. As Géo, simply, she aspired to fame and glory.

Naturally there was no question of love in the case. Does one yield to sentiment, or even to sensuality, when one is determined to live one's own life? Géo, quite alone, facing her own future, her dowry recovered, wedded her art.

War.

Besides transforming the five parts of the world, it is going, according to circumstances, to disarrange and rearrange everything, even in the smallest cells of the social beehive. Like an acid, it is going to cause dissolution in one place and precipitation in another.

In the month of August, 1914, Géo suddenly realized that she had no talent and had been living in a world of self-deception. Her parents were dead. She had lost track of her former husband. With all the violence of the moral revulsion which had laid hold of her, with all the romantic feeling with which the first months of the war were impregnated, she multiplied her efforts to get in touch once more with her divorcé. He was a soldier—he, too—and as such she knew that he would prove a hero.

A hero! But her efforts were vain. Perhaps he had fallen in love with another woman; perhaps he had been killed or taken prisoner.

Géo takes up again the letter, the reading of which had been interrupted by her long reverie. Once more she sighs:

'This lieutenant here, I know to whom I shall turn him over. Yes, she is just the sort of person he needs.'

Another envelope opened; another letter unfolded.

'Ladies, I am ashamed to address myself to your bureau. To deliver one's soul to an agency, even an agency as discreet as yours—it is horrible. But I am so lonely, ladies—doubly lonely amid the terrors of war; doubly lonely because I formerly dreamed myself a dream of happiness. If she whom I loved and who for three years was my wife had understood me——'

With trembling hands Géo almost tears the page, so eagerly does she turn it in order to see the signature. Among the numerals and abbreviations it is there—this perfectly legible, electrifying signature:

'Adjutant Charles Bouvier.'

Géo jumps to her feet. Erect, she resumes her reading, while the cat, awakened with a start, yawns and stretches on the divan.

'Find me a correspondent—a friend to whom I can tell my troubles. I cannot keep them to myself any longer. My parents died when I was a child. I have neither brother nor sister. It is said: "It is not good for man to be alone." For five years I have been alone. I cannot endure it any longer. But now that my life is in perpetual danger, I need more than ever a soul linked with my own—with my soul, so menaced in this frail habitat of a soldier's body. And then, I have just received the Croix de Guerre. It is so melancholy that there is no one to be proud of me.'

'Quick, my pen! Quick, my ink!'

Géo has no married name and no family name. But she needs no other name than Géo to be a godmother to soldiers. No one was likely to know her, in spite of her painting. Nor will she need to disguise her handwriting. Did she recognize at once her former husband's handwriting?

'Monsieur l'Adjutant, I wish to be your godmother. For I also am lonely and broken in spirit. But I must make one condition. It is that you shall not know my real name. For you I shall be Géo and nothing else. And you can tell me all the wrongs that have been done to you. I shall understand them, believe me, better than anybody else.'

Pen in air, the young wife smiles sadly, tenderly. Then she bends over and continues her letter. And her fingers tremble constantly as she writes.

I have already told you how Géo, divorced, became by the merest accident the godmother of her poor husband, that lawful adorer of whom, before the war, she had disembarrassed herself so quickly, with all the unconscious cruelty of youth, in order 'to live her own life', as so many others do.

Now the correspondence between them is well established. Adjutant Charles Bouvier doesn't know that the godmother to whom he writes with so much ardour is his former wife. He doesn't know her name or her age, since it was on that condition that she agreed to accept him as a godson.

Géo, alone as usual in her studio, where she has not painted since the war began, settles down to open the thick military letter, a letter weighted with the self-revelations of an unknown soul, an unknown soul which is also the soul of her ex-husband.

From habit rather than from desire she begins by lighting a cigarette. Then she installs herself on the divan and passes her right hand carelessly through her short, henna-stained curls. At twenty-eight there is no necessity for colouring them. But the henna is a detail in the Latin Quarter make-up which Géo, in spite of her dissatisfaction with it, has not yet reached the point of giving up. Women who have no children often become their own dolls; and that leads them into extravagances and eccentricities.

'My godmother, you asked me in your last letter to tell you what I think of women, since I speak of them all the time and neglect to write you anything about the war. Such a curiosity on your part leads me to believe that you are still young, in spite of all your bitterness. And that thought delights me, because one can never be truly understood except by his contemporaries. Children love the company of other children. Young people love the society of young people, and so on. As for me, I am now entering my second youth; and so are you, it seems to me.

'So, now that I have told you all my life, I am going to try to express my soul to you. What I say will not be very original. I am a man, like other men, or, rather, a Frenchman, like other Frenchmen—preoccupied, that is, before everything else, with women. To be so is the indestructible inheritance of our Latin race.

'You understand well that this preoccupation is not due solely to sensual unrest, but comes primarily from a deep feeling of tenderness, in which there remains, as it were, a souvenir of that infancy which was so gently cradled at a mother's breast.

'What do I think of women? You alone, godmother, shall know. My wife, my cruel little wife, never knew at all. She was too young to understand my secrets and I was too young to tell them to her. Moreover, there are things which one can write, but which one could never say in the actual presence of another, hindered by all the restraints of self-consciousness and modesty.

'To you, who are unknown, who are invisible, I can give these "confidences of a man".

'I can't tell you better what I think of women than by setting forth what I like in women.

'A woman! I, a man, a simple man, a man like all the rest, demand and wish that a woman be, before all else, a woman—that is to say, my opposite. I want her to be a continual surprise to me, with that charm which is always an element of surprise. I want to smile and even to laugh sometimes, with amused astonishment, on discovering her to be in every way different from me. I wish her soul to be feminine. I wish that soul to be, as in electricity, the negative pole, just as mine is the positive pole. Then there will be a play of sparks between us.

'While I, the positive element, earn outside the means to maintain the domestic establishment, I want her, the negative element, to be the mysterious spirit of the home, that spirit through which the miracle of daily life is accomplished—the miracle of order and direction in the household. All my being, absorbed in work without counts on her for repose in that interior, made miraculous by her presence. In hours of difficulty I expect from her, also, good advice, rather murmured than spoken, which, once again outside, I shall follow without realizing too much the influence on my life which my wife, that priestess-like authority, exercises.

'My beloved, my collaborator, my guide—that is my wife. I give her, you see, the rôle of a domestic providence. But, perhaps, you smile pityingly over this masculine dream, in which the management of the household— incomprehensible marvel in the eyes of a man—holds almost as large a place as passion.

'Godmother, do not smile! Let me tell you, rather if you have a daughter, how to bring her up so that she may make a man happy, and at the same time be happy herself. Teach her, certainly, to be as attractive as possible; gracious under all circumstances, and even coquettish in her style and tastes. Let her learn some agreeable art—music, especially, which quickens the intimate emotion of the hearth. Let her study a foreign language—English, if you wish—a valuable resource added to other resources.

'But, godmother, above everything else—and you must pardon me for going back to things so material—teach her to use her hands, to keep house, to manage the kitchen, because it is a great superiority for a lady to be able in an emergency to care for her husband and her children as a daughter of the people does.

'See, godmother, what gratitude can enter into the tenderness of a man well cared for by his wife. There can be no doubt about it. I, a poor soldier in this great war—it is because of the lack of them on my part that I have emphasized all those things of which I speak. Abandoned while I was very young by the wife whom I loved so much, I lived two years as an orphan before I lived three years in the trenches. And nobody can be more of an orphan, believe me, than a man without a wife.

'All men have not been to as hard a school as I have been to. But, speaking for all men, I can say to you: 'Women, women, while we, the fighters at the front, are eminently men, you must be eminently women in order to re-establish the equilibrium. Don't be trivial and frivolous, as my wife was; cultivated to the point of oddity, restless, self-assertive, a sort of men in miniature, creatures in transition whom their own logic would lead to grow moustaches. I know well that there is such a thing as feminism; and I have no quarrel with it. It is a necessity; that's all there is about it. And, certainly, I would permit women to be as long as they care to be on wit and intelligence. But let them not cut their hair short!'

Géo didn't finish her letter. A little cry, a little jump. Throwing the sheets on the floor, she ran to the mirror. What consternation! She had her hair cut short. With a jerk she pulled open the door and entered her dressing room. There, before the big triple mirror, in a fever, she tried with the aid of some hairpins to twist her short locks into a knot.

Lucie Delarue-Mardrus, 'The Godmother', from *Tales of Wartime France by Contemporary Writers Illustrating the Spirit of the French People at War*, trans. William L. McPherson (New York: Dodd, Mead, 1918), 97–108

Matilde Serao
(1856–1927)

Matilde Serao was born in Naples and lived there for most of her life. Although trained as a teacher, she established herself as a journalist of international repute whose pieces were frequently translated into other languages, especially English. She helped her husband run newspapers and, after leaving him, started her own paper. She was also a prolific novelist whose fictions explore the role and destinies of women, the nature of female relationships and women's experience of love, poverty, and war. The extract below comes from one of her journalistic pieces written during the war. It exemplifies the way in which traditional religious feeling and new ideas of women's autonomy could combine into an enthusiastic acceptance of war.

---

30   IT WAS THE WILL OF GOD

I AM not talking here to idle and somnolent feminine spirits in whom the Faith is something vague and indistinct which they avoid looking at, and in whom religion is a monotonous and tiresome repetition of the same gestures, which no longer have any character, the same words, which no longer express anything. Neither do I speak to those fanciful and frivolous feminine spirits, in whom the Faith is an extempore and fleeting flame of the imagination; in whom religion is a passing exaltation, for its shapes and colours, for its music and the fragrance of its incense.

I wish to speak here to that immense crowd of simple and tenacious believers, who at all stages of their existence, in every contingency of their lives, have Faith enclosed in the deepest level of their awareness, like a divine spiritual filter from which they draw all virtue. To this immense multitude of unknown believers, who pour out their hearts, every dawn and every dusk, in the ancient words of prayer, and restore themselves with these outpourings; who in each supreme hour of their existence, know how to tell the Lord of their unconsoled sadness, and understand, in the shadow, in the silence and in the solitude, how to listen for His reply. Noblewomen, whose trembling hands open the book of sacred prayer, but whose eyes, veiled with tears, can no longer distinguish in the shadows, the printed words. Those bourgeois women, bent over rosaries held tightly in their hands, lose the thread of their prayers, distracted and conquered by their invincible pain. Simple women of the people, on their knees on the bare, cold marble, who have neither prayer book nor rosary, but whose lips, between the sighs and the half-suppressed moans, repeat a single phrase continuously, in which a name, a name always resounds, the name of 'he who is gone'. And it is to those, my dearest unknown sisters, my sisters in suffering, I, not known to them, but their sister, wish to say here, the most sincere and the most sisterly words.

My sisters, have you, like me, daylong asked our Lord, the mercy that this terrible chalice of the War, might be distanced from your lips? Have you, like me asked him recently, in the last day or so, almost as if you were at the bedside of one about to die, that there might be a miracle and we might, all of us, be saved from the horrors of the War? Were your prayers impetuous, ardent, delirious? Yes! they were.

But the grace was not granted; the miracle did not come, and all those far away things which you and I in our prayers sought to avert, have come about. Are you true Christians, are you true believers, have you a firm and intact faith in a Supreme Will which you must not judge, but to which you must bend, with a tortured, but reverent heart? If this is your case, if your inner life possesses this splendid virtue, if your spirit has this shining light, in every stormy sea, you must say to yourself, you *know already*, that the Almighty has allowed, for His high and mysterious reasons, this War. You know already that He wishes all this, and that all the tribulation which has come upon you, upon us, is from God.

How will you, my sisters, in your Christian soul, as believers, accept this incomparable tribulation? Crying, sobbing, howling, blinded by suffering, maddened by suffering? Do you wish to be such bad Christians, such rebel Christians? And would you still merit that lofty name? And would you still be deserving of the Sacred Cross? Could the infinite family of Christ still consider you as belonging to them, you who do not wish to suffer, you who do not know how to suffer? Will you give this bad example to those who love you, to your friends, to your servants? Would you be an object of shame, because you do not know how and do not wish to suffer?

Or would you be an indifferent, weak creature? In this way you would increase the pain of all those who surround you, instead of being the centre of their sublime resignation, and of their sublime patience, as is your womanly, Christian duty. Instead of mastering yourself with that moral energy which the Faith gives you, instead of transforming your mortal sadness into trusting serenity, would you make the suffering of others more acute and insupportable?

Would you, in this way, carry out that which the good common people so justly call 'Doing God's Will'? Do you think that it was for this that you were given an immortal soul, and were told to make it lovely and strong? Is it sighs, tears and howling which will show the beauty and the value of your immortal soul?

No! No! Those who see clear signs of the manifestation of the Will of a just God must open their arms, re-open their hearts and welcome His Will as a divine law, for which certainly, the hidden reasons will be revealed later. And they will be merciful as well as just. Those who see an ineffable pain come upon them, sent by He who distributes, according to His wisdom, joy and pain, they must receive this pain like a welcome guest and give it the best place and venerate it.

Matilde Serao, 'Dio l'ha voluto!', trans. David Mendel, from *Parla una donna* (*A Woman Speaks*) (Milan: Fratelli Treves, 1916), 1–3

Sidonie Gabrielle Colette
(1873–1954)

Colette achieved early acclaim with her five 'Claudine' novels written largely under the supervision of her husband Willy. After their divorce in 1906, she worked as a *variété artiste* in Paris but gradually succeeded in building up a career as art critic, novelist, and war correspondent. Her mature work is characterized by great sensitivity and psychological depth. It includes novels like *La Vagabonde* (1911), *Chéri* (1920), and *Duo* (1934) and many autobiographical and semi-autobiographical writings. All in all Colette wrote over seventy books. The following text was first published in *Le Matin* on 24 March 1915. It is one of the series of wartime cameos which she wrote for various newspapers. In 1919 these little essays on war were collected and published in Paris as *Les Heures longues*.

---

31   THEY ARE THE SAME

'. . . THE bombardment started immediately and without warning. One district which remained intact was then pillaged, drenched in petrol with the aid of brooms and finally burnt down. In the middle of it all was an old woman who kept guard over her bedridden husband; they hit her with the butt of a gun, chased her away and then set light to the bed of the invalid; Captain Nichau, an old retired veteran, attacked the Germans single handed, calling them cowards; they shot him with a revolver and threw him into the flames.'

'Prussian officers dined cheerfully at the Hôtel du Grand-Monarque. Immediately afterwards they burnt it down. A hundred or so local people were arrested in the streets and put into a burnt out cellar without food. The Germans were heard to say: "This must be the fate of all France. All of them, women, children, old men, must experience this."'

'Out of two hundred and thirty-five burnt out houses, only a dozen caught fire because of missiles. One hundred and ninety-eight were set alight by hand with the aid of petrol; in these fourteen burnt bodies were found afterward.'

'In the town of This the old Abbé, seventy-five years old, was bound to the saddle of a horse with his hands tied and then the animal was made to run. In order to make his injuries more serious, they tied a rope to the priest's legs which the soldiers kept pulling.'

'Bombardment of a hospital without military reason. They throw fire bombs . . . deposit excrement in living rooms, in cupboards, in post offices. Officers walk off with the silver cutlery after a meal. General von der Tann comports himself like a savage in the Mayor's Office.'

'In the Château of Monsieur Thomas, an outhouse gives shelter to thirty wounded men: the Germans put fire to it and all of the wounded perish in the flames.'

'Weaver Lacroix has both his hands chopped off before they burn him alive.'

'Monsieur Legrand, gentleman of Cléry, billets officers of the Uhlan Regiment. The German lieutenant nearly strangles him, beats him up and finally kills him. Later they pull a rope through the mouth of the corpse and hang it from a beam. German regiments file past this trophy.'

'The gardener Renoult who stayed behind in Frou is beaten with a gun and nearly killed by a Prussian soldier. An officer who happens to pass, grabs his sword and half buries it in Renoult's skull. The poor innocent man is trailed, half strangled and his face covered in blood, along fifty meters of town wall where a Prussian, before finishing him off, is barbaric enough to cut off his nose, his ears and to gouge out his eyes.'

I do not have the courage to read on. There is more, there is more . . . And the date? 1915?—No, the year is 1871. Yet, one might easily confuse the two. An Englishman, fond of precise documentation, published, a few years before the war, the volume which contains this terrible list. It stands right next to another list which enumerates 'Deposed or Assassinated Popes' and another with 'Famous People who Led Unhappy Marriages' . . .

Colette, 'Les mêmes . . .', trans. Daniel Cardinal, from *Les Heures longues*, *Œuvres II* (Paris: Nouvelle Revue Française, Gallimard, 1986), 510–11

Marcelle Capy

Nothing is known of Marcelle Capy's life other than that she held strong pacifist views and, at the outbreak of the war, was active in France as a writer. The text below comes from *Une Voix de femme dans la mêlée* (*A Woman's Voice amidst the Conflict*) of 1916 which contains an enthusiastic preface by her friend and fellow pacifist Romain Rolland. It seems to have been written as a complement to his similarly polemical tract *Au-dessus de la mêlée* (*Above and Beyond the Conflict*) of the same year. The book was published in Paris but its many blank pages, imposed by the censors, are an indication of the hostility with which Capy's stance was received. In 1930 she published the anti-war novel *Les Hommes passèrent* (*Men Pass*).

―――――――

32   THE WAR GOT HIM

ALL the women fancied him.

He was but a simple farmhand, yet even the daughters of wealthy farmers dreamed of standing by his side in the little office in the Town Hall beneath the eyes of the plaster figure of the Republic which presides over all marriages.

His language was brutal and the coarseness of his jokes made many a cheek burn. He was said to be violent. When drunk he made free with his fists, the persuasiveness of his punches adding to his swagger. He had muscle and was tough and lithe with it. He smoothed down his hair with care and never stinted on the brilliantine. When he laughed out loud you couldn't miss the healthy row of teeth.

The secret of his success was that, though he courted them all, he never actually chose one. A squeezed waist here, a stolen kiss there, yet not one could boast of any advantage over another. All of them did their utmost to conquer him. Even their mothers joined in.

On winter evenings they would take turns to invite him back home. They would roast chestnuts for him on log fires and pour out helpings of sweet mulled wine, trying to get him to appreciate the advantages of domestic bliss.

He wouldn't much fancy always working for others . . . He'd sooner set himself up in a house where he could be master in his own right . . . There certainly didn't seem to be any lack of marriageable girls . . . And if you're a good looking lad and strong enough for any sort of work, it's not so difficult to set yourself up pretty nicely . . .

The girls encouraged him with urgent and tender words.

He listened, kindly and jovial, sipping his warm drink. Between his fingers he cracked open the burnt shells of chestnuts. He teased the girls but beat a retreat at any sign of a direct attack.

At the decisive moment he would get up, curse the cold, light his lantern, shout a sonorous 'Good night' and plunge into the darkness. Neither mother nor daughter had gained any ground since his arrival.

And still they loved him.

And still they were jealous. They spied on him, fought over him in their
various coquettish ways.
Who would get him?
In the end neither this one nor that one got him.
The war got him. His wedding bed was the damp soil of the Argonne.

Marcelle Capy, 'La Guerre l'eut', trans. Agnès Cardinal, from *Une Voix de
femme dans la mêlée* (Paris: Ollendorf, 1916), 116–17

Ellen La Motte
(1873–1961)

In the introduction to *The Backwash of War* Ellen La Motte described 'the stag-
nant place' in which she worked as a nurse, ten kilometres behind the lines in
Belgium. She reflected on it by commenting: 'we are witnessing a phase in the
evolution of humanity, a phase called War—and the slow onward progress stirs
up the slime in the shallows, and this is the Backwash of War. It is very ugly.'

---

33   A Belgian Civilian

A BIG English ambulance drove along the high road from Ypres, going in the
direction of a French field hospital, some ten miles from Ypres. Ordinarily,
it could have had no business with this French hospital, since all English
wounded are conveyed back to their own bases, therefore an exceptional
case must have determined its route. It was an exceptional case—for the
patient lying quietly within its yawning body, sheltered by its brown canvas
wings, was not an English soldier, but only a small Belgian boy, a civilian,
and Belgian civilians belong neither to the French nor English services. It is
true that there was a hospital for Belgian civilians at the English base at
Hazebrouck, and it would have seemed reasonable to have taken the patient
there, but it was more reasonable to dump him at this French hospital,
which was nearer. Not from any humanitarian motives, but just to get rid of
him the sooner. In war, civilians are cheap things at best, and an immature
civilian, Belgian at that, is very cheap. So the heavy English ambulance
churned its way up a muddy hill, mashed through much mud at the

entrance gates of the hospital, and crunched to a halt on the cinders before the *Salle d'Attente*, where it discharged its burden and drove off again.

The surgeon of the French hospital said: 'What have we to do with this?' yet he regarded the patient thoughtfully. It was a very small patient. Moreover, the big English ambulance had driven off again, so there was no appeal. The small patient had been deposited upon one of the beds in the *Salle d'Attente*, and the French surgeon looked at him and wondered what he should do. The patient, now that he was here, belonged as much to the French field hospital as to any other, and as the big English ambulance from Ypres had driven off again, there was not much use in protesting. The French surgeon was annoyed and irritated. It was a characteristic English trick, he thought, this getting other people to do their work. Why could they not have taken the child to one of their own hospitals, since he had been wounded in their lines, or else have taken him to the hospital provided for Belgian civilians, where, full as it was, there was always room for people as small as this. The surgeon worked himself up into quite a temper. There is one thing about members of the *Entente*—they understand each other. The French surgeon's thoughts travelled round and round in an irritated circle, and always came back to the fact that the English ambulance had gone, and here lay the patient, and something must be done. So he stood considering.

A Belgian civilian, aged ten. Or thereabouts. Shot through the abdomen, or thereabouts. And dying, obviously. As usual, the surgeon pulled and twisted the long, black hairs on his hairy, bare arms, while he considered what he should do. He considered for five minutes, and then ordered the child to the operating room, and scrubbed and scrubbed his hands and his hairy arms, preparatory to a major operation. For the Belgian civilian, aged ten, had been shot through the abdomen by a German shell, or piece of shell, and there was nothing to do but try to remove it. It was a hopeless case, anyhow. The child would die without an operation, or he would die during the operation, or he would die after the operation. The French surgeon scrubbed his hands viciously, for he was still greatly incensed over the English authorities who had placed the case in his hands and then gone away again. They should have taken him to one of the English bases, St Omer, or Hazebrouck—it was an imposition to have dumped him so unceremoniously here simply because 'here' was so many kilometres nearer. 'Shirking,' the surgeon called it, and was much incensed.

After a most searching operation, the Belgian civilian was sent over to the ward, to live or die as circumstances determined. As soon as he came out of ether, he began to bawl for his mother. Being ten years of age, he was unreasonable, and bawled for her incessantly and could not be pacified. The patients were greatly annoyed by this disturbance, and there was indignation that the welfare and comfort of useful soldiers should be interfered with by the whims of a futile and useless civilian, a Belgian child at that. The nurse of that ward also made a fool of herself over this civilian, giving him far more attention than she had ever bestowed upon a soldier. She was sentimental, and his little age appealed to her—her sense of proportion and standard of values were all awrong. The *Directrice* appeared in the ward and tried to comfort the civilian, to still his howls, and then, after an hour of vain effort, she decided that his mother must be sent for. He was obviously dying, and it was necessary to send for his mother, whom alone of all the world he seemed to need. So a French ambulance, which had nothing to do with Belgian civilians, nor with Ypres, was sent over to Ypres late in the evening to fetch this mother for whom the Belgian civilian, aged ten, bawled so persistently.

She arrived finally, and, it appeared, reluctantly. About ten o'clock in the evening she arrived, and the moment she alighted from the big ambulance sent to fetch her, she began complaining. She had complained all the way over, said the chauffeur. She climbed down backward from the front seat, perched for a moment on the hub, while one heavy leg, with foot shod in slipping *sabot*, groped wildly for the ground. A soldier with a lantern watched impassively, watched her solid splash into a mud puddle that might have been avoided. So she continued her complaints. She had been dragged away from her husband, from her other children, and she seemed to have little interest in her son, the Belgian civilian, said to be dying. However, now that she was here, now that she had come all this way, she would go in to see him for a moment, since the *Directrice* seemed to think it so important. The *Directrice* of this French field hospital was an American, by marriage a British subject, and she had curious, antiquated ideas. She seemed to feel that a mother's place was with her child, if that child was dying. The *Directrice* had three children of her own whom she had left in England over a year ago, when she came out to Flanders for the life and adventures of the Front. But she would have returned to England immediately, without an instant's hesitation, had she received word that one of these children was dying. Which was a point of view opposed to that of this Belgian mother, who seemed to feel that her place was back in Ypres, in her home, with her husband and other children. In fact, this Belgian mother had been rudely dragged away from her home, from her family, from certain duties that she seemed to think important. So she complained bitterly, and went into the ward most reluctantly, to see her son, said to be dying.

She saw her son, and kissed him, and then asked to be sent back to Ypres. The *Directrice* explained that the child would not live through the night.

The Belgian mother accepted this statement, but again asked to be sent back to Ypres. The *Directrice* again assured the Belgian mother that her son would not live through the night, and asked her to spend the night with him in the ward, to assist at his passing. The Belgian woman protested.

'If *Madame la Directrice* commands, if she insists, then I must assuredly obey. I have come all this distance because she commanded me, and if she insists that I spend the night at this place, then I must do so. Only if she does not insist, then I prefer to return to my home, to my other children at Ypres.'

However, the *Directrice*, who had a strong sense of a mother's duty to the dying, commanded and insisted, and the Belgian woman gave way. She sat by her son all night, listening to his ravings and bawlings, and was with him when he died, at three o'clock in the morning. After which time, she requested to be taken back to Ypres. She was moved by the death of her son, but her duty lay at home. *Madame la Directrice* had promised to have a mass said at the burial of the child, which promise having been given, the woman saw no necessity for remaining.

'My husband', she explained, 'has a little *estaminet*, just outside of Ypres. We have been very fortunate. Only yesterday, of all the long days of the war, of the many days of bombardment, did a shell fall into our kitchen, wounding our son, as you have seen. But we have other children to consider, to provide for. And my husband is making much money at present, selling drink to the English soldiers. I must return to assist him.'

So the Belgian civilian was buried in the cemetery of the French soldiers, but many hours before this took place, the mother of the civilian had departed for Ypres. The chauffeur of the ambulance which was to convey her back to Ypres turned very white when given his orders. Everyone dreaded Ypres, and the dangers of Ypres. It was the place of death. Only the Belgian woman, whose husband kept an *estaminet*, and made much money selling drink to the English soldiers, did not dread it. She and her husband were making much money out of the war, money which would give their children a start in life. When the ambulance was ready she climbed into it with alacrity, although with a feeling of gratitude because the *Directrice* had promised a mass for her dead child.

'These Belgians!' said a French soldier. 'How prosperous they will be after the war! How much money they will make from the Americans, and from the others who come to see the ruins!'

And as an afterthought, in an undertone, he added: '*Ces sales Belges!*'

Ellen La Motte, 'A Belgian Civilian', from *The Backwash of War: The Human Wreckage of the Battlefield as Witnessed by an American Hospital Nurse* (New York and London: G. P. Putnam's Sons, 1916), 63–73

Vera Brittain
(1893–1970)

Testament of Youth records Vera Brittain's life between 1900 and 1925: her upbringing in the north of England; the fact that she won an exhibition at Somerville College, Oxford, and that her studies were cut short when she enlisted as a VAD. She served as a nurse throughout the war, in London, Malta, and in France. The extract below describes the aftermath of the death of her fiancé Roland Leighton, who was killed in the trenches in December 1915—a death which Brittain describes as 'so painful, so unnecessary, so grimly devoid of...heroic limelight'. Published in 1933, *Testament of Youth* charts the growth of Brittain's pacifism and feminism; it expressed also the profound disillusionment with the war which characterized the 1920s and early 1930s. *Testament of Youth* was followed by two other autobiographical works—*Testament of Friendship* (1940), a tribute to Winifred Holtby, and *Testament of Experience* (1957). Vera Brittain also published works of fiction, history, and travel.

---

34   ROLAND LEIGHTON

THE more I came to detest my work at Camberwell, the more I relied upon my short intervals with Roland's family to give some purpose to an existence which seemed to have become singularly pointless. Two or three weeks after Roland's death, his mother 'began to write, in semi-fictional form, a memoir of his life, which she finished in three months, as well as replying at length to letters of condolence from friends and readers all over the country. At the end of that time she had a short breakdown from shock and overwork, and was in bed warding off serious heart trouble for several weeks. The many occasions on which I went down to see her and discuss the publication of her memoir, filled me with longing to write a book about Roland myself, but I concluded that three months was too short a time for me to see personal events in their true perspective. I would wait, I decided, rather longer than that before contributing my own account of his brief, vivid existence. I should have been astonished indeed had anyone told me that I should wait for seventeen years.

In Sussex, by the end of January, the season was already on its upward grade; catkins hung bronze from the bare, black branches, and in the damp lanes between Hassocks and Keymer the birds sang loudly. How I hated them as I walked back to the station one late afternoon, when a red sunset turned the puddles on the road into gleaming pools of blood, and a new horror of mud and death darkened my mind with its dreadful obsession. Roland, I reflected bitterly, was now part of the corrupt clay into which war had transformed the fertile soil of France; he would never again know the smell of a wet evening in early spring.

I had arrived at the cottage that morning to find his mother and sister standing in helpless distress in the midst of his returned kit, which was lying, just opened, all over the floor. The garments sent back included the outfit that he had been wearing when he was hit. I wondered, and I wonder still, why it was thought necessary to return such relics—the tunic torn back and front by the bullet, a khaki vest dark and stiff with blood, and a pair of blood-stained breeches slit open at the top by someone obviously in a violent hurry. Those gruesome rags made me realise, as I had never realised before, all that France really meant. Eighteen months afterwards the smell of Étaples village, though fainter and more diffused, brought back to me the memory of those poor remnants of patriotism.

'Everything', I wrote later to Edward, 'was damp and worn and simply caked with mud. And I was glad that neither you nor Victor nor anyone who may some day go to the front was there to see. If you had been, you would have been overwhelmed by the horror of war without its glory. For though he had only worn the things when living, the smell of those clothes was the smell of graveyards and the Dead. The mud of France which covered them was not ordinary mud; it had not the usual clean pure smell of earth, but it was as though it were saturated with dead bodies—dead that had been dead a long, long time. . . . There was his cap, bent in and shapeless out of recognition—the soft cap he wore rakishly on the back of his head—with the badge thickly coated with mud. He must have fallen on top of it, or perhaps one of the people who fetched him in trampled on it.'

Vera Brittain, *Testament of Youth* (London: Virago, 1978), 250–2

IV

TOWARDS THE FRONT

Sidonie Gabrielle Colette
(1873–1954)

Colette's record of her visit to an English military camp is typical of her keen, if strangely detached, powers of observation and her gimlet eye for the bizarre. The piece was first published in May 1915 in *Le Matin*.

---

35   AN ENGLISH CAMP

SPREADING along the edge of grey, smoke-covered Rouen is a flat khaki town. Sand-coloured soldiers stroll along avenues which have been cut into the living earth; they emerge from beige canvas tents or shelter under wooden barracks. An entire world has taken on that slightly scorched tinge: khaki, khaki, everything is khaki.

Visiting the camp one can but marvel. The shelters and the men, as if born of each other, are at the exact same point of solidity, of stability. A vast, squat lecture hall encircled at its base by a childish, smiling ornament of flowers and round stones, releases some sixty sturdy, geometric Tommies. From a busy bakery issue forth, along with bronzed soldiers, batches of white and brown loaves . . . Men digging an artesian well nearby, resemble, in their nimble jumps in and out of the pits, those insects on sandy beaches, that teem at low tide like living grains of sand.

They lack nothing. The English camp has concerts, boxes neatly aligned for horses, shimmering troughs of fresh water, cinemas, chapels, garages, restaurants, rooms for lounging, rooms for reading and for writing letters, hospitals where the searching hands of the sick can find electric buzzers on the wall.

It's all there. The abundance, perfection even, and that soldier's gait so distinctive in its relaxed agility, inspire in us in the first instance a kind of respectful dismay; as an image of mobilization transfixed, it gives a worrying impression of permanence . . . the notion doesn't last. Regularly swelled by landings from England, the camp feeds a measured flow of combatants to various fronts.

Just now, another twelve hundred are marching down to the railway station and the transport vehicles, spotless, scrubbed, neatly gartered, irreproachable, complete with that bright red daub inflicted by the sun on their blond flesh. Wearing the smiles of children at First Communion, they look at us with curious eyes made bluer still by contrast with their tanned skin . . .

'Where are they going?'

An irrepressible question to which the young khaki officer simply raises his hand in a sign of ignorance:

'I don't know,' he says without the trace of an accent. 'They're part of the British army.'

And he adds, in response to our look of surprise: 'I'm an Indian officer, born in India. I don't know anything about the British army. I'm from over there . . .'

This pink and blond 'Indian' points behind him to another part of the camp which looks deserted after the recent departure of Indian troops. The avenues are empty except for a cook who, with bare legs and dancing feet, wanders from tent to tent—and for the occasional odd apparition of a passing nurse, head covered and eyelids lowered over mysterious leonine eyes.

'Do you want to see one of the kitchens in the Indian camp?'

It's the same wooden edifice, a fine and honest portable house complete with electric lighting. But here we search in vain for cast-iron stoves: under a single light-bulb, balanced on three stones, there smokes a witches' cauldron, and from an indistinct crouching figure next to it a hand appears, dark, delicate and of wild nobility, and throws I know not what charm into the vapour . . .

The time has come to leave and to return to the other Rouen by means of one of those trams which we had encountered earlier. The carriages are packed with serious-faced Sikhs in turbans and far less serious English nurses in boy-scout caps and short capes bordered with red. Just one more moment in which to linger . . . time to pluck a flower from one of the thousands of little flower beds, the pride of the camp—time to study the poster on the door of the lecture hall which reads: Tomorrow at 4 o'clock, *A Talk on Joan of Arc*.

Colette, 'Un Camp anglais', trans. Daniel Cardinal, from *Les Heures longues, Œuvres II* (Paris: Nouvelle Revue Française, Gallimard, 1986), 519

Gertrude Stein
(1874–1946)

Gertrude Stein spent her childhood in Vienna and Paris and her adolescence in Oakland, California, where her German-Jewish parents had settled. In 1893 she studied psychology at Radcliffe College under William James. In 1903 she returned to Europe as one of a generation of American expatriates who saw Paris as the mecca of avant-garde art. A shrewd collector and trendsetter, she befriended such painters and writers as Picasso and Hemingway, her apartment on 27 rue de Fleurus achieving renown as the definitive salon of Modernism. Stein's reputation as a writer is that of a quirky experimentalist who pioneered a kind of literary Cubism in texts characterized by bold imagery, eccentric spellings and syntax, and notorious tricks of repetition. The following extract is from *The Autobiography of Alice B. Toklas*, a work composed by Stein but attributed to her lifelong companion.

---

36   THE WAR

WE left for Alsace and on the road had our first and only accident. The roads were frightful, mud, ruts, snow, slush, and covered with french armies going into Alsace. As we passed, two horses dragging an army kitchen kicked out of line and hit our Ford, the mud guard came off and the toolchest, and worst of all the triangle of the steering gear was badly bent. The army picked up our tools and our mud guard but there was nothing to do about the bent triangle. We went on, the car wandering all over the muddy road, up hill and down hill, and Gertrude Stein sticking to the wheel. Finally after about forty kilometres, we saw on the road some american ambulance men. Where can we get our car fixed. Just a little farther, they said. We went a little farther and there found an american ambulance outfit. They had no extra mud guard but they could give us a new triangle. I told our troubles to the sergeant, he grunted and said a word in an undertone to a mechanic. Then turning to us he said gruffly, run-her-in. Then the mechanic took off his tunic and threw it over the radiator. As Gertrude Stein said when any american did that the car was his.

We had never realized before what mud-guards were for but by the time we arrived in Nancy we knew. The french military repair shop fitted us out with a new mud-guard and tool chest and we went on our way.

Soon we came to the battle-fields and the lines of trenches of both sides. To anyone who did not see it as it was then it is impossible to imagine it. It was not terrifying it was strange. We were used to ruined houses and even ruined towns but this was different. It was a landscape. And it belonged to no country.

I remember hearing a french nurse once say and the only thing she did say of the front was, c'est un paysage passionant, an absorbing landscape. And that was what it was as we saw it. It was strange. Camouflage, huts, everything was there. It was wet and dark and there were a few people, one did not know whether they were chinamen or europeans. Our fan-belt had stopped working. A staff car stopped and fixed it with a hairpin, we still wore hairpins.

Another thing that interested us enormously was how different the camouflage of the french looked from the camouflage of the germans, and then once we came across some very very neat camouflage and it was american. The idea was the same but as after all it was different nationalities who did it the difference was inevitable. The colour schemes were different, the designs were different, the way of placing them was different, it made plain the whole theory of art and its inevitability.

Finally we came to Strasbourg and then went on to Mulhouse. Here we stayed until well into May.

Our business in Alsace was not hospitals but refugees. The inhabitants were returning to their ruined homes all over the devastated country and it was the aim of the A.F.F.W. to give a pair of blankets, underclothing and children's and babies' woollen stockings and babies' booties to every family. There was a legend that the quantity of babies' booties sent to us came from the gifts sent to Mrs Wilson who was supposed at that time to be about to produce a little Wilson. There were a great many babies' booties but not too many for Alsace.

Our headquarters was the assembly-room of one of the big school-buildings in Mulhouse. The german school teachers had disappeared and french school teachers who happened to be in the army had been put in temporarily to teach. The head of our school was in despair, not about the docility of his pupils nor their desire to learn french, but on account of their clothes. French children are all always neatly clothed. There is no such thing as a ragged child, even orphans farmed out in country villages are neatly dressed, just as all french women are neat, even the poor and the aged. They may not always be clean but they are always neat. From this standpoint the parti-coloured rags of even the comparatively pros-perous Alsatian children was deplorable and the french schoolmasters suffered. We did our best to help him out with black children's aprons but these did not go far, beside we had to keep them for the refugees.

We came to know Alsace and the alsatians very well, all kinds of them. They were astonished at the simplicity with which the french army and french soldiers took care of themselves. They had not been accustomed to that in the german army. On the other hand the french soldiers were rather mistrustful of the alsatians who were too anxious to be french and yet were not french. They are not frank, the french soldiers said. And it is quite true. The french whatever else they may be are frank. They are very polite, they are very adroit but sooner or later they always tell you the truth. The alsatians are not adroit, they are not polite and they do not inevitably tell you the truth. Perhaps with renewed contact with the french they will learn these things.

We distributed. We went into all the devastated villages. We usually asked the priest to help us with the distribution. One priest who gave us a great deal of good advice and with whom we became very friendly had only one large room left in his house. Without any screens or partitions he had made himself three rooms, the first third had his parlour furniture, the second third his dining-room furniture and the last third his bed-room furniture. When we lunched with him and we lunched well and his alsatian wines were very good, he received us in his parlour, he then excused himself and withdrew into his bed-room to wash his hands, and then he invited us very formally to come into the dining-room, it was like an old fashioned stage setting.

We distributed, we drove around in the snow we talked to everybody and everybody talked to us and by the end of May it was all over and we decided to leave.

We went home by way of Metz, Verdun and Mildred Aldrich.

Gertrude Stein, from *The Autobiography of Alice B. Toklas* (London: Penguin, 1933), 202–5

Mademoiselle Miss

It has not proved possible to discover any information about this author. The extract below is from Letter VII of *'Mademoiselle Miss', Letters from an American Girl Serving with the Rank of Lieutenant in a French Army Hospital at the Front*, which was published in Boston in 1916. The book contains six photographs of the author at work. It appears to be genuine and seems to have been written to encourage subscriptions to the American Fund for French Wounded.

---

37   LETTER VII

GASTON is of the stuff that will make France victorious. He's a little fish dealer of Paris, staunch and sane of soul and limb, the kind that goes out alone on patrol, and brings down his Boche every time, and wears the cross at 19 without bragging,—the kind that is equal to anything from writing patriotic verse that brings tears to your eyes, to outwitting his nurse and always getting his way. He was only slightly wounded and got into my service by mistake; but that wretched little wound in his thigh would never heal despite my most intelligent efforts. At last he was well enough to get up and suddenly, without any suggestion or instruction, Gaston became my chief assistant. He cut my cottons, folded compresses, helped with bandages, polished my instruments, did a thousand little fine things that I could never trust to my orderlies, and when we were alone at work after 'lights out' we talked philosophy. We didn't cry when we separated only because we're good soldiers.

A pearl fisher—a good Catholic and a brave fighter—had come from the sunny shores of Guadeloupe, to die for France. When they amputated his leg they didn't discover that there was a ball in his back. I found it when I took Pavilion V. But then it was too late. Every day the fever mounted higher, and every day his black cheeks grew thinner; but he always kept saying 'It is going well,' in the sweet caressing tones that recalled early lullabies. Never a murmur, always a smile. The last day our faithful priest confessed him—he knew just enough French for that—and it was moonlight when he went, one of us kneeling either side. After Extreme Unction he pressed my hand; and suddenly a marvellous change passed over his face as if it had grown white and luminous. 'Mama,' he murmured, 'Louis,' then fainter and sweeter—

'O mon bon Dieu,' and it was over, and nothing remained but a radiating smile. I went to lay him away among the heroes; and if ever I doubted how to die, my black pearl fisher from Gaudeloupe has shown me the way.

They brought Croya in half-unconscious, with seven suppurating wounds. It was late, and I did the first examination and dressing unassisted. The next day, they overhauled him in the operating room, decided he was hopeless, and handed him over to me. It is one of the few dressings I have had that really frightened me; for it was so long, and every day for a week or more, I extracted bits of cloth and fragments of metal, sometimes at a terrifying depth. Besides my patient was savage and sullen, all that is ominous in the Arab nature. Gradually, however, the suppuration ceased, the fever fell, and suddenly one day Croya smiled.

It was so utterly surprising and transforming that we all rubbed our eyes. From the first I had tried to win his confidence, but I was always repulsed with a kind of grave scorn. The day after he smiled, he said 'Thanks, Mama,' when I gave him an orange, and when No. 15 asked why he called me that, he explained in his weird French that I was just like a Mama. After that it was all simple enough. When Croya got better he used to help to do his own dressing, and when Mama had a minute she'd go and sit beside him and he'd lay his cheek against her arm, and teach her Arab words. As he grew better he was crazy to play some music. So when Karabiche went to Paris on leave, he brought back a flute; then Croya would half sit up in bed with his shaved head tipped against his temperature chart, and play soft, strange, wild melodies that had all the mystery of the Algerian plains in them. Every night the last thing I did was to slip some edible jest into his hand—a cold orange or a sticky bonbon, or cracker crumbs that got lost in the bed unless I lit my electric lamp to find them; and we'd stifle our amusement so as not to wake the others. I explained to the Head Surgeon that I had tamed my Arab, and I wanted to keep him till he was well enough to go back. But then that heartless General B. came and sent away nearly every one, and Croya had to go.

His despair was poignantly touching. Orientals do not weep; but he wouldn't eat, he developed a temperature, all the light left those wide, brown eyes, and he kept repeating all day, 'I am not going—I am not going!' When he started he had a ticket pinned to his cap on which I had written careful instructions to treat him attentively. I asked him how much money he had: he answered, 'I am very rich.' That was all the satisfaction I had till I found his pitiful little purse with just five cents inside. I put in two dollars with the rest, midst incoherent protestations from Croya. I tucked him in his blankets in the auto, and the last I heard was 'Au revoir, Mama' in tones that I can never forget.

He reached Toulouse a week ago and every day since, I've had a card written by some comrade and signed 'The child who does not forget his Mama.' One, illustrated, had a rather too passionate couplet. The next day I got one representing a child who says to its mother, 'Little mother, how much I love you,' and Croya explains that it was a comrade who played a joke 'because I don't know how to read. Forgive me, Mama.' Perhaps Croya is the only son I shall ever have, but I thank Heaven for giving me, to nurse and love, this poor wild child of the desert.

From '*Mademoiselle Miss*', *Letters from an American Girl* (Boston: W. A. Butterfield, 1916), 60–7

Gladys de Havilland

Nothing seems to be known about Gladys de Havilland other than her authorship of *The Woman's Motor Manual* (1918). Published in the last phases of the war, the manual covers both military driving and the various kinds of civilian work available to women—private chauffeuse; driving vans and taxis. On the latter de Havilland wrote that 'what women have to do, who aspire to become taxi drivers, is to think nothing about sex disabilities but to embark at once upon a study of the map of London'. The manual is of interest for its testimony on the new roles open to women and for the down-to-earth practicality which it recommends that women acquire. This attitude emerges in her barbed comments on 'butterfly chauffeuses' and her admiration for the work of the 'Fannys', carried out under difficult conditions. The general format of the manual underlines its practical approach: it is extensively illustrated (with advertisements on the endpapers which include both spark plugs and corsets for driving) and has a large section on the structure, function, and upkeep of motor engines.

---

38 THE 'FANNYS'

AT the present time the chief ambition of the majority of women motorists is to drive an ambulance in France. There are many women who are well adapted for the work, but there are others—butterfly chauffeuses, who are mainly out for new experiences and a good time—who should think twice before adopting this branch of motorcar driving, for it is not by any means all honey.

THE UNWANTED 'BUTTERFLY'

As a case in point, I know a girl who thought that it would be a 'change' and very exciting to drive an ambulance in France. After a few weeks spent in endeavouring to obtain a position, she managed to achieve her aim, and, clad in a becoming and particularly well-cut khaki uniform (with cream silk stockings carefully chosen to correspond), she departed for Calais, there to take up her duties as an ambulance driver.

Three weeks later I received the following letter from her, which I hope may prove a warning to other butterfly chauffeuses:

'I am thinking with longing of those glorious days in England, for that is, in fact, what they were when compared with the time I am having in this bleak Spartan spot. I am giving vent to my agony by writing to you, and also, in my "spare time", I am designing a frieze for my wigwam, consisting of a series of tragedies founded on fact, under the title of "Women Who Share Tommies' Peril." The tragedies here are colossal! Just picture me at this moment, sitting on my wardrobe-dressing-table-washstand-combined (in other words, my packing case), a smelly oil stove filling the hut with black fumes, and every part of my body absolutely frozen. I am asked daily how I like being here. In reply, I can only stare and say, "Don't be so silly!" Somehow, I never discover that there is any work to be done until the convoy has started and got well away, and I and my ambulance are left to ponder over the super-ghastliness of life in khaki. "It's an experience," you say. Yes; and so would be being tossed by a bull. I am all for a quiet "comfy" life now—a sofa, a large fire, and a book. And oh! to be able to wear a crêpe de Chine blouse instead of this ever-lasting manly uniform!'

A short time after receiving this letter I heard that the writer had given up her work, and had returned to her home in England, after having put the society with whom she had enlisted to a great deal of inconvenience and expense.

A STRENUOUS LIFE

Without a doubt, to drive an ambulance in France is not so thrilling and enjoyable as some inexperienced girls imagine it to be. In fact, on the contrary, it is very strenuous work indeed, and generally entails an extremely Spartan mode of living. Perhaps nothing substantiates this statement so decisively as the fact that many women ambulance drivers in France have cut their hair quite short, as they have found that they have not sufficient time to attend to long hair properly, and, in some places, they have even found difficulty in keeping it clean. Therefore it will be readily understood that the butterfly woman is absolutely out of her element in such a position. The more solid and responsible woman, with plenty of grit and pluck, is the only type who is likely to 'stick it out'.

WOMEN DOING NOBLE WORK

I am proud to say that I have met many such women, splendidly unselfish and courageous, who have done and are still doing noble work as ambulance drivers in France. For example, two women members, drivers of the First Aid Nursing Yeomanry Corps (Miss Cuff and Miss Rous Allen), spent six months with the Belgian Field Hospital at Hoogstadt, during which time they lived in a tent which was cold and wet, amid rats and the discomfort of camp life in war time, and were constantly on duty of a very trying kind.

Again, on one occasion, a member of the F.A.N.Y. corps (they are popularly known as 'Fannys') once worked single-handed, while another 'Fanny', who was very ill with pleurisy, lay alone all day. They lived in old rooms, very cold and dreadfully damp, and yet, in spite of this, in spite of dull food (for the minimum was spent on the staff in order to save for the men), and in spite of the extreme difficulty in getting to England for any leave, they worked on, determined to 'keep the flag flying'.

And, again, there was one occasion when two girls, members of the F.A.N.Y., assisted in moving 400 French wounded. After seeing them safely entrained, they motored a distance of 125 miles, were at the station to meet the trains, and worked from midnight until 8 in the morning. So efficient were they that they received a letter of thanks and congratulations from the Governor-General of Calais.

HOW THE CORPS STARTED

The F.A.N.Y. Corps was raised in 1909 to assist the Royal Army Medical Corps in time of war. Its object then was to provide mounted detachments and ambulance wagons to take over wounded from the R.A.M.C. units at clearing hospitals or dressing stations and convey them to base hospitals at the railhead. For this work, the members were trained under R.A.M.C. instructors and nurses, and received a thorough grounding in stretcher drill, moving helpless patients, improvising and applying splints, also in bandaging and cooking. Horsemanship was also taught, and the members were mounted in order that detachments might move rapidly from one point to another as required. The present war has practically abolished mounted work, however, and the Corps have substituted an efficient service of motor ambulances.

It was at Calais, in 1916, that the F.A.N.Y. started the first women's motor ambulance convoy. They had applied for this work frequently before permission was granted. At Hoogstadt, in July, 1916, the F.A.N.Y. established the first convoy of women drivers, only four miles behind the firing line. In January, 1917, another ambulance convoy of six to eight cars was started at Binson, driven, of course, by F.A.N.Y. women drivers. All these units were organized by Mrs McDougall, who has been offered the Role of Leopold II, in recognition of her services for the Belgians, for whom she has worked hard since the outbreak of war.

WORK ACCOMPLISHED

The F.A.N.Y. has a fleet of motor ambulances which for many months proceeded to the Front with clothing and comforts for the soldiers, and carried wounded from the advanced dressing stations to the nearest hospitals. Several members have worked at regimental aid posts behind the first line of trenches on the Yser, helping the battalion doctors to cope with rushes of wounded. These motor ambulances have done a great part of the convoy work in Calais since October, 1917, bearing wounded daily from the clearing station to the various hospitals, and from the hospitals to boats and trains.

Also they take returning convalescents from the boats to their depots. The approximate number of cases carried during the year is 80,000.

The F.A.N.Y. motor bath worked for some time at an aviation ground near the Front. This motor bath gives 250 baths a day and disinfects the soldiers' clothes.

The F.A.N.Y. motor kitchen did excellent work in providing soup and coffee for the wounded. For some time it was attached to the 7th (Belgian) Regiment of Artillery, and did all the cooking for about 300 men, some two miles behind the firing line, this with a woman cook and a woman chauffeur—Miss Lewis and Miss Hutchinson respectively. During a gas attack these brave women rendered great service and saved the lives of some of the gassed Canadians. An interesting account of their experiences appeared in an issue of 'The First Aid Nursing Yeomanry Corps Gazette', which goes to show that they do not monopolize all the thrills in the firing line!

After a difficult journey and a night at B——, marked by a farewell supper given by the N.C.O.s, Miss Lewis and Miss Hutchinson started early next morning at the rear of the battery for Ypres. Miss Lewis writes:

Thrilling Experiences

'The batteries marched at the rate of 20 kilometres a day, starting at 6.30 a.m. and halting for the night towards 4 or 5 in the evening, so that a journey that would have taken the kitchen one afternoon took us instead, at the pace we moved, just five days; but, slow though it was, and made slower by the incessant halts on route (lasting sometimes three-quarters of an hour and for no apparent reason), the journey never once lacked interest. Different soldiers of the battery who knew the country well would drop behind and talk to us, and tell us things of interest about the places and country we passed through. We learned from our guide Palmanus the names of the officers. Palmanus it was who, as naturally as a mother, took our comfort and happiness under his personal care from the moment he was made responsible for the kitchen. Palmanus it was who, en route, shared his ration of bread with us and gave us to drink out of his coffee can until experience had taught us to buy bread over night at the village where we put up. Palmanus who stayed with us late each evening to clean up the kitchen after the 140 men of the battery had been provided for, and who personally conducted us to our billets each evening, and then found for himself any odd corner in a barn that might be left after his—by that time snoring—comrades had settled in for the night. Usually it was Palmanus who, when up at the Front, and the battery ordered to fire in the afternoon, persistently refused to aid Miss Hutchinson and myself to peel potatoes for the men's suppers on the ground that if the men were too much occupied with the war to peel their own potatoes, it must naturally follow that they went without them.

A Dangerous Delay

'Not many miles from the village from which we started the car stopped—no petrol reaching the engine! And we were delayed half an hour whilst Miss Hutchinson took down the carburetter and removed the obstruction. It did not give me a comfortable feeling somehow as a first start off to see our battery disappearing in the distance down a tortuous road that had many others leading out of it. Imagination pictured us in similar circumstances at the Front with the battery fighting a rearguard action! It did not seem possible then that the kitchen would prove worthy of the battery, but it never gave us trouble again except what was unavoidable under the conditions, and under Miss Hutchinson's magnificent driving surmounted unbelievable difficulties for a car with so light a frame and with so heavy a body.

'Towards 3 o'clock the halt for the first night was made just north of the town of ——. The guns and ammunition wagons were drawn up at the side of the road forming a line stretching away out of sight over the hill, the horses were unhitched and taken to be watered. We were told to prepare the men's evening meal immediately. We backed the kitchen into the yard of a farm by the roadside, and prepared to do as we had been ordered.

Supper Under Difficulties

'Supper to prepare for 140 men at the end of a trying day full of unusual experiences! It seemed nearly an impossible job. The materials were so scanty and the quantity so immense for so small a kitchen, and the meat— that part of it that was not huge bone—so hopelessly fresh. We ought to have been thankful, had we then known, for it to have been fresh meat at all with which to make soup and stew: not many days later we were given small half-pound tins of English bully-beef and told that we must make the usual soup for the men—140 of them! Being "Fannys", of course, nothing daunted us, and each man brought his billy-can to be filled with soup and stew, and we heard no complaints about the way in which it had been cooked.

'A little later, a message came that it would give the officers pleasure if we would have our meals at the mess. We removed as many traits as possible of the day's work and walked the mile and a half that separated us from the inn at the bottom of the hill where the officers had their mess. After some time spent in sitting on a bench inside the inn talking to our command-ant, to whom we gave a little sketch of the history of the Corps, dinner was ready. In a rough room, reeking of beer, we sat down, Miss Hutchinson and myself one on each side of the major who presided over the mess, to what seemed to us, after hospital diet, princely fare! We were both con-sumed with silence, dead tired, and longing to be in bed, yet conversing politely throughout dinner (our war-worked hands concealed as much as possible under the table!), as though we were in a London mansion and war did not exist except in history. Major Beving apologized for there being no tablecloth, as he had not considered it worth while to unpack until the Front was reached. During the meal the orders for the next day arrived by despatch rider. We were informed that the Ypres salient was to be the desti-nation of the battery, and the silence of thought fell upon the mess. Supper over, with the aid of an electric torch we returned to our billet, glad to return to bed as 3.30 a.m. was the hour at which we had to rise the next morning.'

Gladys de Havilland, 'The First Aid Yeomanry Corps' ('The Fannys'), from *The Woman's Motor Manual* (London: The Temple Press, 1918), 69–78

Helen Zenna Smith
(1901–1985)

A journalist, brought up in Australia and England, Evadne Price wrote under her own name when she published her popular children's books during the 1920s and 1930s. She adopted the pseudonym Helen Zenna Smith to write *Not So Quiet*, which was suggested by a publisher as a woman's reply to Erich Maria Remarque's *All Quiet on the Western Front*. Price's acceptance of this commission did not include the original idea that she parody Remarque: she produced, instead, a realistic account of a woman's experience of war. *Not So Quiet* is based on the war diary of Winifred Young, who had served as an ambulance driver at the front. Upon publication the novel became an immediate success: it was serialized and the film rights were sold. Four other Helen Zenna Smith novels followed: *Women of the Aftermath* (1931); *Shadow Women* (1932); *Luxury Ladies* (1933); *They Lived with Me* (1934). Price became a war correspondent in the Second World War, serving in France and Germany and reporting on the liberation of the concentration camps.

———

39   Not So Quiet . . .

I DROVE till dawn to and fro—station, Number Five Hospital—Number Five Hospital, station . . . sick, numb, frozen-fingered, frozen-hearted . . . station, Number Five Hospital—Number Five Hospital, station. . . .

It ended, just as I thought it would never end. Back again at the depot I collapsed with my head on the steering wheel. Tosh helped me down, forced steaming cocoa into me. . . . 'Pretty bloody kick-off, Smithy. But wait till you get gas cases or, worse, liquid-fire. . . .'

I whimpered like a puppy. . . . I couldn't go on. . . . I was a coward. . . . I couldn't face those stretchers of moaning men again . . . men torn and bleeding and raving. . . .

Tosh laughed a funny, queer laugh. 'And the admiring family at home who are basking in your reflected glory? "My girl's doing her bit—driving an ambulance very near the line. . . ."' She laughed again. 'Will they let you off, Smithy? Not likely! You'll never have the pluck to crawl home and admit you're ordinary flesh and blood. Can't you hear them? "Well, back *already*? You didn't stay *long*, did you?" No, Smithy, you're one of England's Splendid Daughters, proud to do their bit for the dear old flag, and one of England's Splendid Daughters you'll stay until you crock up or find some other decent excuse to go home covered in glory. It takes nerve to carry on here, but it takes twice as much to go home to flag-crazy mothers and fathers. . . .'

I watch her now running a comb through her hair, softly damning and blasting the knots. Generous hair, Tosh's, as generous as the rest of her, thick, long, red as a sunset in Devon when not grime- and grease-blackened. As I stare she parts the strands over her right ear, peers anxiously into the square of looking-glass, and emits a string of swear-words before turning to The Bug.

'Lend me your scissors, Bug.'

The Bug silently hands them over, lights a cigarette, and passes me the paper packet.

'Everyone read this paper?' asks Tosh.

Everyone has. Tosh spreads the newspaper on the floor near her bed and kneels down, brandishing the scissors.

The B.F. cries out in alarm. 'You're not going to cut off your hair, Tosh? Your *lovely* hair.'

'Why should I be a free lodging-house for waifs and strays?' Tosh laughs hoarsely at her own crude wit. She has, when amused, the big porky, jolly laugh of a fat publican.

'Oh, Tosh, how *can* you? Short hair's terribly unfeminine. I wouldn't cut off my hair for anything.'

'No, you vain little scut, you'd rather crawl.'

Snip, snip, snip go the scissors. Snip, snip, snip. The long, red strands fall into the much-scanned crumpled newspaper. I crane my neck. *Have* I read it? Is it the *Daily Mail* or the *Daily Express*? If it's the *Mail* I have read it, but if it's the *Express* there's something I haven't quite finished. . . .

A red curl of Tosh's hair hides the top of the page. I can't see. Perhaps a post will come to-morrow bringing fresh newspapers; we haven't had any letters, or, better still, parcels, for six days.

Snip, snip, snip. . . .

'No wonder I've scratched my head off—no wonder I couldn't sleep!' Tosh points triumphantly to the paper. We interestedly follow the direction of her fingers and go on munching our ginger biscuits. A few weeks ago we should have vomited. But after cleaning the inside of an ambulance it would take more than a few lice to make our gorges rise.

'A bloody platoon,' says Tosh.

Snip, snip, snip. . . .

'I'll bet you're all as alive-o, if you only carried out a smashing attack,' chuckles Tosh.

I catch the eye of The Bug and we both grimace—we know Tosh is very near the truth, for we have both been itching furiously for days past. Small-tooth combing, though a temporary check, has no lasting effect. We get them from the 'sitters'—the cases well enough to sit beside us in front on the ambulances. Straight from the field dressing stations, before that straight from the trenches, who can wonder the sitters are alive with vermin?

Snip, snip, snip....

Tosh's hair is half off, giving her a curiously lop-sided effect. I wish I had her courage, but a mental vision of Mother restrains me. Poor Mother, she would die of horror if I came home on leave with my hair cut short like a man's. She wouldn't understand the filth and beastliness after my cheery letters home. Only dreadful blue-stocking females cut their hair. Besides, Mother has always been so proud of my hair—why, I cannot imagine. It is not beautiful hair. It is long, but thin and mouse-coloured. Nondescript. Like its owner. Like its owner's name, Helen Smith. Helen Z. Smith. How jealously I preserve the secret of that Z., that ludicrous Z. bestowed on me by my mother. Z. was the heroine of a book mother read the month before I arrived on earth. She wanted me to grow up like Z. Z. was the paragon of beauty, virtue, and womanliness. Mother has been sadly disappointed over the first; I am still the second, but the third—well, Z. was never an ambulance driver somewhere in France. I am very dubious about the third.

Snip, snip, snip....

No, I had better not emulate Tosh. It would definitely put the tin helmet on the womanliness. It would also spoil Mother's pet story of myself and my sister Trix—of how, a wee fair head and a wee dark head, lately released from the tortures of curl-papers, we used to walk demurely to Sunday school while Mother waved from the front gate. Since Father grew rich and promoted us to Wimbledon Common, Mother omits the reference to the front gate—it isn't done on Wimbledon Common to wave from the front gate—but she still bores everyone who will listen (and a lot who won't) with the story of the two wee curly heads. With Trix a V.A.D. and me ambulance driving, I can see those wee curly heads working overtime, while Mother drops a sentimental tear on the socks she is knitting for my second-loot brother, her 'hero boy'.

Snip, snip, snip....

'You'll look awfully unsexed, Tosh,' warns The B.F.

'Unsexed? Me? With the breasts of a nursing mother?' Tosh winks behind The B.F.'s back. The poor B.F. gasps and goes scarlet. Tosh is revolutionising her ideas of the British aristocracy in private life more and more each day.

Snip, snip, snip. . . .

We go on munching our biscuits and smoking our gaspers. Directly the kettle boils there will be hot Bovril, something to warm us before starting out—thin, miserable stuff, for the bottle is nearly empty and there are six of us, but enough to send a glow through our bodies. We think of it with mouth-watering anticipation and watch Tosh marshalling the lively contents of the newspaper more towards the centre with a pen-holder.

'What an R.T.O. was lost when I became an ambulance driver,' says Tosh.

That goes down well with us, even The B.F. Inwardly we are proud to think our stomachs no longer heave up and down at the sight of a louse. After all, a few vermin more or less make little difference. Our flea-bags are full of them, in spite of Keatings and Lysol, and our bodies a mass of tiny red bites with the tops scratched off. We are too hard worked to spare the necessary time to keep clean, and that is the trouble. It is four weeks since we had a bath all over, nine days since we had a big wash—we haven't had time. We dare not hot-bath in case we have to go out immediately afterwards into the snow. The last girl who did it is now in hospital with double pneumonia and not expected to live.

Tosh finishes her barbering. She shakes her head like a shaggy dog. I see to my satisfaction that the paper is the *Mail* and not the *Express*. I have read it, after all. Tosh crumples it into a ball, takes the enamelled chamber from under her camp-bed, and proceeds to make a bonfire inside it. It smokes at first, but after a few seconds begins to crackle merrily.

'Wholesale slaughter,' says Tosh. 'Well, it's the fashion in our circles, *n'est-ce pas?* Anyone got a fag?'

Helen Zenna Smith, from Not So Quiet . . . Stepdaughters of War
(London: Virago, 1988), 12–18

Maria Näpflin
(1896-?)

Maria Näpflin was born in Beckenried, a small town in central Switzerland. When the war broke out she travelled to Vienna to become a Red Cross nurse and soon found herself tending the wounded on the Eastern Front. The passage below is taken from her strongly idiosyncratic account of her war experiences. In it she describes her long struggle with drug dependency and her descent into psychological collapse. At the same time her book offers an eloquent account of the contrast between the soldier's heroic sacrifice and the corruption rampant behind the battle lines of the Austro-Hungarian empire. In a sequel entitled *Heimatlos, Staatenlos* (*Homeless, Stateless*) of 1946, Näpflin tells of her ordeal at the hands of the Swiss authorities when, in 1938, she tried to return home without a passport, a penniless refugee from Hitler's Germany.

---

40 MORPHINE

SINCE there is no rule without exception, no working day went by without some unforeseen disruption to our routine. Mishaps of all kinds as well as fatalities were apt to occur at any moment, at any hour. There were the sudden deteriorations of those suffering from tuberculosis or malaria, there were acute attacks of colic, and so on. The nurse in charge of the unit tended to be someone with extensive experience in first aid and emergencies. As such she was put in charge of the drugs cabinet which, together with medical instruments and bandages, contained all the emergency medicines. Every transaction to do with this cabinet had to be monitored and recorded by the doctor in charge. He fulfilled this task with variable care, depending on how far he trusted the responsible nurse. Unfortunately for me I was deemed extremely reliable, and my rule over the drugs cabinet remained utterly unchecked. Our medicine store contained, amongst many other things, morphine, both in the form of capsules and as a powder. Its beneficial properties as an analgesic and tranquillizer meant that all the patients continually clamoured to have it. For a long time I administered the drug with great strictness and impartiality. Then, one day, it occurred to me to try a tiny dose myself. After that I took more and more, until I was unable to shake off its hold over me.

In Serbia I began to notice that some of the doctors, indeed some of the best doctors, took morphine on a regular basis. The drug is well known for its pain-killing and somniferous properties and I couldn't help wondering why doctors who, with their demanding and exhausting job, ought to try to boost their energies, should want to take morphine. Thus I remained wary of the practice and tried to keep my hands off the poison. Sick in body and spirit, I returned from the front for a month's vacation in Vienna. Physically I seemed to recover in no time at all, but I was unable to shake off the deep depression which had gotten hold of me. Work, I came to believe, would be the best antidote and thus I agreed to become nurse in charge under the supervision of the admirable Sister Rosa. She brought out the best in me and I, eager to prove how reliable and caring I was, threw myself into my new work with every ounce of energy at my disposal.

However it soon became obvious that my commitment was not entirely genuine. I felt broken and lacking in strength to such an extent that at times I was barely able to carry on. In the evening, after a busy day on the ward, I would come close to a complete collapse. It was then that the craving for morphine began to re-assert itself. And once more I was right at the source, since I had shared access to the drugs cabinet. But how was I going to fiddle the books? Already I had noticed that morphine in powdered form, because it was used in such large quantities, was less strictly controlled than the capsules. Thus it was easier to steal small quantities. I began to experiment with three to four measures per day and the benefits were immediate and spectacular. My depression lifted and all my sombre thoughts disappeared as if blown away by a fresh wind. At the same time of course I was now well and truly addicted. I placated my conscience by telling myself that I was just as sick as our patients and therefore entitled to the same relief . . .

Maria Näpflin, from *Fortgerungen, Durchgedrungen bis zum Kleinod hin* (*Struggles towards the Jewel at the Centre*), trans. Agnès Cardinal (Meiringen: Loeptien, 1922), 55–8

Rheta Childe Dorr

(1866–1948)

From an early age, Rheta Childe Dorr was a committed feminist. Following an unsuccessful attempt to study art, she became a journalist with a particular interest in writing about the condition of women. Over a number of years Dorr investigated the industrial status of women: she worked in many factories and travelled extensively in Europe to research the social and political conditions of women. After the war she was the Czechoslovakia correspondent to the *New York Herald* and became a member of the National Woman's Party when the Constitutional Amendment equalizing the legal position of women was passed. A contributor to American journals and to leading newspapers, her writing ranged across history, sociology, politics, and biography. It included *What Eight Million Women Want* (1910–11); *Inside the Russian Revolution* (1917); *A Soldier's Mother in France* (1918); *A Woman of Fifty* (1924). She also wrote a biography of Susan B. Anthony (1928).

———

41   To the Front with Botchkareva

Women of all ranks rushed to enlist in the Botchkareva battalion. There were many peasant women, factory workers, servants and also a number of women of education and social prominence. Six Red Cross nurses were among the number, one doctor, a lawyer, several clerks and stenographers and a few like Marie Skridlova who had never done any except war work. If the working women predominated I believe it was because they were the stronger physically. Botchkareva would accept only the sturdiest, and her soldiers, even when they were slight of figure, were all fine physical specimens. The women were outfitted and equipped exactly like the men soldiers. They wore the same kind of khaki trousers, loose-belted blouse and high peaked cap. They wore the same high boots, carried the same arms and the same camp equipment, including gas masks, trench spades and other paraphernalia. In spite of their tightly shaved heads they presented a very attractive appearance, like nice, clean, upstanding boys. They were very strictly drilled and disciplined and there was no omission of saluting officers in that regiment.

The battalion left Petrograd for an unknown destination on July 6 in our calendar. In the afternoon the women marched to the Kazan Cathedral, where a touching ceremony of farewell and blessing took place. A cold, fine rain was falling, but the great half circle before the cathedral, as well as the long curved colonnades, were filled with people. Thousands of women were there carrying flowers, and nurses moved through the crowds collecting money for the regiment.

I passed a very uneasy day that July 6. I was afraid of what might happen to some of the women through the malignancy of the Bolsheviki, and I was mortally afraid that I was not going to be allowed to get on their troop train. I had made the usual application to the War Ministry to be allowed to visit the front, but I did not follow up the application with a personal visit, and therefore when I dropped in for a morning call I was dismayed to find the barrack in a turmoil, and to hear the exultant announcement, 'We're going this evening at eight.'

It was an unseasonal day of rain, and I spent reckless sums in droshky hire, rushing hither and yon in a fruitless effort to wring emergency permits from elusive officials who never in their lives had been called upon to do anything in a hurry, or even to keep conventional office hours. Needless to say I found nobody at all on duty where he should have been that day. Even at the American Embassy, where, empty-handed and discouraged, I wound up late in the afternoon, I found the entire staff absent in attendance on a visiting commission from home. The one helpful person who happened to be at the Embassy was Arno Dosch-Fleurot of the New York *World*. 'If I were you,' he said, 'I wouldn't worry about a permit. I'd just get on the train—if I could *get* on—and I'd stay until they put me off, or until I got where I wanted to go. Of course they may arrest you for a spy. In any other country they'd be pretty sure to. But in Russia you never can tell. Shepherd, of the United Press, once went all over the front with nothing to show but some worthless mining stock. Why not try it?'

I said I would, and before eight that evening I was at the Warsaw Station, unwillingly participating in what might be called the regiment's first hostile engagement. For at least two thirds of the mob that filled the station were members of the Lenine faction of Bolsheviki, sent there to break up the orderly march of the women, and even if possible to prevent them from entraining at all. From the first these spy-led emissaries of the German Kaiser had sworn enmity to Botchkareva's battalion. Well knowing the moral effect of women taking the places of deserting soldiers in the trenches, the Lenineites [*sic*] had exhausted every effort to breed dissension in the ranks, and at the last moment they had stormed the station in the hope of creating an intolerable situation. In the absence of anything like a police force they did succeed in making things painful and even a little dangerous for the soldiers and for the tearful mothers and sisters who had gathered to bid them good-by. But the women kept perfect discipline through it all, and slowly fought their way through the mob to the train platform.

As for me, a mixture of indignation, healthy muscle and rare good luck carried me through and landed me in a somewhat battered condition next to Adjutant Skridlova. 'You got your permit,' she exclaimed on seeing me. 'I am so pleased. Stay close to me and I'll see you safely on.'

Mendaciously perhaps, I answered nothing at all, but stayed, and every time a perspiring train official grabbed me by the arm and told me to stand back Skridlova rescued me and informed the man that I had permission to go. At the very last I had a bad moment, for one especially inquisitive official asked to see the permission. This time it was the Nachalnik, Botchkareva herself, who came to the rescue. Characteristically she wasted no words, but merely pushed the man aside, thrust me into her own compartment and ordered me to lock the door. Within a few minutes she joined me, the train began to move and we were off. That was the end of my troubles, for no one afterwards questioned my right to be there. At the Adjutant's suggestion I parted with my New York hat and early in the journey substituted the white linen coif of a Red Cross nurse. Thus attired I was accepted by all concerned as a part of the camp equipment.

The troop train consisted of one second class and five fourth class carriages, the first one, except for one compartment reserved for officers, being practically filled with camp and hospital supplies. In the other carriages, primitive affairs furnished with three tiers of wooden bunks, the rank and file of the regiment traveled. I had a place in the second class compartment with the Nachalnik, the Adjutant and the standard bearer, a big, silent peasant girl called Orlova. Our luxury consisted of cushioned shelves without bedding or blankets, which served as seats by day and beds by night. We had, of course, a little more privacy than the others, but that was all. As for food, we all fared alike, and we fared well, friends of the regiment having loaded the train with bread, butter, fruit, canned things, cakes, chocolate and other delicacies. Tea-making materials we had also, and plenty of sugar. So filled was our compartment with food, flowers, banners, guns, tea kettles and miscellaneous stuff that we moved about with difficulty and were forever apologizing for walking on each other's feet.

For two nights and the better part of two days we traveled southward through fields of wheat, barley and potatoes, where women in bright red and blue smocks toiled among the ripening harvests. News of the train had gone down the line, and the first stage of our journey, through the white night, was one continued ovation. At every station crowds had gathered to cheer the women and to demand a sight of Botchkareva. It was largely a masculine crowd, soldiers mostly, goodnatured and laughing, but many women were there too, nurses, working girls, peasants. Occasionally one saw ladies in dinner gowns escorted by officer friends.

The farther we traveled from Petrograd, the point of contact in Russia with western civilization, the more apparent it grew that things were terribly wrong with the empire. More and more the changed character of the station crowds reminded us of the widespread disruption of the army. The men who met the train wore soldiers' uniforms but they had lost all of their upright, soldierly bearing. They slouched like convicts, they were dirty and unkempt, and their eyes were full of vacuous insolence. Absence of discipline and all restraint had robbed them of whatever manhood they had once possessed. The news of the women's battalion had drawn these men like a swarm of bees. They thrust their unshaven faces into the car windows, bawling the parrot phrases taught them by their German spy leaders. 'Who fights for the damned capitalists? Who fights for English bloodsuckers? We don't fight.'

And the women, scorn flashing from their eyes, flung back: 'That is the reason why we do. Go home, you cowards, and let women fight for Russia.'

Their last, flimsy thread of 'peace' propaganda exhausted the men usually fell back on personal insults, but to these the women, following strict orders, made no reply. When the language became too coarse the women simply closed the windows. No actual violence was ever offered them. When they left the train for hot water or for tea, for more food or to buy newspapers, they walked so fearlessly into the crowds that the men withdrew, sneering and growling, but standing aside.

There was something indescribably strange about going on a journey to a destination absolutely unknown, except to the one in command of the expedition. Above all it was strange to feel that you were seeing women voluntarily giving up the last shred of protection and security supposed to be due them. They were going to meet death, death in battle against a foreign foe, the first women in the world to volunteer for such an end. Yet every one was happy, and the only fear expressed was lest the battalion should not be sent at once to the trenches.

As for me, when we arrived at our destination, some two miles from the barracks prepared for us, I had a moment of longing for the comparative safety of the trenches. For what looked to me like the whole Russian army had come out to meet the women's battalion, and was solidly massed on both sides of the railroad track as far as I could see.

I looked at the Nachalnik calmly buckling on her sword and revolver. She had a confident little smile on her lips. 'You may have to fight those men out there before you fight the Germans,' I said.

'We are ready to begin fighting any time,' she replied.

She was the first one out of the train, and the others rapidly followed her.

In Camp and Battlefield

The women's regiment did not have to fight its brothers in arms, however. The woman commander took care of that. She just walked into that mob of waiting soldiers and barked out a command in a voice I had never before heard her use. It reminded me somewhat of that extra awful motor car siren that infuriates the pedestrian, but lifts him out of the road in one quick jump. Botchkareva's command was spoken in Russian, and a liberal translation of it might read: 'You get to hell out of here and let my regiment pass.'

It may not have been ladylike, but it had the proper effect on the Russian army, which promptly backed up on both sides of the road, leaving a clear lane between for the women. The women shouldered their heavy kits and under a broiling sun marched the two miles which lay between the railroad and the camp. The Russian army followed the whole way, apparently deciding that the better part of valor was to laugh at the women, not to fight them. . . .

Cool and refreshed, the battalion marched back to the barracks, which consisted of two long, hastily constructed wooden buildings, exactly like hundreds of others on all sides about as far as the eye could reach. Some of the buildings were half underground, for warmth in winter, and must have been rather stuffy. Our buildings were well ventilated with many dormer windows in the sharply slanting roof, and they were new and clean and free from the insects which in secret I had been dreading. Inside was nothing at all except two long wooden platforms running the length of the building, about ninety feet. They were very roughly planed and full of bumps and knot holes, but they were the only beds provided by a step-motherly government. Here the women dumped their heavy loads, their guns, ammunition belts, gas masks, dog tents, trench spades, food pails and other paraphernalia. Here they unrolled their big overcoats for blankets, and here for the next week, all of us, officers, soldiers and war correspondent, ate, slept and lived. Two hundred and fifty women in the midst of an army of men. Behind us a government too engrossed in fighting for its own existence to concern itself about the safety of any group of women. Before us the muttering guns of the German foe. Between us and all that women have ever been taught to fear, a flimsy wooden door. But sleeplessly guarding that door a woman with a gun.

In that first midnight in camp I woke on my plank bed to hear the shuffling of men's feet on the threshold, a loud knock at the door, and from our sentry a sharp challenge: 'Who goes there?'

'We want to come in,' said a man's voice ingratiatingly.

'No one can come in at this hour,' answered the sentry. 'Who are you and what do you want?'

The man's answer was brutally to the point. 'Aren't there girls here?' he demanded.

'There are no girls here,' was the instant reply. 'Only soldiers are here.' . . .

The impatience of those women to go forward, to get into action, was constant. They fretted and quarreled during the frequent rainy spells which kept them housebound, and were really happy only when something happened to promise an early start. One day it was the arrival of 250 pairs of new boots, great clumsy things which it would have crippled me to wear, and in fact all the women who could afford it had boots made to order. Another day it was the appearance of a camp cooking outfit especially for the battalion. Four good horses were attached to the outfit, and the country girls hailed them with delight as something to pet and fuss over.

The women spent much time cleaning and learning their guns. They seemed to love their firearms, one girl always alluding to her rifle as 'my sweetheart'.

'How can you love a gun?' I asked her.

'I love anything that brings death to the Germans,' she answered grimly. This girl, a highly educated, wellbred young woman, was in Germany when the war broke out. She was arrested and charged with espionage, a charge which, for all I know, may have been true. It was not proved, of course, or she would have been shot. On the mere suspicion, however, she was kept in prison for a year and must have suffered pretty severely. She looked forward to the coming fight with keen zest. I asked her one day what she would do if she was taken prisoner again. She pulled from under her blouse a slender gold chain on the end of which was a capsule in a chamois bag. 'I shall never be taken prisoner,' she said. 'None of us will.'

Rheta Childe Dorr, 'To the Front with Botchkareva', from *Inside the Russian Revolution* (New York: The Macmillan Company, 1918), 58–65, 67–8, 70–1

Frances Wilson Huard

(1885–?)

At the outbreak of war Frances Huard was living in France, near the Marne, sixty miles from Paris. She recounts her experiences of life near the battle zone in two books, *My Home in the Field of Honour* (1916) and *My Home in the Field of Mercy* (1917). Subtitled 'the experiences of a resident near the river Marne at the opening of the European war of 1914', these are personal memoirs, anecdotal and conversational, which record her war work, including the establishment of a hospital in Soissons. The books also record her gradual awakening to the realities of war, in the same way as the fictionalized

version provided in Canfield's 'La Pharmacienne' (no. 9). The extract
which follows, from *My Home in the Field of Mercy*, records the discovery of
the rape of a young Frenchwoman. Frances Huard wrote other books
about the war: *With Those who Wait* (1918) and *Lilies, White and Red*
(1919).

42   My Home in the Field of Mercy

My nurse and I were resting a moment before our own meal, silently medi-
tating in front of the fire. Our reverie was short lived, however, for someone
knocked at the door and announced that the widow X— from the Black
Farm was downstairs and wanted to see me. It was urgent.

I knew of many but could think of no pressing reasons why the woman
should demand me. I had seen neither her nor her ten year old daughter
since our return after the invasion. Perhaps she was short of funds. Madame
Guix said she would go and attend to the matter.

As I passed my office on the way to supper a sob attracted my attention
and as I opened the door I could hear Madame Guix saying, 'There, there,
I am sure he'll go.'

The haggard looking woman hastily brushed the tears from her eyes and
stood up.

'She says her little daughter is ill; has been for some time. Wants to know
if our doctor won't go and see her.'

'What's the trouble with her?' I asked.

This brought forth new tears.

'I don't know—I don't know,' sobbed the woman. 'O, do come, do
come!'

Already well acquainted with the primitive methods of caring for the
ill still so prevalent among the peasants in this particular district; realising
that often for economy's sake medical assistance was not summoned
until too late to be of any use, I judged that this case must indeed be
urgent.

I sought out our doctor and laid the matter before him. He expressed his
willingness to make the visit, and the woman having refused our offer of
something hot to stimulate her, patiently waited until we had finished our
evening meal. Then the four of us set out together, leaving the pharmacist in
charge of the hospital.

What a wild night it was. The wind howled most dismally through the pine trees and drove the rain in sheets against our faces. We chose a short cut down our avenue, and as we plodded along through the layers of moist leaves each footstep added another noise to the tempest. There were moments when it was hard to tell whether it were guns or thunder that rent the air, and as now and again we would emerge into the open, I fancied I saw lightning—or was it the flash of distant searchlights seeking out enemy's aeroplanes?

At the little iron gate which marks the extreme limit of our property, we clustered together and I held the lantern closer to enable my nurse to better insert the key. A tremendous gust of wind that sent the frightened nightbirds screaming from their perches, blew out the light and left us in total darkness. We were now nearly a mile from the house; it was useless to think of retracing our steps. To try to light a match was hopeless. There was nothing to do but continue.

What a mad, ghastly tramp we had, our doctor, Madame Guix and myself, following in the path of that sorrow stricken mother, slipping and sliding on the steep inclines, the noise about us such as to make one wonder whether God and man were not doing their utmost to shatter poor old mother earth.

After nearly an hour's climb, puffing and panting, dripping with rain and perspiration we finally reached an isolated farmhouse. Our guide entered first and we followed close behind to see an old white-bonneted peasant woman crouching in the corner of the hearth, her face lighted by the glow of the dying embers.

'Mother, he's come,' said Madame X— rousing the dozing figure.

'God be praised, God be praised,' mumbled the little old woman bustling about to light a candle.

'Where is the child?' asked the doctor after having removed his raincoat that had covered his uniform.

He followed the woman to a doorway and over his shoulder I could see stretched out on a humble bed a puny, emaciated child. Surely her visage was familiar. Of course I knew her! She had been in my catechism class that year and had made her First Communion in June. Could it be possible? What a change had come over her! The mother bent over her and gently called 'Elvire, Elvire'. At the touch of her hand the child started and shivered.

'Elvire,' called the woman, 'here's the doctor and Madame Huard. They've come to see you.'

The girl cast a glance in our direction, her eyes falling on the doctor in uniform who stood nearest her. With a wild yell she caught at the covers and in one bound was in the other corner of the room.

'I am afraid! I am afraid!' she shrieked. 'Don't come near me! don't, don't!' Her little body was quaking, tortured by her spirit.

The old grandmother darted into the room and seizing the doctor by the arm motioned him to come away.

'Elvire,' pleaded the broken-hearted mother, 'Elvire, he's gone.'

'But he'll come back! no! no! I'm afraid, no, don't let him come, don't let him touch me.'

'Elvire,' I called, my voice shaking with horror and emotion. 'Elvire, don't you remember me? Surely—Madame Huard? Don't you remember how we used to sing together last Spring.'

A queer choking sound came from her throat. Her eyes softened but no tears came. There were none left.

Then followed the hardest moral struggle I ever hope to experience; a full half hour in which I sought to convince this little fear-cowed animal of my integrity. And when at last I held that tiny heaving body against my breast, saw the eyes close peacefully, I knew that I had won a victory.

Elvire slept, slept for the first time since the fifth of September. We had already guessed the woeful truth but to corroborate our direst suppositions, the tales of German cowardice and brutality that mid tears and lamentations we wrung from those grief-bowed peasant women made me feel that war might pass and peace might come again, but I could never pardon.

Frances Wilson Huard, from My Home in the Field of Mercy (New York:
George H. Doran Company, 1917), 66–71

Alexandra Pilsudski
(1880?–?)

Alexandra Szczerbinska was born of Polish middle-class parents in Suvalki, a part of Poland which was at the time under Russian rule. Of her childhood she writes: 'As the child of a patriot family I grew up in an atmosphere of secret rebellion.' Before the war she was active in the clandestine Polish nationalist movement until she was arrested in Warsaw by the Russian police. During the war she married Josef Pilsudski, the head of the Polish nationalist movement, who was to become the chief architect of Polish independence after the war. The extract below is taken from her *Memoirs*, which describe her life as a Polish freedom fighter from her earliest years and through two world wars.

———

43   MEMOIRS

LATER I was removed to a separate cell which I occupied with one other woman, Madame Klempinska, a political prisoner like myself, and a member of the P.P.S.

The conditions of the prison were much the same as they had been under the Russian regime; the food was little better. Breakfast consisted of a cup of weak tea and a slice of bread without butter; dinner was a plate of kascha; in the evening there was nothing but a cup of boiling water. After my trial, however, I was allowed to have a parcel of provisions sent in by my lawyer, Mr Pazchalski, and I and my companion in misfortune lived on it for a couple of days. Never did food taste so delicious!

The German court found me guilty of political agitation and ordered me to be put in a detention camp. At the end of a further fortnight in the Paviak I was taken to Szczypiorno, near Kalisz, one of the biggest camps for prisoners of war in Poland.

My first impressions of Szczypiorno were discouraging to say the least.

Imagine a windswept, desolate field, knee-deep in mud in many places, crossed and re-crossed by lines of dug-outs in which some four thousand prisoners of war and a hundred civilians were herded together. That was the picture which greeted me when I arrived in the gloom of a bleak December afternoon with Madame Klempinska and four men, Polish civilians, who were also to be interned. Wooden-faced Bavarian soldiers received us from the police who had accompanied us from Warsaw; a young lieutenant ran his finger down a list setting forth our names, occupations and sentences, reeled off a perfunctory warning on the folly of trying to escape and then handed us over to the guards. The four men were marched off in one direction, Madame Klempinska and I in another.

The camp had been originally planned in the form of huts, but at the last moment timber had apparently run short, and there had been a compromise resulting in dug-outs, sunk deep into the earth and topped by a flimsy structure of wood about three feet in height and containing small windows. Seen from the front the effect was rather like rows of dolls-houses.

Madame Klempinska and I crossed the field in a thin drizzle of rain which our guard cheerfully informed us fell nearly every day during the winter months, and descended a flight of wooden steps into a sort of cave. It reminded us irresistibly of a vault and had the same musty, earthy smell. When our eyes grew accustomed to the dim light we saw that it was a comparatively large apartment, divided into two by a trench which was spanned by duckboards, a necessary measure for after days of heavy rain it became like a moat. This primitive accommodation was designed for eighty men but as we were the only women in the camp we had it to ourselves until we were joined by a young servant girl. It was bitterly cold in those winter days for the one small stove in the centre only gave out heat within a limited radius and the icy winds of December curled through the doors and windows. In one corner were two heaps of sacks filled with sawdust and covered with army blankets. Our beds. There was no furniture of any description, not even a table. For the first few minutes we were too stunned even to give voice to our dismay, but when the guard returned with some papers which we were to sign I asked for an interview with the Commandant of the camp. At first he refused even to pass on the request, saying that it was against the regulations at that hour of the day, but I was so persistent that at length he departed, very reluctantly, to consult the officer on duty. Half an hour later he returned with the message that the Commandant would see me, after I had been disinfected. He stared at me in blank astonishment when I burst out laughing and then explained that the process of disinfection was part of the routine of arrival at the camp. A few minutes later Madame Klempinska and I were initiated into it.

We were taken into a room where a tall grim-looking German woman divested us of our clothes which she rolled up in bundles. Then she led us to two small bath tubs which she proceeded to fill with a very small quantity of water and a great deal of strong disinfectant. After telling us to get into them she departed carrying our clothes, and leaving the door open so that the wind whistled round our naked forms until I ran shivering to shut it. The process of bathing was the reverse of pleasant. The atmosphere in the room was almost glacial, for there were no panes in the windows, and the water in the baths was almost boiling. Consequently we were alternately chilled and scalded, while the disinfectant stung our skins until we were the colour of lobsters. After we had endured about fifteen minutes of this the German woman returned bringing two wraps of coarse towelling in which we were bidden to clothe ourselves until our own garments were dry. In the meantime she washed our hair in a strong carbolic lotion which left it as hard and as brittle as straw and so sticky and unmanageable that it took weeks to recover.

The next process was a hasty examination by the German army doctor attached to the camp, who pronounced us in good health and gave us each a couple of injections for typhus. Evidently the theory of disinfection did not extend to this, for he plunged the hypodermic needle first into me and then into Madame Klempinska without even troubling to wipe it.

While we were undergoing all this our clothes were being disinfected in another room with Germanic thoroughness. Apparently they were dealt with even more drastically than we were for when they were returned to us my blue dress had turned green while poor Madame Klempinska's gloves had shrunk so much that she could not get them on.

The rite of purification having thus been accomplished I was taken to see the Commandant, an elderly man, a Prussian officer of the old school with charming manners. He received me courteously and listened sympathetically to my complaint regarding the quarters which had been allotted to me. The camp, he explained, had not been intended for the accommodation of women prisoners, and we were in fact the first whom he had received there. He had already sent in a request to headquarters for beds and mattresses for us and hoped that they would be forthcoming before long. In the meantime he suggested that I should go round with him next morning and see whether I could find among the unoccupied huts one better than our present one.

With this I was forced to be content, but the night that followed was one of the most unpleasant I have ever lived through. I lay awake hour after hour in the darkness listening to the rats scurrying up and down the planks. The trenches were infested with them, and they grew so bold that they used to run over us as we lay on our sacks. I still shudder at the remembrance of those wet, hairy bodies crawling over my arms and neck! After the first few nights I got into the habit of wrapping my blankets round me so tightly that not even my head was left uncovered. Although the Commandant kept his word and moved us to another hut which was slightly less damp and in time even secured camp beds for us the rats continued to be one of our worst trials.

The days passed slowly for us and we had no means of killing time and no contact with the outside world. In theory we were allowed to receive letters but for some reason or other they never seemed to reach us. During the greater part of a year I only heard once from Pilsudski, yet he wrote to me many times. The absence of news was one of the hardest things to bear. One tortured oneself wondering what was happening. Occasionally one of the guards brought in a German newspaper, which was passed round from hut to hut until it almost fell to pieces. We had only one book, the life of Julius Cæsar. We read it over and over again, from cover to cover.

The prisoners of war were divided into two camps, French and Russian. They had their separate cookhouses and were responsible for cooking their own meals. Although the food which was supplied to them was the same—exceedingly good and in enormous quantities—their manner of preparing it was entirely different, characteristic of the two races. The French, although there were no professional cooks among them, expended time and care on their meals and managed to achieve a very creditable example of the cuisine française. The Russians, fatalistic and indifferent, used to heap everything that was given to them—fish, meat, potatoes, cucumber, or anything else that happened to be going—into one stewpan, put it on the fire and then ladle it out in vast platefuls. Madame Klempinska and I and the little servant used to eat in our own hut but we had to fetch our food from the Russian canteen, and we were so disgusted at the unappetizing mess that was served out to us that we petitioned to be allowed to share the food of the French prisoners. However, official red tape would not stretch so far.

The last weeks of December were inexpressibly dreary. The rain poured down in torrents, filling the trenches and turning the field into a bog. Christmas Eve dawned in an atmosphere of gloom for guards and prisoners alike. Madame Klempinska and I sat crouched over the stove and talked of past Christmases, which is a foolish time for anyone, except the very happy, to do. And so my thoughts went back along the years to Suvalki, and I saw myself as a child again, standing at the window watching the snowflakes spreading a soft, glistening blanket over Grandmother's garden, and searching the sky for the first pale star; the Star of Bethlehem, Aunt Maria had said. Only after it had appeared could the Christmas feast begin, and I was hungry for I had fasted since the night before. In imagination I could hear the laughter and chatter in the kitchen where Anusia and Rosalia were putting the finishing touches to the dishes they had been preparing all day, the twelve symbolical dishes of fish and the sweet cakes filled with honey and spices and poppy seeds. My sisters and I had helped too, strewn fragrant herbs and grasses on the tablecloth in remembrance of the first Christmas that had dawned in a stable, and hung the Christmas tree with sweets and red apples from the garden.

'No, not apples'... said Madame Klempinska... 'Paper dolls. I used to make them for a full month before Christmas, and we had cakes on our tree instead of sweets.'

'Toys are the best' . . . said a deep bass voice from the doorway . . . 'My father used to carve them out of wood for us in the winter evenings.' . . .

The camp life at Lauban was far more pleasant than at Szczypiorno. We were allowed a certain amount of liberty and could even go to the town to buy what we could get (which was not much) at the local store. It was soon sold out of such luxuries as tinned meat, chocolates, and soap. As the months passed the shortage of food grew serious and rations were cut down more and more drastically both for us and for the soldiers who guarded us. The French prisoners of war suffered the least for nearly all of them had 'marraines', under the French war charities scheme, who sent them parcels of food. The German officers were glad to buy chocolate from them, although they were too proud to deal with them directly, and one of the women in our hut, the wife of the Polish officer, used to act as go-between. She was an exceedingly pretty woman, very popular with the gallant Frenchmen. The long conversations which she used to hold with them over the palisade kept the occupants of our hut supplied with news both of the camp and of the outside world. The latter was generally either inaccurate, founded on the gossip of sentries, or stale, taken from newspapers weeks old, but we welcomed it and passed it round among ourselves.

In a community like ours national characteristics asserted themselves strongly. The two Englishmen, true to the proverbial reserve of their race, kept rigidly to their own society, bowed and smiled amiably at their fellow prisoners when they encountered them on their way to town, but resisted all attempts at closer acquaintance. The Russians, almost without exception simple, uneducated peasants, accepted their lot with dreary fatalism but made no effort to get the best out of it. The Frenchmen, many of whom were professional men, lawyers, doctors and clerks, were, on the other hand, philosophical and good-humoured, organized concerts and provided the entire social life of the camp.

The concerts which were held every week were very popular and revealed a surprising amount of talent, although after many months the programme grew rather stale. A Polish girl from Lithuania who was well-known on the professional stage used to sing, and the French usually contributed a sketch. But personally I got more amusement out of the grouping of the audience than from the actual programme.

This was arranged with the German love of etiquette and social procedure which could even extend to a prison camp. We were all rigidly graded. In the front row were the German officers, in the second the 'Bessere Dame' (Better Women) as the occupants of our hut and a few of the Lithuanians were classified. Then came the 'bessere' French, which meant French prisoners of war who had been professional men in civilian life. With these were the Russian doctors. (The two Englishmen were conveniently disposed of in a corner which eliminated the problem of their social status.) Behind the 'bessere' French were the 'ordinary French', and last of all the 'ordinary' Russians, who were a picturesque assembly . . . Cossacks, Kalmuks, tall slender Sartes, handsome Caucasians.

In one hut were several women who were kept apart from the rest, classified, with true Germanic directness, as 'prostitutes'. Actually only one of them merited the name as a professional. The rest had been forced by starvation to sell themselves in the streets of Warsaw. Two of them had been teachers in private schools which had closed because of the war, another had been a saleswoman in an exclusive dressmaker's shop which had also put up its shutters, a fourth had been secretary to a rich foreign woman who had hurried back to her own country at the first threat of war. Behind each one was an individual tragedy.

Their lot at the camp was unspeakably wretched. They were subjected to countless humiliating restrictions, and were openly insulted by the guards when they went out for exercise. Yet at night the young soldiers used to climb over the palisade into their huts and force them to accede to them. One of them, a girl of seventeen who had been sent for detention with her mother, cried so bitterly when she told me of this nightly degradation that I protested to the German doctor attached to the camp. He seemed surprised at what he evidently thought a most unreasonable complaint, reminded me that the women were prisoners, and that it was wartime. He flatly refused to do anything in the matter. Eventually matters were brought to a head by an open scandal.

We were sitting in our hut one evening when a Lithuanian woman burst in screaming that all the women in Hut Number X were dying. 'Number X' was what was officially known as 'The Prostitutes' Quarters'.

We hurried there and found some of the women writhing in agony while others sat on their mattresses crying. In the extremity of their misery they had broken up the contents of several packets of needles and swallowed them.

We sent one of the guards for the doctor but he came back with the report that he could not be found and that the dispensary was locked. The nearest hospital was miles away and time was precious. We had no medicine or any means of treating the poor women, and we could think of only one remedy. Fortunately the kascha for our evening meal had just been cooked. We fetched great bowls of it and forced it down their throats. It saved their lives for although some of them were very ill they recovered.

Their tragic attempt at suicide was reported to the Commandant of the camp and an inquiry was instituted. As a result the youngest of the girls was, at our request, allowed to come to our hut.

The spring days lengthened into summer and the summer into autumn and still we remained at Lauban. The news from the outer world grew more and more confused. We heard of the collapse of Russia and of German victories on the Western Front. Yet the guards at the camp were withdrawn and replaced by men too old for the firing line; we shivered in the intense cold of September and October because there was no fuel for heating the camp, and every day the food got less. At length our daily ration was a tiny slice of bread made of a mixture of coarse flour and potatoes, and a plateful of turnips boiled in ox blood. We could only bring ourselves to eat it by holding our noses and swallowing it like medicine. I remember almost weeping with gratitude when one of the prisoners of war who had been working on a neighbouring farm gave me some potatoes which he had secreted in his pocket.

It was difficult to keep one's morale. Even the French lost their cheerful optimism; the German guards were as depressed as the prisoners. But worse than the actual hardships, to me at least, was the continued absence of news. The year 1916 was drawing to its close and month after month had gone by without a letter from Joseph Pilsudski. I had heard, more or less vaguely, from the German soldiers at the camp that he was with his Legions behind the Styr and that the fighting had been very heavy there during the summer. I tried to comfort myself with the thought that if he had been killed or taken prisoner I should have seen it in the German newspapers which reached the camp fairly regularly. I wrote to him many times, but my letters were unanswered. Afterwards I discovered that none of them had reached him. I tried to get in touch with other friends and to obtain news of the different organizations for which I had worked, but with no better success. I could only wait.

Alexandra Pilsudski, from *Memoirs of Madame Pilsudski* (London: Hurst & Blackett, 1940), 241–51

Zofia Nałkowska
(1885–1954)

As the daughter of a prominent family of geographers and famous social thinkers, Zofia Nałkowska belonged to the Polish intellectual élite at the turn of the century. Her ability to combine an interest in the new discoveries of psychoanalysis and the experiments of Modernism with a deference towards the rationalist modes of her father's generation, make her one of the most interesting Polish novelists of the inter-war years. She is particularly well known for her unusually subtle and often cruel portrayals of the human psyche. The extract below comes from her novel *Hrabia Emil* (*Count Emil*), first published in instalments in the journal *Swiat* (*The World*) from 1917 to 1918.

———

44   Count Emil

THE shooting was drawing ever closer, speeded up, and as if swollen in the cloudy, rainy autumn air. The window panes rattled and the whole of Emil's mansion shuddered. Reverberations from the artillery fire tore the air as if it were right outside the wall of the great garden.

Emil sat waiting, quite ready now, but without any joy. From the moment he had seen the suffering and the dead with his own eyes, he began to calculate defeat and victory in that very same currency.

It meant that he now knew that in order to get through, the Polish soldiers would have to break through the bulwark of human flesh, and be soaked in blood like a sponge. Many of their own ranks would be left on the other side. He realized that it would take a lot of suffering and a lot of hard warfare to make it happen.

He kept getting news of their approach: that they were already 'here' or 'over there', that they were coming closer, and closer still. In different directions the low, cloudy sky was lit up by distant fire.

At last the front line entered Kluniewiec.

During the night, the estate and the administrative buildings were overrun by a tide of soldiers. As is customary, the higher ranking officers at once took over the left-hand wing of the Manor, with all its guest-rooms on the first floor. Next morning a long line of ambulance cars began rolling in through the open gate. The wounded were being brought across the terrace into the large halls which had already been cleared out.

At once everything changed. Everything became understandable, clear cut and began to make sense: the faces, the movements everywhere, reflected restlessness, seriousness and desperation. Even that human moaning which, when first heard, seemed to be so unbearable, now had its place, its foreseen, established value within this reality.

For Emil and his immediate family, the Worostanskys, there remained just a few rooms to which he and his mother had the more precious items brought from the occupied halls. These were now gathered around them in haste and disorder and made movement amongst them difficult and awkward.

All the bed linen had been handed over for use with the wounded. Even so, many of them were lying on the floor on naked straw mattresses or on straw covered with any old rag.

In the largest hall the carpet which was fixed to the floor had remained in place. On it the wounded lay, row after row, neatly lined up, one behind the other, like the letters in an inscription of enigmatic meaning.

For the time being they remained like this with virtually no help at all. The officers kept explaining that a hospital detachment was expected but that somehow, it had been delayed. The majority of the wounded were dressing their own wounds or helped one another to do so. Some were approaching the house from the front line, unaided, crawling towards the gate, and finishing by lying on the gravel path next to the central lawn beneath the steps leading up to the entrance terrace. The battle was still raging and provided a steady flow of new arrivals. Two more rooms had to be commandeered for the hospital.

All the soldiers were swearing and grumbling about the tardy hospital detachment and about some Princess who was supposed to have financed it. They were cursing her with dreadful oaths.

In spite of his resentment Emil found himself organizing help for the Russian wounded although it was not on their terms that he would have wished to observe the suffering and desperation of war. An old barber-surgeon was brought in from the town, its two young surgeons and the local doctor all having departed since the beginning of the war. Two young girls who had done a first-aid course, daughters of Kluniewiec officials, also offered their help. All this was of little use since there were no bandages. From among the inmates of the house, only mother spent the whole of the first day in the hospital. She who had always been so idle, so capricious and frivolous, became indispensable when faced with disaster. In contrast, aunt, who had always felt the suffering of the whole world so acutely, could not be persuaded to lend a hand. She could not bear the screams of the wounded and the sight of their blood. The very next morning she left for Skaliczny. The same pair of horses brought back Ada and Nina, both fully qualified nurses.

Emil found them standing in the large hall with its crimson wallpaper, slabs of marble and gilding. The whole floor had become alive with arms stretching out towards them from all sides, catching hold of their clothes, trying to hold on to these frail shadows of relief and hope. The heavy air was filled with a chorus of incessant voices, of groaning, howling, prolonged moaning, callings for bread, of swearing and plaintive pleading. Suddenly Emil thought: 'They should never have been hurt. In fact, none of this is necessary. There is no need for this to happen.' Yet he hardly believed it himself and did not really want to believe it.

After a while the voices merged into a single monotonous hum, which eventually failed to elicit any further sympathy and became mere backdrop. From this background noise there rose a voice—strident, resonant and hysterical—of a man in his last agony. He was lying far from the central passage, parallel to the others in a row. A grenade had skinned his arms and legs and bared them to the bone. His flank had been ripped open to reveal his entrails. He stirred a little, with eyes and mouth wide open. His cries were animal-like, or seemed to belong to a woman or little child. They struck terror in every heart. He screamed that they should finish him off. In his prolonged groans he hit, in the end, on a single high note—as if it was the most appropriate—and maintained it to the end. He kept calling, entreating people to kill him. It was his one and only plea. But everyone avoided him. Nobody knew how to deal with him. In the end only Nina found the courage to approach him. Muttering a few words, she bent over him and then knelt down. It was obvious that his pain was terrible and beyond all measure. Suffering unspeakably, he never fainted, but was dying slowly and in full consciousness. What could she say to him? What words were there for her to say? Emil did not understand. The soldier wanted to die: did he not have the right to that?

Some strange obduracy mixed with a little self-loathing prevented Emil from following Nina to see the soldier. Ada was quite right when she remarked that to go to see him was a waste of time since there was nothing to be done. She did not go either. Both of them were standing over an elderly soldier with a bearded face helping to change the dressing on the palm of his hand which had been shot through.

Death may differ from death more, sometimes, than from life. What does it mean, Emil thought, to get a bullet through one's heart and drop dead without as much as a cry? Or to feel one's life ebb away with the loss of blood, growing cool and faint, down to nothingness—how does it compare with this arduous labour of dying, this toil of suffering which lasts for a day and a night and yet another day? And he felt that in death there lurked injustices far greater than the most grievous wrongs of life.

It was already dusk when, suddenly, all became quiet, even though the shouting and groaning went on as before. The soldier had stopped screaming. Nina came over and said that he had died.

Immediately she resumed her care of the others, reproaching herself for having stayed with one soldier such a long time. Clearly Ada had been right. It was obvious that one couldn't have helped him.

It was on the fourth day only that the hospital detachment finally appeared. In the cool bright midday sun a young woman in officer's uniform and breeches rode through the gate, surrounded by a handful of medical officers. After alighting from her horse in front of the main entrance she asked to see the lady of the house and introduced herself as Princess Jaszwin. She then commandeered one more room in a way that would tolerate no opposition.

She was a merry creature. Not pretty but lively, with slanting black eyes and vividly flushed face. One of the officers, Lieutenant Kolenkin, quite openly took up residence in the same room with her. He was shorter than she, frail, melancholic, with slightly uneven shoulder-blades.

Both wanted to be installed at once and requested a meal without even visiting the halls where the wounded were. These were meanwhile being attended by the hospital personnel of the detachment and by the servants.

For most of the time the Princess remained in her room. Occasionally she would play billiards, show off her skills at tennis, or go for a ride through the park or into the neighbouring countryside with the officers. In the morning her room remained shut until noon and no one dared to wake her.

Since the detachment had recently lost its only doctor, terrible things were happening in the hospital. Nina, who had left, returned once more but without Ada.

Because of the lack of space, each time a new batch of wounded arrived from the battlefield, the dying were carried outside before they had even time to pass away. Corpses were not buried but carried into the yard near the kitchens, where, among the birch trees, there stood timbered pits for household rubbish. Into these the corpses were thrown.

One day Emil knocked at the Princess's door. A merry voice from within asked what was up. Upon hearing Emil's name she opened the door and emerged in a crimson silk negligee unbuttoned at the neck. Emil demanded that the dead be buried and pointed out that it was highly unseemly to leave them lying on a rubbish heap.

'All right. Would you, please, wait a minute?'

She closed the door and Emil could hear a conversation going on inside, which was followed by peels of laughter by the Princess. A moment later she reappeared, fully dressed in uniform and a riding cap on her curly hair. She called a soldier and sent him away with instructions. It was not long before a suitable place without any tree roots was found. Graves were dug in a little meadow between two copses of the park, quite close to the windows of the house.

The Princess, together with a couple of officers, stood smiling and blushing on the terrace in the sunshine. A little further away, on a low handrail next to the steps, sat Lieutenant Kolenkin looking pale and frail.

All of them were watching the dead being carried along the terrace. The corpses were stiffly elongated and nearly naked. One of them had his right hand strangely twisted and raised as if towards his own temple—a last unexplained gesture, perhaps of pain, or the fear of death.

The Princess pointed to it with her riding-whip: 'Look, what a disciplinarian,' she cried laughingly. 'Even in death he salutes us.'

Without taking their eyes off the young woman the officers too were laughing and the sun was spreading a warm glow over the scene on the terrace of the Manor House of Kluniewiec.

Zofia Nałkowska, *Count Emil*, trans. Jerzy Strzetelski, Barbara Strzylewska, and Agnès Cardinal (Warsaw: Czytelnik, 1977), 160–6

V

WRITING THE WAR

Enid Bagnold

(1889–1981)

Enid Bagnold spent much of her early childhood in the West Indies before returning to Europe, where she completed her education in England and Switzerland. She attended Walter Sickert's school of painting and drawing, where she developed a talent for etching and met the sculptor Gaudier-Brzeska and the writer Katherine Mansfield. She developed friendships with many other writers, including Vita Sackville-West and H. G. Wells. In 1914 Bagnold became a VAD at the Royal Herbert Hospital, Woolwich. *A Diary Without Dates* (1917) records her experiences there: it is reported that 'within half an hour of the book's publication she was sacked by her matron for indiscipline'. Her novel, *The Happy Foreigner* (1920) records her subsequent war career as a driver for the FANY in France at the end of the war. Bagnold's later writing included fiction (*National Velvet*, 1935) and drama (*The Chalk Garden*, 1955). At the time, *A Diary Without Dates* attracted much admiration—H. G. Wells described it as 'one of the two most human books written about the war'.

---

45   INSIDE THE GLASS DOORS

PAIN . . .

To stand up straight on one's feet, strong, easy, without the surging of any physical sensation, by a bedside whose coverings are flung here and there by the quivering nerves beneath it . . . there is a sort of shame in such strength.

'What can I do for you?' my eyes cry dumbly into his clouded brown pupils.

I was told to carry trays from a ward where I had never been before—just to carry trays, orderly's work, no more.

No. 22 was lying flat on his back, his knees drawn up under him, the sheets up to his chin; his flat, chalk-white face tilted at the ceiling. As I bent over to get his untouched tray his tortured brown eyes fell on me.

'I'm in pain, Sister,' he said.

No one has ever said that to me before in that tone.

He gave me the look that a dog gives, and his words had the character of an unformed cry.

He was quite alone at the end of the ward. The Sister was in her bunk. My white cap attracted his desperate senses.

As he spoke his knees shot out from under him with his restless pain. His right arm was stretched from the bed in a narrow iron frame, reminding me of a hand laid along a harp to play the chords, the fingers with their swollen green flesh extended across the strings; but of this harp his fingers were the slave, not the master.

'Shall I call your Sister?' I whispered to him.

He shook his head. 'She can't do anything. I must just stick it out. They're going to operate on the elbow, but they must wait three days first.'

His head turned from side to side, but his eyes never left my face. I stood by him, helpless, overwhelmed by his horrible loneliness.

Then I carried his tray down the long ward and past the Sister's bunk. Within, by the fire, she was laughing with the M.O. and drinking a cup of tea—a harmless amusement.

'The officer in No. 22 says he's in great pain,' I said doubtfully. (It wasn't my ward, and Sisters are funny.)

'I know,' she said quite decently, 'but I can't do anything. He must stick it out.'

I looked through the ward door once or twice during the evening, and still his knees, at the far end of the room, were moving up and down. . . .

A little flying boy with bright eyes said in his high, piping voice to me across the ward:

'So there are soldiers coming into the ward to-night!'

I paused, struck by his accusing eyes.

'What do you mean? Soldiers . . .?'

'I mean men who have been to the front, nurse.'

The gallants raised their eyebrows and grew uproarious.

The gallants have been saying unprofessional things to me, and I haven't minded. The convoy will arm me against them. 'Soldiers are coming into the ward.'

Eight o'clock, nine o'clock. . . . If only one could eat something! I took a sponge-finger out of a tin, resolving to pay it back out of my tea next day, and stole round to the dark corner near the German ward to eat it. The Germans were in bed; I could see two of them. At last, freed from their uniform, the dark blue with the scarlet soup-plates, they looked—how strange!—like other men.

One was asleep. The other, I met his eyes so close; but I was in the dark, and he under the light of a lamp.

I knew what was happening down at the station two miles away; I had been on station duty so often. The rickety country station lit by one large lamp; the thirteen waiting V.A.D.'s; the long wooden table loaded with mugs of every size; kettles boiling; the white clock ticking on; that frowsy booking clerk . . .

Then the sharp bell, the tramp of the stretcher-bearers through the station, and at last the two engines drawing gravely across the lighted doorway, and carriage windows filled with eager faces, other carriage windows with beds slung across them, a vast Red Cross, a chemist's shop, a theatre, more windows, more faces. . . .

The stretcher-men are lined up; the M.O. meets the M.O. with the train; the train Sisters drift in to the coffee-table.

'Here they come! Walkers first. . . .'

The station entrance is full of men crowding in and taking the steaming mugs of tea and coffee; men on pickaback with bandaged feet; men with only a nose and one eye showing, with stumbling legs, bound arms. The station, for five minutes, is full of jokes and witticisms; then they pass out and into the waiting chars-à-bancs.

A long pause.

'Stretchers!'

The first stretchers are laid on the floor.

There I have stood so often, pouring the tea behind the table, watching that littered floor, the single gas-lamp ever revolving on its chain, turning the shadows about the room like a wheel—my mind filled with pictures, emptied of thoughts, hypnotized.

But last night, for the first time, I was in the ward. For the first time I should follow them beyond the glass door, see what became of them, how they changed from soldiers into patients. . . .

The gallants in the ward don't like a convoy; it unsexes us.

Nine o'clock . . . ten o'clock. . . . Another biscuit. Both Germans are asleep now.

At last a noise in the corridor, a tramp on the stairs. . . . Only walkers? No, there's a stretcher—and another . . . !

Now reflection ends, my feet begin to move, my hands to undo bootlaces, flick down thermometers, wash and fetch and carry.

The gallants play bridge without looking up. I am tremendously fortified against them: for one moment I fiercely condemn and then forget them. For I am without convictions, antipathies, prejudices, reflections. I only work and watch, watch. . . .

Waker is not everything a man should be: he isn't clever. But he is so very brave.

After his tenth operation two days ago there was a question as to whether he should have his pluggings changed under gas or not. The discussion went on between the doctors over his bed.

But the anæsthetist couldn't be found.

He didn't take any part in the discussion such as saying, 'Yes, I will stand it . . .' but waited with interest showing on his bony face, and when they glanced down at him and said, 'Let's get it through now!' he rolled over to undo his safety-pin that I might take off his sling.

It was all very fine for the theatre people to fill his shoulder chockful of pluggings while he lay unconscious on the table; they had packed it as you might stuff linen into a bag: it was another matter to get it out.

I did not dare touch his hand with that too-easy compassion which I have noticed here, or whisper to him 'It's nearly over . . .' as the forceps pulled at the stiffened gauze. It wasn't nearly over.

Six inches deep the gauze stuck, crackling under the pull of the forceps, blood and puss leaping forward from the cavities as the steady hand of the doctor pulled inch after inch of the gauze to the light. And when one hole was emptied there was another, five in all.

Sometimes, when your mind has a grip like iron, your stomach will undo you; sometimes, when you could say 'To-day is Tuesday, the fifth of August,' you faint. There are so many parts of the body to look after, one of the flock may slip your control while you are holding the other by the neck. But Waker had his whole being in his hands, without so much as clenching them.

When we had finished and Sister told me to wipe the sweat on his forehead, I did so reluctantly, as though one were being too exacting in drawing attention to so small a sign.

Enid Bagnold, from *A Diary Without Dates* (London:
Heinemann, 1918), 25–7, 70–3, 140–1

Fanny Kemble Johnson
(1868–?)

An American writer, born and educated in Virginia, Fanny Kemble Johnson was publishing stories by the turn of the century, at which time she also began to contribute to periodicals like *Atlantic Monthly*. She is the author of other works, including *The Beloved Son* (1916). Fanny Kemble Johnson's story 'The Strange-Looking Man' was first published in *The Pagan* and then reprinted in E. J. O'Brien's *Best Short Stories of 1917*. A short biographical note described her chief interests as 'her four children, her writing, and contemporary history as it is made from day to day'. A companion volume offers a source for the story and suggests the way the author wished it to be read: 'I got the idea for "The Strange-Looking Man" . . . from reading the story of the home-coming of a Canadian soldier, limbless, partially blind, wholly demented, to his young wife—homebringing, I should have said. . . . I could not help feeling as I wrote that my little boy symbolized Germany as she is and my young man life, as we are now so strongly hoping it may come to be.'

46   THE STRANGE-LOOKING MAN

A TINY village lay among the mountains of a country from which for four years the men had gone forth to fight. First the best men had gone, then the older men, then the youths, and lastly the school boys. It will be seen that no men could have been left in the village except the very aged, and the bodily incapacitated, who soon died, owing to the war policy of the Government which was to let the useless perish that there might be more food for the useful.

Now it chanced that while all the men went away, save those left to die of slow starvation, only a few returned, and these few were crippled and disfigured in various ways. One young man had only part of a face, and had to wear a painted tin mask, like a holiday-maker. Another had two legs but no arms, and another two arms but no legs. One man could scarcely be looked at by his own mother, having had his eyes burned out of his head until he stared like Death. One had neither arms nor legs, and was mad of his misery besides, and lay all day in a cradle like a baby. And there was a quite old man who strangled night and day from having sucked in poison-gas; and another, a mere boy, who shook, like a leaf in a high wind, from shell-shock, and screamed at a sound. And he too had lost a hand, and part of his face, though not enough to warrant the expense of a mask for him.

All these men, except he who had been crazed by horror of himself, had been furnished with ingenious appliances to enable them to be partly self-supporting, and to earn enough to pay their share of the taxes which bur-dened their defeated nation.

To go through that village after the war was something like going through a life-sized toy-village with all the mechanical figures wound up and click-ing. Only instead of the figures being new, and gay, and pretty, they were battered and grotesque and inhuman.

There would be the windmill, and the smithy, and the public house. There would be the row of cottages, the village church, the sparkling water-fall, the parti-colored fields spread out like bright kerchiefs on the hillsides, the parading fowl, the goats and cows,—though not many of these last. There would be the women, and with them some children; very few, how-ever, for the women had been getting reasonable, and were now refusing to have sons who might one day be sent back to them limbless and mad, to be rocked in cradles—for many years, perhaps.

Still the younger women, softer creatures of impulse, had borne a child or two. One of these, born the second year of the war, was a very blonde and bullet-headed rascal of three, with a bullying air, and of a roving disposition. But such traits appear engaging in children of sufficiently tender years, and he was a sort of village plaything, here, there, and everywhere, on the most familiar terms with the wrecks of the war which the Government of that country had made.

He tried on the tin mask and played with the baker's mechanical leg, so indulgent were they of his caprices; and it amused him excessively to rock the cradle of the man who had no limbs, and who was his father.

In and out he ran, and was humored to his bent. To one he seemed the son he had lost, to another son he might have had, had the world gone differently. To others he served as a brief escape from the shadow of a future without hope; to others yet, the diversion of an hour. This last was espe-cially true of the blind man who sat at the door of his old mother's cottage binding brooms. The presence of the child seemed to him like a warm ray of sunshine falling across his hand, and he would lure him to linger by letting him try on the great blue goggles which he found it best to wear in public. But no disfigurement or deformity appeared to frighten the little fellow. These had been his playthings from earliest infancy.

One morning, his mother, being busy washing clothes, had left him alone, confident that he would soon seek out some friendly fragment of soldier, and entertain himself till noon and hunger-time. But occa-sionally children have odd notions, and do the exact opposite of what one supposes.

On this brilliant summer morning the child fancied a solitary ramble along the bank of the mountain-stream. Vaguely he meant to seek a pool higher up, and to cast stones in it. He wandered slowly straying now and then into small valleys, or chasing wayside ducks. It was past ten before he gained the green-gleaming and foam-whitened pool, sunk in the shadow of a tall gray rock over whose flat top three pine-trees swayed in the fresh breeze. Under them, looking to the child like a white cloud in a green sky, stood a beautiful young man, poised on the sheer brink for a dive. A single instant he stood there, clad only in shadow and sunshine, the next he had dived so expertly that he scarcely splashed up the water around him. Then his dark, dripping head rose in sight, his glittering arm thrust up, and he swam vigorously to shore. He climbed the rock for another dive. These actions he repeated in pure sport and joy in life so often that his little spectator became dizzy with watching.

At length he had enough of it and stooped for his discarded garments. These he carried to a more sheltered spot and rapidly put on, the child still wide-eyed and wondering, for indeed he had much to occupy his attention.

He had two arms, two legs, a whole face with eyes, nose, mouth, chin, and ears, complete. He could see, for he had glanced about him as he dressed. He could speak, for he sang loudly. He could hear, for he had turned quickly at the whir of pigeon-wings behind him. His skin was smooth all over, and nowhere on it were the dark scarlet maps which the child found so interesting on the arms, face, and breast of the burned man. He did not strangle every little while, or shiver madly, and scream at a sound. It was truly inexplicable, and therefore terrifying.

The child was beginning to whimper, to tremble, to look wildly about for his mother, when the young man observed him.

'*Hullo!*' he cried eagerly, 'if it isn't a child!'

He came forward across the foot-bridge with a most ingratiating smile, for this was the first time that day he had seen a child and he had been thinking it remarkable that there should be so few children in a valley, where, when he had travelled that way five years before, there had been so many he had scarcely been able to find pennies for them. So he cried 'Hullo,' quite joyously, and searched in his pockets.

But, to his amazement, the bullet-headed little blond boy screamed out in terror, and fled for protection into the arms of a hurriedly approaching young woman. She embraced him with evident relief, and was lavishing on him terms of scolding and endearment in the same breath, when the traveler came up, looking as if his feelings were hurt.

'I assure you, Madam,' said he, 'that I only meant to give your little boy these pennies.' He examined himself with an air of wonder. 'What on earth is there about me to frighten a child?' he queried plaintively.

The young peasant-woman smiled indulgently on them both, on the child now sobbing, his face buried in her skirt, and on the boyish, perplexed, and beautiful young man.

'It is because he finds the Herr Traveler so strange-looking,' she said, curtsying. 'He is quite small,' she showed his smallness with a gesture, 'and it is the first time he has even seen a whole man.'

Fanny Kemble Johnson, 'The Strange-Looking Man', in E. J. O'Brien (ed.),
Best Short Stories of 1917 (Boston: Houghton, 1917?), 361–4

Vernon Lee
(1856–1936)

Violet Paget was born in France, the only child of the second marriage of the widowed Matilda Lee-Hamilton and the family's tutor. Her father had been educated in Warsaw but left Poland after becoming involved in the 1848 uprising. She was a prolific essayist, novelist, and writer of short stories: her pseudonym Vernon Lee registers her debt to her half-brother, the poet Eugene Lee-Hamilton. She had a first and great success with *Studies in the Eighteenth Century in Italy* (1880) which broke new ground in opening up the culture of Italy to an English readership. However, her first novel *Miss Brown* (1884) and some subsequent stories in which she ridicules the contemporary literary coteries in England were badly received. During the war the cosmopolitan, pacifist stance of *The Ballet of the Nations* (1915) and the trilogy *Satan the Waster* (1920) earned her further condemnation. Yet she was also widely admired. Elegant, erudite, and a brilliant conversationalist, she was a well-known figure in the international cultural élite and belonged to the group of lesbian women in Paris—Gertrude Stein, Radclyffe Hall, Djuna Barnes amongst them—who frequented Natalie Barney's salon in the rue Jacob. The original text *The Ballet of the Nations* was published with extensive illustrations by Maxwell Armfield.

---

47   THE BALLET OF THE NATIONS

FOR a quarter or so of a century, Death's celebrated Dances had gone rather out of fashion.

Then, with the end of the proverbially *bourgeois* Victorian age, there set in a revival of taste, and therefore of this higher form of tragic art, combining, as it does, the truest classical tradition with the romantic attractions of the best Middle Ages. In South Africa and the Far East, and then in the Near East quite recently, the well-known Ballet-Master Death had staged some of his vastest and most successful productions.

'It is time,' said Satan, the Lessee of the World, 'to re-open the Theatre of the West. The Politicians and Armament Shareholders have long got all the stage-property in readiness, and the Scene-Shifters of the Press are only waiting for the signal.'

'Your orders shall have my very best attention,' answered Ballet-Master Death, 'for, to tell you the truth, my dear Lord Satan, this West, with its Doctors and Economists and Trade Unions, is fast losing the habit of those sublimer forms of Art of which Aristotle pithily remarks, that they purge the world of its inhabitants by terror and pity. I myself will answer for the Dancers, if you will see to getting an adequate orchestra; for, as you are aware, Death himself cannot set the Nations dancing, still less keep up the dance, without the Music of the Passions.'

'That shall be my business,' said Satan, the World's immortal Impresario; 'let us lose no time.'

The first Instrumentalist whom they called upon was Self-Interest, who is usually engaged to play the ground-bass of Human Life. But he had joined a Trade Union. 'I am busy,' yawned Self-Interest, 'come some other day'; and he turned upon his ear, and dreamed of reconstituting Society upon a broader basis.

'Self-Interest was always a dull dog; not a particle of divine fire in *him*,' grumbled Death. 'What was the good of wasting time on such a fellow?'

'May I remark that you Skeletons are apt to be a trifle testy?' answered Satan, quite unruffled in his delicate iron wings. 'Don't you see that by knocking at Self-Interest's door, I have brought Fear, that over-retiring old slut, to her window? Hi! Widow Fear, it's only a couple of old friends inviting you to a little entertainment. Come down, my dear, and bring some of your ungraceful but amusing offspring.'

So Fear, squalid beyond all other Passions, came down, hesitating just a little, because she had heard Self-Interest refuse the invitation. But she was speedily dragged along by her shabby, restless twins, Suspicion and Panic; and the family carried penny-whistles and foghorns and a cracked storm-and-massacre bell, genuine mediæval but wrapped in yesterday's *Daily Mail* and *Globe*.

'Rather an unpresentable lot, though such first-rate performers,' mused Satan; 'we must have something handsome to make up for them, for the Nations have grown dreadfully superfine of late, and some of the other indispensable members of the band aren't very attractive either. Deign to join our little amateur orchestra,' he cried in a fine round voice, and rustling his arch-angelic wings ceremoniously, 'dear my Lady Idealism and my young Prince Adventure.' And the couple, bride and bridegroom, came out of their palace of cloud and sunbeams; very magnificent they were, and of noblest bearing, if a little overdressed. Idealism carried a silver trumpet and Adventure a woodland horn. There came also Death's mother (or wife, for their family relations are best not inquired into) Sin, whom the gods call Disease; nor was there any need of calling her. With her came her well-known crew, Rapine, Lust, Murder and Famine, fitted out with bull-roarers and rattles and other cannibalic instruments.

'Here comes Hatred with Self-Righteousness,' said Satan, nodding in the direction of a pair who pretended not to be acquainted, but were nevertheless hurrying together out of the Inn of Vanity, and trundling between them a huge double-bass and a small harmonium, upon which, once they had taken place, side by side, Self-Righteousness, most obligingly, gave Hatred his right pitch.

'That'll do to begin with,' cried Death, who was always in a hurry. 'Heroism is sure to join as soon as we have well begun; and he can be plopped down anywhere. See! here come the Dancers! Just strike up a bit; Fear and you; Idealism; and you, Hatred, growl on the deep string; just a bar or two to make the Nations hurry up and get over that tiresome *mauvaise honte* of theirs.'

The Nations had meanwhile assembled, each brilliant and tidy in its ballet dress, which was far better cut, and of handsomer stuff, of course, than its everyday broad-cloth or rags. And Idealism and Adventure, Hatred and Self-Righteousness, were already busy tuning, for unlike the rest of the orchestra they were sticklers for correctness, when Ballet-Master Death's preliminary instructions were cut short by the appearance of an unsuspected and very odd pair of additional musicians. For while the rest of the band were dressed, or in some cases undressed, in classical, mediæval, biblical or savage costumes, these two were habited in a manner uncompromisingly modern, the one like a city clerk who should have joined the Red Cross, and the other, who was a lady, in the spectacles and smock most commonly seen in laboratories.

'Get out with you!' yelled Ballet-Master Death, jumping from his stool at the sight of the new-comers; and, turning to his orchestra, 'Kick them out! Kick out the new-fangled intruders who want to spoil our fun! Knock them down! Trample on them! Don't you see they are alien spies? Spies in the service of Life and Progress!'

'Hush, hush!' answered Satan, with an arch-angelic gesture which sent all the orchestra cowering to their places, and temporarily paralysed the skeleton arm of Death. 'Which of us is master here, I wonder? Will you never learn manners, you bony old relic of the Stone Age, with your rabble of instruments fit for an ethnological museum?' Then, turning to the new-comers, 'Please excuse his country manners, dear Madam Science and dear Councillor Organisation. You know the habits of Skeletons, their skulls are inevitably empty!'

'Pray don't mention it, my Lord,' answered Science, who had a first-rate gramophone tucked under her arm, *'qui sait comprendre sait tout pardon-ner*, so it is part of my professional duty to find excuses for your Ballet-Master's behaviour towards us.'

'It's all as it should be,' added Organisation, who had begun unpacking a very handy miniature pianola and its various rollers. 'Of course Science and I *are* permanently in the service of Life and Progress. But that firm is work-ing slack at present, so we feel at liberty to take a temporary engagement.'

'Nothing could be more conducive to the success of our Ballet,' answered Satan, pressing their hands affectionately but lightly between his claws, which Science took this opportunity of examining; 'and I only hope our col-laboration may become permanent. Of course Death,' and he lowered his arch-angelic voice to the politest whisper, 'is getting a bit old for his job and dreadfully prejudiced. Besides, I fear it can't be denied that you have done one or two things which have made ignorant people gossip in a manner cal-culated to rub him the wrong way. Come here, you peppery old Ballet-Master,' and Satan playfully sent an electric stream through the Skeleton which sent him shivering and rattling like a brake of dry reeds, 'come and shake hands with this illustrious lady and gentleman, who will keep up our Ballet with their wonderful mechanical instruments when the rest of our classic band have neither breath nor strings left. And now, as soon as our new friends are seated in the front place they deserve, please begin your instructions. And, by the way, you haven't yet given out the title of our new Ballet.'

'This Ballet of ours,' began Death, after rapping three times on his desk, 'is called the Ballet of the Nations. Nothing very new in the title, but one that always draws. As regards instructions, long experience has taught me that I can leave both my orchestra and my *corps de ballet*—the Nations at present have all got excellent heads—to their own inspiration, provided only they will keep their eyes constantly fixed on my bâton. The more they depart from the regulation steps, cutting capers according to circumstances and inventing terrifically new figures, the more they will find, odd as it may appear, that their vis-à-vis as well as their partners will respond; and the more indissolubly interlocked will become the novel and majestic pattern of destruction which their gory but indefatigable limbs are weaving for the satisfaction of our enlightened Stage-Lessee, my Lord Satan, and the admiration of History. As to the music, all that is wanted is that the rythm be well marked, the discords plentiful but adequately relieved by allied harmonies and powerful national unisons; and that our Orchestra of Human Passions should refresh itself with strong spirits as often as is compatible with not falling asleep. The scheme of the Ballet is very simple, and its variety arises out of the great number—I hope I may say the constantly increasing number—of Dancing Nations. The main *motif* is, of course—for we are thoroughly up to date, although our dear Impresario does not give us credit for it—the main theme is that each Nation is repelling the aggression of its vis-à-vis, and at the same time defending its partner. There are two minor themes of outstanding Dancers flying to the rescue of the main groups: the two themes together giving rise to all manner of surprising inventions. It is, I need scarcely say, very conducive to a fine effect that all the Nations should keep a strictly innocent expression of countenance, while endeavouring to tear off as much of the costume and ornaments, and lop off as many as possible of the limbs of their vis-à-vis. At the end of the main action the Chief Dancers may be called upon to shift sides or take part in a general breakdown of a highly modern and anarchical style, something like the Paris *impromptu* after the *pas de deux* of 1870, only on a vast scale. And now! the first position, please!'

'One moment!' cried Satan; 'I'm sorry to be always interrupting, but what about Heroism? He's sure to join, and where shall we place him when he turns up?'

'Oh, just anywhere,' whispered Ballet-Master Death; 'he is always the most obliging of my orchestra, although he usually comes in after we have begun. And not a bit difficult to please, like Idealism and even Adventure. *He* won't mind sitting alongside that filthy slut Fear, or surrounded by the cannibal music of the Companions of Sin. But here he comes!' For at that moment there entered Heroism, with limbs like a giant, blushes like a girl, and merry eyes like a child's.

'Welcome, Heroism, our Prince of Tenors,' cried Satan, with sham cordiality, for there was no love lost between the new-comer and himself, although Heroism was sincerely attached to Death. 'We were just saying, my dear young friend, that there is nothing you shrink from, and that you are the most modest and reliable of our orchestra. Why, I remember the

French Revolution Ballet, when Heroism and Panic played not only a duet, but at the same instrument, four hands! That was Lessee Satan's finest Ballet hitherto, with the Marat theme in Paris and the Hoche theme on the frontier. But, with good-will, this new dance of our Ballet-Master Death may be still finer and as long.'

Death smiled, for he loved Heroism.

'Come here, my boy,' he said, 'you have always been dutiful and loving to your old daddy Death, and cared for him more than for any other of the Immortals.' So saying, the Skeleton Ballet-Master tapped the budding cheeks of Heroism, that star-like youth, with eyes which laughed but saw not, for even as his cousin Love, he is blind from the cradle. And Heroism, at the sound of Death's well-known voice, kissed his bony fingers with rapture; and, grasping the drum with which he accompanies his heavenly voice, sat down obedient between Fear and Hatred, unconscious of their foulness.

The way the Ballet began was this: Among the Nations appointed by Satan to dance, for a few had to be kept to swell the audience, which would otherwise have consisted only of sundry sleepy Virtues and of the Centuries-to-Come, which are notoriously bodiless and difficult to please—among those Dancing Nations there was a very little one, far too small to have danced with the others, and particularly unwilling to dance at all, because it knew by experience that the dances of Ballet-Master Death oftenest took place upon its prostrate body. So it was told, as it always had been told, it need do nothing but stay quite quiet for the others to dance round. And as it stood there, in the middle of the Western Stage, two or three of the tallest and finest Dancers danced up in a silent step, smiling, wreathing their arms and blowing kisses, all of which is the ballet-language for 'Don't be afraid, we will protect you,' and danced away again wagging their finger at a particular one of their vis-à-vis, who was also curtsying and smiling in the most engaging manner on the other side. During this prelude Idealism, Self-Righteousness and a one-eyed hidden Fiddler called Statecraft, played a few conventional variations on the well-known diplomatic hymn to Peace, to which the Nations pirouetted unconcernedly about, although Fear, with Suspicion and Panic, were beginning to whistle and to thump on that mediæval tocsin-bell concealed in greasy newspapers.

And as the Smallest-of-all-the-Corps-de-Ballet stood quite alone in the middle of the Western Stage, that same tall and very well-trained Dancer sidled up to it with polite gestures of 'by your leave', and, suddenly placing his colossal horny paws on the Tiny One's shoulders, prepared for leap-frog. But at a sign from Death's bâton, and with a hideous crash of all the instruments of Satan's orchestra, and a magnificent note from Heroism's clear voice, the poor Smallest-Dancer-of-All tripped up that Giant and made him reel. But the Giant instantly recovered his feet, although his eyes became bloodshot and his brain swam. And, flinging the poor Smallest-Dancer on the floor, he set to performing on its poor little body one of the most terrific *pas seuls* that Ballet-Master Death had ever invented, while the vis-à-vis Nations danced slowly up, till they all came to grips over that Smallest-of-all-the-Dancers, who lay prone on the ground, and continued so to lie, pounded out of all human shape into a dancing-mat for the others.

'This first figure of our Ballet,' said the world's Impresario Satan, rising from his seat and bowing to the audience, that is to say, the Nations who wouldn't dance, and the sleepy Virtues and the Centuries-to-Come; 'this first figure of our Ballet is called *The Defence of the Weak*. It will continue unremittingly at the Western End of the Stage, while the Eastern End is occupied by a not entirely symmetrical (for symmetry is apt to be *fade*) choreographic invention called the *Steam-Roller Movement*, which will end up in the Triumph of such small Nationalities (and I sincerely hope many will join!) as may have any limbs left to dance with.'

During this first figure of the Ballet the scenery of that Western End of the Stage had undergone a slow change, and continued changing in a manner such that the Ages-to-Come, seated among the audience, admitted to one another these new scenic displays surpassed all others with which the courtesy of Satan had wiled away their *ennui*. For, whereas the Ballet had begun with the tender radiance of an August sunset above half-harvested fields, where the reaping machines hummed peacefully among the corn-stooks and the ploughs cut into the stubble, the progress of the performance had seen the deep summer starlit vault lit up by the flare of distant blazing farms, and its blue solemnity rent by the fitful rocket-tracks of shells and the Roman-candles and Catherine-wheels of far-off explosions. Until, little by little, the heavens, painted such a peaceful blue, were blotted out by volumes of flamelit smoke and poisonous vapours, rising and sinking, coming forward and receding like a stifling fog, but ever growing denser and more blinding, and swaying obedient to Death's bâton no less than did the bleeding Nations of his Corps-de-Ballet. In and out of that lurid chasm they moved, by twos or threes, now lost to view in the billows of darkness, now issuing thence towards the Ballet-Master's desk; or suddenly revealed, clasped in terrific embrace, by the meteor-curve of a shell or the leaping flame of an exploding munition-magazine, while overhead fluttered and whirred great wings which showered down bomb-lightnings. Backwards and forwards moved the Dancers in that changing play of light and darkness, and undergoing uncertain and fearful changes of aspect.

Since, you should know, that Nations, contrary to the opinion of Politicians, are immortal. Just as the Gods of Valhalla could slash each other to ribbons after breakfast and resurrect for dinner, so every Nation can dance Death's Dance however much bled and maimed, dance upon stumps, or trail itself along, a living jelly of blood and trampled flesh, providing only it has its Head fairly unhurt. And that Head, which each Nation calls its Government, but the other Nations call 'France', or 'Russia', or 'Britain', or 'Germany', or 'Austria' for short, that Head of each Dancing Nation (except that of the Smallest-Dancer, who never ceased being prostrate on the ground) is very properly helmetted, and rarely gets so much as a scratch, so that it can continue to catch the Ballet-Master's eye, and order the Nation's body to put forth fresh limbs and, even when that is impossible, keep its stump dancing ever new figures in obedience or disobedience to what are called the Rules of War. This being the case, Death kept up the dance regardless of the state of the Dancers, and also of the state of the Stage, which was such that, what between blood and entrails and heaps of devastated properties, it was barely possible to move even a few yards.

Yet dance they did, lopping each others' limbs and blinding one another with spirts of blood and pellets of human flesh. And as they appeared and disappeared in the moving wreaths of fiery smoke, they lost more and more of their original shape, becoming, in that fitful light, terrible uncertain forms, armless, legless, recognisable for human only by their irreproachable-looking heads which they carried stiff and high even while crawling and staggering along, lying in wait, and leaping and rearing and butting as do fighting animals; until they became, with those decorous well-groomed faces, mere unspeakable hybrids between man and beast, they who had come on to the stage so erect and beautiful. For the Ballet of the Nations, when Satan gets it up regardless of expense, is an unsurpassed spectacle of transformations, such as must be witnessed to be believed in.

Thus on they danced their stranger and stranger antics. And, as they appeared by turns in that chaos of flame and darkness, each of those Dancing Nations kept invoking Satan, crying out to him, 'Help me, my own dear Lord.' But they called him by Another Name.

And Satan, that creative Connoisseur, rejoiced in his work and saw that it was very good.

'Dear Creatures,' he murmured to himself, where he throned invisible above the audience of Neutral Peoples and Sleepy Virtues and Ages-to-Come, 'how true it is that great artistic exhibitions, especially when they address themselves to the Group-Emotion, invariably bring home to the Nations that there is, after all, a Power transcending their ephemeral existence! Indeed that is one reason why I prefer the Ballet of the Nations to any of the other mystery-plays, like Earthquake and Pestilence, which Death puts on our stage from time to time. The music is not always very pretty, at once too archaic and too ultra-modern for philistine taste, and the steps are a trifle monotonous. But it gives immense scope for moral beauty, and revives religious feeling in all its genuine primeval polytheism. It answers perfectly to what the Spaniards call an *Auto Sacramental*, a sacred drama having all the attractions of a bull-fight. I grant the Heads of the Nations are occasionally a bit hard-featured. But the Bodies of the Nations are always sound and virginal; and their heart is always in the right place. And for true sublimity,' purred Satan gently on his invisible throne, 'give me, I always say, one of Death's dances performed by Nations each with its heart absolutely in the right place, and perfectly obedient to its traditional Head.'

So the Ballet went on. But for this it was necessary to keep up the music of that orchestra of Passions and Habits which sat around the slippery and reeking stage: Widow Fear with her nimble children, Suspicion and Panic, playing on penny-whistles, foghorns and that mediæval tocsin-bell in its wrapper of newspapers; Idealism and Adventure, that splendid pair, blowing their silver trumpet and woodland horn; Hatred, who was always tuning afresh at the harmonium of Self-Righteousness; Sin, whom the Gods call Disease, and her classic crew Rapine, Lust and Murder, with their cannibal band of bull-roarers and rattles; Science and Organisation seated a little apart, for none of the others liked their new-fangled looks, but whose gramophone and pianola went on unflaggingly when all the other musicians began showing signs of fatigue; and only Heroism, a smile in his clear blind eyes, found ever fresh breath and ever more jubilant notes.

I have just said that the rest of the band were beginning to flag; either because the Passions are notoriously deficient in staying-power, or because, in the case of the less noble ones, they had fuddled themselves with the strong liquor of literature from Satan's tap-room, and were coming in all at random, Suspicion and Panic, notably, deafening the Heads of the Nations, and Fear, poor slut, being seized with *delirium tremens*. None of these things were noticed by the Dancers, but they danced a little less fiercely, and began mistaking their vis-à-vis for partners and vice versa, to the despair of the Ballet-Master, who wheeled from side to side at his desk, cracking his fleshless joints like castagnettes, and hitting the somnolent Human Motives of the orchestra tremendous whacks with his bâton of

fire-hardened root-of-prejudice. But Satan began to fear lest the performance might end untimely, for, except the voice of Heroism and the
mechanical instruments of Science and Organisation, the sounds were
getting feeble and intermittent, and the Nations were beginning to halt and
stumble, and even to curtsy to each other as if the end might be at hand.

'This will never do,' said Satan to himself. 'Why! we haven't yet come to
the figure of Famine and Insurrection!' So, beckoning with his arch-angelic
claw to the followers of Sin, he whispered Rapine, Murder and Lust to fetch
him two new players from among the Sleepy Virtues of the Audience.

Sleepy indeed they seemed, and some, like Wisdom, Equanimity and
Temperance, let alone Truthfulness, had long since fallen into consoling
dreams, after closing their eyes and bunging-up their ears against sights and
sounds repugnant to their principles, but which they had not grit enough to
interrupt. But among the Virtues two were not asleep, and sat motionless
under the spell of hideous fascination; their eyes fixed, their hearing intent,
with horror so great it almost turned to pleasure. These two were called Pity
and Indignation, sister and brother of divinest breed; she, wan like waters
under moonlight and as gentle, murmurous and lovely, and also, like such
waters, dangerous in her innocence. The other, golden and vivid as flame,
and like flame, tipped with terrible scarlet, purifying but devastating.

To them, who were fascinated with horror before that dance, there
sprang, at Satan's bidding, Rapine, Murder and Lust, the crew of Death's
Mother-Paramour Sin, whom the Gods call Disease. And straightway that
noble pair of twins, Pity and Indignation, responded to the hideous summons. Hand in hand they leaped from among the sleeping Virtues, and flew,
on rushing pinions, into the midst of Satan's orchestra. Fear and her brood
fell back. Idealism and Adventure, by this time wellnigh spent with breathless blowing of their silver trumpet and hunting-horn, eagerly made room
for them. Heroism, that blind, smiling young giant, recognised at once
Pity's delicious healing breath and Indignation's fiery blast; he shook himself, and with renewed vigour his godlike youthful voice sang out words
which no one distinguished but all the world understood. And Sin, with
her crew, fell down at the new-comers' feet and fawned upon them.

Even before either of that immortal pair had uttered a sound, the flagging
Dancers, the bleeding Nations, weary of that stage slippery with blood and
entrails, felt the wind of the wings of Pity and Indignation; and, in its pure
breath, suddenly revived.

The holy pair required no instruments. Pity merely sobbed, and her sobs
were like the welling-up notes of many harps, drowning the soul in tender
madness. But Indignation hissed and roared like a burning granary when

the sparks crackle as they fly into the ripe standing harvest, and the flames wave scores of feet high in the blast of their own making.

Death was overpowered with delight.

'Now nothing can stop the dancing,' he cried; 'and this shall yet be the greatest triumph of Ballet-Master Death!' and, rapping on his desk, spoke as follows: 'Ladies and Gentlemen, dear valiant Nations of my Corps-de-Ballet! we will now proceed to the third and last figure; the last because, as you know, it is made never to end! For it is called *Revenge.*'

'You might have trusted to me, dear Ballet-Master Death,' purred Satan, the World's great Stage-Lessee, quite softly to himself. 'Pity and Indignation can renew Death's dance when all the Nations have danced themselves to stumps, and the ordinary band, except perhaps Fear and her Children, can fiddle and blow no longer.'

And thus the Ballet of the Nations is still a-dancing.

> Vernon Lee, *The Ballet of the Nations: A Present Day Morality with a Pictorial Commentary by Maxwell Armfield* (London: Chatto & Windus, 1915)

Claire Goll
(1891–1977)

The daughter of wealthy Jewish parents, Claire Goll spent an unhappy childhood in Nuremberg. After a brief first marriage she went to Geneva to study philosophy. During the war she became interested in Expressionism and pacifism and met her future husband the poet Ivan Goll. Much of her subsequent work was done in collaboration with him. After his death Goll resumed her own literary career publishing poetry, stories, and a series of autobiographical texts. The following story comes from a collection of war stories entitled *Die Frauen erwachen* (*Women Awake*), first published in 1918 in Switzerland.

---

48   THE HAND OF WAX

THE train disgorged its passengers; hordes upon hordes of soldiers—among the very first, a young officer, his eyes searching. On the platform stood his young wife, similarly searching, anxious. When their eyes met fear shot through her like an electric shock. Her glance fell to the level of his hand and remained there as if glued to it, so that he began to move it uncomfortably to and fro. Like a white animal, pale and ghostlike, the hand seemed to her to creep out of his sleeve. A hand made of wax. A poisonous flower budding out of him. The woman trembled as she imagined being accidentally touched by it. He made his way towards her, slowly, as if to give her time to get accustomed to this hand. She pulled herself together and hid behind a smile which was meant to be warm. They embraced. Hastily she began to pour over him a stream of words about their happy reunion. But it was as if between them there lay some invisible obstacle and not just a year spent apart.

She stood by the window, glancing absentmindedly down to the road. Even more distractedly she picked up something black from the floor and returned to the room. Somehow she felt broken, tired. But why now? Now that she would no longer have to wait for the bell to ring, for a bell to toll, whenever the postman called? Now that there were no longer any lonely nights, where black boats under fluttering sails of fear sped along a sea red with war. Now that this room was no longer a darkened stage of despair on which her overwrought imagination pictured her husband dancing, puppet-like, amongst the gruesome props of war. Now that madness and chance had settled for his hand. Now that nothing connected her any longer with the massacre. What? Did she not see, just now, two young girls glide past her window in a cloud of deepest mourning? Did nothing connect her to them any more?

On the contrary! For all eternity she must share the pain with those living dead who still continued to listen into every night, capable only of keeping vigil: a trembling mother who, having already lost everything, now awaits the moment when they come to take away the last of her sons who is still half a child. Children, cheated of their childhood, which for the last three years has been hemmed in by shadows; children growing up with neither feast nor laugh. And brides robbed of their lovers, whose future has been stolen and whose lives lie in ruins.

In the depth of her heart she despised this pointless martyrdom, these dishonourable heroics which consisted of plunging human beings like herself into despair. Many like her recognized the absurdity of this blind subordination to an obsolete patriotic impulse. Yet they all seemed to lack the courage to speak out against this undignified submission of mankind to a uniform demanded by a group of cynics hidden behind a wall of bodies; against that urge to lay down one's life in the name of some rhetoric, some inherited phrase, some grand word one never once questioned as one grew up. Thus she thought as she stood there while over there was her husband Marc with his fervent allegiance to convention. How was she ever going to breach this chasm and find her way back to the innocent happiness of her first year of married life? She now felt dull and heavy, almost hostile towards him. Since he had always been straight and clear in everything, she had been careful never to surprise or frighten him with her true self. At all times she would close the door behind her, and when she approached him, she had left the true Ines, of whom he knew nothing, elsewhere. She had always controlled herself for him, and thus he hardly knew her, though he must have felt that they did not truly meet on the bridge of their words. Should she now continue to deceive him with her silence and betray her other self in favour of the one he wanted? If she did not speak out on this first day, she would have to keep her peace for ever after and for the rest of their lives they would move past each other like strangers.

When he entered the room she knew she would have to speak.

Against the dark shade of the civilian suit which he had just put on, the artificial hand looked even more grotesque. For her the hand had become a gruesome symbol which would always remind her of the corpses which stood between him and her.

With a sudden surge of courage she reached her decision. Carefully, tentatively, she approached him: 'Do you know, Marc, that I suffer just as much over our victories as over our defeats? As our flags fly against the sky I see our enemy kneeling down in pain into the earth.'

He couldn't quite believe he had heard right. Earnestly, he reprimanded her: 'Ines, how can you, now that famine and death for which the enemy is responsible creep through our cities, now that many of us lie dying, how can you betray us with your compassion?'

She became more precise: 'Famine for women and the children, or death by water and fire—it is all the same. We are all equally guilty as long as we are full of hate. Hence I am neither for us nor for them but against murder. Every one of our victories I see as a defeat because it merely proves that we are better at killing.'

Completely taken aback now he raised his voice: 'These are shameful pacifist ideas, Ines. I will not permit them!'

'Permit them? The year I spent on my own has been stronger than you!' she replied harshly.

He too became harsh and played his trump card: 'Is this the thanks we get for sacrificing our hand on the altar of the fatherland?'

Thus confronted she remained silent. How often in future would the hand and his heroism be used against her?

She thought aloud: 'Oh, we are but the pretext for your sacrifice! Why do you insist on shielding us with your bodies instead of your spirit? Why do human beings protect themselves by murdering other human beings? As if true heroism resided in brute force and numerical superiority and not in the ability to love.' She thus continued to shock him and knew that her marriage was now on the line.

At last he took her seriously. Slighted in his status as hero, he spoke to her sharply: 'We are men. We do not fight with our hearts but with arms. We kill in self-defence and to protect ourselves. And we protect you and the fatherland with our very lives. It is a sacred duty and an honour and it is not for nothing that we receive our prize.' He proudly pointed to his Iron Cross.

She looked at it with contempt. For her there was an iron wall between them. There was something alien and harsh in her eyes as she looked at him. It irritated him and a poisonous feeling welled up in him. First that awkward welcome and now these speeches! Even without them he felt deeply offended that she so completely ignored his martyrdom. He grinned cruelly. He wanted to punish her. Get her where it hurt.

Slowly, harmlessly, he began:

'It is just as well that you were not asked to fight out there! Clearly you would have wanted to spare the French fools too, weird crackpots that they are. No doubt halfway through the battle you would have felt like fraternizing with them.' He waited.

After a while, out of her corner in the room she asked: 'What do you mean?'

He searched for smooth words with which to torture her: 'During my last battle, in the thundering chaos of an offensive, I suddenly found myself in a clearing, a quiet little enclave surrounded by death. In front of me there stood this man holding a bayonet. Immobile, like an apparition. Out of his dreamy face two large blue eyes looked at me. On his lips which nearly smiled there hovered a plea. His eyes burrowed into mine, questioning, almost tenderly. Something inexplicable was happening between us. For a moment I could see only a human being and forgot the enemy. I saw the ring on his finger, imagined his wife. And for a few seconds—the whole episode took no longer than that—I softened. Then, suddenly from behind I heard my people approach. I heard the screams, the sighs and came to my senses. "Traitor!" I shouted at myself and all tenderness vanished. Automatically I pulled my revolver, expecting his defence. He stood immobile. "Coward!" I yelled and then pulled the trigger. His bayonet fell first. Contorted by mortal pain he looked at me, incredulous, and with outstretched arms as if in a fraternal gesture, he fell grotesquely against my chest. Before I could distentangle myself, the heavens opened and blackness fell upon us: a grenade. It crushed my hand . . . ' He stopped and suddenly began to tremble.

His story had an unexpected reaction. He had wanted to chastise Ines for her lack of faith but achieved the opposite. Her face was white and contorted. Words rushed from her mouth, hunting around, lashing out at him: 'You, you, you are a . . . You saw the ring on his finger, you saw the woman who every night waited for him, who believed in his life, in his return, and you killed him! You saw the children who, every night, pleaded for him with praying hands, and you killed him all the same! You are no better than a common murderer!'

Like stones she threw the words at him: 'A murderer, that's what you are!' With this sentence she broke through the protective wall of phrases which he, and millions of other men, had built around his deeds in order to drown out his screaming heart.

'A man tried to stand apart from the concept "enemy", a fellow human being offered himself up to you and you felt his brotherhood. You did not destroy a uniform but a life and with it a second one, that of his wife, a woman who will be devastated over the fact that you have become a hero. You murderer—murderer!'

She stood tall in her new self-realization.

Taken completely aback, he let her talk, shaken rigid with consternation. Then his anger flared up. He rushed towards her instinctively lifting his right hand. 'Your hand!' she screamed. At the last moment he withdrew it and ran out of the room. The door fell shut; the door between them. She knew it was the door to her marriage.

Her face was like a mask of stone. That hand had rendered it thus. A sudden desperate astonishment rent her apart, shook her. Why did she say all this now and not sooner? Why had she not talked to him of wives and mothers when he left? Was he indeed alone the guilty one? Why did she let him go? Why didn't all the women throw themselves in front of the trains instead of laughing, waving and sticking flowers into their men's guns? Women had always known about other men's wives and mothers. Why then, did the mothers of all men not unite in resistance to this madness?

Weren't they thus even more responsible for the collapse of their world than the men? Always acquiescent, weak and passive, women, who were supposed to live for love, seemed incapable of smoothing over the harshness of their men, of building bridges over the torrents of bellicose impulses and the violence which tears peoples apart.

Instead of teaching their sons to be brothers, women tolerate doctrines which divide their children into friends and foes. Ines saw herself assailed by more and more accusations: 'Men are supposed to be the spirit, women the heart of the world. Yet we remain silent when the children born of us are being sacrificed and become heroes as they learn to perfect the art of killing. And still we women say nothing. They refused us the dubious honour of going to war but not once did we avail ourselves of the much greater honour of mounting a campaign against it. We remained silent. We said nothing. It is we who carry the greater part of the responsibility!'

The thought struck to the centre of her being. Out of nowhere she saw a hand floating threateningly towards her: the solemn accusation of the dead. She too must carry her guilt. Crying uncontrollably, she collapsed onto the floor.

During the night, with eyes wide open, she kept vigil over her exhausted husband's sleep. She was no longer the same woman as yesterday: the murdered man was in her heart. Heavy and hard as stone, it lay inside her like a rock surrounded by a sea of fear. With every beat this man entered deeper into her consciousness, pulsating, giving off signals far beyond his death, filling the whole night. He demanded her. Everywhere in the darkness her searching eyes met him, the walls became the backdrop for his image which threatened to engulf her and the room became a tomb. All rooms were now tombs where women slept with shades whose lives had been lost because of their silence. The entire town was one huge cemetery.

Faster and faster her heart began to beat in the dark room in which she lay alone with her conscience. She groaned and turned over when, suddenly, her hand came into contact with something smooth and soft which glowed white between the beds on the bedside table. The hand! The hand of wax! Her husband must have secretly taken it off and put it there! As if by chance it lay there, bent at the wrist, so that all its protruding fingers seemed to be pointing at her. Every woman now had such a dead man's hand next to her bed. It separated her from her husband, threatened her and grew larger in the night. It was the new emblem under which they all now went to sleep.

Beside herself with terror she curled up. The hand filled the entire room, every one of its fingers pointing at her with an accusing: You!

Her fear grew monstrous. The hand began to creep up on her. Any moment now it was going to touch her. It was going to lie on top of her for the rest of night, every night. She would have to sleep with it for the rest of her life. A scream began to rise in her. Her anguish extended itself over her whole existence like a rope on which she must dance towards that dead man. There was but one escape.

Quietly, on her toes, she crept past her sleeping husband into the next room. She unlocked a small casket and, from a black wrapper on which there grinned a white skull, she carefully unpeeled a small round pill. Faintly pink, it looked like candy. She threw it into a glass of water and then locked herself into an adjacent room so that her screams would not be heard. Her face grew composed as she drank it down slowly and to the last drop.

> Claire Goll, 'Die Wachshand', trans. Agnès Cardinal, from *Die Frauen erwachen* (Frauenfeld: Huber & Cie, 1918), 11–27; also in Gisela Brinker-Gabler (ed.), *Frauen gegen den Krieg* (Frankfurt-on-Main: Fischer, 1980), 58–64

Constance Holme
(1880–1955)

The youngest of fourteen children, Constance Holme lived all her life in Owlet Ash, Westmoreland. In 1916 she married Frederick Punchard and in 1919 established herself as a writer of note by winning the French literary prize *Femina Vie Heureuse* with *The Splendid Faring*. A prolific writer, she consolidated her literary reputation with novels such as *The Trumpet in the Dust* (1921), *The Lonely Plough* (1931), *Beautiful End* (1935) as well as many short stories, some of which Oxford University Press included in its World Classics series. The following text is taken from *The Wisdom of the Simple and Other Stories* of 1937.

—————

49   SPEEDING UP, 1917

BECAUSE Death has quickened his pace, we, too, must run fast. We must speed up our lives to escape him, and at the next corner we shall run into his arms. But those that come after will meet him only at the end of the long lane, in the sunset.

The ordinary pageant of death is quickened insanely, like cinema-pictures speeded beyond truth. The living must move at cinema-speed, too. They race through their hasty days, and cannot dream through their scamped nights. They tear through the veil of mystery that hides their coming, and are gone again before the rents are closed.

In factory and office, yard and mine, they have worked double tides.

Armies were made between the winter sowing and the spring. Then they came to the land, and said 'Speed up the land'.

But they could not speed up Nature. There were snow and frost and big winds and snow again, and always when the land was loosed a little, the frost returned. When at last it eased off, they sent ploughs that hurried behind machines and huge wheels, bumping and tearing up the land. In near fields they were ploughing with horses, smooth as gliding keels, in a cloud of gulls so thick that you could hear the wings brush as they passed; and in all the furrows were little birds. But where they speeded up the land there was neither gull nor little bird.

And then there was more snow. . . .

They have speeded the plough, but they cannot speed the green shoots for the ewes and the young lambs. They turn the furrow, but they cannot quicken the seed. The buds have not hastened a whit for the frenzied rush of man, nor the coloured crocus-carpets over the lawns. Only in the appointed time the little cypress and the weeping ash stood charmed in a ring of snowdrops round their feet.

They have speeded our daylight. Our racing lives shall see longer days and fewer moons. The clocks strike wrong against the sun. But the shadows lie where they used to do at the hour of worship. The rooks go home as of old.

Constance Holme, 'Speeding Up, 1917', from *The Wisdom of the Simple and Other Stories* (London: Oxford University Press, World's Classics, 1937), 176–7

Florence Kiper Frank
(1885–1976)

Florence Kiper Frank was born in Kansas and educated at the University of Chicago. She wrote poetry, plays (including plays for children), and reviews for major journals such as the *Bookman*, the *Nation*, the *New Republic*, and the *New York Herald Tribune*. Before the war she was a member of the Chicago Literary Circle among whose members were Sherwood Anderson, Edgar Lee Masters, and Amy Lowell. Florence Kiper Frank had a long writing career: her first published work was in 1904, her last in 1956. 'War Impressions' appeared in the *Little Review*, a journal founded by Margaret

Anderson which published many of the major modernist writers—Joyce, Eliot, Pound, H.D., Dorothy Richardson, Gertrude Stein, and William Carlos Williams. The Modernist affiliations of the piece are clear.

---

50   THE MOVING-PICTURE SHOW

WE sat at a moving-picture show. Over a little bridge streamed the Belgian refugees, women, children, boys, dogs, horses, carts, household goods—an incongruous procession. The faces were stolid, the feet plodded on— plodded on!

'See!' said my friend, 'sometimes a woman turns to look at a bursting shell.'

I murmured, 'How interesting!'

And my soul shuddered. It shuddered at sophistication.

The man who had taken the pictures told us about them. He had been not more than three weeks ago in Belgium. . . .

'Huzza!' sang my ancestor of five thousand years back. He led a band of marauders into an enemy's village. They ripped things up and tore about the place singing and looting. There was nothing much left to that village by the time they got through with it.

But the people many miles away did not behold his exploits. Alas, there were no moving-picture shows in those days!

Florence Kiper Frank, from 'War Impressions', *Little Review*, 2 (Aug. 1915), 11

Phyllis Campbell

Phyllis Campbell is on record as having written two novels—*Lined with Rags* and *The White Hen*, both published by Mills & Boon in 1920. These, together with *Back of the Front* (1915), might suggest a prolific young writer—however, there is little biographical information to confirm this. *Back of the Front* is primarily an account of Campbell's experience of the early phase of the war: her hasty removal from school in Germany and her work assisting the wounded in France, near the battle zone. The memoir also records soldiers' stories of visions, while under fire, of St Michael and Joan of Arc. A preface attests to the authenticity of Campbell's record and appears to rebut charges of sensationalism. Yet the way it is produced—as one of a series of stirring and fantastical war-stories—suggests that it may also be seen as a parallel to Arthur Machen's *The Angel of Mons*. Campbell's account is striking for its ability to express the haunting and dream-like nature of the arrival of the convoys of the wounded and the almost hallucinatory states of mind they produced in those caring for them.

———

51   BACK OF THE FRONT

HUDDLED together at the very end of the platform was a company of children of different ages, and sitting with his back to the wall was an old man with a little boy of about five in his arms. Latty knelt down beside him and talked to him soothingly, but the old man made no sign he had heard her. Every now and again he would pat the child's back with a shrivelled hand as if to make sure he was there—staring blankly in front of him the while. Suddenly his arms relaxed and he fell sideways down, and the child rolled over, but the child's body fell one way and its little golden dusty head another—it was almost severed from its body. For one moment I felt as if I were walking on air and that the top of my head was lifting and falling on again—then I was horribly sick. Two soldiers carried the bodies away. . . .

In my childhood and up till last year, I have had a sort of recurring nightmare. I used to dream I was standing in a little lonely station in a forest, waiting for a train—the railway line ran out of the forest on one side, and into it again on the other—and I waited for something. Something terrible, and harmful, that was to arrive at the platform. Presently a train would come creeping, creeping, out of the dark trees towards me, and as it came a sound would run before it of sobbing and wailing—a sound so terrifying that I would wake dripping with terror, and shriek for protection.

On this night of my birthday I had all the feeling of that dream. There was a *majeur* in charge of the Post and several assistants in addition to the *ambulanciers* and a long table on trestles stood between the little waiting-room and the canteen. There were piles of shrouded bandages, utensils, and sterilisers, and rows of bottles and basins. We were given little paper lanterns, such as are used for the decorations of Christmas trees, and told to light them when the train came in—there was no other light allowed—and in the meantime there was the moonlight.

The heat was intense—it was unnatural heat, it made even thinking impossible, perhaps fortunately. Raoul stood beside me, and gave me his good wishes, and while he talked I saw the train of my dreams come slowly crawling, creeping out of the forest towards the platform, and before it came a low awful crying—inarticulate and wild. All the blood in my body seemed to leap into my head, and I turned to fly—anywhere—anywhere away from that crying.

Raoul laid a hand on my arm, and I came back to myself. He lit my lantern and his own, and I moved to Latty's side as the train came to a standstill.

The train was made up of cattle boxes, heaped with men. Some of the doors were shut to, and a red stream oozed slowly under them. Others were open with a little straw here and there *over* the wounded. As the train drew up before us Latty and I were facing an open waggon. At one side of the door sat a soldier who had lost both his legs, he was supporting a boy whose arms were gone, both were bleeding copiously and unconscious—and as I followed Latty with the *pansement* box, the cry of the wounded resolved itself into words. '*A boire! A boire! A boire!*' 'A drink! A drink!'

In all the horrors of that night the cry for water clings most in my memory. How long these poor shattered soldiermen had been lying there, heaped up, many dying with the dead, we never knew. Nor did we even know from whence came that first terrible load of suffering.

At sight of them most of the Post had fled. But Latty, who had the blood of heroes in her veins, showed them what the woman of the old French Noblesse is made of. Her big eyes brimmed over once, and it was done with, this was no time for tears or fears. Nothing dismayed her, and at her order I became like herself. Climbing into waggons ankle-deep in blood and bandaging hideous wounds almost in the dark, giving drink and food, washing aching bodies coated with blood and dust, cutting off soleless boots and washing the feet that had worn them out. Talking, encouraging, feeding them, carrying out the dead and laying them in stark rows at the back of the platform. All in racing time—not an instant—not a second to lose.

I saw Nancy and Aunt Margaret in their red-stained dresses flying here and there, and suddenly I found myself transferred from Latty to the *majeur*, and carrying his boxes and bottles, following him through the dark waggons.

It was the dream—the dreadful, dreadful dream; I had always known that train would come in. But alas! it was only the first of a long series. The driver with the bandaged head, having eaten and drunk, climbed into the

engine again and slowly, slowly, the train of sorrows crept out into the darkness of the forest again.

The *majeur* bundled up the instruments Latty had sterilised for him, we
washed and sterilised the basins, scrubbed out the waiting-room and the
canteen, and never said a word to each other. The *majeur* shook hands
with me.

Phyllis Campbell, from *Back of the Front* (London: Newnes, 1915), 29, 60–3

Katherine Mansfield
(1888–1923)

Born in New Zealand, Katherine Mansfield spent most of her life in Europe
and died of tuberculosis in France. Her reputation rests almost entirely on her
short stories, many of which look back to her life in New Zealand. Some of her
later stories (for example, 'Six Years After' and 'The Fly'), reflect, in hind-
sight, on the war's emotional effect. By contrast, the following story,
'An Indiscreet Journey', is based on Mansfield's direct experience—a journey
in 1915 to the French town of Gray, forbidden to women visitors as it was in the
Zone des Armées, and a sexual escapade with Corporal Francis Carco.

52   AN INDISCREET JOURNEY

I

SHE is like St Anne. Yes, the concierge is the image of St Anne, with that
black cloth over her head, the wisps of grey hair hanging, and the tiny
smoking lamp in her hand. Really very beautiful, I thought, smiling at
St Anne, who said severely: 'Six o'clock. You have only just got time. There
is a bowl of milk on the writing-table.' I jumped out of my pyjamas and into
a basin of cold water like any English lady in any French novel. The
concierge, persuaded that I was on my way to prison cells and death by
bayonets, opened the shutters and the cold clear light came through. A
little steamer hooted on the river; a cart with two horses at a gallop flung
past. The rapid swirling water; the tall black trees on the far side, grouped

together like negroes conversing. Sinister, very, I thought, as I buttoned on my age-old Burberry. (That Burberry was very significant. It did not belong to me. I had borrowed it from a friend. My eye lighted upon it hanging in her little dark hall. The very thing! The perfect and adequate disguise—an old Burberry. Lions have been faced in a Burberry. Ladies have been rescued from open boats in mountainous seas wrapped in nothing else. An old Burberry seems to me the sign and the token of the undisputed venerable traveller, I decided, leaving my purple peg-top with the real seal collar and cuffs in exchange.)

'You will never get there,' said the concierge, watching me turn up the collar. 'Never! Never!' I ran down the echoing stairs—strange they sounded, like a piano flicked by a sleepy housemaid—and on to the Quai. 'Why so fast, *ma mignonne?*' said a lovely little boy in coloured socks, dancing in front of the electric lotus buds that curve over the entrance to the Métro. Alas! there was not even time to blow him a kiss. When I arrived at the big station I had only four minutes to spare, and the platform entrance was crowded and packed with soldiers, their yellow papers in one hand and big untidy bundles. The Commissaire of Police stood on one side, a Nameless Official on the other. Will he let me pass? Will he? He was an old man with a fat swollen face covered with big warts. Horn-rimmed spectacles squatted on his nose. Trembling, I made an effort. I conjured up my sweetest early-morning smile and handed it with the papers. But the delicate thing fluttered against the horn spectacles and fell. Nevertheless, he let me pass, and I ran, ran in and out among the soldiers and up the high steps into the yellow-painted carriage.

'Does one go direct to X.?' I asked the collector who dug at my ticket with a pair of forceps and handed it back again. 'No, Mademoiselle, you must change at X.Y.Z.'

'At—?'

'X.Y.Z.'

Again I had not heard. 'At what time do we arrive there, if you please?'

'One o'clock.' But that was no good to me. I hadn't a watch. Oh, well—later.

Ah! the train had begun to move. The train was on my side. It swung out of the station, and soon we were passing the vegetable gardens, passing the tall, blind houses to let, passing the servants beating carpets. Up already and walking in the fields, rosy from the rivers and the red-fringed pools, the sun lighted upon the swinging train and stroked my muff and told me to take off that Burberry. I was not alone in the carriage. An old woman sat opposite, her skirt turned back over her knees, a bonnet of black lace on her head. In her fat hands, adorned with a wedding and two mourning rings, she held a letter. Slowly, slowly she sipped a sentence, and then looked up and out of the window, her lips trembling a little, and then another sentence, and again the old face turned to the light, tasting it . . . Two soldiers leaned out of the window, their heads nearly touching—one of them was whistling, the other had his coat fastened with some rusty safety-pins. And now there were soldiers everywhere working on the railway line, leaning against trucks or standing hands on hips, eyes fixed on the train as though they expected at least one camera at every window. And now we were passing big wooden sheds like rigged-up dancing halls or seaside pavilions, each flying a flag. In and out of them walked the Red Cross men; the wounded sat against the walls sunning themselves. At all the bridges, the crossings, the stations, a *petit soldat*, all boots and bayonet. Forlorn and desolate he looked, like a little comic picture waiting for the joke to be written underneath. Is there really such a thing as war? Are all these laughing voices really going to the war? These dark woods lighted so mysteriously by the white stems of the birch and the ash—these watery fields with the big birds flying over—these rivers green and blue in the light—have battles been fought in places like these?

What beautiful cemeteries we are passing! They flash gay in the sun. They seem to be full of cornflowers and poppies and daisies. How can there be so many flowers at this time of the year? But they are not flowers at all. They are bunches of ribbons tied on to the soldiers' graves.

I glanced up and caught the old woman's eye. She smiled and folded the letter. 'It is from my son—the first we have had since October. I am taking it to my daughter-in-law.'

'. . .?'

'Yes, very good,' said the old woman, shaking down her skirt and putting her arm through the handle of her basket. 'He wants me to send him some handkerchiefs and a piece of stout string.'

What is the name of the station where I have to change? Perhaps I shall never know. I got up and leaned my arms across the window rail, my feet crossed. One cheek burned as in infancy on the way to the seaside. When the war is over I shall have a barge and drift along these rivers with a white cat and a pot of mignonette to bear me company.

Down the side of the hill filed the troops, winking red and blue in the light. Far away, but plainly to be seen, some more flew by on bicycles. But really, *ma France adorée*, this uniform is ridiculous. Your soldiers are stamped upon your bosom like bright irreverent transfers.

The train slowed down, stopped. . . . Everybody was getting out except me. A big boy, his sabots tied to his back with a piece of string, the inside of his tin wine cup stained a lovely impossible pink, looked very friendly. Does one change here perhaps for X.? Another whose képi had come out of a wet paper cracker swung my suit-case to earth. What darlings soldiers are! *'Merci bien, Monsieur, vous êtes tout à fait aimable. . . .'* 'Not this way,' said a bayonet. 'Nor this,' said another. So I followed the crowd. 'Your passport, Mademoiselle. . . .' *'We, Sir Edward Grey . . .'* I ran through the muddy square and into the buffet.

A green room with a stove jutting out and tables on each side. On the counter, beautiful with coloured bottles, a woman leans, her breasts in her folded arms. Through an open door I can see a kitchen, and the cook in a white coat breaking eggs into a bowl and tossing the shells into a corner. The blue and red coats of the men who are eating hang upon the walls. Their short swords and belts are piled upon chairs. Heavens! what a noise. The sunny air seemed all broken up and trembling with it. A little boy, very pale, swung from table to table, taking the orders, and poured me out a glass of purple coffee. *Ssssh*, came from the eggs. They were in a pan. The woman rushed from behind the counter and began to help the boy. *Toute de suite, tout' suite!* she chirruped to the loud impatient voices. There came a clatter of plates and the pop-pop of corks being drawn.

Suddenly in the doorway I saw someone with a pail of fish—brown speckled fish, like the fish one sees in a glass case, swimming through forests of beautiful pressed sea-weed. He was an old man in a tattered jacket, standing humbly, waiting for someone to attend to him. A thin beard fell over his chest, his eyes under the tufted eyebrows were bent on the pail he carried. He looked as though he had escaped from some holy picture, and was entreating the soldiers' pardon for being there at all. . . .

But what could I have done? I could not arrive at X. with two fishes hanging on a straw; and I am sure it is a penal offence in France to throw fish out of railway-carriage windows, I thought, miserably climbing into a smaller, shabbier train. Perhaps I might have taken them to—*ah, mon Dieu*—I had forgotten the name of my uncle and aunt again! Buffard, Buffon—what was it? Again I read the unfamiliar letter in the familiar handwriting.

'My dear Niece,

Now that the weather is more settled, your uncle and I would be charmed if you would pay us a little visit. Telegraph me when you are coming. I shall meet you outside the station if I am free. Otherwise our good friend,

Madame Grinçon, who lives in the little toll-house by the bridge, *juste en face de le gare*, will conduct you to our home. *Je vous embrasse bien tendrement*.

Julie Boiffard'

A visiting card was enclosed: *M. Paul Boiffard*.

Boiffard—of course that was the name. *Ma tante Julie et mon oncle Paul*—suddenly they were there with me, more real, more solid than any relations I had ever known. I saw *tante Julie* bridling, with the soup-tureen in her hands, and *oncle Paul* sitting at the table with a red and white napkin tied round his neck. Boiffard—Boiffard—I must remember the name. Supposing the Commissaire Militaire should ask me who the relations were I was going to and I muddled the name—Oh, how fatal! Buffard—no, Boiffard. And then for the first time, folding Aunt Julie's letter, I saw scrawled in a corner of the empty back page: *Venez vite, vite*. Strange impulsive woman! My heart began to beat. . . .

'Ah, we are not far off now,' said the lady opposite. 'You are going to X, Mademoiselle?'

'*Oui, Madame.*'

'I also. . . . You have been there before?'

'No, Madame. This is the first time.'

'Really, it is a strange time for a visit.'

I smiled faintly, and tried to keep my eyes off her hat. She was quite an ordinary little woman, but she wore a black velvet toque, with an incredibly surprised looking sea-gull camped on the very top of it. Its round eyes, fixed on me so inquiringly, were almost too much to bear. I had a dreadful impulse to shoo it away, or to lean forward and inform her of its presence. . . .

'*Excusez-moi, Madame*, but perhaps you have not remarked there is an *espèce de* sea-gull *couché sur votre chapeau.*'

Could the bird be there on purpose? I must not laugh. . . . I must not laugh. Had she ever looked at herself in a glass with that bird on her head?

'It is very difficult to get into X. at present, to pass the station,' she said, and she shook her head with the sea-gull at me. 'Ah, such an affair. One must sign one's name and state one's business.'

'Really, is it as bad as all that?'

'But naturally. You see the whole place is in the hands of the military, and'—she shrugged—'they have to be strict. Many people do not get beyond the station at all. They arrive. They are put in the waiting-room, and there they remain.'

Did I or did I not detect in her voice a strange, insulting relish?

'I suppose such strictness is absolutely necessary,' I said coldly, stroking my muff.

'Necessary,' she cried. 'I should think so. Why, Mademoiselle, you cannot imagine what it would be like otherwise! You know what women are like about soldiers'—she raised a final hand—'mad, completely mad. But—' and she gave a little laugh of triumph—'they could not get into X. *Mon Dieu*, no! There is no question about that.'

'I don't suppose they even try,' said I.

'Don't you?' said the sea-gull.

Madame said nothing for a moment. 'Of course the authorities are very hard on the men. It means instant imprisonment, and then—off to the firing-line without a word.'

'What are *you* going to X. for?' said the sea-gull. 'What on earth are *you* doing here?'

'Are you making a long stay in X., Mademoiselle?'

She had won, she had won. I was terrified. A lamp-post swam past the train with the fatal name upon it. I could hardly breathe—the train had stopped. I smiled gaily at Madame and danced down the steps to the platform. . . .

It was a hot little room, completely furnished, with two colonels seated at two tables. They were large grey-whiskered men with a touch of burnt red on their cheeks. Sumptuous and omnipotent they looked. One smoked what ladies love to call a heavy Egyptian cigarette, with a long creamy ash, the other toyed with a gilded pen. Their heads rolled on their tight collars, like big over-ripe fruits. I had a terrible feeling, as I handed my passport and ticket, that a soldier would step forward and tell me to kneel. I would have knelt without question.

'What's this?' said God I, querulously. He did not like my passport at all. The very sight of it seemed to annoy him. He waved a dissenting hand at it, with a '*Non, je ne peux pas manger ça*' air.

'But it won't do. It won't do at all, you know. Look,—read for yourself,' and he glanced with extreme distaste at my photograph, and then with even greater distaste his pebble eyes looked at me.

'Of course the photograph is deplorable,' I said, scarcely breathing with terror, 'but it has been viséd and viséd.'

He raised his big bulk and went over to God II.

'Courage!' I said to my muff and held it firmly, 'Courage!'

God II held up a finger to me, and I produced Aunt Julie's letter and her card. But he did not seem to feel the slightest interest in her. He stamped my passport idly, scribbled a word on my ticket, and I was on the platform again.

'That way—you pass out that way.'

Terribly pale, with a faint smile on his lips, his hand at salute, stood the little corporal. I gave no sign, I am sure I gave no sign. He stepped behind me.

'And then follow me as though you do not see me,' I heard him half whisper, half sing.

How fast he went, through the slippery mud towards a bridge. He had a postman's bag on his back, a paper parcel and the *Matin* in his hand. We seemed to dodge through a maze of policemen, and I could not keep up at all with the little corporal who began to whistle. From the toll-house 'our good friend, Madame Grinçon', her hands wrapped in a shawl, watched our coming, and against the toll-house there leaned a tiny faded cab. *Montez vite, vite!* said the little corporal, hurling my suit-case, the postman's bag, the paper parcel and the *Matin* on to the floor.

'A-ie! A-ie! Do not be so mad. Do not ride yourself. You will be seen,' wailed 'our good friend, Madame Grinçon'.

'*Ah, je m'en f . . .*' said the little corporal.

The driver jerked into activity. He lashed the bony horse and away we flew, both doors, which were the complete sides of the cab, flapping and banging.

'*Bon jour, mon amie.*'

'*Bon jour, mon ami.*'

And then we swooped down and clutched at the banging doors. They would not keep shut. They were fools of doors.

'Lean back, let me do it!' I cried. 'Policemen are as thick as violets everywhere.'

At the barracks the horse reared up and stopped. A crowd of laughing faces blotted the window.

'*Prends ça, mon vieux,*' said the little corporal, handing the paper parcel.

'It's all right,' called someone.

We waved, we were off again. By a river, down a strange white street, with little houses on either side, gay in the late sunlight.

'Jump out as soon as he stops again. The door will be open. Run straight inside. I will follow. The man is already paid. I know you will like the house. It is quite white. And the room is white too, and the people are—'

'White as snow.'

We looked at each other. We began to laugh. 'Now,' said the little corporal.

Out I flew and in at the door. There stood, presumably, my Aunt Julie. There in the background hovered, I supposed, my Uncle Paul.

'*Bon jour, Madame!*' '*Bon jour, Monsieur!*'

'It is all right, you are safe,' said my Aunt Julie. Heavens, how I loved her! And she opened the door of the white room and shut it upon us. Down went the suit-case, the postman's bag, the *Matin*. I threw my passport up into the air, and the little corporal caught it.

II

What an extraordinary thing. We had been there to lunch and to dinner each day; but now in the dusk and alone I could not find it. I clop-clopped in my borrowed *sabots* through the greasy mud, right to the end of the village, and there was not a sign of it. I could not even remember what it looked like, or if there was a name painted on the outside, or any bottles or tables showing at the window. Already the village houses were sealed for the night behind big wooden shutters. Strange and mysterious they looked in the ragged drifting light and thin rain, like a company of beggars perched on the hill-side, their bosoms full of rich unlawful gold. There was nobody about but the soldiers. A group of wounded stood under a lamp-post, petting a mangy, shivering dog. Up the street came four big boys singing:

'Dodo, mon homme, fais vit' dodo . . .'

and swung off down the hill to their sheds behind the railway station. They seemed to take the last breath of the day with them. I began to walk slowly back.

'It must have been one of these houses. I remember it stood far back from the road—and there were no steps, not even a porch—one seemed to walk right through the window.' And then quite suddenly the waiting-boy came out of just such a place. He saw me and grinned cheerfully, and began to whistle through his teeth.

'*Bon soir, mon petit.*'

'*Bon soir, Madame.*' And he followed me up the café to our special table, right at the far end by the window, and marked by a bunch of violets that I had left in a glass there yesterday.

'You are two?' asked the waiting-boy, flicking the table with a red and white cloth. His long swinging steps echoed over the bare floor. He disappeared into the kitchen and came back to light the lamp that hung from the ceiling under a spreading shade, like a haymaker's hat. Warm light shone on the empty place that was really a barn, set out with dilapidated tables and chairs. Into the middle of the room a black stove jutted. At one side of it there was a table with a row of bottles on it, behind which Madame sat and took the money and made entries in a red book. Opposite her desk a door led into the kitchen. The walls were covered with a creamy paper patterned all over with green and swollen trees—hundreds and hundreds of trees reared their mushroom heads to the ceiling. I began to wonder who had chosen the paper and why. Did Madame think it was beautiful, or that it was a gay and lovely thing to eat one's dinner at all seasons in the middle of a forest. . . . On either side of the clock there hung a picture: one, a young gentleman in black tights wooing a pear-shaped lady in yellow over the back of a garden seat, *Premier Rencontre*; two, the black and yellow in amorous confusion, *Triomphe d'Amour*.

The clock ticked to a soothing lilt, *C'est ça, c'est ça*. In the kitchen the waiting-boy was washing up. I heard the ghostly chatter of the dishes.

And years passed. Perhaps the war is long since over—there is no village outside at all—the streets are quiet under the grass. I have an idea this is the sort of thing one will do on the very last day of all—sit in an empty café and listen to a clock ticking until—

Madame came through the kitchen door, nodded to me and took her seat behind the table, her plump hands folded on the red book. *Ping* went the door. A handful of soldiers came in, took off their coats and began to play cards, chaffing and poking fun at the pretty waiting-boy, who threw up his little round head, rubbed his thick fringe out of his eyes and cheeked them back in his broken voice. Sometimes his voice boomed up from his throat, deep and harsh, and then in the middle of a sentence it broke and scattered in a funny squeaking. He seemed to enjoy it himself. You would not have been surprised if he had walked into the kitchen on his hands and brought back your dinner turning a catherine-wheel.

Ping went the door again. Two more men came in. They sat at the table nearest Madame, and she leaned to them with a birdlike movement, her head on one side. Oh, they had a grievance! The Lieutenant was a fool—nosing about—springing out at them—and they'd only been sewing on buttons. Yes, that was all—sewing on buttons, and up comes this young spark. 'Now then, what are you up to?' They mimicked the idiotic voice. Madame drew down her mouth, nodding sympathy. The waiting-boy served them with glasses. He took a bottle of some orange-coloured stuff and put it on the table edge. A shout from the card-players made him turn sharply, and crash! over went the bottle, spilling on the table, the floor—smash! to tinkling atoms. An amazed silence. Through it the drip-drip of the wine from the table on to the floor. It looked very strange dropping so slowly, as though the table were crying. Then there came a roar from the card-players. 'You'll catch it, my lad! That's the style! Now you've done it! . . . *Sept, huit, neuf.*' They started playing again. The waiting-boy never said a word. He stood, his head bent, his hands spread out, and then he knelt and gathered up the glass, piece by piece, and soaked the wine up with a cloth. Only when Madame cried cheerfully, 'You wait until *he* finds out,' did he raise his head.

'He can't say anything, if I pay for it,' he muttered, his face jerking, and he marched off into the kitchen with the soaking cloth.

'*Il pleure de colère,*' said Madame delightedly, patting her hair with her plump hands.

The café slowly filled. It grew very warm. Blue smoke mounted from the tables and hung about the haymaker's hat in misty wreaths. There was a suffocating smell of onion soup and boots and damp cloth. In the din the door sounded again. It opened to let in a weed of a fellow, who stood with his back against it, one hand shading his eyes.

'Hullo! you've got the bandage off?'

'How does it feel, *mon vieux*?'

'Let's have a look at them.'

But he made no reply. He shrugged and walked unsteadily to a table, sat down and leant against the wall. Slowly his hand fell. In his white face his eyes showed, pink as a rabbit's. They brimmed and spilled, brimmed and spilled. He dragged a white cloth out of his pocket and wiped them.

'It's the smoke,' said someone. 'It's the smoke tickles them up for you.'

His comrades watched him a bit, watched his eyes fill again, again brim over. The water ran down his face, off his chin on to the table. He rubbed the place with his coat-sleeve, and then, as though forgetful, went on rubbing, rubbing with his hand across the table, staring in front of him. And then he started shaking his head to the movement of his hand. He gave a loud strange groan and dragged out the cloth again.

'*Huit, neuf, dix,*' said the card-players.

'*P'tit,* some more bread.'

'Two coffees.'

'*Un Picon!*'

The waiting-boy, quite recovered, but with scarlet cheeks, ran to and fro. A tremendous quarrel flared up among the card-players, raged for two minutes, and died in flickering laughter. 'Ooof!' groaned the man with the eyes, rocking and mopping. But nobody paid any attention to him except Madame. She made a little grimace at her two soldiers.

'*Mais vous savez, c'est un peu dégoûtant, ça,*' she said severely.

'*Ah, oui, Madame,*' answered the soldiers, watching her bent head and pretty hands, as she arranged for the hundredth time a frill of lace on her lifted bosom.

'*V'là, Monsieur!*' cawed the waiting-boy over his shoulder to me. For some silly reason I pretended not to hear, and I leaned over the table smelling the violets, until the little corporal's hand closed over mine.

'Shall we have *un peu de charcuterie* to begin with?' he asked tenderly.

III

'In England,' said the blue-eyed soldier, 'you drink whisky with your meals. *N'est-ce pas, Mademoiselle?* A little glass of whisky neat before eating. Whisky and soda with your *bifteks*, and after, more whisky with hot water and lemon.'

'Is it true that?' asked his great friend who sat opposite, a big red-faced chap with a black beard and large moist eyes and hair that looked as though it had been cut with a sewing-machine.

'Well, not quite true,' said I.

'*Si, si,*' cried the blue-eyed soldier. 'I ought to know. I'm in business. English travellers come to my place, and it's always the same thing.'

'Bah, I can't stand whisky,' said the little corporal. 'It's too disgusting the morning after. Do you remember, *ma fille*, the whisky in that little bar at Montmartre?'

'*Souvenir tendre,*' sighed Blackbeard, putting two fingers in the breast of his coat and letting his head fall. He was very drunk.

'But I know something that you've never tasted,' said the blue-eyed soldier, pointing a finger at me; 'something really good.' *Cluck* he went with his tongue. '*E-patant!* And the curious thing is that you'd hardly know it from whisky except that it's'—he felt with his hand for the word—'finer, sweeter perhaps, not so sharp, and it leaves you feeling gay as a rabbit next morning.'

'What is it called?'

'Mirabelle!' He rolled the word round his mouth, under his tongue. 'Ah-ha, that's the stuff.'

'I could eat another mushroom,' said Blackbeard. 'I would like another mushroom very much. I am sure I could eat another mushroom if Mademoiselle gave it to me out of her hand.'

'You ought to try it,' said the blue-eyed soldier, leaning both hands on the table and speaking so seriously that I began to wonder how much more sober he was than Blackbeard. 'You ought to try it, and to-night. I would like you to tell me if you don't think it's like whisky.'

'Perhaps they've got it here,' said the little corporal, and he called the waiting-boy. '*P'tit!*'

'*Non, Monsieur*,' said the boy, who never stopped smiling. He served us with dessert plates painted with blue parrots and horned beetles.

'What is the name for this in English?' said Blackbeard, pointing. I told him 'Parrot.'

'Ah, *mon Dieu!* . . . Pair-rot. . . .' He put his arms round his plate. 'I love you, *ma petite* pair-rot. You are sweet, you are blonde, you are English. You do not know the difference between whisky and mirabelle.'

The little corporal and I looked at each other, laughing. He squeezed up his eyes when he laughed, so that you saw nothing but the long curly lashes.

'Well, I know a place where they do keep it,' said the blue-eyed soldier. '*Café des Amis*. We'll go there—I'll pay—I'll pay for the whole lot of us.' His gesture embraced thousands of pounds.

But with a loud whirring noise the clock on the wall struck half-past eight; and no soldier is allowed in a café after eight o'clock at night.

'It is fast,' said the blue-eyed soldier. The little corporal's watch said the same. So did the immense turnip that Blackbeard produced and carefully deposited on the head of one of the horned beetles.

'Ah, well, we'll take the risk,' said the blue-eyed soldier, and he thrust his arms into his immense cardboard coat. 'It's worth it,' he said. 'It's worth it. You just wait.'

Outside, stars shone between wispy clouds and the moon fluttered like a candle flame over a pointed spire. The shadows of the dark plume-like trees waved on the white houses. Not a soul to be seen. No sound to be heard but the *Hsh! Hsh!* of a far-away train, like a big beast shuffling in its sleep.

'You are cold,' whispered the little corporal. 'You are cold, *ma fille*.'

'No, really not.'

'But you are trembling.'

'Yes, but I'm not cold.'

'What are the women like in England?' asked Blackbeard. 'After the war is over I shall go to England. I shall find a little English woman and marry her—and her pair-rot.' He gave a loud choking laugh.

'Fool!' said the blue-eyed soldier, shaking him; and he leant over to me. 'It is only after the second glass that you really taste it,' he whispered. 'The second little glass and then—ah!—then you know.'

Café des Amis gleamed in the moonlight. We glanced quickly up and down the road. We ran up the four wooden steps, and opened the ringing glass door into a low room lighted with a hanging lamp, where about ten people were dining. They were seated on two benches at a narrow table.

'Soldiers!' screamed a woman, leaping up from behind a white soup-tureen—a scrag of a woman in a black shawl. 'Soldiers! At this hour! Look at that clock, look at it.' And she pointed to the clock with the dripping ladle.

'It's fast,' said the blue-eyed soldier. 'It's fast, Madame. And don't make so much noise, I beg of you. We will drink and we will go.'

'Will you?' she cried, running round the table and planting herself in front of us. 'That's just what you won't do. Coming into an honest woman's house this hour of the night—making a scene—getting the police after you. Ah, no! Ah, no! It's a disgrace, that's what it is.'

'Sh!' said the little corporal, holding up his hand. Dead silence. In the silence we heard steps passing.

'The police,' whispered Blackbeard, winking at a pretty girl with rings in her ears, who smiled back at him, saucy. 'Sh!'

The faces lifted, listening. 'How beautiful they are!' I thought. 'They are like a family party having supper in the New Testament. . . .' The steps died away.

'Serve you very well right if you had been caught,' scolded the angry woman. 'I'm sorry on your account that the police didn't come. You deserve it—you deserve it.'

'A little glass of mirabelle and we will go,' persisted the blue-eyed soldier.

Still scolding and muttering she took four glasses from the cupboard and a big bottle. 'But you're not going to drink in here. Don't you believe it.' The little corporal ran into the kitchen. 'Not there! Not there! Idiot!' she cried. 'Can't you see there's a window there, and a wall opposite where the police come every evening to . . .'

'Sh!' Another scare.

'You are mad and you will end in prison,—all four of you,' said the woman. She flounced out of the room. We tiptoed after her into a dark smelling scullery, full of pans of greasy water, of salad leaves and meat-bones.

'There now,' she said, putting down the glasses. 'Drink and go!'

'Ah, at last!' The blue-eyed soldier's happy voice trickled through the dark. 'What do you think? Isn't it just as I said? Hasn't it got a taste of excellent—*excellent* whisky?'

Katherine Mansfield, 'An Indiscreet Journey', from *The Stories of Katherine Mansfield*, ed. A. Alpers (Oxford: Oxford University Press, 1984), 628–44

H.D. (Hilda Doolittle)
(1886–1961)

Hilda Doolittle was born in Bethlehem, Pennsylvania, the daughter of an eminent professor of astronomy. While still in her teens she forged a close friendship with Ezra Pound, who, although only a year older, became her mentor during her formative years as a writer. She began her literary career with stories for children but acquired status as a poet when, in 1911, she moved to Europe and, under Pound's sponsorship, became a key member of the Imagist group. Using her initials as a *nom de plume* she subsequently produced a corpus of poems, stories, and essays, as well as a number of semi-autobiographical experimental novels in which the impact of natural phenomena on the human sensibility and the nature of female sexuality emerge as dominant themes. She was a patient of Freud and much of her work is influenced by her lasting interest in psychoanalysis. *Asphodel* was written between 1921 and 1922, after some of the most turbulent years in H.D.'s life. Her brother was killed in action in 1916, she married Richard Aldington in 1918, and gave birth to her daughter Perdita in 1919. The text is one of the few surviving examples of her early struggle to forge modes of expression equal to the task of representing the impact of the war on the feminine sensibility.

―――

53   ASPHODEL

1

DARRINGTON came across the room. Candles made a smudge in the distance. How far away was the other side of the room? It wavered and fell. It fell and wavered. Perhaps next time it really would fall down. 'Jerrold.'

Darrington came across the room. He sat on her bed, their bed. She hadn't really gone to bed, just piled the cushions behind her back and sat up and sat up and listened. Darrington came as he had always come at her voice, coming toward her, his head bent forward, his yellow French book half open in his hand. 'Jerrold.' 'Darling.' Darrington called her darling, had always called her darling, had been calling her darling forever. 'Where—am I?'

'You're right here, here right enough. Thank God we got you out of that damned nursing home.' 'Yes. I forget. Keep forgetting. The funniest thing was when they stood at the end of my bed and told me about the crucified—'

'Hush. Hush darling.' 'Jerrold.' 'Darling?' 'Are there any men left, any at all in the streets, not, not in khaki?'

'Keep quiet. Don't talk. Don't talk about it, darling.' 'I can't think. Can't think about anything else and yet all night (is it night?) my head has been going round and round. You remember that girl I almost forgot.' 'Which girl Astraea?' 'That American girl that crossed with me—when just was it?' 'You mean when you first crossed, two years before the war.' 'Yes two years before the war. Where was it?' 'Where was what?' 'Someone, something got—killed.' 'Hush darling—don't talk about killed.' 'I don't mean the nursing home. I don't mean the horror of the nurses. I can talk of that now. I don't mean their taking me into the cellar—while—it—was happening. I know they took me into the cellar. I know the baby was dead. I know all that. I'm not afraid of talking about it. Really Jerrold.' 'Hush. Hush darling.' 'I mean long ago, something happened long and long ago—the other side of a chasm. Someone. Something. A silver bullet—' 'Don't talk of bullets darling.'

'Read Browning to me.' 'What just do you want dear and the room's too dark; can't turn on the electricity till the raid's over.' 'Read anything—your voice—it was always your voice—sometimes in the worst times, I hear your voice. I wouldn't have minded if they hadn't been so horrid to—you—' 'Do keep still. Don't fidget. Now rest there.' Darrington pulled the cushion to a flat plateau, lifted her by the shoulders, pushed her into the down cushions, 'now don't talk.'

'What shall I read, darling?' 'That thing about Fortù—Fortù, was it? The Englishman in Italy, you know what I mean. It takes me back to Sorrento, to Ana-Capri. It makes things come right. *Gaudy melon flower.* I said those things over and over and over before—it—before it arrived, I was going to say. But it didn't. I used to think I would keep all Italy, the melon flowers, the gold broom above Amalfi. It wasn't England I loved having it. How could I have loved England? God—God—God—' 'Stop talking . . . stop . . . stop, darling.' 'I can't stop talking. I've been quiet for weeks, all those weeks in that filthy place. They didn't kill me anyhow. Their beastliness at least made me glad for one thing. I was glad, so glad it was killed, killed by them, by their beastliness, their constant nagging. The Queen brought Atkinson's eau-de-cologne. But would eau-de-cologne mean anything to anyone who was having a baby, *having I say a baby*, while her husband was *being killed* in Flanders? They got exaltées, those nurses and their cheeks flushed with ardour and they said . . . O Mrs Darrington, how *lucky* for *you* to have your husband when poor Mrs Rawlton's husband is actually now lying wounded . . . and Mrs Dwight-Smith's husband is MISSING. Their cheeks went pink with almost consumptive joy and fervour while they drove and drove and drove one toward some madness. Why isn't Mr Darrington in Khaki? What is khaki? Khaki killed it. They killed it. Italy died and cras amet and I send you Rhodocleia for your hair and swiftly walk o'er the western wave, spirit of night. Italy died with it—*Why isn't Mr. Darrington in khaki?* Good old ecstatic baby-killers like the Huns up there. What is khaki?' 'Hush hush—' 'Another gun. Perhaps we'll go this time—read Fortù.'

> *'Fortù, Fortù, my beloved one,*
> *Sit here by my side.'*

'Go on, go on reading. Don't let anything stop you. Go on. It will make things come right. Go on reading. Don't let anything stop you. After all percussion or something only broke all the upstairs windows last time . . . they may do better this time . . .'

> *'Pomegranates were chapping and splitting*
> *In halves on the tree . . . straight out of the rock side*
> *Some burnt sprig of bold hardy rock-flower . . . great*
> *butterflies fighting, some five for one cup . . .'*

'Butterflies fighting makes me forget. Funny my being alone. And it was gone, all Italy was gone. Amalfi was gone . . . Amalfi's gone with that crash. They're trying for Euston station but they've got Amalfi . . . the things one didn't know were real, until shattered by unreality . . . guns, guns, guns, guns. Our own gun makes more noise but it rattles nicely, just over us that anti-aircraft . . . Amalfi. They've got Amalfi this time. The zeppelins and the anti-aircraft guns are both shattering Amalfi. Butterflies fighting, some five for one cup . . . did you say some five for one cup? Somewhere butterflies are fighting . . . but what butterfly can fight against this thing any longer? I should never have dreamed five butterflies could fight some five for one cup. And why did we come here? Because that plaster Flora was spilling her plaster basket of plaster rose rosette roses like the one (almost) on the long road to Ana-Capri. Do you remember why we took these rooms? That was why. No. Don't speak. Hold me closer. They always try for Euston. It was because that plaster Flora spilled her plaster flowers and we remembered she was just a little like the one in the Signorina's garden. Oranges were in flowers . . . winter blossom and winter Hebridean apples, gold winter oranges above Mediterranean water. My grandfather said of all the things he wanted to see in Europe (we always spoke of Europe in those days, not France, not England, not Germany, just Europe) was the Bay of Naples.

The Bay of Naples . . . that was near enough. I can't get any exaltation out of bombs bursting. God knows I've conscientiously *tried* to do it. Perhaps it's because I'm not English, not European. I feel Europe is splitting like that pomegranate *in halves on the tree*, Europe, all of it that I so love . . . how long have we been married?'

'Why do you ask that? It's almost three years now.' 'One year before the war. Italy and coming back just in time and everything broken, everyone scattered . . . everything different. Italy . . . is Italy different? But it can't be. Italy would be the same if all the Huns of all the universe (who exactly are Huns?) should over-run it. Things now are like Gibbon. The decline and Fall. This is history, I suppose. Go on reading.'

> '. . . *about noon from Amalfi . . . his basket before us*
> *All trembling alive*
> *With pink and grey jellies, your sea-fruit . . .*'

'Yes. And lizards everywhere. Flowers burnt out of rocks, like volcanic embers. Those red anemones. O yes. Everything will come right. Everything has come right. *Open my heart and you will see engraved inside of it Italy*. But I love France too. But Italy is to France what a red ember is to a polished gem. Yes France is a gem polished and cold and flawless and beautiful I can't think of men dying, only of France, la patrie a polished amethyst or some eighteenth century cameo. No, no Hun (what is a Hun anyway?) should break and steal and plunder. A pity though it's happened. That's because I'm not English I suppose. We always spoke of Europe. I love Europe.'

> '*Meantime, see the grape-bunch they've brought you,*
> *The rain-water slips*
> *O'er the heavy blue bloom on each globe*
> *Which the wasp to your lips, still follows*
> *Still follows with fretful persistence:*
> *Nay taste, while awake . . .*'

'I did taste . . . but it's gone. They've broken it . . .'

> '*Next, sip this weak wine*
> *From the thin green glass flask, with its stopper*
> *A leaf of the vine.*'

'It was you who taught me to love those things, Capri Nero, Capri Bianco, cigarettes, the pear trees against Solaro were a mass of blossom and there were prickly pear and cactus. The small goats scampered before us and there was that singular goat-herd (for a long time we thought we'd dreamed it) piping under that one clump of cool willows. Cool willows and below, so far below that one could for a breath have flung oneself down, the sea. The sea. Thalassa. Yes, it was Greece, not like Tuscany. We had Greece, having Italy.'

> *'The wild fruit trees bend . . .*
> *All is silent and grave;*
> *'Tis a sensual and timorous beauty,*
> *How fair but a slave.*
> *So I turned to the sea . . .'*

'So I turned to the sea. Do you remember? I went first. You were heavier. You were surprised and I loved plaguing you. You had only seen me in London and in Paris and you had no idea what I was like really. You found what I was like really. I think it frightened you. Open my heart and you will see engraved inside of it Italy. How could I have known, loving France, loving England that I would love so much better, Italy? France is a polished gem, a priceless intaglio, England is a great wide rose spread just before its falling, Italy is a live ember burning the hearts of men.'

Now why must he do this? Why must he do this? She might have known he would do this, clutching her in his arms, the moment she was happy with him. Everything had come clear talking of Italy. Images smudged, as it were, on a square of thick glass were smudged out by this Sirocco rain they read of. Italy and the talk of Italy had washed out the black, dark grey and khaki-coloured images. Khaki images were splashed like mud across the clear window of her mind and now the clear images of beauty, the gaudy melon flower, the rock islets showed clear. She looked through her mind into a far country. Pays lointain . . . pro patria. She looked through a clear glass far and far and just before her as if the wall of the room had parted, she was looking through between columns (the two sides of the enormous book-case) into a fair country, rocks, the silver lentisk, the white plaques of sea-rosemary, a flute in the distance and the lines of Theocritus. Why must Darrington now spoil it? Hadn't she had enough? Months and months of waiting and now this. Now this, this curious weakness and this reward of weakness; the mind clarified past all recognition, herself gazing through her mind into a fair country. There was no wind. The sea so far below gave no sound. A boy far and far and far was pulling a boat and colours familiar through cheap water colours all their lives took vivid form, were prismatic colours seen through crystal. The walls of cone-shaped Vesuvius and the jagged edge of Capri, the wall that was Capri was rising out of the sea, an island, a Greek island, the island where Odysseus heard the Syren voices. Little plots of earth set like bright rugs on the vertical island mountain, were bright marigolds, and clumps of early winter flowering irises. Irises, white, yellow, blue and lavender. Marguerites growing in enormous balls of white flower made the immaculate white walls a shade more subtle—shell grey. Oranges were flowering and against citron flowers great globes of ripe fruit, rocks and the crevices and the slopes of trees and flax flowers laid like rugs, true gardens of the Hesperides. A church bell (a cathedral bell) was ringing and it was Easter. 'Do you remember that odd poor Christ we said looked like Adonis?' Darrington remembered, but he didn't really care as she cared. He was living in the present and its terror.

Why didn't he go then if he felt like this? He said he would wait now for conscription, he was dead sick of hypocrisy and can't his 'gov'nor' try to get him into a snobby regiment for the family kudos. Family. Kudos. But she was sick, so weak that she only wanted him to go, to go away somewhere, somehow quickly. Everyone took it out on her, would do when she got a little stronger. Nurses bending over her . . . watching her . . . asking . . . no, no. It was impossible. There was no such criminal cruelty in any world, never never in England. She had dreamed a horrible dream and reality was different. Reality that she looked at, propped on the heavy cushions while the guns went on, went on, went on, was something very different. Guns dropped sound like lead-hail and if the guns were quiet they might hear some more pertinent manifestation. One like last time, an enormous shattering, breaking and tearing . . . guns over-head were better though they dropped lead hail that beat and seared her brain, brought pain back to her consciousness. 'O Mrs Darrington. Everything's arranged beautifully. There is at the moment, only one other—in—your—state.' Only two of them. Only two of them waiting. But the other woman had a husband in France so they were nicer to her. O God. Why isn't my husband in France? Guns, guns, guns. Let him at least have the decency to leave me, let me lie here listening. I love listening. Maybe the next one will crash on us. Then I will go simply through the two tall columns (two upright edges of the enormous book-case) into a land that claims me. Patriotism. 'There was that Austrian poet at Corpo di Cava, do you remember?' Darrington remembered but there was an odd wide glare to his eyes. He was thinking like those nurses of the cellar.

'Darling wouldn't it be better—in—your—condition—' 'No. No. No. I can't go downstairs with all the other people. At least it's cool here and so quiet—' '*Quiet*?' 'I mean with you—yes—quiet—' She wasn't with Darrington really, not here. But how explain it to him? His eyes went wide, vacant. He didn't dare think about it. O God don't let his eyes go vacant, then he'll spoil it, then he'll bend and kiss me. Why can't we be happy? Why can't I just remember?

'But you don't care?' 'Darling. You—know—I—do—' Guns were quiet. Tea steamed into her face and she drank the fumes of the tea like some drug fiend, the scent of drug. Tea smelt of far sweet hours, of afternoons of all the happy little times they'd had together. Darrington had made the tea while she lay listening. He was nice, did nice things. She supposed he really did care, had been sorry. It's so hard for a man to say such things. He knew it hurt her to talk about the baby. She supposed he had cared. He wouldn't have let her go through it, almost a year and her mind glued down, broken, and held back like a wild bird caught in bird-lime. The state she had been in was a deadly crucifixion. Not one torture (though God that had been enough) but months and months when her flaming mind beat up and she found she was caught, her mind not taking her as usual like a wild bird but her mind-wings beating, beating and her feet caught, her feet caught, glued like a wild bird in bird-lime. Darrington hadn't known this. No one had known this. No one would ever know it for there were no words to tell it in. How tell it? You can't say this, this . . . but men will say O she was a coward, a woman who refused her womanhood. No, she hadn't. But take a man with a flaming mind and ask him to do this. Ask him to sit in a dark cellar and no books . . . but you mustn't. You can't. Women can't speak and clever women don't have children. So if a clever woman does speak, she must be mad. She is mad. She wouldn't have had a baby, if she hadn't been. Darrington had said he would 'take care of her.' Did they always say that? Darrington had said he would take . . . but he was, he had made the tea, had brought her the tea. He had been reading Browning and the words had cleared her mind, swept away horrors like clean rain on a mud spattered window. Darrington had read her,

> *Next sip this weak wine*
> *From the thin green glass flask, with its stopper,*
> *A leaf of the vine.*

Words had fused with her horror and the memories that weren't real, like a drug. Words were a drug. Darrington had given her this drug.

Darrington had given her words and the ability to cope with words, to write words. People had been asking her (just before the war) for poems, had written saying her things had power, individuality, genius. Darrington had done this. Therefore she must remember, try to remember, try to be things

she had been before the war—no before *it* started. The world was caught as
she had been caught. The whole world was breaking and breaking for some
new spirit. Men were dying as she had almost died to the sound (as she had
almost died) of gun-fire. Guns, guns, guns, guns. Thank God for that. The
guns had made her one in her suffering with men—men—men— She had
not suffered ignobly like a woman, a bird with wings caught, for she was
alone and women weren't left alone to suffer. There were always doctors,
and mothers, and grand-mothers. She had been alone . . . alone . . . no, there
were nurses. No there weren't nurses. Nurses had all run upstairs to get the
others to bring the others . . . babies were crying . . . ghastly mistake . . . some
doctor . . . and guns . . . but there were guns in France and she was in France
for women didn't suffer this way. She was suffering for two, for herself and
Darrington. Darrington had refused suffering . . . 'O no, Jerrold. Don't let
them push you in now. Wait decently for conscription.'

Unmarried men were going, had gone. They would soon get Darrington.
God, God, God, God, God. Why hadn't he gone? Why didn't he go?
People's faces—'O Mrs Darrington. It's so funny. You're the only woman
here whose husband isn't . . .' Isn't? God. But it was true. Guns. Guns.
Guns. Thank God she had suffered to the sound of guns and the baby
wasn't . . . dead . . . not born . . . still born . . . but it didn't matter. 'Darling
but—you—don't—care—any—more.'

2

'Jerrold, but I do care.' By a super-human effort, she lifted her face to his and
smothered under his kisses, she went on with it, 'yes, I do care awfully,' for
what did it matter? It didn't matter. It wasn't real and what she was doing
had no reality, no meaning. It was one with drab walls, walls of drab men
that stood between her and—guns, guns, guns. But Darrington would go
soon, would go to France soon, so that she could lift up her face to his and
let his arms (khaki arms now) hold her close, close, 'being away from you
has made the difference. I see what you are now, have always been.' She
would have to go on with it, no matter what might happen for his arms were
khaki arms now and soon he might be dead, dead—what a relief. No, she
mustn't think things like that. Had she thought it? No, she hadn't thought
it. She had never thought it. 'You've made everything so lovely here. I never
realized how huge the room was. Dinner was so charming with the white
wine.' White wine? Where had it come from? White wine. Delia had sent
her some white wine, saying she looked peaked, Delia being heavenly,
everyone being heavenly because of Jerrold being in Khaki, they were being
nice to her though everyone was gone. Did they think she wanted another

baby? Were they being nice to her hoping she might have one? Was there
nothing else in the world? Men and guns, women and babies. And if you
have a mind what then? But there were men with minds, must be men with
minds, feeling as she did and it wasn't so bad, now Darrington was in khaki.
Going to France soon. She must keep up. 'Where did the white wine come
from?' 'O Delia sent it, delicious Delia, done up in uniform, hateful meetings—' but she mustn't be horrid about Delia. They were all busy, all the
pretty drawing room turned into a red cross section and she knew she ought
to have gone on making swabs but it was so horrible, not seeing swabs but
what they were meant for, and talking, how they gossiped and Delia working so hard. Poor Delia something had gone out of her. Delia however hard
Hermione might try to think it, wasn't the same. She had lost her soul somehow in this mess, this work room, this lint, this cotton wool. But no. It was
Hermione who was horrid. How horrid to hate them, all the women who
went on talking as if they were enjoying it, and the worst of it was one felt
they *were* enjoying it. It was horrible of her not to but how could she help it?
How could she help her vivid mind not seeing? Her mind had been trained
to see. Cultivated. For just this horror? Women talking, picking cotton,
making bandages. O God, don't they see what they're making them for? Am
I the only coward? But I'm not. I had a baby, I mean I didn't—in an air raid.
I know what pain is. They don't know. They can't see. But for Delia's sake
(delicious Delia) one must go on, go on, done up in a dust cloth and an
apron, with one's nun's face. But she wasn't a nun, all the rest had clean
faces, her face wasn't clean. It was smudged with gun-powder for she
had been under fire—wasn't a dressed up nurse, was a real casualty. 'O Mrs
Darrington, we hear your husband—' What had they now heard? But they
hadn't. They had mixed her up with someone else. Her husband wasn't
better, wasn't worse. Her husband was just the same thank you. She had
unwittingly said the right thing. They thought Jerrold was wounded, then
someone whispering and they let her alone for they had found out that she
had had a baby in an air raid just like Daily Mail atrocities. Novels were
right. Even newspapers. She had had things happen in true journalese style,
she Hermione who had drawn music from people, who was a child, they
had said then, a spirit. Where was that? Who was a child, a spirit? And
when had all that happened? Jerrold had gone back now. Hermione had
gone back now to the Red Cross Unit that was Delia Prescott's great drawing room . . . where Walter had used to give concerts . . . where gold gauze
had been the first Liberty gold gauze curtains Hermione had then seen,
where Delia had always had wedges of winter hyacinths in the round sort of
marble basin in the other little room off the big room where the tables were

crowded now against the room wall. Jerrold had gone back. Hermione had gone back . . . Delia was resting by her. 'O is that you Delia?' Must talk to Delia about something else. She couldn't go on hearing their callous appraisal of how someone 'took' something. People all 'took' things like that. But she hadn't. But they didn't know she hadn't, she would go on pretending. But she might get across to Delia. Delia, delicious Delia, who wasn't (nobody could accuse her) delicious in that fawn-mud uniform. 'Delia.' 'Dryad.' Dryad. She would scream simply. Delia had forgotten herself. She had called her Dryad. People now didn't call her Dryad. She had been Dryad in the old days before the earth opened and left part on one side, part on the other.

Thank God at least she was on this side of the chasm. She hadn't thank God, gone (as Jerrold wanted her) to America. 'Jerrold was mad wanting me to go to the States.' 'Poor Jerrold.' Why did Delia say poor Jerrold. 'Why did you say that Delia?' 'I don't know. After all he *is* in it and there's George out of it. I can't know how he does it.' 'But George is American.' 'That doesn't matter, Dryad. He's here with us.' 'But we're American.' 'That makes it twice as hard, people sneering (and they're right) about the dove-cote.' 'Yes they're right, but it isn't our fault, America's not in it.' 'They make us feel— it—is—' Delia must work five times as hard as anybody, Americans must suffer five times as hard as anyone else to show—to show what? An *American*. What did they mean by that? They said it so often nowadays. 'Lady Prescott—' Delia tired to death trailed her weary khaki across to another table. Lady Prescott's unit. Delia.

Henry James died of it, their great American, and they said Americans didn't care. Didn't care. Some didn't. But when they did, O Gawd, as George used to put it. George. How could he go on wearing the same spotted speckled mosaic of cravats? But poor Georgio. One never shoved anyone into it, couldn't. Not even Darrington. Guns, guns, guns, and how small they looked like a little pack of hornets, so near and so small, a whole flotilla of little planes this time and how brave of them. How low they were flying, people talking of poisonous gas and people straining upward and all in the daylight, you couldn't say they weren't remarkable, extraordinarily brave, extraordinary super-human courage to fly low over London in full noonlight. And the crash that followed and would follow and all of us blinking up into a lead-grey light that was the full noon glare, how could they do it, and all of us really marvelling that they were so brave really, English people, so surprised, all of us were so surprised that noon seeing them fly so low. We all said they must be 'us', we all said hearing the stifle and the low

growl, 'no, it's them'. We all marvelled saying 'baby killers', watching one,
two three, all flying in a neat formation. 'Those beasts. Baby-killers.' Yes,
that was true. How odd that the most blatant of journalese should be true,
the most banal and obvious things were now true, the war had made things
like that true. Hermione had never read, listened as little as she could until
this became true. 'Baby-killers.' The most obvious and low level of horrors,
O Gawd, and prose and poetry and the Mona Lisa and her eye lids are a
little weary and sister my sister, O fleet sweet swallow were all smudged out
as Pompeii and its marbles had been buried beneath obscene filth of lava,
embers, smouldering ash and hideous smoke and poisonous gas. Was
London still there? It was hard, would be hard to find it. Some of them
might be left, there might be an afterwards and then some of them would get
to work and dig, dig deep down and unearth all the old treasures. There was
no use remembering the treasures, the cold, sweet uplifted arm of some
marble Hermes, the tiny exquisite foot and bird-like ankle of some
Aphrodite. Those things were being buried and all they could do was to
watch, to stand in little groups and knots and after all with the volcano
belching its filth over them, they were all one, must be all one, fear, terror,
the obstinate courage that refused its terror made them one, facing bright
hawks in an odd grey poisonous noon that swooped and swooped and we
all said, 'it can't be them, it's *us*, it must be, flying so low', but it was *them*,
insinuating themselves, what courage, what dastardly beauty of destruction. 'Baby-killers.' Gods, men, flying high, flying low, 'ours' were as brave
of course, better, braver, better altogether, but not so tight, not so hard, not
so devastating in their cruel cynicism. Baby-killers. Little Willie, big Willie,
newspapers making all life on one level, but how could we help it? How
could we help it? O thank God, I'm here, didn't go back to America. How
could we help it. 'Delia.'

'What darling?' 'How can you—go on—with—this? You're looking more
and more ill. It's killing you.' 'It—has—killed—' O God. Hermione was forgetting. So many were dead. She had forgotten that Tony whom she hardly
knew was out of it, 'gone west', but he was away so much, the house always
seemed Delia's property and Delia was above suspicion though people had
a way (as people did in those days) of a little pitying Delia. Women would,
of course, Delia being so beautiful, so chaste in that odd American-Greek
manner in spite of what people said, when Americans were like that, they
were high and pure and divine and Delia was like that and Lillian Merrick
was like that. Tall and cold, new England, that was another name for a trans-
planted England that was more English than England, more Greek than
Greek. Delia was like that. Lillian was like that. Hermione had forgotten

Tony, there were so many Englishmen (had been so many Englishmen) like that and Tony was so often in Africa and so often he was running across to France. France. Tony was in France for good. Hermione had forgotten Tony. 'Delia?' 'Darling—' But what could she say to Delia? She couldn't now say chuck it, they're exploiting you, they're killing you, they're beasts, devils, they are more cruel than the wasp-devils who fly low over London and at least have their courage, their panache, what are these devils? Nothing. They don't even have children for the other devils to kill. We are in it. Killing and being killed. Who are these? Obscene rows of suppressed women, not women, but some of them have lost sons. O, don't let me be cruel. I am so muddled. Poor Tony. 'I never—knew—Tony.' 'He was like that, Hermione. No one ever knew him. He said I was aloof and—' 'Cold, Delia?' 'Cold, darling. Yes, how did you know?' 'It's the sort of thing they say.' '*They* say, Hermione?' 'I mean—Jerrold.'

H.D., 'Asphodel; Part II', from *Asphodel*, ed. Robert Spoo (Durham, NC, and London: Duke University Press, 1992), 107–19

Mary Borden
(1886–1968)

Mary Borden was a wealthy American who settled in Britain and became prominent on the pre-war literary scene—she was a friend of Wyndham Lewis, George Bernard Shaw, and Ford Madox Ford. While Captain Turner, her first husband, was busy with counter-espionage work, she equipped a mobile hospital which was attached to the French Army at the Front and she stayed with it throughout the war. *The Forbidden Zone*, from which the story below is taken, is a compilation of sketches, short stories, and poems which reflects her nursing experiences. Much of the book was written during the war and sections were published in the *English Review* in 1917.

———

54   THE BEACH

THE beach was long and smooth and the colour of cream. The woman sitting in the sun stroked the beach with the pink palm of her hand and said to herself, 'The beach is perfect, the sun is perfect, the sea is perfect. How pretty the little waves are, curling up the beach. They are perfectly lovely. They are like a lace frill to the beach. And the sea is a perfectly heavenly blue. It is odd to think of how old the beach is and how old the sea is, and how much older that old, old fellow, the fiery sun. The face of the beach is smooth as cream and the sea to-day is a smiling infant, twinkling and dimpling, and the sun is delicious; it is burning hot, like youth itself. It is good to be alive. It is good to be young.' But she could not say this aloud so she said to the man beside her in the wheel chair:

'How many millions of years has it taken to make the beach? How many snails have left their shells behind them, do you think, to make all this fine powdery sand? A million billion?' She let the sand run through her strong white fingers and smiled, blinking in the sun and looked away from the man in the invalid chair beside her toward the horizon.

The man wriggled and hitched himself clumsily up in his chair; an ugly grimace pulled his pale face to one side. He dared not look down over the arm of his wheel chair at the bright head of the woman sitting beside him. Her hair burned in the sunlight; her cheeks were pink. He stole a timid, furtive look. Yes, she was as beautiful as a child. She was perfectly lovely. A groan escaped him, or was it only a sigh?

She looked up quickly. 'What is it, darling? Are you in pain? Are you tired? Shall we go back?' Her voice sounded in the immense quiet of the beach like a cricket chirping, but the word 'darling' went on sounding and sounding like a little hollow bell while she searched his features, trying to find his old face, the one she knew, trying to work a magic on him, remove and replace the sunken eyes, the pinched nose, the bloodless wry mouth. 'He's not a stranger,' she said to herself. 'He's not.' And she heard the faint mocking echo, 'Darling, darling', ringing far away as if a bell-buoy out on the water were saying 'Darling, darling', to make the little waves laugh.

'It's only my foot, my left foot. Funny, isn't it, that it goes on throbbing. They cut it off two months ago.' He jerked a hand backward. 'It's damn queer when you think of it. The old foot begins the old game, then I look down and it's not there any more, and I'm fooled again.' He laughed. His laughter was such a tiny sound in the great murmur of the morning that it might have been a sand-fly laughing. He was thinking, 'What will become of us? She is young and healthy. She is as beautiful as a child. What shall we do about it?' And looking into her eyes he saw the same question, 'What shall we do?' and looked quickly away again. So did she.

She looked past him at the row of ugly villas above the beach. Narrow houses, each like a chimney, tightly wedged together, wedges of cheap brick and plaster with battered wooden balconies. They were new and shabby and derelict. All had their shutters up. All the doors were bolted. How stuffy it must be in those deserted villas, in all those abandoned bedrooms and kitchens and parlours. Probably there were sand-shoes and bathing dresses and old towels and saucepans and blankets rotting inside them with the sand drifting in. Probably the window panes behind the shutters were broken and the mirrors cracked. Perhaps when the aeroplanes dropped bombs on the town, pictures fell down and mirrors and the china in the dark china closets cracked inside these pleasure houses. Who had built them?

'Cowards built them,' he said in his new bitter, rasping voice, the voice of a peevish, irritable sandfly. 'Built them to make love in, to cuddle in, to sleep in, hide in. Now they're empty. The blighters have left them to rot there. Rotten, I call it, leaving the swanky plage to go to the bad like that, just because there's a war on. A little jazz now and a baccarat table would make all the difference, wouldn't it? It would cheer us up. You'd dance and I'd have a go at the tables. That's the casino over there, that big thing; that's not empty, that's crowded, but I don't advise you to go there. I don't think you'd like it. It's not your kind of a crowd. It's all right for me, but not for you. No, it wouldn't do for you—not even on a gala night.

'They've a gala night in our casino whenever there's a battle. Funny sort of place. You should watch the motors drive up then. The rush begins about ten in the evening and goes on till morning. Quite like Deauville the night of the Grand Prix. You never saw such a crowd. They all rush there from the front, you know—the way they do from the race-course—though, to be sure, it is not quite the real thing—not a really smart crowd. No, not precisely, though the wasters in Deauville weren't much to look at, were they? Still, our crowd here aren't precisely wasters. Gamblers, of course, down and outs, wrecks—all gone to pieces, parts of 'em missing, you know, tops of their heads gone, or one of their legs. When they take their places at the tables, the croupiers—that is to say, the doctors—look them over. Come closer, I'll whisper it. Some of them have no faces.'

'Darling, don't.' She covered her own face, closed her ears to his tiny voice and listened desperately with all her minute will to the large tranquil murmur of the sea. 'Darling, darling', far out the bell-buoy was sounding.

'Bless you,' said the thin, sharp, exasperated sandfly voice beside her. 'Little things like that don't keep us away. If we can't walk in we get carried in. All that's needed is a ticket. It's tied to you like a luggage label. It has your name on it in case you don't remember your name. You needn't have a face, but a ticket you must have to get into our casino.'

'Stop, darling—darling, stop!'

'It's a funny place. There's a skating rink. You ought to see it. You go through the baccarat rooms and the dance hall to get to it. They're all full of beds. Rows of beds under the big crystal chandeliers, rows of beds under the big gilt mirrors, and the skating rink is full of beds, too. The sun blazes down through the glass roof. It's like a hot-house in Kew Gardens. There's that dank smell of a rotting swamp, the smell of gas gangrene. Men with gas gangrene turn green, you know, like rotting plants.' He laughed. Then he was silent. He looked at her cowering in the sand, her hands covering her face, and looked away again.

He wondered why he had told her these things. He loved her. He hated her. He was afraid of her. He did not want her to be kind to him. He could never touch her again and he was tied to her. He was rotting and he was tied to her perfection. He had no power over her any more but the power of infecting her with his corruption. He could never make her happy. He could only make her suffer. His one luxury now was jealousy of her perfection, and his one delight would be to give in to the temptation to make her suffer. He could only reach her that way. It would be his revenge on the war.

He was not aware of these thoughts. He was too busy with other little false thoughts. He was saying to himself, 'I will let her go. I will send her away. Once we are at home again, I will say good-bye to her.' But he knew that he was incapable of letting her go.

He closed his eyes. He said to himself 'The smell of the sea is good, but the odour that oozes from the windows of the casino is bad. I can smell it from here. I can't get the smell of it out of my nose. It is my own smell,' and his wasted greenish face twitched in disgust.

She looked at him. 'I love him,' she said to herself. 'I love him,' she repeated. 'But can I go on loving him?' She whispered, 'Can I? I must.' She said, 'I must love him, now more than ever, but where is he?'

She looked round her as if to find the man he once had been. There were other women on the beach, women in black and old men and children with buckets and spades, people of the town. They seemed to be glad to be alive. No one seemed to be thinking of the war.

The beach was long and smooth and the colour of cream. The beach was perfect; the sun perfectly delicious; the sea was perfectly calm. The man in the wheel chair and the woman beside him were no bigger than flies on the sand. The women and children and old men were specks.

Far out on the sea there was an object; there were two objects. The people on the beach could scarcely distinguish them. They peered through the sunshine while the children rolled in the sand, and they heard the sound of a distant hammer tapping.

'They are firing out at sea,' said someone to someone.

How perfect the beach is. The sea is a perfectly heavenly blue. Behind the windows of the casino, under the great crystal chandeliers, men lie in narrow beds. They lie in queer postures with their greenish faces turned up. Their white bandages are reflected in the sombre gilt mirrors. There is no sound anywhere but the murmur of the sea and the whispering of the waves on the sand, and the tap tap of a hammer coming from a great distance across the water, and the bell-buoy that seems to say, 'Darling, darling.'

Mary Borden, 'The Beach', from The Forbidden Zone (London:
Heinemann, 1929), 42–50

Mary Butts
(1890–1937)

A prolific yet neglected writer, Mary Butts grew up in Dorset but her adult life was spent in the metropolitan artistic world. In the war years she was a member of literary circles in London; she lived in Paris during the 1920s where she became acquainted with Pound, H.D., Bryher, Rebecca West, and May Sinclair. Her works were published in journals of Modernist writing such as the *Little Review*, the *Dial*, and *Pagany*. Throughout her life Butts was interested in the occult and she was for a period a friend of Aleister Crowley. Later in her life she returned to England and lived in Cornwall, where she died in 1937. The relationship between the land and its dwellers is a preoccupation in much of her writing: in 'Speed the Plough' this theme and its associated values are explored in relation to the psychological and physical traumas inflicted by the war.

---

55   SPEED THE PLOUGH

HE lay in bed, lax and staring, and obscure images rose and hung before him, dissolved, reshaped. His great illness passed from him. It left him too faint for any sequence of thought. He lay still, without memory, without hope. Such concrete impressions as came to him were sensuous and centred round the women of the hospital. They distressed him. They were not like the Kirchner girls in the worn *Sketch* he fingered all day.

La Coquetterie d'une Ange. One need not know French to understand Coquetterie, and Ange was an easy guess. He stared at the neat counterpane. A tall freckled girl with draggled red hair banged down a cup of cocoa and strode away.

Coquetterie, mannequin, lingerie, and all one could say in English was underwear. He flicked over the pages of the battered *Sketch*, and then looked at the little nurse touching her lips with carmine. 'Georgette,' he murmured sleepily, 'crêpe georgette.'

He would always be lame. For years his nerves would rise and quiver and knot themselves, and project loathsome images. But he had a fine body, and his soldiering had set his shoulders and hardened his hands and arms.

'Get him back on to the land,' the doctors said.

The smells in the ward began to assail him, interlacing spirals of odour, subtle but distinct. Disinfectant and distemper, the homely smell of blankets, the faint tang of blood, and then a sour draught from the third bed where a man had been sick.

He crept down under the clothes. Their associations rather than their textures were abhorrent to him, they reminded him of evil noises . . . the crackle of starched aprons, clashing plates, unmodulated sounds. Georgette would never wear harsh things like that. She would wear . . . beautiful things with names . . . velours and organdie, and that faint windy stuff aerophane.

He drowsed back to France, and saw in the sky great aeroplanes dipping and swerving, or holding on their line of steady flight like a travelling eye of God. The wisps of cloud that trailed a moment behind them were not more delicate than her dress. . . .

'What he wants, doctor, to my mind, is rousing. There he lies all day in a dream. He must have been a strong man once. No, we don't know what he was. Something out of doors I should think. He lies there with that precious Kirchner album, never a word to say.'

The doctor nodded.

He lay very still. The presence of the matron made him writhe like the remembered scream of metal upon metal. Her large hands concealed bones that would snap. He lay like a rabbit in its form, and fright showed his dull gums between his drawn-back lips.

Weeks passed. Then one day he got up and saw himself in a glass. He was not surprised. It was all as he had known it must be. He could not go back to the old life. It seemed to him that he would soil its loveliness. Its exotics would shrivel and tarnish as he limped by. 'Light things, and winged, and holy' they fluttered past him, crêpe velours, crêpe de Chine, organdie, aerophane, georgette. . . . He had dropped his stick . . . there was no one to wash his dirty hands. . . . The red-haired nurse found him crying, and took him back to bed.

For two months longer he laboured under their kindness and wasted under their placidity. He brooded, realising with pitiful want of clarity that there were unstable delicate things by which he might be cured. He found a ritual and a litany. Dressed in vertical black, he bore on his outstretched arms, huge bales of wound stuffs. With a turn of the wrist he would unwrap them, and they would fall from him rayed like some terrestrial star. The Kirchner album supplied the rest. He named the girls, Suzanne and Verveine, Ambre and Desti, and ranged them about him. Then he would undress them, and dress them again in immaculate fabrics. While he did that he could not speak to them because his mouth would be barred with pins.

The doctors found him weaker.

Several of the nurses were pretty. That was not what he wanted. Their fresh skins irritated him. Somewhere there must still be women whose skins were lustrous with powder, and whose eyes were shadowed with violet from an ivory box. The brisk provincial women passed through his ward visiting from bed to bed. In their homely clothes there was an echo of the lovely fashions of *mondaines*, buttons on a skirt where a slit should have been, a shirt cut to the collar bone whose opening should have sprung from the hollow between the breasts.

Months passed. The fabric of his dream hardened into a shell for his spirit. He remained passive under the hospital care.

They sent him down to a farm on a brilliant March day.

His starved nerves devoured the air and sunlight. If the winds parched, they braced him, and when the snow fell it buried his memories clean. Because she had worn a real musquash coat, and carried a brocade satchel he had half believed the expensive woman who had sat by his bed, and talked about the worth and the beauty of a life at the plough's tail. Of course he might not be able to plough because of his poor leg . . . but there was always the milking . . . or pigs . . . or he might thatch. . . .

Unfamiliarity gave his world a certain interest. He fluttered the farmer's wife. Nothing came to trouble the continuity of his dream. The sheen on the new grass, the expanse of sky, now heavy as marble, now luminous; the embroidery that a bare tree makes against the sky, the iridescent scum on a village pond, these were his remembrancers, the assurance of his realities. Beside them a cow was an obscene vision of the night.

Too lame to plough or to go far afield, it seemed as though his fate must overtake him among the horned beasts. So far he had ignored them. At the afternoon milking he had been an onlooker, then a tentative operator. Unfortunately the farmer recognised a born milkman. At five o'clock next morning they would go out together to the byres.

At dawn the air was like a sheet of glass; behind it one great star glittered. Dimmed by a transparent shutter, the hard new light poured into the world. A stillness so keen that it seemed the crystallisation of speed hung over the farm. From the kitchen chimney rose a feather of smoke, vertical, delicate, light as a plume on Gaby's head. As he stamped out into the yard in his gaiters and corduroys he thought of the similitude and his mouth twisted.

In the yard the straw rose in yellow bales out of the brown dung pools. Each straw was brocaded with frost, and the thin ice crackled under his boots. He paused. 'Diamanté,' he said at last, 'that's it.'

On a high shoulder of down above the house, a flock of sheep were gathered like a puffy mat of irregular design. The continual bleating, the tang of the iron bell, gave coherence to the tranquillity of that Artemisian dawn. A hound let loose from the manor by some early groom passed menacing over the soundless grass. A cock upon the pigsty wall tore the air with his screams. He stopped outside the byre now moaning with restless life. The cock brought memories. 'Chanticleer, they called him, like that play once. . . .'

He remembered how he had once stood outside the window of a famous shop and thrilled at a placard. . . . 'In twenty-four hours M. Lewis arrives from Paris with the Chanticleer toque.' It had been a stage hit, of course, one hadn't done business with it, but, O God! the London women whose wide skirts rose with the wind till they bore them down the street like ships. He remembered a phrase he had heard once, a 'scented gale'. They were like that. The open door of the cow-shed steamed with the rankness that had driven out from life. . . . Inside were twenty female animals waiting to be milked.

He went in to the warm reeking dark.

He squatted on the greasy milking stool, spoke softly to his beast, and tugged away. The hot milk spurted out into the pail, an amazing substance, pure, and thick with bubbles. Its contact with caked hides and steaming straw sickened him. The gentle beast rubbed her head against her back and stared. He left the stall and her warm breath. The light was gaining. He could see rows of huge buttocks shifting uneasily. From two places he heard the milk squirting in the pails. He turned to it again, and milked one beast and another, stripping each clean.

The warm milk whose beauty had pleased began to nauseate him. There was a difference in nature between that winking, pearling flow and the pale decency of a Lyons' tea jug. So this was where it all started. Dimly he realised that this was where most of life started, indifferent of any later phase. 'Little bits of fluff,' Rosalba and all the Kirchner tribe . . . was Polaire only a cow . . . or Delysia? . . . The light had now the full measure of day. A wind that tasted delicately of shingle and the turf flew to meet him. The mat on the down shoulder was now a dissolving view of ambulating mushrooms.

'Yes, my son,' the farmer was saying, 'you just stay here where you're well off, and go on milking for me. I know a born milkman when I see one, and I don't mind telling you you're it. I believe you could milk a bull if you were so inclined. . . .'

He sat silent, overwhelmed by the disarming kindness.

'See how the beasts take to you,' the voice went on. 'That old cow she's a terror, and I heard you soothing her down till she was pleasant as yon cat. It's dairy work you were cut out for. . . . There's a bull coming round this forenoon . . . pedigree . . . cost me a bit. You come along.'

As yet they did not work him very hard, he would have time to think. He dodged his obligations towards the bull, and walked over to an upland field. He swept away the snow from under a thorn bush, folded his coat beneath him, and lit a cigarette.

'And I stopped, and I looked, and I listened.' Yes, that was it, and about time too. For a while he whistled slowly Robey's masterpiece.

He had to settle with his sense of decency. It was all very well. These things might have to happen. The prospect of a milkless, meatless London impressed him as inconvenient. Still most of that stuff came from abroad, by sea. That was what the blockade was for. 'I've got to get away from this. I never thought of this before, and I don't like it. I've been jockeyed into it somehow, and I don't like it. It's dirty, yes dirty, like a man being sick. In London we're civilised. . . .'

A gull floated in from the sea, and up the valley where the horses steamed at the spring ploughing.

'A bit of it may be all right, it's getting near that does one in. There aren't any women here. They're animals. Even those girls they call the squire's daughters. I never saw such boots. . . . They'd say that things were for use, and in London they're for show. . . . Give me the good old show. . . .' He stopped to dream. He was in a vast circular gallery so precipitous that standing one felt impelled to reel over and sprawl down into the stalls half a mile below. Some comedian had left the stage. Two gold-laced men were changing the numbers on either side. The orchestra played again, something that had no common tune. Then there swung on to the stage a woman plumed and violent, wrapped in leopard skins and cloth-of-gold. Sometimes she stepped like a young horse, sometimes she moved with the easy trailing of a snake. She did nothing that was not trivial, yet she invested every moment with a significance whose memory was rapture.

Quintessence was the word he wanted. He said . . . 'There's a lot of use in shows.'

Then he got up stiffly, and walked down the steep track to the farm, still whistling.

When the work was over he went out again. Before the pub, at the door marked 'hotel', a car was standing, a green car with glossy panels and a monogram, cushioned inside with grey and starred with silver. A chauffeur, symphonic also in green and bright buttons, was cranking her up. Perched upon the radiator was a naked silver girl. A woman came out of the inn. She wore white furs swathed over deep blue. Her feet flashed in their glossy boots. She wore a god in green jade and rose. Her gloves were rich and thick, like moulded ivory.

'Joy riding,' said a shepherd, and trudged on, but he stood ravished. It was not all dead then, the fine delicate life that had been the substance of his dream. Rare it might be, and decried, but it endured. The car's low humming died away, phantom-like he saw it in the darkling lane, a shell enclosing a pearl, the quintessence of cities, the perfection of the world.

He had heard her deep voice. 'I think we'll be getting back now.' She was going back to London. He went into the bar and asked the landlady who she was.

'Sort of actress,' the landlord said. And then. 'The war ought to have stopped that sort of thing.'

'Why, what's the harm?'

'Spending the money that ought to go to beating those bloody Germans.'

'All the same her sort brings custom,' the wife had said.

He drank his beer and went out into the pure cold evening. It was six o'clock by the old time, and the radiance was unnatural.

He walked down the damp lane, pale between the hedgerows. It widened and skirted a pond covered with vivid slime.

'And that was all they had to say about her. . . .'

He hated them. A cart came storming up the hill, a compelling noise, grinding wheels and creaking shafts and jingling harness; hard breathing, and the rough voice of the carter to his beast.

At the pond the horse pulled up to breathe, his coat steamed, the carter leaned on the shaft.

'Some pull that.'

'Aye, so it be.' He noticed for the first time the essential difference in their speech.

Carter and horse went up the hill. He lit another cigarette.

Something had happened to him, resolving his mind of all doubts. He saw the tail lights of a car drawing through the vast outskirts of a city. An infinite fine line went out from it and drew him also. That tail lamp was his star. Within the car a girl lay rapt, insolent, a cigarette at her lips.

He dreamed. Dark gathered. Then he noticed that something luminous was coming towards him. Down the hollow lane white patches were moving, irregular, but in sequence, patches that seemed to his dulled ears to move silently, and to eyes trained to traffic extraordinarily slow. The sun had passed. The shadow of the hill overhung the valley. The pale light above intensified its menace. The straggling patches, like the cups of snow the downs still held in every hollow, made down the lane to the pond's edge. It was very cold. From there no lighted windows showed. Only the tip of his cigarette was crimson as in Piccadilly.

With the sound of a charging beast, a song burst from him, as, soundless, each snowy patch slid from the land on to the mirrored back of the pond. He began to shout out loud.

'Some lame, some tame, some game for anything, some like a stand-up fight,
Some stay abed in the morning, and some stay out all night.
Have you seen the ducks go by, go a-rolling home?
Feeling very glad and spry, have you seen them roam?
There's mamma duck, papa duck, the grand old drake,
Leading away, what a noise they make.
Have you heard them quack, have you heard them quack, have you seen those
    ducks go by?
Have you seen the ducks go by, go a-rolling home? . . .'

The way back to the farm his voice answered Lee White's, and the Vaudeville chorus sustained them. At the farm door they forsook him. He had to be coherent to the farmer. He sought inspiration. It came. He played with the latch, and then walked into the kitchen, lyrical. . . .

'And I stopped, and I looked, and I left.'

A month later found him on his knees, vertical in black cloth, and grey trousers, and exquisite bow tie. A roll of Lyons brocade, silver, and peach, was pliant between his fingers as the teats of a cow. Inside it a girl stood frowning down upon him.

Despair was on her face, and on the faces of the attendant women.

'But if you can't get me the lace to go with it, what am I to wear?'

'I am sorry, madame. . . . Indeed we have done all that is possible. It seems that it is not to be had. I can assure madame that we have done our best.' He rose and appealed to the women. His conviction touched them all.

'Madame, anything that we can do . . .'

The lovely girl frowned on them, and kicked at her half-pinned draperies.

'When the war starts interfering with my clothes,' she said, 'the war goes under. . . .'

His eyes kindled.

Mary Butts, 'Speed the Plough', from *Speed the Plough* (London:
Chapman and Hall, 1923), 11–26

Mrs Henry Dudeney
(1866–1945)

Alice Dudeney wrote under her married name, Mrs Henry Dudeney. She was an extremely prolific writer, publishing some sixty works of fiction between 1901 and 1935. Some of her work touched on social issues: her first novel, *The Maternity of Harriott Wicken* (1902) was described as 'a study of a mother's commitment to her idiot child'. Most of her novels, however, were romantic— both because they were love-stories and also in the manner that they revealed Alice Dudeney's attachment to Sussex, where she lived. She was described by her publishers as 'the novelist of the Weald and the Marsh and the Down Countries'. In her story of the soldier and his dog the importance of these landscapes is clear, as is the sentimental narrative: but 'Missing' contains also a picture of the difficulties of domestic life in the immediate post-war period.

——

56   'MISSING'

WHEN all your life you have been a shepherd and then they turn you into a soldier!

You see strange lands; you are wounded, imprisoned, hunted; you get away at last; and you come home. You are here, standing on the top of the hills—these gracious green giants that all your life made your boundaries; were your girdle; hemmed you in.

The misty blue nose of Firle Beacon, suddenly appearing as he crowned a ridge, made him understand how he had fretted for these hills in a strange land.

He was thinking about this as he went along, walking high, with the arable land and the little villages far below. It was a wonderful walk that he was taking, for he was still weak, bewildered, and half starved, so that nothing seemed quite real and he was ready for anything.

He would have a lot to tell Annie. She wouldn't believe half. There were things that he did not expect her to believe, and other things that he did not want to tell her—horrible things that he, with the others, had suffered. He did not wish her to know, yet he knew very well that it would all trickle out of him as they sat together by the fire that night, just the three of them.

As he walked along he looked at the sky, asking it that futile question which men ask. He asked why wars were. Why should this shocking thing be which took a man away from his sheep and his wife and his home?

But it was over and it would not be again in his time. So he could once more be a shepherd and be a husband.

As he walked along he noticed things. The hill was vividly green, and a black cow sitting on the slope of it had a domestic pose. She looked, so he thought, like a cat sitting on a hearth-rug.

He went lilting down. In a few minutes he would come to that rough sheep-track, milk-white, chalky, which led to his cottage.

He clumped along in a quiet yet thrilling gratitude of mind. He had come back; he was safe and sound.

There had been rain for many days. The blurred, blossoming look of that flooded marshland was not lost upon him. Seven miles or more away lay the blue sea. He knew just where to look for it, but he did not want to see it any more. He'd done with the sea and done with travel, pray God.

There was a soft mist that day. Through it came the sound of bells. Then he saw, some distance off, a vague, pearly mass of sheep, just faintly moving on the edge of the hill, on its steep north side.

He listened to those bells, he saw the rigid black figure of the shepherd, and he saw the shepherd's watchful dog. He had come back, and he also was going to be a shepherd until he died.

Men that he knew, that he had soldiered with, been a prisoner with, swore that they would not return to quiet country labour. They talked of towns and new lands; they laughed at him. But all he wanted was to live all day upon the hills he knew, leading sheep, days on the hills, nights in the warm cottage, just the three of them. What more did a man want?

He had come back to it all. He would be home in a minute. Very soon there would be arms around him, kissing, and a glad noise—behind a shut door.

He came to the track, which was just one of many tracks, leading off the great Downs. They are all alike, and each man loves his own best. So, when he saw that track his eye—that started from a sharp cheek-bone—was alert with rapture. There was stinging in his eyes, oppression at his breast. He was so weak and so glad.

Annie had very likely given him up for dead. Hundreds had died, men that he knew, comrades. But he had doggedly lived through it all. He was strong. And he meant to get back to Sussex, to sheep.

He went squelching down the track, and that creamy fluid, the Sussex mud, was over the tops of his boots. At a wind of the track he came upon the cottage. He could see it, lying a long way down. It was square-built, and all upon one floor. It had a wandering garden in which a yew-tree grew. It was not pretty; the roof was slate, the walls were cemented and they looked damp. Yet it seemed to melt into the hills and it assaulted nothing.

He had brought Annie to this cottage as a bride; it had seen the babyhood of Bob. So to him it was full of ardour, full of delight, full of pathos. To him it was a palace of the heart.

He went very carefully down that sticky track; even he, who knew Sussex soil so well, for the wet chalk is more slippery than ice.

Three parts of the way down was a heave gate, leading into a tiny field. Before the gate was a churned-up patch of mud. It was patterned over, feathered with the thousand little footmarks of sheep.

The marks of their feet, the hurdles that enclosed them, the faint, unpleasing smell of the flock, and the sound of the bell thrilled him. He felt stifled, and he stood still in a stupid, mad delight, looking at those munching, blowing sheep that were hurdled off in the small field. Then he turned round with his back to the gate, leaning on it, and he looked at the hill he had descended, that round, green giant behind which in wintertime the sun dropped so early, leaving the cottage dull and the chalk track ghostly, grim.

He looked up. The aimless shepherd with his sheep had followed. He was standing on the top of the hill, sharply outlined against the sky. He moved very slowly, like a wraith, and he drove his sheep through a flock of gulls that rose screaming and circling.

This returned soldier stood by the gate, looking up, grinning fondly. He had done that, with gulls, with sheep, a dozen times. He recalled it—the stupid, uncaring sheep, the gulls that were so noisy and that looked like silver in the sun. To-day they were thick white and pallid through the mist. He recalled it with a great joy, the things that he had seen, that he had done upon these hills—and would see and do again. He thought of flint stones in the chalk and the way they twinkled as the light caught them. He thought of all the pretty summer things—tiny blossoms, tinkling silence, happy haze.

He went on to the cottage, and, now that he was so near, he felt afraid. If, in four years, anything had happened to Annie! Sometimes a soldier came home and found his wife dead—or worse! Suppose she had thought him dead! Suppose she had got married again! Such things were. Many affairs might come between a man and a woman in four years. He had been reported missing. He knew that.

There was her curtain at the window. A white curtain with a green stripe and a pink flower. She was fond of colour. There was a long, long row of washing in the garden. She had set up three new clothes-posts. Proper posts they were, too!

He looked at this limp washing, critically, fearfully. He did not know what to expect. He wished he was inside. He shook.

He was back, he was at home, he stood at his own gate. It was wonderful; it made him stupid, silly. He had returned to a good wife—and not only to a wife. There was other love to reckon with. He smiled, for there were three of them, not two.

He meant to be easy, happy, comfortable, for the rest of his days. Fair wages, good food, a clean bed—what else did a man want? And he had earned it. There they would be, all three of them, in the cottage, sleeping through the black night, at the end of the track, at the foot of the hill.

Yet he had brought back memories. There were things—and sights—that he could not forget. It would all be painted on his pillow. Pictures would put themselves between him and Annie as she lay with her head on the other pillow. He could see her head on the pillow, as it used to look and as it would look to-night. Lots of hair! And it was the colour of the sun when the sun is sulky.

He went in at the gate. The front door looked so shut, as if it did not mean to open, as if it had not been opened since he went away. He walked through the garden and the strange, wet washing flapped into his face. He kept fighting it back; in a way, he was cursing, for, somehow, things were strange. The back door was open, so he stepped noiselessly into the wash-house. There was the bucket she took to the well. There was her old cap behind the door. There were the brooms and the bowls. It all seemed unreal and heartless to him, for he had been so far and seen so much, while nothing here had changed.

Four years he had been a soldier, and two years out of that four he had been a prisoner. They had given him up. He was a dead man, standing in the wash-house, looking about him. That was it. They all took him for a dead man. And—Annie?

The door leading into the front room was open and there she stood, unchanged—as her brooms and buckets! She had her back to him; she was ironing. He stood breathless, staring at her bowed shoulders and her greying hair. She was not very young.

Could anything be more lovely, more safe, more at home than that warm smell of ironing? He did not feel afraid any more. He did not put questions to his heart, piling up quick agony on agony, for there she stood, and unchanged.

He looked at her, rejoicing in that glory of her auburn hair that was turning grey. There was so much of it. Her head seemed overweighted. He had married her for that flaming mop of hair, and often told her so—in their best moments and their bitter ones.

He surveyed her sharp shoulders and sinewy hand as she stood there patiently ironing. She had never been pretty, even as a girl, and now she was a lean woman with a big nose, with staring eyes that were the colour of her hair. But she was his and he had come to her; that was enough.

Mixed up with the smell of ironing was the smell of food. What had she got in the pot? His staring eyes, finding the pot on the hob, were famished. He had a lust for hot food.

He looked at the pot, he looked at his wife, and then he looked round for the other one. For there were two of them that he dearly loved and had come back to. A whimsical, kind smile crossed his mouth and made his gaunt face roguish.

Then he felt afraid again and then he listened. For he saw nothing, only Annie ironing. And he heard nothing. He stood there, looking, listening. He was sniffing—at the smell of the irons, at the smell from the pot.

After dinner and a wash, he'd sleep. Then he would have his tea. After tea he would walk to the village and drink at the *Tiger* and talk with the neighbours. But he would not stay long, for Annie would want him with her by the fire. How many nights in the past had he come home along the zigzag track from the village? Nights when there was a reeling moon in a sky of drunken, fleeing cloud—and he a bit drunk, perhaps; just now and then, not often!

He kept staring round the room, for he was puzzled, and again he was cold with fear. He stood pinching in his breath, behind his wife who was ironing. He looked toward the old-fashioned, wide sofa that had been his mother's and had been a place where he had cuddled up when he was small or sick. It was piled with rough-dry linen waiting for the iron.

Annie had been forced to take in washing. Was that it? He looked at her bowed back and rhythmic hand. She wouldn't let Bob cuddle up on the sofa in the middle of the clean linen, would she? Yet where was he? This was what he kept asking himself as he looked and as he listened.

He saw nothing on the floor but the well swept drugget that had a hole in it near the arm-chair. In that chair he used to doze off after supper and scuffle his feet. How warm it used to be after supper, with the window and the door shut, with the wood burning and the wind blowing hard outside. He remembered how he used to come down, stiff, from the hill and how he used to shut the door and blow and breathe hard and stamp his feet.

Annie went to the fire for a fresh iron, half turned, and saw him! He marked that her face was glowing, yet abashed, and that she had been crying. All this he saw—but in a moment only. Then they were in each other's arms, stifling, close, strangling. They murmured and choked and laughed. They were in a delirium of reunion. Their world was transformed.

At last she dragged back, she looked at him. He saw the bitterness at the corners of her mouth and the tears in the corners of her eyes. She was astringent and melting. Then she started sobbing violently, fiercely, so it seemed to him. And she fell on the sofa in the middle of the white linen she had washed. It grouped about her formally, all of it bone dry.

'You was wounded and missing. I thought you'd never come back no more.'

'I've been a prisoner, my dear.' He stood over her, seeming helpless, dazed. 'Me and some more chaps got away. I shall have things to tell you, Annie—digging tunnels, crawling out; hiding in the daytime, travelling nights. An' when we did get across the frontier we heard it was all over. The war was done, so we needn't have troubled.'

She pulled him down to her, holding his hand tight, averting her face. So they sat together on this old sofa.

'I'm glad you've got back,' she said brokenly, 'for I never looked to see you again.'

He was staring at her profile; he could not miss that stark terror on her face. She was afraid of something—dreadfully, dreadfully afraid. That was plain to him. Their frantic hands were locked together. He looked at her menacing side-face; he looked round the room. His eyes were full of baffled, stupid terror. For when he went away there had been three of them. And now they were but two. He asked her at last, and he was afraid to ask.

'Where's Bob, then?'

Now it was out. She turned round, seeming ghastly, and she left him, walking defiantly to the mantelpiece.

There were two china dogs on it with gilt chains round their necks, one at each end. In the middle was a china shepherd with his dog at his feet and a lamb in his arms. She felt behind this shepherd; she returned to her husband, carrying something.

'I kept his collar,' she said, sullenly. 'I thought that if s'be you ever did come back you'd like his collar.'

She pushed it into his hands and he foolishly turned it about—Bob's collar, with Bob's name on it and the faint smell of Bob drifting up from it. The soul of his sheep-dog came to him through that collar.

'He's dead, then?' His sad eye gleamed in the great socket as he asked.

She looked savagely at that stricken face.

'Do you know,' she demanded, 'what food has rose to? Dog's food, I mean. And he was so big; he jes' wolfed it. Anybody 'ud think he was a child, the fuss you make!'

'He was like a child, Annie. He was the only one we got. Think I ain't fretted for him?'

'Very likely.' She was dry. 'Fretted more 'n you did for me.'

'Don't you be a fool. That's different. Why, coming over the hill I thought out how it 'ud be—him thumpin' his tail and barkin' and jumpin' an' tearin' me to rags.'

'You're in rags now, come to that.'

She seemed implacable—but he knew her. She was always like that when her heart was softest.

'Yes, I'm in rags, and I'm dirty and hungry, my gell.'

'Poor old chap! You hungry!' She sat down; she flung one arm round his neck. She saw the tears in his eyes, and tears struggled down her own contorted face. For a moment they cried together. And the faint smell from the dog's collar drifted up to them.

'Well, I'm heartbroke,' he said; 'that's all. Why, we've had him since he was a baby! He couldn't stand on his four legs that night I brung him home in my pocket. For weeks he couldn't straddle acrost the door-step. Remember that night he first come?'

She nodded. Then she methodically brought out her handkerchief. She wiped her own eyes, then she wiped her husband's.

'No good us bein' two old fools about him,' she said brusquely. 'He's gone.'

'You made him lap milk from your two fingers that night. Remember?'

She nodded impatiently.

'When he growed up, summer and winter he stood out on them hills with me. That's company, if you like. You women, biding at home in the warm, you don't reckon what it means to a man. Out in all weathers, me and him, together. I was lookin' forward to us doing it again. Reckon I looked to that more 'n I did to anything else.'

'Like as not,' she snapped. 'Don't matter about me.'

'Freezin' cold up there; the wind fit to cut your soul out. Up there with the lambs all night, lambin'-times, me an' him. Watchin' me with his funny old eyes, one brown, one blue.'

He turned from her. He rested his arm on the end of the sofa, he dropped his head and hid his face.

'An' you've gone an' killed him because he would have his belly full.'

His wife arose. She stood before him in a valedictory way.

'Can't you hear his old tail thump, Annie? Wonder he ain't haunted you. Can't you feel his big paw comin' up to your knee meal-times? Wonder you can get your victuals down! Remember the way he'd stand on his hind legs supper-time, leanin' his back agen' the arm-chair. He hadn't got many tricks, but that was one. I never teached him that. He thought of it hisself.'

'It's all very well,' she said shrilly, rating him, 'for you, comin' back like this! But how do you think I've managed on your soldierin' pay? Women what's got children are better off. The price of things is cruel. Was I to goo hungry? Was he to be full? Is that what you want? An' I couldn't'—she was wailing—'goo out to work, like some does. I ain't strong; you know that. I have took in a bit of washin', as you see, but it's 'most broke my back.'

He lifted his face and he looked at her very tenderly.

'I knows, my dear. I don't want to be hard on you, Annie. But I'm come back, an' I could have worked to fill you both. I'm as strong as I ever was—once I get some good food in me. If I hadn't been strong, I'd ha' died. Lots did. Why, they dropped off like sheep wi' the scab. Prisoners, I mean. We got not to take no notice. We'd ha' gone mad if we'd noticed.'

He shivered. She dropped down to the sofa; she snuggled up to him at once. For that was her way, to change about. You never knew how to take her.

'You've come back,' she said dramatically. 'Oh, I've got you. Don't you fret, old man, over a dog. Why, I've missed him, too! Think I ain't? Last night I never slept a wink. An' I've been fair lost all day. I couldn't give over cryin'. But what was the good? It was a good offer, an'——'

'A good offer! Then he ain't dead? Bob's alive, then?'

He pushed her away. He stood on his feet, erect, gaunt, swaying, looking the colour of dirty chalk, chalk with great shadows in it.

There was one second of supreme silence. Annie sat still.

'He ain't dead,' she said grimly, 'unless he've broke his heart since yesterday. There's been a lady stayin' in the village an' she took a gurt fancy to Bob. She wouldn't leave me alone; she never give over till I ses yes. An' she paid me a good price.'

'Where's the money?'

'Money! Lord! I spent it in the village yesterday afternoon. Things I owed for. Money goos like water. Wait till you've been home a week.'

The rigour of the war had crushed her. He could see that. She had been soured, afraid, desperate. The thought came to him that he must love her back—to sweetness, to laughing, to lightness.

He was a lover still. Just standing on the hills all day with sheep had kept him fiery, made him thoughtful. He would woo her again—but first he must fetch Bob. He was dizzy. His dog was not dead.

'Where's she took him to?'

His wife arose; she walked to the mantelpiece again, felt behind one of the china dogs and brought out an envelope.

'It's Westdean,' she said. 'Fossiter's the name. She's stayin' at the rectory.'

She gave him the paper. He snatched it, and at the same moment with his other hand he caught at the table, to save himself from falling. He felt light and small, weak, dim.

'I tell you I've spent the money,' said Annie, following him when, after a pause, he moved toward the door.

'I've got money. Don't you worry about money no more.'

She seemed to see his leanness for the first time.

'Why, you're a walkin' shadow!' she added. 'You don't goo off like this without a bite. I've got some liver stewin' in the pot.' She was close behind him, putting her arms round his neck again, loving him, luring him. 'Now you set down in the easy-chair. I'll spread the cloth.'

He shook his head. He was pulling at the front door and it stuck.

'I been gooin' in an' out at the back sence you went away. Where you off to? *Tiger?*'

That was her all over. But she never meant it. He remembered how she used to scold Bob—and then give him the best bits off her plate.

'I'm off to Westdean,' he told her, coolly.

She knew that voice. It brought her to heel, for she knew, as Bob knew, just how far she could go with him.

'Westdean! 'Tis ten mile—five there, five back. An' all acrost them hills. You ain't fit for it. You'll drop.'

He had the door open at last, and he turned to her solemnly.

'I'll be back afore dark,' he said. 'We'll be back, me an' Bob.' Then he laughed in her face and looked loving.

He walked away, through the garden and out at the gate. She watched him; she was stunned. Then she wheeled round to the cupboard and cut bread, in a panic. She found a rind of cheese. She wrapped it all in paper and ran after him.

'Eat that as you goo along,' she said with wonderful tenderness, when she caught him up. She stuffed it into his gaping pocket. 'There, you old softie!' she said unsteadily. 'An' give me a kiss.'

So they repeated their moment, their ravishment, here out on the open track, which narrowed to the hill, which widened to the village and became a lane. He had her in his arms before their own gate. Wild clematis was in crowns that looked like dirty soapsuds upon the high hedges. Little writhen thorn-trees were aflame with berry on this mild December day.

'Yes, you goo and fetch him.' She laughed a little, and took her face out from the folds of his greatcoat. 'He'll be half off his silly old chump when he sees you.'

So he—who had been a shepherd and a soldier—went off alone, with his face turning steadfast toward Westdean. He rejoiced in the solemn loneliness of the hills. He whistled as he went. But the whistling sounded hollow. When did he whistle last—in a devil-may-care, free way?

He walked on. Westdean was lying at his foot. The enchanting Cuckmere river wriggled toward the sea. He kept his eyes from the sea, for he did not love it. All he asked for was the hills by day and the cottage by night. Just the three of them in the cottage, nights! The cooking, the barking, the scolding, the fondling! He remembered.

Mrs Henry Dudeney, 'Missing', from A Baker's Dozen (London: Heinemann, 1922), 249–66

Helen Thomas
(1877–1967)

Helen Noble was born in Liverpool and brought up in Lancashire and London. Her father was a critic and essayist; she was one of five children. When she was 17 and had just left school she met Edward Thomas. Their courtship and marriage and the birth of their first child are recorded in her memoir, *As It Was*, which she wrote shortly after her husband was killed at the battle of Arras in 1917. The story of their family life and his death is contained in the sequel, *World Without End*, which was written a few years later. These memoirs are among the most moving personal records to emerge from the war. They describe the Thomas marriage and reveal the range of Thomas's literary friendships: W. H. Davies, Eleanor Farjeon, Ivor Gurney, D. H. Lawrence, Robert Frost, William Morris. The following extract describes the last family Christmas before Edward Thomas's death.

———

57   WORLD WITHOUT END

CHRISTMAS had come and gone. The snow still lay deep under the forest trees, which tortured by the merciless wind moaned and swayed as if in exhausted agony. The sky, day after day, was grey with snow that fell often enough to keep the surface white, and to cover again and again the bits of twigs, and sometimes large branches that broke from the heavily laden trees. We wearied for some colour, some warmth, some sound, but desolation and despair seemed to have taken up her dwelling place on the earth, as in our hearts she had entered, do what we would to keep her out. I longed with a passionate longing for some sign of life, of hope, of spring, but none came, and I knew at last none would come.

The last two days of David's leave had come. Two days and two nights more we were to be together, and I prayed in my heart, 'Oh, let the snow melt and the sky be blue again!' so that the dread which was spoiling these precious hours would lift.

The first days had been busy with friends coming to say good-bye, all bringing presents for David to take out to the front—warm lined gloves, a fountain pen, a box of favourite sweets, books.

This was not a time when words of affection were bearable; so they heaped things that they thought he might need or would like. Everyone who came was full of fun and joking about his being an officer after having had, as it were, to go to school again and learn mathematics, which were so uncongenial to him, but which he had stuck to and mastered with that strange pertinacity that had made him stick to all sorts of unlikely and uncongenial things in his life. They joked about his short hair, and the little moustache he had grown, and about the way he had perfected the Guards' salute. We got large jugs of beer from the inn near by to drink his health in, and an end to the War. The hateful cottage became homely and comfortable under the influence of these friends, all so kind and cheerful.

Then in the evenings, when just outside the door the silence of the forest was like a pall covering too heavily the myriads of birds and little beasts that the frost had killed, we would sit by the fire with the children and read aloud to them, and they would sing songs that they had known since their baby-hood, and David sang new ones he had learnt in the army—jolly songs with good choruses in which I, too, joined as I busied about getting the supper. Then, when the baby had gone to bed, Elizabeth would sit on his lap, con-tent just to be there, while he and Philip worked out problems or studied maps. It was lovely to see those two so united over this common interest.

But he and I were separated by our dread, and we could not look each other in the eyes, nor dared we be left alone together.

The days had passed in restless energy for us both. He had sawn up a big tree that had been blown down at our very door, and chopped the branches into logs, the children all helping. The children loved being with him, for though he was stern in making them build up the logs properly, and use the tools in the right way, they were not resentful of this, but tried to win his rare praise and imitate his skill. Indoors he packed his kit and polished his accoutrement. He loved a good piece of leather, and his Sam Browne and high trench boots shone with a deep, clear lustre. The brass, too, reminded him of the brass ornaments we had often admired when years ago we had lived on a farm and knew every detail of a plough team's harness. We all helped with the buttons and buckles and badges to turn him out the smart officer it was his pride to be. For he entered into this soldiering which he hated in just that same spirit of thoroughness of which I have spoken before. We talked, as we polished, of those past days: 'Do you remember when Jingo, the grey leader of the team, had colic, and Turner the ploughman led her about Blooming Meadow for hours, his eyes streaming with tears because he thought she was going to die? And how she would only eat the hay from Blooming Meadow, and not the coarse hay that was grown in Sixteen Acre Meadow for the cows? And do you remember Turner's whip which he carried over his shoulder when he led Darling and Chestnut and Jingo out to the plough? It had fourteen brass bands on the handle, one for every year of his service on the farm.' So we talked of old times that the children could remember.

And the days went by till only two were left. David had been going through drawers full of letters, tearing up dozens and keeping just one here and there, and arranging manuscripts and note-books and newspaper cut-tings all neatly in his desk—his face pale and suffering while he whistled. The children helped and collected stamps from the envelopes, and from the drawers all sorts of useless odds and ends that children love. Philip knew what it all meant, and looked anxiously and dumbly from his father's face to mine.

And I knew David's agony and he knew mine, and all we could do was to speak sharply to each other. 'Now do, for goodness' sake, remember, Jenny, that these are the important manuscripts, and that I'm putting them here, and this key is for the box that holds all important papers like our marriage certificate and the children's birth certificates, and my life insurance policy. You may want them at some time; so don't go leaving the key about.' And I, after a while, 'Can't you leave all this unnecessary tidying business, and put up that shelf you promised me? I hate this room, but a few books on a shelf might make it look a bit more human.' 'Nothing will improve this room; so you had better resign yourself to it. Besides, the wall is too rotten for a shelf.' 'Oh, but you promised.' 'Well, it won't be the first time I've broken a promise to you, will it? Nor the last, perhaps.'

Oh, God! melt the snow and let the sky be blue.

The last evening comes. The children have taken down the holly and mistletoe and ivy, and chopped up the little Christmas-tree to burn. And for a treat Elizabeth and Polly are to have their bath in front of the blazing fire. The big zinc bath is dragged in, and the children undress in high glee, and skip about naked in the warm room, which is soon filled with the sweet smell of the burning greenery. The berries pop, and the fir-tree makes fairy lace, and the holly crackles and roars. The two children get into the bath together, and David scrubs them in turn—they laughing, making the fire hiss with their splashing. The drawn curtains shut out the snow and the starless sky, and the deathly silence out there in the biting cold is forgotten in the noise and warmth of our little room. After the bath David reads to them. First of all he reads Shelley's *The Question* and *Chevy Chase*, and then for Polly a favourite Norse tale. They sit in their nightgowns listening gravely, and then, just before they kiss him good-night, while I stand by with the candle in my hand, he says: 'Remember while I am away to be kind. Be kind, first of all, to Mummy, and after that be kind to everyone and everything.' And they all assent together, and joyfully hug and kiss him, and he carries the two girls up, and drops each into her bed.

And we are left alone, unable to hide our agony, afraid to show it. Over supper we talk of the probable front he'll arrive at, of his fellow-officers, and of the unfinished portrait-etching that one of them has done of him and given to me. And we speak of the garden, and where this year he wants the potatoes to be, and he reminds me to put in the beans directly the snow disappears. 'If I'm not back in time you'd better get someone to help you with the digging,' he says. He reads me some of the poems he has written that I have not heard—the last one of all called *Out in the Dark*. And I venture to question one line, and he says, 'Oh no, it's right, Jenny, I'm sure it's right.' And I nod because I can't speak, and I try to smile at his assurance.

I sit and stare stupidly at his luggage by the wall, and his roll of bedding, kit-bag, and suit-case. He takes out his prismatic compass and explains it to me, but I cannot see, and when a tear drops on to it he just shuts it up and puts it away. Then he says, as he takes a book out of his pocket, 'You see, your Shakespeare's *Sonnets* is already where it will always be. Shall I read you some?' He reads one or two to me. His face is grey and his mouth trembles, but his voice is quiet and steady. And soon I slip to the floor and sit between his knees, and while he reads his hand falls over my shoulder and I hold it with mine.

'Shall I undress you by this lovely fire and carry you upstairs in my khaki overcoat?' So he undoes my things, and I slip out of them; then he takes the pins out of my hair, and we laugh at ourselves for behaving as we so often do, like young lovers. 'We have never become a proper Darby and Joan, have we?'

'I'll read to you till the fire burns low, and then we'll go to bed.' Holding the book in one hand, and bending over me to get the light of the fire on the book, he puts his other hand over my breast, and I cover his hand with mine, and he reads from *Antony and Cleopatra*. He cannot see my face, nor I his, but his low, tender voice trembles as he speaks the words so full for us of poignant meaning. That tremor is my undoing. 'Don't read any more. I can't bear it.' All my strength gives way. I hide my face on his knee, and all my tears so long kept back come convulsively. He raises my head and wipes my eyes and kisses them, and wrapping his greatcoat round me carries me to our bed in the great, bare ice-cold room. Soon he is with me, and we lie speechless and trembling in each other's arms. I cannot stop crying. My body is torn with terrible sobs. I am engulfed in this despair like a drowning man by the sea. My mind is incapable of thought. Only now and again, as they say drowning people do, I have visions of things that have been—the room where my son was born; a day, years after, when we were together walking before breakfast by a stream with hands full of bluebells; and in the kitchen of our honeymoon cottage, and I happy in his pride of me. David did not speak except now and then to say some tender word or name, and hold me tightly to him. 'I've always been able to warm you, haven't I?' 'Yes, your lovely body never feels cold as mine does. How is it that I am so cold when my heart is so full of passion?' 'You must have Elizabeth to sleep with you while I am away. But you must not make my heart cold with your sadness, but keep it warm, for no one else but you has ever found my heart, and for you it was a poor thing after all.' 'No, no, no, your heart's love is all my life. I was nothing before you came, and would be nothing without your love.'

So we lay, all night, sometimes talking of our love and all that had been, and of the children, and what had been amiss and what right. We knew the best was that there had never been untruth between us. We knew all of each other, and it was right. So talking and crying and loving in each other's arms we fell asleep as the cold reflected light of the snow crept through the frost-covered windows.

David got up and made the fire and brought me some tea, and then got back into bed, and the children clambered in, too, and we sat in a row sipping our tea. I was not afraid of crying any more. My tears had been shed, my heart was empty, stricken with something that tears would not express or comfort. The gulf had been bridged. Each bore the other's suffering. We concealed nothing, for all was known between us. After breakfast, while he showed me where his account books were and what each was for, I listened calmly, and unbelievingly he kissed me when I said I, too, would keep accounts. 'And here are my poems. I've copied them all out in this book for you, and the last of all is for you. I wrote it last night, but don't read it now. . . . It's still freezing. The ground is like iron, and more snow has fallen. The children will come to the station with me; and now I must be off.'

We were alone in my room. He took me in his arms, holding me tightly to him, his face white, his eyes full of a fear I had never seen before. My arms were round his neck. 'Beloved, I love you,' was all I could say. 'Jenny, Jenny, Jenny,' he said, 'remember that whatever happens, all is well between us for ever and ever.' And hand in hand we went downstairs and out to the children, who were playing in the snow.

A thick mist hung everywhere, and there was no sound except, far away in the valley, a train shunting. I stood at the gate watching him go; he turned back to wave until the mist and the hill hid him. I heard his old call coming up to me: 'Coo-ee!' he called. 'Coo-ee!' I answered, keeping my voice strong to call again. Again through the muffled air came his 'Coo-ee.' And again went my answer like an echo. 'Coo-ee' came fainter next time with the hill between us, but my 'Coo-ee' went out of my lungs strong to pierce to him as he strode away from me. 'Coo-ee!' So faint now, it might be only my own call flung back from the thick air and muffling snow. I put my hands up to my mouth to make a trumpet, but no sound came. Panic seized me, and I ran through the mist and the snow to the top of the hill, and stood there a moment dumbly, with straining eyes and ears. There was nothing but the mist and the snow and the silence of death.

Then, with leaden feet which stumbled in a sudden darkness that overwhelmed me I groped my way back to the empty house.

Helen Thomas, As It was . . . World Without End (London:
Faber, 1972), 299–312

Liesbeth Dill (Liesbeth von Drigalski)
(1877–1962)

Liesbeth Dill wrote some hundred novels, stories, and essays in the realist and
naturalist idiom on the twin themes of the role of women in German society
and the political and ethnic situation of the Saarland and Lothringia. Her
intense love of these border regions and her interest in their tragic history
caused her, in the 1930s, to align herself with the National Socialists. Her
novel *Wir von der Saar* (*We Who are Born in the Saarland*) of 1934 ends with
a statement of allegiance to Hitler. The extract below is taken from *Das
verlorene Land: Ein Buch über Lothringen und Lothringer* (*The Lost Country:
A Book about the Lorraine and Her People*) of 1920 which is, in the main, a
lament about the loss of her country.

58   POLITICAL PORCELAIN

IT was the large living-room of a lonely farmhouse in the region of Metz in
which I sought shelter from the air battle which was raging above us in the
autumn of 1916. Sixteen airplanes had come buzzing across from Mot-à-
Mousson to unload their bombs on to the bridges and barracks of the
nearby recruiting station, whereupon four planes from the Fort arrived and
tried to defend the flight path into the town.

In the great hearth there burnt a log fire. The quiet room was enveloped
in comfortable cosiness, intensified by the slow ticking of a large clock on
the wall. The soft humming of a copper kettle suspended above the fire, in
which water for coffee was boiling, stood in marked contrast to the struggle
which was being played out above our roof.

From in between polished pewterware, colourful pictures of Madonnas
were smiling down on us. Next to them hung copper vases of holy water,

decked with the dry twigs blessed by the Bishop. These were supposed to protect the house from the raging elements of nature. Above us Man was raging.

The large dark, oaken wardrobes contained veritable treasures of linen and materials; the heavy chests were adorned with carvings of shepherds' games from the time of Louis XV and the cupboard, the so-called *dressoir*, was filled with colourful faience. The old farmer told me the story of these strange plates, cups and bowls. Some, cracked and ancient, were painted with birds and proud peacocks. A domestic cockerel, symbol of Gallic nationhood, adorned a row of yellow cups; lustily crowing 'Vive le roi!', he seemed ready for war. There was also a row of delicate plates in matted greys and blues showing three lilies, emblem of the self-important French monarchy by the 'Grace of God'. These had belonged to the farmer's great-grandparents, farmers who remained loyal to the King throughout the years of the Revolution . . . Opinions seemed to have been divided, though, over their 'Bien-Aimé'. It appears that although Louis XV was still being celebrated on contemporary coffee cups, the churches of Paris remained quite empty during the years before his death. No one was the slightest bit interested in praying for his recovery. 'De quoi se plaint-on, n'est-il pas mort?' asked the Bishop mockingly, when the Royal Court complained . . .

An ancient jug with two handles sported an image of happy Lothringian peasants drinking from a cup of wine. The piece was found in a wood behind the farm and dated back to late Roman times. It was certainly extremely old and proved that wine-growing was already playing an important role in ancient times. The fortunes of Lothringia have indeed depended on it through the ages. Since time immemorial, the gentle hills which extend themselves over both sides of the Mosel from the French border at Novéant to Luxembourg have been covered with vines.

On the popular Lothringian plates made of porous grey or yellow clay, glazed and painted in lively colours and adorned with flowers, windmills or landscapes, there were some interesting inscriptions. They referred to the period of French emigration, the 'période tragique', when the French noblemen had to flee to Germany in order to save themselves from the rage of the mob and had to be glad if they could make a modest living in Mainz, Koblenz, Hamburg or Trier. It was a time when duchesses and marquises sold their jewels and then their lace; and when all the money was gone and their estates and their wealth had been confiscated on the other side of the border, they began to build up businesses selling fans, pearl-encrusted bags and paintings, or else they went out into the streets to sell newspapers. Only a few were lucky enough to find a position in a German family, like the

Countess Neuilly who found shelter with a family from Lützow. 'Mais des Lützow sont rares,' said the old Countess Neuilly, whose oval portrait, complete with powdered locks, smiled down on us from a chubby sugar bowl. Most of the noble folk from Versailles ended their days sadly in an attic on a bed of straw or in a street. Their homeland had abandoned them.

On the lowest shelf of the *dressoir* there stood, innocently, a political chamber pot. Frenchmen are fond of such jokes; they are given as presents on New Year's Eve, like those lovely mustard pots which represent something one does not like to be reminded of at the dinner table, or those saucy ashtrays with a lid 'à l'anglaise' . . . The dinner service in blue and white came from the famous factory at Niederweil which had its heyday in the year 1700 until the manufacture of porcelain at Strasbourg was forbidden. These models with the 'Figurines de Lorraine' would have been the delight of any connoisseur. For this farmer they were just pieces of crockery belonging to his household.

There was a pink chocolate service with pictures of the Revolution and the Republic, collected by a subversive relative in Paris. On the rotund chocolate jug there figured the guillotine and on the cream jug was the inscription 'Vive la liberté!' or 'Vive la nation!' In those days the cockerel became an important political animal, he adorned every plate, he peered out at us from the depth of cake tins and sat on every Lothringian bowl. These large coffee bowls without saucers are frequently used here. Because people here are fond of dunking their white bread into milky coffee, they prefer large cups or so-called 'bols', brightly painted and without handles. Our mothers, who had been educated in Lothringian boarding-schools or convents, still had their coffee served out of soup tureens. To this day cheap taverns serve it in beer glasses. Wax cloth on tables is universally used. Lothringians are not particularly interested in elegant tableware but their food is excellent. 'J'aime mieux cela,' declares the farmer. Bellicose and ready for anything, the French cockerel sits on barricades, on cannons. Sometimes he sports the red cap of the Jacobins—product of the hottest, reddest days—'Je veille pour la nation'—sometimes he balances boldly on a bayonet or a lance . . . But with every change of government there was also a change of tableware . . . When Napoleon entered the world stage, proud and solemn imperial eagles appeared on the nation's crockery. The old man showed them to me with pride.

There followed further revolutions, years of turmoil. Inscribed on the crockery was the year 1848 adorned with tricolours and colourful ribbons. Now that farmers were allowed to stand as equals next to noblemen and priests, the emblems of the three estates were prominently and victoriously displayed on the crockery: sword and rapier for the nobility, crook for the clergy and the spade for the peasants. After the war of 1870 there appeared the modern products of the faience factory at Saargemünder. Dark blue vases with majestic roses glazed in matt. Beautifully formed red and yellow cups and ornamental plates with lusty representations of life complete with witty, mostly lascivious inscriptions. These were plates which one buys in the market-place and which the farmer's wife, had she understood the meaning of the verses, would certainly not have tolerated in her living-room, between the Madonnas and the blessed rosaries. The old farmer showed them to me with a smile: 'C'est la mode maintenant.'

The coffee table was decked with faience in the floral patterns which one sees everywhere these days and which, with its graceful colours, endows every coffee table with an air of cheerfulness.

As the noise above our heads ebbed and flowed, I discovered on the *dressoir* an elegantly curved, oval teacup in blue. On its back stood written: 'Déposé 1900'. 'Ah, that's just a single piece,' said the old man and quickly took it from me. Even so I just had time to glimpse the crossed flags of the French and Russian nations united: 'Vive la Russie!' This was the last political product of the porcelain industry before the outbreak of war. And as one listened to the human storm raging above us, one couldn't help thinking that at any moment a bomb might crash through the thin roof of the farmhouse and transform the entire political crockery here into a pile of rubble...

I wonder what kind of faience the descendants of this old farmer will collect and what inscriptions they will carry!

Liesbeth Dill, 'Politisches Porzellan', trans. Agnès Cardinal, from *Das verlorene Land: Ein Buch über Lothringen und Lothringer* (Leipzig-Gaschwitz: Dürr & Weber GmbH, Zellenbücherei, no. 10, 1920), 42–7

Edith Wharton
(1862–1937)

Born to a wealthy New York family, Edith Wharton lived her adult life as a privileged socialite. She also became a fine novelist—*The House of Mirth* (1905), *The Custom of the Country* (1913), *The Age of Innocence* (1920)—and a travel writer. She was a friend of Henry James and, after 1907, spent much of her life in Paris. Her war work, for which she was made a Chevalier of the

Legion of Honour, displayed an unexpected organizational genius. Targeted especially at Belgian refugees, it eventually included clinics and dispensaries, a clothing depot, grocery and coal distribution points, day nurseries and schools, and an employment agency. Her war writing includes *The Marne* (1918), *Fighting France* (1919), and *A Son at the Front* (1923). 'Writing a War Story' was written in 1919.

---

59   WRITING A WAR STORY

Miss Ivy Spang of Cornwall-on-Hudson had published a little volume of verse before the war.

It was called 'Vibrations', and was preceded by a Foreword in which the author stated that she had yielded to the urgent request of friends in exposing her first-born to the public gaze. The public had not gazed very hard or very long, but the Cornwall-on-Hudson *News-Dispatch* had a flattering notice by the wife of the Rector of St Dunstan's (signed 'Asterisk'), in which, while the somewhat unconventional sentiment of the poems was gently deprecated, a graceful and ladylike tribute was paid to the 'brilliant daughter of one of our most prominent and influential citizens, who has voluntarily abandoned *the primrose way of pleasure* to scale *the rugged heights of Parnassus*'.

Also, after sitting one evening next to him at a bohemian dinner in New York, Miss Spang was honored by an article by the editor of *Zigzag*, the new 'Weekly Journal of Defiance', in which that gentleman hinted that there was more than she knew in Ivy Spang's poems, and that their esoteric significance showed that she was a *vers-librist* in thought as well as in technique. He added that they would 'gain incommensurably in meaning' when she abandoned the superannuated habit of beginning each line with a capital letter.

The editor sent a heavily-marked copy to Miss Spang, who was immensely flattered, and felt that at last she had been understood. But nobody she knew read *Zigzag*, and nobody who read *Zigzag* seemed to care to know her. So nothing in particular resulted from this tribute to her genius.

Then the war came, and she forgot all about writing poetry.

The war was two years old, and she had been pouring tea once a week for a whole winter in a big Anglo-American hospital in Paris, when one day, as she was passing through the flower-edged court on her way to her ward, she heard one of the doctors say to a pale gentleman in civilian clothes and spectacles, 'But I believe that pretty Miss Spang writes. If you want an American contributor, why not ask her?' And the next moment the pale gentleman had been introduced and, beaming anxiously at her through his spectacles, was urging her to contribute a rattling war story to *The Man-at-Arms*, a monthly publication that was to bring joy to the wounded and disabled in British hospitals.

'A good rousing story, Miss Spang; a dash of sentiment, of course, but nothing to depress or discourage. I'm sure you catch my meaning? A tragedy with a happy ending—that's about the idea. But I leave it to you; with your large experience of hospital work of course you know just what hits the poor fellows' taste. Do you think you could have it ready for our first number? And have you a portrait—if possible in nurse's dress—to publish with it? The Queen of Norromania has promised us a poem, with a picture of herself giving the baby Crown Prince his morning tub. We want the first number to be an 'actuality', as the French say; all the articles written by people who've done the thing themselves, or seen it done. You've been at the front, I suppose? As far as Rheims, once? That's capital! Give us a good stirring trench story, with a Coming-Home scene to close with . . . a Christmas scene, if you can manage it, as we hope to be out in November. Yes—that's the very thing; and I'll try to get Sargent to do us the wounded V. C. coming back to the old home on Christmas Eve—snow effect.'

It was lucky that Ivy Spang's leave was due about that time, for, devoted though she was to her patients, the tea she poured for them might have suffered from her absorption in her new task.

Was it any wonder that she took it seriously?

She, Ivy Spang, of Cornwall-on-Hudson, had been asked to write a war story for the opening number of *The Man-at-Arms*, to which Queens and Archbishops and Field Marshals were to contribute poetry and photographs and patriotic sentiment in autograph! And her full-length photograph in nurse's dress was to precede her prose; in the table of contents she was to figure as 'Ivy Spang, author of *Vibrations: A Book of Verse*'.

She was dizzy with triumph, and went off to hide her exultation in a quiet corner of Brittany, where she happened to have an old governess, who took her in and promised to defend at all costs the sacredness of her mornings— for Ivy knew that the morning hours of great authors were always 'sacred'.

She shut herself up in her room with a ream of mauve paper and began to think.

At first the process was less exhilarating than she had expected. She knew so much about the war that she hardly knew where to begin; she found herself suffering from a plethora of impressions.

Moreover, the more she thought of the matter, the less she seemed to understand how a war story—or any story, for that matter—was written. Why did stories ever begin, and why did they ever leave off? Life didn't—it just went on and on.

This unforeseen problem troubled her exceedingly, and on the second morning she stealthily broke from her seclusion and slipped out for a walk on the beach. She had been ashamed to make known her projected escapade, and went alone, leaving her faithful governess to mount guard on her threshold while she sneaked out by a back way.

There were plenty of people on the beach, and among them some whom she knew; but she dared not join them lest they should frighten away her Inspiration. She knew that Inspirations were fussy and contrarious, and she felt rather as if she were dragging along a reluctant dog on a string.

'If you wanted to stay indoors, why didn't you say so?' she grumbled to it. But the Inspiration continued to sulk.

She wandered about under the cliff till she came to an empty bench, where she sat down and gazed at the sea. After a while her eyes were dazzled by the light, and she turned them toward the bench and saw lying on it a battered magazine—the midsummer 'All Story' number of *Fact and Fiction*. Ivy pounced upon it.

She had heard a good deal about not allowing one's self to be 'influenced', about jealously guarding one's originality, and so forth; the editor of *Zigzag* had been particularly strong on that theme. But her story had to be written, and she didn't know how to begin it, so she decided just to glance casually at a few beginnings.

The first tale in the magazine was signed by a name great in fiction, one of the most famous names of the past generation of novelists. The opening sentence ran: 'In the month of October, 1914—' and Ivy turned the page impatiently. She may not have known much about story writing, but she did know that *that* kind of a beginning was played out. She turned to the next.

' "My God!" roared the engineer, tightening his grasp on the lever, while the white, sneering face under the red lamp . . . '

No; that was beginning to be out of date, too.

'They sat there and stared at it in silence. Neither spoke; but the woman's heart ticked like a watch.'

That was better but best of all she liked, 'Lee Lorimer leaned to him across the flowers. She had always known that this was coming . . .' Ivy could imagine tying a story on to *that*.

But she had promised to write a war story; and in a war story the flowers must be at the end and not at the beginning.

At any rate, there was one clear conclusion to be drawn from the successive study of all these opening paragraphs; and that was that you must begin in the middle, and take for granted that your reader knew what you were talking about.

Yes; but where was the middle, and how could your reader know what you were talking about when you didn't know yourself?

After some reflection, and more furtive scrutiny of *Fact and Fiction*, the puzzled authoress decided that perhaps, if you pretended hard enough that you knew what your story was about, you might end by finding out toward the last page. 'After all, if the reader can pretend, the author ought to be able to,' she reflected. And she decided (after a cautious glance over her shoulder) to steal the magazine and take it home with her for private dissection.

On the threshold she met her governess, who beamed on her tenderly.

'Chérie, I saw you slip off, but I didn't follow. I knew you wanted to be alone with your Inspiration.' Mademoiselle lowered her voice to add: 'Have you found your plot?'

Ivy tapped her gently on the wrinkled cheek. 'Dear old Madsy! People don't bother with plots nowadays.'

'Oh, don't they, darling? Then it must be very much easier,' said Mademoiselle. But Ivy was not so sure—

After a day's brooding over *Fact and Fiction*, she decided to begin on the empiric system. ('It's sure to come to me as I go along,' she thought.) So she sat down before the mauve paper and wrote 'A shot rang out—'

But just as she was appealing to her Inspiration to suggest the next phrase a horrible doubt assailed her, and she got up and turned to *Fact and Fiction*. Yes, it was just as she had feared, the last story in *Fact and Fiction* began: 'A shot rang out—'

Its place on the list showed what the editor and his public thought of that kind of an opening, and her contempt for it was increased by reading the author's name. The story was signed 'Edda Clubber Hump'. Poor thing!

Ivy sat down and gazed at the page which she had polluted with that silly sentence.

And now (as they often said in *Fact and Fiction*) a strange thing happened. The sentence was there—she had written it—it was the first sentence on the first page of her story, it *was* the first sentence of her story. It was there, it had gone out of her, got away from her, and she seemed to have no further control of it. She could imagine no other way of beginning, now that she had made the effort of beginning in that way.

She supposed that was what authors meant when they talked about being 'mastered by their Inspiration'. She began to hate her Inspiration.

On the fifth day an abased and dejected Ivy confided to her old governess that she didn't believe she knew how to write a short story.

'If they'd only asked me for poetry!' she wailed.

She wrote to the editor of *The Man-at-Arms*, begging for permission to substitute a sonnet; but he replied firmly, if flatteringly, that they counted on a story, and had measured their space accordingly—adding that they already had rather more poetry than the first number could hold. He concluded by reminding her that he counted on receiving her contribution not later than September first; and it was now the tenth of August.

'It's all so sudden,' she murmured to Mademoiselle, as if she were announcing her engagement.

'Of course, dearest—of course! I quite understand. How could the editor expect you to be tied to a date? But so few people know what the artistic temperament is; they seem to think one can dash off a story as easily as one makes an omelet.'

Ivy smiled in spite of herself. 'Dear Madsy, what an unlucky simile! So few people make good omelets.'

'Not in France,' said Mademoiselle firmly.

Her former pupil reflected. 'In France a good many people have written good short stories, too—but I'm sure they were given more than three weeks to learn how. Oh, what shall I do?' she groaned.

The two pondered long and anxiously; and at last the governess modestly suggested: 'Supposing you were to begin by thinking of a subject?'

'Oh, my dear, the subject's nothing!' exclaimed Ivy, remembering some contemptuous statement to that effect by the editor of *Zigzag*.

'Still—in writing a story, one has to have a subject. Of course I know it's only the treatment that really matters; but the treatment, naturally, would be yours, quite yours. . . . '

The authoress lifted a troubled gaze upon her Mentor. 'What are you driving at, Madsy?'

'Only that during my year's work in the hospital here I picked up a good many stories—pathetic, thrilling, moving stories of our poor poilus; and in the evening, sometimes, I used to jot them down, just as the soldiers told them to me—oh, without any art at all . . . simply for myself, you understand. . . . '

Ivy was on her feet in an instant. Since even Mademoiselle admitted that 'only the treatment really mattered', why should she not seize on one of

these artless tales and transform it into Literature? The more she considered the idea, the more it appealed to her; she remembered Shakespeare
and Molière, and said gayly to her governess: 'You darling Madsy! Do lend
me your book to look over—and we'll be collaborators!'

'Oh—collaborators!' blushed the governess, overcome. But she finally
yielded to her charge's affectionate insistence and brought out her shabby
copybook, which began with lecture notes on Mr Bergson's course at the
Sorbonne in 1913, and suddenly switched off to 'Military Hospital No. 13.
November, 1914. Long talk with the Chasseur Alpin Emile Durand,
wounded through the knee and the left lung at the Hautes Chaumes. I have
decided to write down his story. . . . '

Ivy carried the little book off to bed with her, inwardly smiling at the fact
that the narrative, written in a close, tremulous hand, covered each side
of the page, and poured on and on without a paragraph—a good deal like
life. Decidedly, poor Mademoiselle did not even know the rudiments of
literature!

The story, not without effort, gradually built itself up about the adventures
of Emile Durand. Notwithstanding her protests, Mademoiselle, after a day
or two, found herself called upon in an advisory capacity and finally as a collaborator. She gave the tale a certain consecutiveness, and kept Ivy to the
main point when her pupil showed a tendency to wander; but she carefully
revised and polished the rustic speech in which she had originally tran-
scribed the tale, so that it finally issued forth in the language that a young
lady writing a composition on the Battle of Hastings would have used in
Mademoiselle's school days.

Ivy decided to add a touch of sentiment to the anecdote, which was
purely military, both because she knew the reader was entitled to a certain
proportion of 'heart interest', and because she wished to make the subject
her own by this original addition. The revisions and transpositions which
these changes necessitated made the work one of uncommon difficulty; and
one day, in a fit of discouragement, Ivy privately decided to notify the editor
of *The Man-at-Arms* that she was ill and could not fulfill her engagement.

But that very afternoon the 'artistic' photographer to whom she had
posed for her portrait sent home the proofs; and she saw herself, exceedingly long, narrow and sinuous, robed in white and monastically veiled,
holding out a refreshing beverage to an invisible sufferer with a gesture
halfway between Mélisande lowering her braid over the balcony and
Florence Nightingale advancing with the lamp.

The photograph was really too charming to be wasted and Ivy, feeling herself forced onward by an inexorable fate, sat down again to battle with the art of fiction. Her perseverance was rewarded, and after a while the fellow authors (though Mademoiselle disclaimed any right to the honors of literary partnership) arrived at what seemed to both a satisfactory result.

'You've written a very beautiful story, my dear,' Mademoiselle sighed with moist eyes; and Ivy modestly agreed that she had.

The task was finished on the last day of her leave; and the next morning she traveled back to Paris, clutching the manuscript to her bosom, and forgetting to keep an eye on the bag that contained her passport and money, in her terror lest the precious pages should be stolen.

As soon as the tale was typed she did it up in a heavily-sealed envelope (she knew that only silly girls used blue ribbon for the purpose), and dispatched it to the pale gentleman in spectacles, accompanied by the Mélisande-Nightingale photograph. The receipt of both was acknowledged by a courteous note (she had secretly hoped for more enthusiasm), and thereafter life became a desert waste of suspense. The very globe seemed to cease to turn on its axis while she waited for *The Man-at-Arms* to appear.

Finally one day a thick packet bearing an English publisher's name was brought to her. She undid it with trembling fingers, and there, beautifully printed on the large rough pages, her story stood out before her.

At first, in that heavy text, on those heavy pages, it seemed to her a pitifully small thing, hopelessly insignificant and yet pitilessly conspicuous. It was as though words meant to be murmured to sympathetic friends were being megaphoned into the ear of a heedless universe.

Then she began to turn the pages of the review; she analyzed the poems, she read the Queen of Norromania's domestic confidences, and she looked at the portraits of the authors. The latter experience was peculiarly comforting. The Queen was rather good-looking—for a Queen—but her hair was drawn back from the temples as if it were wound round a windlass, and struck out over her forehead in the good old-fashioned Royal Highness fuzz; and her prose was oddly built out of London drawing-room phrases grafted onto German genitives and datives. It was evident that neither Ivy's portrait nor her story would suffer by comparison with the royal contribution.

But most of all was she comforted by the poems. They were nearly all written on Kipling rhythms that broke down after two or three wheezy attempts to 'carry on' and their knowing mixture of slang and pathos seemed oddly old-fashioned to the author of 'Vibrations'. Altogether, it struck her that *The Man-at-Arms* was made up in equal parts of tired compositions by people who knew how to write, and artless prattle by people who didn't. Against such a background, 'His Letter Home' began to loom up rather large.

At any rate, it took such a place in her consciousness for the next day or two that it was bewildering to find that no one about her seemed to have heard of it. *The Man-at-Arms* was conspicuously shown in the windows of the principal English and American bookshops but she failed to see it lying on her friends' tables and finally, when her tea-pouring day came round, she bought a dozen copies and took them up to the English ward of her hospital, which happened to be full at the time.

It was not long before Christmas and the men and officers were rather busy with home correspondence and the undoing and doing-up of seasonable parcels but they all received *The Man-at-Arms* with an appreciative smile, and were most awfully pleased to know that Miss Spang had written something in it. After the distribution of her tale, Miss Spang became suddenly hot and shy, and slipped away before they had begun to read her.

The intervening week seemed long; and it was marked only by the appearance of a review of *The Man-at-Arms* in the *Times*—a long and laudatory article—in which, by some odd accident, 'His Letter Home' and its author were not so much as mentioned. Abridged versions of this notice appeared in the English and American newspapers published in Paris; and one anecdotic and intimate article in a French journal celebrated the maternal graces and literary art of the Queen of Norromania. It was signed 'Fleur-de-Lys', and described a banquet at the Court of Norromania at which the writer hinted that she had assisted.

The following week, Ivy re-entered her ward with a beating heart. On the threshold one of the nurses detained her with a smile.

'Do be a dear and make yourself specially nice to the new officer in Number 5; he's only been here two days and he's rather down on his luck. Oh, by the way—he's the novelist, Harold Harbard; you know, the man who wrote the book they made such a fuss about.'

Harold Harbard—the book they made such a fuss about! What a poor fool the woman was—not even to remember the title of *Broken Wings!* Ivy's heart stood still with the shock of the discovery. She remembered that she had left a copy of *The Man-at-Arms* in Number 5, and the blood coursed through her veins and flooded her to the forehead at the idea that Harold Harbard might at that very moment be reading 'His Letter Home'.

To collect herself, she decided to remain a while in the ward, serving tea to the soldiers and N. C. O.'s, before venturing into Number 5, which the previous week had been occupied only by a polo player drowsy with chloroform and uninterested in anything but his specialty. Think of Harold Harbard lying in the bed next to that man!

Ivy passed into the ward, and as she glanced down the long line of beds she saw several copies of *The Man-at-Arms* lying on them, and one special favorite of hers, a young lance-corporal, deep in its pages.

She walked down the ward, distributing tea and greetings; and she saw that her patients were all very glad to see her. They always were; but this time there was a certain unmistakable emphasis in their gladness; and she fancied they wanted her to notice it.

'Why,' she cried gayly, 'how uncommonly cheerful you all look!'

She was handing his tea to the young lance-corporal, who was usually the spokesman of the ward on momentous occasions. He lifted his eyes from the absorbed perusal of *The Man-at-Arms*, and as he did so she saw that it was open at the first page of her story.

'I say, you know,' he said, 'it's simply topping—and we're so awfully obliged to you for letting us see it.'

She laughed, but would not affect incomprehension.

'That?' She laid a light finger on the review. 'Oh, I'm glad—I'm awfully pleased, of course—you *do* really like it?' she stammered.

'Rather—all of us—most tremendously—!' came a chorus from the long line of beds.

Ivy tasted her highest moment of triumph. She drew a deep breath and shone on them with glowing cheeks.

'There couldn't be higher praise . . . there couldn't be better judges. . . . You think it's really like, do you?'

'Really like? Rather! It's just topping,' rang out the unanimous response.

She choked with emotion. 'Coming from you—from all of you—it makes me most awfully glad.'

They all laughed together shyly, and then the lance-corporal spoke up.

'We admire it so much that we're going to ask you a most tremendous favor—'

'Oh, yes,' came from the other beds.

'A favor—?'

'Yes; if it's not too much.' The lance-corporal became eloquent. 'To remember you by, and all your kindness; we want to know if you won't give one to each of us—'

('Why, of course, of course,' Ivy glowed.)

'—to frame and take away with us,' the lance-corporal continued sentimentally. 'There's a chap here who makes rather jolly frames out of Vichy corks.'

'Oh—' said Ivy, with a protracted gasp.

'You see, in your nurse's dress, it'll always be such a jolly reminder,' said the lance-corporal, concluding his lesson.

'I never saw a jollier photo,' spoke up a bold spirit.

'Oh, do say yes, nurse,' the shyest of the patients softly whispered; and Ivy, bewildered between tears and laughter, said, 'Yes.'

It was evident that not one of them had read her story.

She stopped on the threshold of Number 5, her heart beating uncomfortably.

She had already recovered from her passing mortification; it was absurd to have imagined that the inmates of the ward, dear, gallant young fellows, would feel the subtle meaning of a story like 'His Letter Home.' But with Harold Harbard it was different. Now, indeed, she was to be face to face with a critic.

She stopped on the threshold, and as she did so she heard a burst of hearty, healthy laughter from within. It was not the voice of the polo player; could it be that of the novelist?

She opened the door resolutely and walked in with her tray. The polo player's bed was empty, and the face on the pillow of the adjoining cot was the brown, ugly, tumultuous-locked head of Harold Harbard, well-known to her from frequent photographs in the literary weeklies. He looked up as she came in, and said in a voice that seemed to continue his laugh: 'Tea? Come, that's something like!' And he began to laugh again.

It was evident that he was still carrying on the thread of his joke, and as she approached with the tea she saw that a copy of *The Man-at-Arms* lay on the bed at his side, and that he had his hand between the open pages.

Her heart gave an apprehensive twitch, but she determined to carry off the situation with a high hand.

'How do you do, Captain Harbard? I suppose you're laughing at the way the Queen of Norromania's hair is done.'

He met her glance with a humorous look, and shook his head, while the laughter still rippled the muscles of his throat.

'No—no; I've finished laughing at that. It was the next thing; what's it called? "His Letter Home," by—' The review dropped abruptly from his hands, his brown cheek paled, and he fixed her with a stricken stare.

'Good lord,' he stammered out, 'but it's *you*!'

She blushed all colors, and dropped into a seat at his side. 'After all,' she faltered, half laughing too, 'at least you read the story instead of looking at my photograph.'

He continued to scrutinize her with a reviving eye. 'Why—do you mean that everybody else—'

'All the ward over there,' she assented, nodding in the direction of the door.

'They all forgot to read the story for gazing at its author?'

'Apparently.' There was a painful pause. The review dropped from his lax hand.

'Your tea—?' she suggested, stiffly.

'Oh, yes; to be sure. . . . Thanks.'

There was another silence, during which the act of pouring out the milk, and the dropping of the sugar into the cup, seemed to assume enormous magnitude, and make an echoing noise. At length Ivy said, with an effort at lightness, 'Since I know who you are, Mr Harbard—would you mind telling me what you were laughing at in my story?'

He leaned back against the pillows and wrinkled his forehead anxiously.

'My dear Miss Spang, not in the least—if I *could.*'

'If you could?'

'Yes; I mean in any understandable way.'

'In other words, you think it so silly that you don't dare to tell me anything more?'

He shook his head. 'No; but it's queer—it's puzzling. You've got hold of a wonderfully good subject; and that's the main thing, of course—'

Ivy interrupted him eagerly. 'The subject is the main thing?'

'Why, naturally; it's only the people without invention who tell you it isn't.'

'Oh,' she gasped, trying to readjust her carefully acquired theory of aesthetics.

'You've got hold of an awfully good subject,' Harbard continued; 'but you've rather mauled it, haven't you?'

She sat before him with her head drooping and the blood running back from her pale cheeks. Two tears had gathered on her lashes.

'There!' the novelist cried out irritably, 'I knew that as soon as I was frank you'd resent it! What was the earthly use of asking me?'

She made no answer, and he added, lowering his voice a little, 'Are you very angry with me, really?'

'No, of course not,' she declared with a stony gaiety.

'I'm so glad you're not; because I do want most awfully to ask you for one of these photographs,' he concluded.

She rose abruptly from her seat. To save her life she could not conceal her disappointment. But she picked up the tray with feverish animation.

'A photograph? Of course—with pleasure. And now, if you've quite finished, I'm afraid I must run back to my teapot.'

Harold Harbard lay on the bed and looked at her. As she reached the door he said, 'Miss Spang!'

'Yes?' she rejoined, pausing reluctantly.

'You were angry just now because I didn't admire your story; and now you're angrier still because I do admire your photograph. Do you wonder that we novelists find such an inexhaustible field in Woman?'

Edith Wharton, 'Writing a War Story', from *The Collected Short Stories of Edith Wharton*, ii, ed. R. W. B. Lewis (New York: Charles Scribner's Sons, 1968), 359–70

Berta Lask
(1878–1967)

Berta Lask was born in Galizien (now Poland) to wealthy Jewish-German parents. Her experience as the wife of a doctor working in the slums of Berlin early this century and the revolutionary events in Russia inspired in her strong socialist, pacifist, and feminist convictions. She joined the Communist Party in 1923. After Hitler came to power she went into exile in Russia and only returned to East Berlin in 1953. She wrote socialist poems, stories, and didactic children's fiction and in 1925 scored an exceptional success with a spectacular production of her drama *Thomas Münzer*. The following story is based on historical fact and illustrates Lask's strongly polemical style of writing. It was published in 1929 in Berlin.

———

60   WOMEN IN BATTLE

INTO the circle of dim light cast by the petrol lamp, there appeared the hollow face of the docker woman, Anna Möller. Over narrow cheekbones her skin stretched taut and lean. Like polished glass her bluegreen eyes shimmered from beneath contracted eyebrows. With quick, brusque movements she pulled her patched-up coat over her cotton dress, put a kerchief over her head and picked up her hard leather boots with their wooden soles, so as not to make any noise. She took a few quick gulps of some cold brown liquid and bit into a slice of dark bread, spongy and sticky from the turnips which had been added. Holding on to her piece of bread, she put out the lamp and tiptoed out of the room.

The steps of the staircase creaked. Doors closed. Out of the hall of the housing block six women workers walked into a cold dawn. Wet snow fell softly on to their faces and drove away their heavy sleepiness. Wide awake now, and with keen eyes, the women peered along the badly lit streets.

Out of a side road comes another group of women. The quiet eyes of Anna Möller suddenly light up—They are coming! They kept their word! A soft call, a short greeting. For a moment the dark cluster of women sticks together. Then it breaks up into smaller groups. The closer they get to the harbour, the thicker, the more numerous the clusters get. Sudden gusts of wind blow dark billowing sails over women's heads along twilight streets towards the harbour.

Anna Möller lifts her head, puts her hand across her eyes against a light which isn't there. That black mass over there—yes, that's them! A sharp cry zigzags through the hurrying sails. Soon hands wave joyful greetings from the crowded harbour. Yes, they're all there, the women of the striking dockers.

Even old Schulten is here with her one remaining stump of a tooth in her lower jaw. Her skin is like a piece of cloth, folded many times, which has taken on the lustreless colour of her eyes. She has lost three sons in the war. The fourth is working as a docker but now he is on strike. Anna extends her hand towards her. Suddenly she notices that she's still holding something. It's that piece of bread, soggy with snow. Greedily she puts it to her mouth as sudden hunger tears at her stomach. With eyes narrowing Old Schulten peers at the piece of bread. Anna gives her half of it. Then both women, one young one old, stand side by side, chewing and waiting. Everyone is waiting, nobody is talking much, only a few whispers can be heard.

—Back there!—No!—Yes!—someone's coming! The dark silhouette comes closer. It is an old man with a rucksack on his back. Three more follow behind him, all of them tired, dragging their feet. And then, marching in loud, aggressive step, comes the long file of strike-breakers from out of town.

The women form a chain, hand in hand they stand in four rows, one behind the next. No one speaks. Only once, Old Schulten turns her head to look at the women behind her. Out of wrinkles her eyes begin to shine, suddenly alight.

The file of strike-breakers hesitates. A man makes a joke. It acts like a signal for battle. A barrage of insults begins to rain down on the men: 'You strike-breakers you! Scabs! Bastards! Traitors!—You'll never get to the harbour alive!'

'Oh, come on, women, do be reasonable! We've got a cargo to unload!'

'You turnip-heads, you! You shitbags! We'll learn you to go and unload cargo . . . Everyone is striking now! We want the war to end. We want our men to come home! And we want bread too.'

The old men shuffle off into side-roads and do not look back. The others stand around, undecided. Slowly their file begins to show gaps. Suddenly, a few hotheads turn around and run towards the women in an attempt to break their chain. But the chain holds and the mocking laugh of the women reverberates among the housing blocks.

The strike-breakers begin to retreat. Their ranks are no longer closed, their aggressive marching has stopped. As if lost, the men pick their way gingerly through the slush.

Once again the street is almost empty. But nearby a handful of curious onlookers persist in hanging around. The women look at each other. Blotches of red dance on their faces marked by hunger. Eyes shine feverishly. A large rotund figure, her arms akimbo, laughs shrilly: 'Ha, the shitbags! We should have banged their heads to pulp.'

'Let's stay together! Who knows what will happen now!' Like a Field Marshall, Anna Möller stands in front of the women.

It is not long before, all glint and gleams, a marching column arrives: pointed helmets, swords, and at its head, a tall Lieutenant.

'Disperse!'

The chain doesn't budge.

'No strike-breaker will get through here!' is the retort.

'The strike-breakers are under order to help break up the front out there!' the Lieutenant bellows.

'They won't break our front!' Anna Möller stands tall, her seagreen eyes signalling storm.

'Do you want to let the enemy into this country?'

'The enemy is already here! Look at them!'

It is old Schulten who shouts it, her spindly old arm pointing at the police.

A command is given. Gleaming swords swish through the air. Slowly Anna sinks into a soft dark chasm. After what might have been a year, perhaps an hour, she begins to rise again. Again a searing, gleaming sword. She gathers all her strength: mustn't die just yet. First the strike must be won:

'Strike!' screams the bleeding mouth as darkness descends once more.
It was a long time before the police had finished with the women.

Berta Lask, 'Frauen im Kampf: Eine Geschichte aus dem Ersten Weltkrieg'
('Women in Battle: A Story from the First World War'), trans. Agnès Cardinal,
from *Frauen kämpfen für den Frieden* (*Women Fight for Peace*) (Berlin: Paul
Merker, 1929), 7–10; also in Gisela Brinker-Gabler (ed.), *Frauen gegen den
Krieg* (*Women Against War*) (Frankfurt-on-Main: Fischer, 1980), 230–2

Virginia Woolf
(1882–1941)

A famous novelist, critic, and essayist, Virginia Woolf was the daughter of Sir
Leslie Stephen: she married Leonard Woolf in 1912. The Woolfs were key
members of the Bloomsbury group and set up the Hogarth Press in 1917, on
which most of her work was first published. Woolf lived in London and
Sussex during the war years. Her first clearly Modernist novel (*Jacob's Room*,
1922) concerns a young man who was killed in the conflict. Her later writings,
especially *Three Guineas* (1938), reveal the depth of her opposition to
warfare, a fact which was inseparable from her feminism. In her diaries, however, she takes a much less overtly political position, choosing to write about
the war as part of the changes which she observed from day to day.

61   DIARY 1921

FRIDAY 18 FEBRUARY

I HAVE been long meaning to write a historical disquisition on the return of
peace; for old Virginia will be ashamed to think what a chatterbox she was,
always talking about people, never about politics. Moreover, she will say,
the times you lived through were so extraordinary. They must have
appeared so, even to quiet women living in the suburbs. But indeed nothing
happens at one moment rather than another. The history books will make it
much more definite than it is. The most significant sign of peace this year is
the sales; just over; the shops have been flooded with cheap clothes. A coat
& skirt that cost £14 in November went for 7 perhaps 5. People had ceased

to buy, & the shops had to dispose of things somehow. Margery Strachey who has been teaching at Debenhams foretells bankruptcy for most of the shopkeepers this very month. Still they go on selling cheaply. Pre-war prices, so they say. And I have found a street market in Soho where I buy stockings at 1/ a pair: silk ones (flawed slightly) at 1/10. A hundred yards down the road they ask 5/6 to 10/6 for the same things, or so they seem. Food has fallen a penny here, a penny there, but our books scarcely show a change. Milk is high, 11d a quart. Butter fallen to 3/- but this is Danish butter. Eggs—I dont know what eggs are. Servant girls aged 20 get £45 wages. And the Times pays me 3 guineas instead of £2.2 for a column. But I think you'll find all this written more accurately in other books, my dear Virginia: for instance in Mrs Gosse's diary & Mrs Webb's I think it true to say that during the past 2 months we have perceptibly moved towards cheapness—*just* perceptibly. It is just perceptible too that there are very few wounded soldiers abroad in blue, though stiff legs, single legs, sticks shod with rubber, & empty sleeves are common enough. Also at Waterloo I sometimes see dreadful looking spiders propelling themselves along the platform—men all body—legs trimmed off close to the body. There are few soldiers about.

Virginia Woolf, from *The Diary of Virginia Woolf*, ii. *1920–24*, ed. Anne Olivier Bell (Harmondsworth: Penguin, 1981), 92–3

VI

RETROSPECT

Jo Mihaly
(1902–1994)

Jo Mihaly was a dancer in Berlin who made a name for herself in the 1920s with mime interpretations such as 'Versions of a War', 'The Talmud Scholar', or 'Flower in a Courtyard'. When Hitler came to power in 1933 she went into exile in Switzerland and stayed there until her death. In later life she wrote stories, poems, and many radio plays. The following extract comes from the diary she kept when she was a teenager living with her grandmother in Schneidemühl, a little provincial town in Eastern Germany which became part of Poland after the war.

———

WAR DIARY

15 AUGUST 1918

IT's all over with Germany. We have suffered a terrible defeat near Amiens. Most of our soldiers have surrendered to the English. At the station a Lieutenant said to grandmother: 'The way things are going, old girl, you can soon pack up your soup stand! We are done for—finished—kaput!'

When grandmother came back from her shift at the station she was quite pale. 'Brew me a strong coffee, child!' she said. I boiled so much roasted barley that the coffee was pitch black. It did revive her. 'You too look as if you are about to keel over' she remarked. We looked at each other searchingly.

'I'm o.k.' I said.

16 AUGUST 1918

Now he is dead too, the poor little mite, just skin and bones, despite the doctor's efforts with saline injections. He had become my favourite and I devoted every free minute to him and he kept looking at me out of huge and over serious eyes like a wise old man. Not once did he smile. This lovely little boy died in my arms; he simply laid his head, which seemed much too large for his skeletal body, on my arm and died without a tremor or sigh.

I laid him out under a sheet of gauze as best as I knew how and surrounded him with as many flowers as I was able to gather in the meadow behind the Catholic Church of the Holy Family. The end result was rather scary, he looked like an ancient dwarf who had been dead for at least one hundred years.

17 AUGUST 1918

My heart is still pounding from the fright my little dead boy gave me during my night watch. I had put his bed into the corridor because it was cooler there. At times I would go and stand next to it trying to cope with my sadness. Between three and four o'clock in the morning I suddenly heard a strange humming sound, such as I had never heard before. It seemed to come from the boy's bed. I bent over the gauze covered shape and it was clear that the noise came from underneath the cover. But there was nothing to see. Yet it was obvious that the humming sound came from the boy. It was so gruesome that I felt chilled to the bone with horror. The sound kept changing; sometimes it was long and loud, sometimes it stopped altogether; then it returned. I was terrified! Could it be that the child was not really dead? Was there life in his lungs which had revived somehow? I tore off the covers and bent over the body. I realized that the noise came from the boy's mouth which had remained slightly open. I summoned all my courage and strength and tried to prise open the tiny mouth a little further so that his poor lungs might get more air. And there, oh God!, there crept out a great fat black fly, one of those bluebottles which feed on carrion. . . .

20 AUGUST 1918

The doctor who came to examine my grandmother also listened to my chest. He diagnoses a strain on the heart and there seems to be something wrong with my rib cage. As of today I am suspended from working in the children's hospital. I shall only be readmitted when I have been given a clean bill of health.

Jo Mihaly, from . . . *da gibt's ein Wiedersehn! Kriegstagebuch eines Mädchens 1914–1918* (*Until we meet again . . . War Diary of a Young Girl: 1914–1918*), trans. Agnès Cardinal (Munich: Deutscher Taschenbuch Verlag, 1986), 347–8

Louise Weiss
(1893–1983)

As the founder and editor, from 1918 to 1934, of the pacifist weekly *L'Europe Nouvelle*, Louise Weiss is one of the earliest well-known advocates, this century, of a united Europe. In the 1930s she was at the spearhead of the campaign for French women's suffrage and during the Second World War became an active member of the French Resistance. A lecturer and journalist, she also made films, wrote plays, and her novel *La Marseillaise*, about Nazi-occupied France, won the first prize of the *Académie Française* in 1947. After the war she consolidated her fame with a series of television documentaries of outstanding quality. She won numerous awards, including that of the French Legion of Honour. In 1979, at the age of 86, she was elected to the European Parliament. The passage below comes from the first volume of her prize-winning autobiography, *Mémoires d'une Européenne*, which is an important political chronicle of this century.

———

63   MEMOIRS

THE armistice came into force at eleven o'clock in the morning.

I was in my office at *L'Europe Nouvelle* busy trying to imagine all the dangers Milan Stefanik was facing in Siberia.

Suddenly, an incredible commotion shook the building. Doors slammed, windows opened. People were shouting and I saw my colleagues running towards the courtyard and into the street. Bells were ringing. A cannon fired. All work ceased, just as I had to make some quick final editorial decisions for our journal which was to salute the end of a conflict of which I had been part these last four years. The end? For France, at least. The end? Not for me, though. My heart was in Siberia, lost in a chaos of extraordinary and confused events. Quietly I closed the window and the bells no longer disturbed me. For a while I continued to work but then I could no longer resist the frenzy of the Parisians which had nevertheless pursued me into my hide-out. I too went out into the streets.

Soon I was carried along by a crowd shrieking with joy and hate. No doubt there was something beautiful in that unleashed human sea, with its flags, its triumphant soldiers, pulling the conquered arms of the enemy along the pavements with trumpet calls and wild embraces—its dances and its mourning women. To me it seemed quite awful. Worse! It seemed stupid. Here a victory was being celebrated that had seemed indeed worth while and in which I too had believed, and towards which I had made my own small contribution as best I could. But little by little, this victory seemed to me undeserving of celebration. The people here seemed to be savages. They glorified their own lack of wisdom and the triumph of aggression. If ever I had encountered Him I would have thrown myself at the feet of that Superman who, alone, could have averted such a catastrophe, such an apotheosis of thousands of massacres which the heart could not tolerate and reason could not fathom. He did not exist, this Superman.

I took refuge in the back-room of a café. At that very hour Milan Stefanik was fighting somewhere between Irkutsk and Vladivostock, trying to reach the immensely long railway-line which was the only means of transport for his troops from the old Austrian–Russian border to the ports in the China Sea. . . .

A group of demonstrators interrupted the peace of the café, where I was dreaming with a sick heart and a tortured mind.—'A drink!' they yelled at the landlord. 'A drink for this broken head!'

They were fussing around a soldier whose badly injured jaw and eye had been hastily patched up. The unhappy man was sitting at the bar. Some joker was blowing the bugle. The corks were popping and everyone became absorbed in the Champagne ceremony.

My croissant stuck in my throat. I was alone. I thought differently from everyone else.

Louise Weiss, from *Mémoires d'une Européenne*, i, trans.
Agnès Cardinal (Paris: Albin Michel, n.d.), 276–7

Sidonie Gabrielle Colette
(1873–1954)

This piece was first published in *Le Matin* on 24 March 1915 but its subject would remain topical far beyond the end of the war. In its argument it is characteristic of Colette's distaste for partisan attitudes and of her common sense.

64   THE CHILD OF THE ENEMY

24 MARCH 1915

SOON it will appear. Still shut in, hardly moving, it is already present. At one moment the newspapers express their sympathy, the next they proclaim their loathing. Some call it 'the innocent' and evoke mawkish picture of it standing between a pardoned mother and some merciful French soldier . . . But it is also decried as a poisonous snake, a living crime, destined for an early death.

The two camps are entrenched. Soon we will have conferences on the Child of the Enemy. And it is all a terrible shame. Why are so many words and so much ink spent on it and on its humiliated mother?

'But we do have to counsel and guide these unfortunate women who . . .'

Not at all! They need none of this. They are no longer in those first hours, those first days of dark madness in which they cried out their shame and asked themselves: 'What am I to do?'

Do you really think that a bitter, nine-month meditation bears no fruit? By all means, give shelter to those who need it, give them support and whatever else they may need: work . . . some baby clothes . . . But after that leave them alone so that they can get on with it. Even the most desperate and vindictive of victim mothers will, in the end, not really be capable of a crime, despite those who are already absolving her in advance.

But what will she do?

Leave her be; no doubt she does not know herself. But it will come to her in time. She suffers, but the optimism transmitted to the female laden with a precious human life, will subdue her torment. It will plead for the child which, trembling there, endows its mother with an extra instinct: that of not thinking too much, of not envisaging the future in precise and sombre outlines. And the most outraged mother, the one who wakes at night cursing the imperious prisoner of her belly, will not want our teachings. She might indeed be waiting, furious and terrified, for the intruder, the monster, to be crushed at its first cry, or at least to be banished . . . But let us have confidence in the moment when she will see, exhausted and subdued, defenceless against her best instincts, that the 'monster' is only a new-born baby, nothing but a baby greedy for life, a baby with vacant eyes and silvery down, with crimped and silky hands like a poppy which has only just opened its cup.

Leave the women alone. Say nothing . . . Hold your peace.

Colette, 'L'Enfant de l'ennemi', trans. Daniel Cardinal, from *Les Heures longues*, *Œuvres II* (Paris: Nouvelle Revue Française, Gallimard, 1986), 508–9

Helen Thomas
(1877–1967)

The extract which follows describes the beginning of Helen Thomas's friendship with the composer and poet Ivor Gurney who, during his service in France, had been wounded, gassed, and shell-shocked. As a consequence he spent many years after the war as a mental patient: at the time of this meeting, he was in the City of London Mental Hospital, Dartford, Kent. He died in hospital in 1937.

———

65   IVOR GURNEY

I THINK it was about 1932 that I had a letter from a woman whose name was strange to me. She was Marion Scott, but as I did not move in musical circles I did not know that she was distinguished in that world. The subject of her letter was strange to me for the same reason. I was therefore filled with surprise and pity when she told me that she was the champion and friend of a young musical genius named Ivor Gurney. This young man had lost his reason in the war and was in a lunatic asylum. He passionately loved my husband's work and was deeply interested in anything to do with him. Indeed Edward Thomas's name—for Ivor Gurney had never met him though they had been near each other at the front in France—evoked in him what one can only call love. She wrote saying that if I could face the ordeal of visiting him, she felt such indirect contact with Edward would mean more to him than we could imagine. So it was arranged that I should go. I met Miss Scott at Victoria Station and I had my hands full of flowers.

On the journey to Dartford she told me about him, how he came of a very humble Gloucestershire family, how he had always been highly sensitive and eccentric and that those fit to judge thought him a musical genius. How his mind—always on the borderline—had quite given way at the front and how he had tried more than once to take his own life.

We arrived at Dartford Asylum which looked like—as indeed it was—a prison. A warder let us in after unlocking a door, and doors were opened and locked behind us as we were ushered into the building. We were walking along a bare corridor when we were met by a tall gaunt dishevelled man clad in pyjamas and dressing gown, to whom Miss Scott introduced me. He gazed with an intense stare into my face and took me silently by the hand. Then I gave him the flowers which he took with the same deeply moving intensity and silence. He then said, 'You are Helen, Edward's wife and Edward is dead.' And I said, 'Yes, let us talk of him.'

So we went into a little cell-like bedroom where the only furniture was a bed and a chair. The window was high and barred and the walls bare and drab. He put the flowers on the bed for there was no vessel to put them in; there was nothing in the room that could in any way be used to do damage with—no pottery or jars or pictures whose broken edge could be used as a weapon.

He remarked on my pretty hat, for it was summer and I had purposely put on my brightest clothes. The gay colours gave him great pleasure. I sat by him on the bed and we talked of Edward and of himself, but I cannot now remember the conversation. But I do remember that though his talk was generally quite sane and lucid, he said suddenly, 'It was wireless that killed Edward', and this idea of the danger of wireless and his fear of it constantly occurred in his talk. 'They are getting at me through wireless.' We spoke of country that he knew and which Edward knew too and he evidently identified Edward with the English countryside, especially that of Gloucestershire.

I learned from the warder that Ivor Gurney refused to go into the grounds of the asylum. It was not his idea of the country at all—the fields, woods, water-meadows and footpaths he loved so well—and he would have nothing to do with that travesty of something sacred to him.

Before we left he took us into a large room in which was a piano and on this he played to us and to the tragic circle of men who sat on hard benches built into the walls of the room. Hopeless and aimless faces gazed vacantly and restless hands fumbled or hung down lifelessly. They gave no sign or sound that they heard the music. The room was quite bare and there was not one beautiful thing for the patients to look at.

We left and I promised to come again.

Ivor Gurney longed more than anything else to go back to his native Gloucestershire, but this was not allowed for fear he should again try to take his own life. I said, 'But surely it would be more humane to let him go there even if it meant no more than one hour of happiness before he killed himself.' But the authorities could not look at it in that way.

The next time I went with Miss Scott I took with me Edward's own well-used ordnance maps of Gloucestershire where he had often walked. This proved to have been a sort of inspiration for Ivor Gurney at once spread them out on his bed and he and I spent the whole time I was there tracing with our fingers the lanes and byways and villages of which Ivor Gurney knew every step and over which Edward had also walked. He spent that hour in revisiting his home, in spotting a village or a track, a hill or a wood and seeing it all in his mind's eye, with flowers and trees, stiles and hedges, a mental vision sharper and more actual for his heightened intensity. He trod, in a way we who were sane could not emulate, the lanes and fields he knew and loved so well, his guide being his finger tracing the way on the map. It was most deeply moving, and I knew that I had hit on an idea that gave him more pleasure than anything else I could have thought of. For he had Edward as companion in this strange perambulation and he was utterly happy, without being over-excited.

This way of using my visits was repeated several times and I became for a while not a visitor from the outside world of war and wireless, but the element which brought Edward back to life for him and the country where they two could wander together.

Helen Thomas, 'Ivor Gurney', in *Time and Again: Memoirs and Letters*, ed. Myfanwy Thomas (Manchester: Carcanet, 1978), 110–12

Antonia White
(1899–1980)

Antonia White was a novelist, translator, and journalist. She is best known for her first novel *Frost in May* (1933) which was followed by *The Lost Traveller* (1950) and *Beyond the Glass* (1954). Her fiction is predominantly autobiographical and contains recurrent themes—her childhood, her Catholicism, the war, her difficulties with writing, and her mental breakdown. The last occurred in the early 1920s when she was confined in the Bethlem asylum in Southwark, which was converted into the Imperial War Museum in 1936. White made a return visit to the building in 1941 which she mentions in a letter: 'I've seen my old cell with a case of shells in it and a radiator which we lunatics would have greatly appreciated!' 'Surprise Visit' (1965) views the visit sombrely: not only does it bring back to life the protagonist's mental breakdown, but the evocation of the building's former function also suggests disturbing parallels between the harsh personal experience of her stay in the asylum and the collective trauma inflicted by the war.

---

66 SURPRISE VISIT

FOR over fifteen years, Julia Tye had been meaning to go back some day and look at the place, partly out of curiosity, partly to prove to herself that she could face it without a qualm. True, she did not know just where it stood, beyond that it was somewhere on London's south bank. On the morning of her release from the huge, grimed building with its dome that so deceptively suggested a church, she had been too excited to notice street names. But she remembered that, soon after leaving the iron gate in the spiked walls, the taxi had crossed a bridge over the Thames. It would have been easy enough to locate it. The place was so old and so notorious that its name had become a generic term for all institutions of its kind. It was probably featured in Baedeker. However, there was no need to consult a guidebook. All Julia had to do was to look it up in a certain classified section of the telephone directory. For some reason or other she had not done so.

This was not because she was trying to forget the period she had spent in the place all that time ago, in her early twenties. On the contrary, whenever the memory tended to fade, she deliberately recalled it. Year by year it gave her a peculiar satisfaction to measure how far and how successfully she had travelled since that deplorably bad start. Nowadays she found it more gratifying than ever. No one at Frant and Redwood's, that eminent publishing firm where she held down such a highly responsible job, could ever have suspected that 'our Miss Tye' had ever been anything but utterly reliable. She had been a reformed character for so long that she could trust herself as much as her employers trusted her. It was only when someone unexpectedly mentioned the name of the place (though she often mentioned it herself in the right company) that she felt a faint, apprehensive chill.

Then, one morning, soon after her thirty-eighth birthday, its name had leapt out at her in a heading in a newspaper. Breaking off from the book reviews she was studying, she switched her eye to the paragraph in the other column. It informed her that the place had been turned into a War Museum. 'The Public Authorities,' she read, 'have realised, for some considerable time, that, judged by modern standards, the building was unsuitable for the purpose it has served for centuries. Since the edifice is attributed to Wren, it was decided not to demolish it, but to use it to house the various weapons, trophies and models which have accumulated during two world wars. Many of these have not hitherto been displayed owing to lack of space. Now that certain necessary internal alterations have been made, the public will be admitted daily (public holidays excepted) to what should prove an interesting exhibition.'

As Julia put down the paper, she saw at once that this was a brilliant opportunity. Now she had a really cogent reason for going back to look at the place. Seeing it from the outside would have been no real test. But to walk right into that building of her own accord, as an ordinary member of the public, free to walk out of it when she chose, would disinfect it once and for all in her imagination.

She could not go at once. Frant and Redwood were in the throes of getting out their autumn list. But even when the rush of work had slowed down, she still delayed her visit. For one thing, she was tired. Without having yet verified its exact situation, she was convinced that it was a long way away both from her home and her office and would mean a tiresome, complicated journey. For another, she had an excellent reason for not being in a hurry. Any sense of anxious compulsion would ruin the experiment. This was something to be undertaken coolly and unemotionally, at the right, the scientific moment. She was sure the analyst who had so successfully diagnosed the causes of her anti-social behaviour would agree.

There was also a third, rather odd reason why she did not yet feel quite ready to confront the place. Though she could recall a number of concrete details about the apparently endless time she had spent in it, the place itself remained unreal. She could shrink her experience into a period between two known dates, but she could not reduce the building to a concrete mass occupying a fixed point in space. Some part of her mind refused to admit that it had gone on existing independently of her, that it was solidly situated somewhere in South London. Even when she read that paragraph in the paper she had felt a faint uncertainty as if, in spite of the old notorious name, the place referred to was not *the* place. Even had there been a photograph, she would still not have been quite sure. She had never been able to rebuild it in memory as a recognisable whole.

It was months after reading the paragraph that going, as she often did in her lunch hour, to buy a ticket for a Shakespeare performance at the Old Vic, she somehow lost her way. After leaving the box-office, she walked a few blocks, absorbed in some office problem, then stopped, expecting to find herself opposite Waterloo Station. Instead, she found herself on the edge of a completely unfamiliar main road. Realising she must have taken the wrong direction, she looked back to see how far she had come from the Old Vic. It was nowhere in sight. Without realizing it, she must have turned a corner. She stood still, gazing around to try to get her bearings. And there, right opposite her, on the other side of the stream of traffic, was the place.

What startled her even more than its sudden appearance, was her instant recognition of that grimy stone facade, with steps leading up to a pillared portico and a dome rising above. Why was she sure that, of many London buildings of its type, it was *the* one? Yet she had known infallibly that it was, before she read *Imperial War Museum* on the board at the open gate. Could she really have registered her one remembered glimpse of its front, more than fifteen years ago, as sharply as that? How shocked, how hurt her father had looked, on the morning they discharged her, when she had turned at the gate to glance back and exclaim:

'Why, it's quite noble, when you see it from the front! Of course, *we* never did.'

He hadn't let her linger, as she longed to, to make out whether that slim dome, firmly anchored above its matching stone pediment, could possibly be the same that used to float now here, now there, erratic as a bubble, over this or that cliff of dingy brown brick. Even at that moment—it came back to her now as she stared—she had had an odd feeling that the building corresponded with some other image, something like a tiny snapshot printed in sepia she had seen innumerable times. Before she could find the connection, her father had bundled her into the waiting taxi, and said, in a low voice, so that the driver should not hear:

'Please God, neither you nor I will ever set eyes on that place again. Julia, my dear, for your own sake—as well as for mine and your mother's—try and blot these last months out of your mind. All we want you to do now is think ahead to a new life. The few people who know where you have been will have the decency not to mention it. So we'll make a pact here and now, shall we, never to refer to the subject again?'

In his presence, she never had referred to it. To forget was, of course, impossible, though at first she hadn't deliberately tried to recall it. It had recalled itself often enough, in the first year or two after her release, in those nightmares where she found herself back there, this time without hope of escape, being herded up and down long corridors and up steep winding stone stairs with other women or locked alone in a cell with a high, barred window, beating frantically on a blank door. But, when the nightmares became more infrequent (she hardly ever had them now) she had found it curiously fascinating to piece it all together. It was extraordinary how much she had consciously forced herself to remember, though time had had so little meaning there that it was impossible to put her memories in an orderly sequence. Long before her father's death, she had discovered there were people to whom she could talk about it quite frankly. Unconventional, broadminded people who saw nothing disgraceful about what had happened to her. With some, it even gave her a peculiar prestige. But of course there were others with whom she had to be careful; there were people who still held her father's old-fashioned views. Sometimes it amused her, in the middle of a dull conference at Frant and Redwood's, to fancy the electrifying effect if 'our Miss Tye' suddenly announced where she had spent most of her twenty-third year.

Now, abruptly confronted with the place, she felt angry and almost insulted. It had no right to burst in on her crudely like that. She glared at it like some intrusive acquaintance who had appeared uninvited. Moreover, there was something indecent in this public exhibition of itself right on a main London road. In her imagination it had always been remote and secretive, approachable only by a maze of tortuous paths. To think it had stood there, all those years, within a few hundred yards of the Old Vic, shamelessly waiting to catch her eye!

Well, now it was there, she would call its bluff. She couldn't of course spare the time. Not that she couldn't take as long a lunch-hour as she pleased, but her desk was piled with proofs she wanted to go through herself for a final revision. It was astonishing how printers' readers, as well as authors, seemed to suffer from mental black-outs. She would go over and accost it, just as she had deliberately accosted Roberts and Patterson, all those years ago, in that night-club. She hadn't, of course, identified them so promptly, disguised in those tatty evening-frocks, with rows of coloured glass bangles wedged on their muscular arms. She had merely been aware of two unpartnered middle-aged women, rather pathetically out of their element, covertly staring at her every time she stepped on to the dance-floor. Julia was quite used to being stared at in those days, even by women. It had seemed rather important, as well as a pleasure, in that first period of her 'new life' to be particularly well-dressed and well-groomed. She had felt unusually confident that night; looking her best, dancing her best, enjoying being a pretty young woman in the arms of a handsome young man. It was he . . . which of her young men had it been? . . . who had said irritably:

'Anyone would think those two ghastly females knew you, the way they keep staring at you, then putting their heads together and whispering.'

She had laughed back:

'Oh, I've known some odd people in my time. You'd be surprised. Next time we pass, I'll have a good look at them.'

The moment she had recognized them over her shoulder, she had broken away from him, in the middle of their dance, saying:

'I certainly do know them. But I don't think they're sure about *me*. I'm going over to speak to them.'

'*No*, Julia,' he had said, clutching her arm. 'They're really too awful, like women policemen.'

'Perhaps that's just what they are!' she had mocked, throwing off his arm and giving Roberts and Patterson her most dazzling smile. 'Anyway, I'm going to have a word with them.'

'Can't it wait? This is such a marvellous tune.'

'It's an even more marvellous joke. I met them in the most *fantastic* circumstances. Perhaps I'll tell you when I get back.'

It shamed her even now to remember she couldn't have carried it off worse. She hadn't been gay and assured, or even lightly cynical. She had faltered and flushed, almost cringed, as if they were still in uniform, with bunches of keys at their belts. Pressed by the young man to tell him the marvellous joke, she had said it wasn't so very funny after all. Though the two women had left almost at once, she had been so silent and danced so badly for the rest of the evening that the young man had asked if she were ill.

Firmly, Julia crossed the road and entered the gate. Slowly and deliberately she walked up the gravel path, fixing her eyes on the building, trying to reduce it to something as impersonal as the Victoria and Albert. All at once, her knees began to tremble. Instead of the huge, three dimensional building, a tiny flat sepia replica of it danced before her retina. She blinked and it was gone again; blinked again . . . it was back, this time encircled by a scroll lettered with its old name, as she had seen it day after day on mugs and plates. She knew at last why she had recognised the place at sight. It ought to have reassured her but it had the reverse effect. If, after fifteen years, she had only just recalled a detail as sharp as that . . . what else might still be buried? Mightn't it be wiser to wait? . . . the place wouldn't run away, as her father used to say when she was too impatient.

No, *she* wouldn't run away either. She forced her legs to carry her up the stairs and through the main door. She thought the official on duty looked at her a little oddly. Ought she to give him some reason for being there? Say she was writing a novel about the 1914–18 period, needed some details of weapons and uniforms? No, that might lead to awkward questions. Or just say she worked in a publisher's and they were bringing out a book on the first world war . . . she was looking for an idea for the jacket? But would he believe her? And did she really work at a publisher's? She shut her eyes, trying in vain to envisage her proof-strewn desk. All she could see was a plate, with a little sepia picture stamped in the middle. It had been like a kind of reward, when one had scraped away the last of some horrid substance under their ruthless eyes, to see it there. It meant Tye had been a good girl. Not like the days Tye flung the plate, still nearly full, on the floor. Such peculiar plates. They didn't break, even though the floor was stone.

She gave the man a vague smile, then hurried into the main hall. She couldn't remember anything like this. Perhaps the place was only a museum after all and had never been anything else. Feeling that a man in some kind of uniform, with a spike moustache and a row of medals, was watching her, she joined a group of schoolboys and peered, as intently as they, at a large gun. Was *that* man's face familiar? Probably just a type. Uniform made people look alike. There'd been a man in uniform at the door the day she left . . . he'd asked her to give him some piece of paper. . . . Anyway, it had been a different kind of uniform. Perhaps they'd kept some of the male staff on as museum keepers? She wouldn't of course, know their faces; they had had no concern with her. Yet hadn't there once been a man—just for a moment, on their side—a man with a spiked moustache?

She pulled herself together. If she was going to get emotionally flurried and start fancying things, she'd better walk out at once. No, that might look bad, as if she felt compelled to prove she *could* walk out. She'd come here to study the place dispassionately, hadn't she? Forcing herself to move slowly from glass case to glass case, staring blankly at shells and aeroplane propellers, she finally reached the end of the great hall, and finding herself alone, safely hidden behind a captured Howitzer, she felt calm enough at last to look around. This vast, high expanse, like the nave of a church, belonged nowhere in her recollections. The quarters she had inhabited must be somewhere away at the back. Perhaps they had been pulled down. With a pang, half of relief, half of disappointment, she realised that it was hardly likely, in any case, that they would be on show to the public. The hall was lit only from above; she could not see any window through which she could catch a glimpse of any part she knew. Then, suddenly, in a bay behind a case in which, like a corpse in an upright glass coffin, stood a life-size figure in tin-hat, gas-mask, and mud-splashed khaki, she saw a window. Edging round the soldier as cautiously as if he were a sentry who might challenge her, she looked through the pane. And there, straight in front of her, was the exercise yard, absolutely unchanged. She could see the dark brown brick walls with their dingy white stone coping just as she had always seen them, as slabs hewn out of some giant wedding-cake, almost petrified with age, like Miss Havisham's. She knew every crack in the asphalt, every broken slat in the bench that encircled the solitary, sooty plane-tree in the centre of the square. The yard was empty. But she felt, at any minute, the door with the barred frosted-glass panes in the wall opposite might open to one of Patterson's keys and out would come the straggling file. She had never learnt them all but she could still sharply envisage the middle-aged woman with the scarred face and the tall gipsy-looking one who would have been handsome but for those disfiguring yellow teeth, with long incisors like a wolf's. 'Old Nick' they called her, because she was always 'giving trouble'. Once she had sunk those yellow fangs in Roberts' wrist, and it had taken three people to overpower her in her fighting rage. After that, it was a long time before Old Nick reappeared in the yard. And there was the quiet little thing who never gave any 'trouble' at all, who looked like a prim, pretty schoolgirl and kept moving her lips as she walked, as if memorising her homework. Julia had always wondered how she came to be there, her fresh little face looked so strange among the others, mostly coarse, haggard or sallow. The rest she could see only as masks, set in a particular expression, sullen or blank or inordinately cheerful; one or two serene, almost saintlike.

She heard footsteps approaching. In panic, she clutched the window ledge, not daring to look round. What was she doing here, hiding behind a glass case? She must have slipped through some forbidden door. No wonder the yard was empty. They'd missed her from the queue and they wouldn't let the others out till they found her. Was it Roberts or Patterson coming to recapture her? She clutched the ledge tighter, head bowed, shoulders hunched, expecting a voice to say:

'Up to your tricks again, Tye? Any more nonsense, and you know where we'll put *you*.'

A voice did speak just behind her. It was a man's and obviously not addressed to her. It was solicitously asking someone if they felt faint and would like a glass of water. Then a hand fell on her shoulder; she turned and almost screamed. She was facing the uniformed man with the grizzled moustache. Was he the museum keeper or the one they had fetched from the men's side to help overpower Old Nick? No, he was both men at once, just as she was two women at once. One this side of the window, in an admirably tailored suit; one out in the yard in a shapeless smock.

'Now, now . . .' someone was saying. That was how they always began— in that false, coaxing voice. In a desperate effort to escape, she dodged away from the glass case containing the soldier and took refuge behind another. Then she saw the figure standing deceptively still inside it: a uniformed nurse, staring fixedly at her and coldly smiling. Now she knew for certain where she was and who she was. She sagged down on her knees before the wax dummy, whimpering:

'No . . . Oh, no! . . . Not *there* . . . Not in the pads. . . . Don't put me back in the pads! . . . I'll be good, Nurse Roberts, I'll be good!'

Antonia White, 'Surprise Visit', in *Strangers* (London: Virago, 1992), 160–73

Radclyffe Hall
(1883–1943)

In her story 'Miss Ogilvy Finds Herself', written in 1926, Radclyffe Hall focuses directly on the wartime weakening of gender taboos. The story was not published until 1934 and in the 'Author's Forenote' to the first edition (Heinemann, 1934) Hall wrote that 'although Miss Ogilvy is a very different person from Stephen Gordon, yet those who have read *The Well of Loneliness* will find in the earlier part of this story the nucleus of those sections of my novel which deal with Stephen Gordon's childhood and girlhood, and with the noble and selfless work done by hundreds of sexually inverted women during the Great War'.

——

67   MISS OGILVY FINDS HERSELF

1

MISS OGILVY stood on the quay at Calais and surveyed the disbanding of her Unit, the Unit that together with the coming of war had completely altered the complexion of her life, at all events for three years.

Miss Ogilvy's thin, pale lips were set sternly and her forehead was puckered in an effort of attention, in an effort to memorize every small detail of every old war-weary battered motor on whose side still appeared the merciful emblem that had set Miss Ogilvy free.

Miss Ogilvy's mind was jerking a little, trying to regain its accustomed balance, trying to readjust itself quickly to this sudden and paralysing change. Her tall, awkward body with its queer look of strength, its broad, flat bosom and thick legs and ankles, as though in response to her jerking mind, moved uneasily, rocking backwards and forwards. She had this trick of rocking on her feet in moments of controlled agitation. As usual, her hands were thrust deep into her pockets, they seldom seemed to come out of her pockets unless it were to light a cigarette, and as though she were still standing firm under fire while the wounded were placed in her ambulances, she suddenly straddled her legs very slightly and lifted her head and listened. She was standing firm under fire at that moment, the fire of a desperate regret.

Some girls came towards her, young, tired-looking creatures whose eyes were too bright from long strain and excitement. They had all been members of that glorious Unit, and they still wore the queer little forage-caps and the short, clumsy tunics of the French Militaire. They still slouched in walking and smoked Caporals in emulation of the Poilus. Like their founder and leader these girls were all English, but like her they had chosen to serve England's ally, fearlessly thrusting right up to the trenches in search of the wounded and dying. They had seen some fine things in the course of three years, not the least fine of which was the cold, hard-faced woman who commanding, domineering, even hectoring at times, had yet been possessed of so dauntless a courage and of so insistent a vitality that it vitalized the whole Unit.

'It's rotten!' Miss Ogilvy heard someone saying. 'It's rotten, this breaking up of our Unit!' And the high, rather childish voice of the speaker sounded perilously near to tears.

Miss Ogilvy looked at the girl almost gently, and it seemed, for a moment, as though some deep feeling were about to find expression in words. But Miss Ogilvy's feelings had been held in abeyance so long that they seldom dared become vocal, so she merely said 'Oh?' on a rising inflection—her method of checking emotion.

They were swinging the ambulance cars in mid-air, those of them that were destined to go back to England, swinging them up like sacks of potatoes, then lowering them with much clanging of chains to the deck of the waiting steamer. The porters were shoving and shouting and quarrelling, pausing now and again to make meaningless gestures; while a pompous official was becoming quite angry as he pointed at Miss Ogilvy's own special car—it annoyed him, it was bulky and difficult to move.

'Bon Dieu! Mais dépêchez-vous donc!' he bawled, as though he were bullying the motor.

Then Miss Ogilvy's heart gave a sudden, thick thud to see this undignified, pitiful ending; and she turned and patted the gallant old car as though she were patting a well-beloved horse, as though she would say: 'Yes, I know how it feels—never mind, we'll go down together.'

2

Miss Ogilvy sat in the railway carriage on her way from Dover to London. The soft English landscape sped smoothly past: small homesteads, small churches, small pastures, small lanes, with small hedges; all small like England itself, all small like Miss Ogilvy's future. And sitting there still arrayed in her tunic, with her forage-cap resting on her knees, she was conscious of a sense of complete frustration; thinking less of those glorious years at the Front and of all that had gone to the making of her, than of all that had gone to the marring of her from the days of her earliest childhood.

She saw herself as a queer little girl, aggressive and awkward because of her shyness: a queer little girl who loathed sisters and dolls, preferring the stable-boys as companions, preferring to play with footballs and tops, and occasional catapults. She saw herself climbing the tallest beech trees, arrayed in old breeches illicitly come by. She remembered insisting with tears and some temper that her real name was William and not Wilhelmina. All these childish pretences and illusions she remembered, and the bitterness that came after. For Miss Ogilvy had found as her life went on that in this world it is better to be one with the herd, that the world has no wish to understand those who cannot conform to its stereotyped pattern. True enough in her youth she had gloried in her strength, lifting weights, swinging clubs and developing muscles, but presently this had grown irksome to her; it had seemed to lead nowhere, she being a woman, and then as her mother had often protested: muscles looked so appalling in evening dress—a young girl ought not to have muscles.

Miss Ogilvy's relation to the opposite sex was unusual and at that time added much to her worries, for no less than three men had wished to propose, to the genuine amazement of the world and her mother. Miss Ogilvy's instinct made her like and trust men for whom she had a pronounced fellow-feeling; she would always have chosen them as her friends and companions in preference to girls or women; she would dearly have loved to share in their sports, their business, their ideals and their wide-flung interests. But men had not wanted her, except the three who had found in her strangeness a definite attraction, and those would-be suitors she had actually feared, regarding them with aversion. Towards young girls and women she was shy and respectful, apologetic and sometimes admiring. But their fads and their foibles, none of which she could share, while amusing her very often in secret, set her outside the sphere of their intimate lives, so that in the end she must blaze a lone trail through the difficulties of her nature.

'I can't understand you,' her mother had said, 'you're a very odd creature—now when I was your age . . .'

And her daughter had nodded, feeling sympathetic. There were two younger girls who also gave trouble, though in their case the trouble was fighting for husbands who were scarce enough even in those days. It was finally decided, at Miss Ogilvy's request, to allow her to leave the field clear for her sisters. She would remain in the country with her father when the others went up for the Season.

Followed long, uneventful years spent in sport, while Sarah and Fanny toiled, sweated and gambled in the matrimonial market. Neither ever succeeded in netting a husband, and when the Squire died leaving very little money, Miss Ogilvy found to her great surprise that they looked upon her as a brother. They had so often jibed at her in the past, that at first she could scarcely believe her senses, but before very long it became all too real: she it was who must straighten out endless muddles, who must make the dreary arrangements for the move, who must find a cheap but genteel house in London and, once there, who must cope with the family accounts which she only, it seemed, could balance.

It would be: 'You might see to that, Wilhelmina; you write, you've got such a good head for business.' Or: 'I wish you'd go down and explain to that man that we really can't pay his account till next quarter.' Or: 'This money for the grocer is five shillings short. Do run over my sum, Wilhelmina.'

Her mother, grown feeble, discovered in this daughter a staff upon which she could lean with safety. Miss Ogilvy genuinely loved her mother, and was therefore quite prepared to be leaned on; but when Sarah and Fanny began to lean too with the full weight of endless neurotic symptoms incubated in resentful virginity, Miss Ogilvy found herself staggering a little. For Sarah and Fanny were grown hard to bear, with their mania for telling their symptoms to doctors, with their unstable nerves and their acrid tongues and the secret dislike they now felt for their mother. Indeed, when old Mrs Ogilvy died, she was unmourned except by her eldest daughter who actually felt a void in her life—the unforeseen void that the ailing and weak will not infrequently leave behind them.

At about this time an aunt also died, bequeathing her fortune to her niece Wilhelmina who, however, was too weary to gird up her loins and set forth in search of exciting adventure—all she did was to move her protesting sisters to a little estate she had purchased in Surrey. This experiment was only a partial success, for Miss Ogilvy failed to make friends of her neighbours; thus at fifty-five she had grown rather dour, as is often the way with shy, lonely people.

When the war came she had just begun settling down—people do settle down in their fifty-sixth year—she was feeling quite glad that her hair was grey, that the garden took up so much of her time, that, in fact, the beat of her blood was slowing. But all this was changed when war was declared; on that day Miss Ogilvy's pulses throbbed wildly.

'My God! If only I were a man!' she burst out, as she glared at Sarah and Fanny, 'if only I had been born a man!' Something in her was feeling deeply defrauded.

Sarah and Fanny were soon knitting socks and mittens and mufflers and Jaeger trench-helmets. Other ladies were busily working at depots, making swabs at the Squire's, or splints at the Parson's; but Miss Ogilvy scowled and did none of these things—she was not at all like other ladies.

For nearly twelve months she worried officials with a view to getting a job out in France—not in their way but in hers, and that was the trouble. She wished to go up to the front-line trenches, she wished to be actually under fire, she informed the harassed officials.

To all her inquiries she received the same answer: 'We regret that we cannot accept your offer.' But once thoroughly roused she was hard to subdue, for her shyness had left her as though by magic.

Sarah and Fanny shrugged angular shoulders: 'There's plenty of work here at home,' they remarked, 'though of course it's not quite so melodramatic!'

'Oh . . .?' queried their sister on a rising note of impatience—and she promptly cut off her hair: 'That'll jar them!' she thought with satisfaction.

Then she went up to London, formed her admirable unit and finally got it accepted by the French, despite renewed opposition.

In London she had found herself quite at her ease, for many another of her kind was in London doing excellent work for the nation. It was really surprising how many cropped heads had suddenly appeared as it were out of space; how many Miss Ogilvies, losing their shyness, had come forward asserting their right to serve, asserting their claim to attention.

There followed those turbulent years at the front, full of courage and hardship and high endeavour, and during those years Miss Ogilvy forgot the bad joke that Nature seemed to have played her. She was given the rank of a French lieutenant and she lived in a kind of blissful illusion; appalling reality lay on all sides and yet she managed to live in illusion. She was competent, fearless, devoted and untiring. What then? Could any man hope to do better? She was nearly fifty-eight, yet she walked with a stride, and at times she even swaggered a little.

Poor Miss Ogilvy sitting so glumly in the train with her manly trench-boots and her forage-cap! Poor all the Miss Ogilvies back from the war with their tunics, their trench-boots, and their childish illusions! Wars come and wars go but the world does not change: it will always forget an indebtedness which it thinks it expedient not to remember.

3

When Miss Ogilvy returned to her home in Surrey it was only to find that her sisters were ailing from the usual imaginary causes, and this to a woman who had seen the real thing was intolerable, so that she looked with distaste at Sarah and then at Fanny. Fanny was certainly not prepossessing, she was suffering from a spurious attack of hay fever.

'Stop sneezing!' commanded Miss Ogilvy, in the voice that had so much impressed the Unit. But as Fanny was not in the least impressed, she naturally went on sneezing.

Miss Ogilvy's desk was piled mountain-high with endless tiresome letters and papers: circulars, bills, months-old correspondence, the gardener's accounts, an agent's report on some fields that required land-draining. She seated herself before this collection; then she sighed, it all seemed so absurdly trivial.

'Will you let your hair grow again?' Fanny inquired . . . she and Sarah had followed her into the study. 'I'm certain the Vicar would be glad if you did.'

'Oh?' murmured Miss Ogilvy, rather too blandly.

'Wilhelmina!'

'Yes?'

'You will do it, won't you?'

'Do what?'

'Let your hair grow; we all wish you would.'

'Why should I?'

'Oh, well, it will look less odd, especially now that the war is over—in a small place like this people notice such things.'

'I entirely agree with Fanny,' announced Sarah.

Sarah had become very self-assertive, no doubt through having mismanaged the estate during the years of her sister's absence. They had quite a heated dispute one morning over the south herbaceous border.

'Whose garden is this?' Miss Ogilvy asked sharply. 'I insist on auricula-eyed sweet-williams! I even took the trouble to write from France, but it seems that my letter has been ignored.'

'Don't shout,' rebuked Sarah, 'you're not in France now!'

Miss Ogilvy could gladly have boxed her ears: 'I only wish to God I were,' she muttered.

Another dispute followed close on its heels, and this time it happened to be over the dinner. Sarah and Fanny were living on weeds—at least that was the way Miss Ogilvy put it.

'We've become vegetarians,' Sarah said grandly.

'You've become two damn tiresome cranks!' snapped their sister.

Now it never had been Miss Ogilvy's way to indulge in acid recriminations, but somehow, these days, she forgot to say 'Oh?' quite so often as expediency demanded. It may have been Fanny's perpetual sneezing that had got on her nerves; or it may have been Sarah, or the gardener, or the Vicar, or even the canary; though it really did not matter very much what it was just so long as she found a convenient peg upon which to hang her growing irritation.

'This won't do at all,' Miss Ogilvy thought sternly, 'life's not worth so much fuss, I must pull myself together.' But it seemed this was easier said than done; not a day passed without her losing her temper and that over some trifle: 'No, this won't do at all—it just mustn't be,' she thought sternly.

Everyone pitied Sarah and Fanny: 'Such a dreadful, violent old thing,' said the neighbours.

But Sarah and Fanny had their revenge: 'Poor darling, it's shell-shock, you know,' they murmured.

Thus Miss Ogilvy's prowess was whittled away until she herself was beginning to doubt it. Had she ever been that courageous person who had faced death in France with such perfect composure? Had she ever stood tranquilly under fire, without turning a hair, while she issued her orders? Had she ever been treated with marked respect? She herself was beginning to doubt it.

Sometimes she would see an old member of the Unit, a girl who, more faithful to her than the others, would take the trouble to run down to Surrey. These visits, however, were seldom enlivening.

'Oh, well . . . here we are . . .' Miss Ogilvy would mutter.

But one day the girl smiled and shook her blonde head: 'I'm not—I'm going to be married.'

Strange thoughts had come to Miss Ogilvy, unbidden, thoughts that had stayed for many an hour after the girl's departure. Alone in her study she had suddenly shivered, feeling a sense of complete desolation. With cold hands she had lighted a cigarette.

'I must be ill or something,' she had mused, as she stared at her trembling fingers.

After this she would sometimes cry out in her sleep, living over in dreams God knows what emotions; returning, maybe, to the battlefields of France. Her hair turned snow-white; it was not unbecoming yet she fretted about it.

'I'm growing very old,' she would sigh as she brushed her thick mop before the glass; and then she would peer at her wrinkles.

For now that it had happened she hated being old; it no longer appeared such an easy solution of those difficulties that had always beset her. And this she resented most bitterly, so that she became the prey of self-pity, and of other undesirable states in which the body will torment the mind, and the mind, in its turn, the body. Then Miss Ogilvy straightened her ageing back, in spite of the fact that of late it had ached with muscular rheumatism, and she faced herself squarely and came to a resolve.

'I'm off!' she announced abruptly one day; and that evening she packed her kit-bag.

4

Near the south coast of Devon there exists a small island that is still very little known to the world, but which, nevertheless, can boast an hotel; the only building upon it. Miss Ogilvy had chosen this place quite at random, it was marked on her map by scarcely more than a dot, but somehow she had liked the look of that dot and had set forth alone to explore it.

She found herself standing on the mainland one morning looking at a vague blur of green through the mist, a vague blur of green that rose out of the Channel like a tidal wave suddenly suspended. Miss Ogilvy was filled with a sense of adventure; she had not felt like this since the ending of the war.

'I was right to come here, very right indeed. I'm going to shake off all my troubles,' she decided.

A fisherman's boat was parting the mist, and before it was properly beached, in she bundled.

'I hope they're expecting me?' she said gaily.

'They du be expecting you,' the man answered.

The sea, which is generally rough off that coast, was indulging itself in an oily ground-swell; the broad, glossy swells struck the side of the boat, then broke and sprayed over Miss Ogilvy's ankles.

The fisherman grinned: 'Feeling all right?' he queried. 'It du be tiresome most times about these parts.' But the mist had suddenly drifted away and Miss Ogilvy was staring wide-eyed at the island.

She saw a long shoal of jagged black rocks, and between them the curve of a small sloping beach, and above that the lift of the island itself, and above that again, blue heaven. Near the beach stood the little two-storied hotel which was thatched, and built entirely of timber; for the rest she could make out no signs of life apart from a host of white seagulls.

Then Miss Ogilvy said a curious thing. She said: 'On the south-west side of that place there was once a cave—a very large cave. I remember that it was some way from the sea.'

'There du be a cave still,' the fisherman told her, 'but it's just above high-water level.'

'A-ah,' murmured Miss Ogilvy thoughtfully, as though to herself; then she looked embarrassed.

The little hotel proved both comfortable and clean, the hostess both pleasant and comely. Miss Ogilvy started unpacking her bag, changed her mind and went for a stroll round the island. The island was covered with turf and thistles and traversed by narrow green paths thick with daisies. It had four rock-bound coves of which the south-western was by far the most difficult of access. For just here the island descended abruptly as though it were hurtling down to the water; and just here the shale was most treacherous and the tide-swept rocks most aggressively pointed. Here it was that the seagulls, grown fearless of man by reason of his absurd limitations, built their nests on the ledges and reared countless young who multiplied, in their turn, every season. Yes, and here it was that Miss Ogilvy, greatly marvelling, stood and stared across at a cave; much too near the crumbling edge for her safety, but by now completely indifferent to caution.

'I remember . . . I remember . . .' she kept repeating. Then: 'That's all very well, but what do I remember?'

She was conscious of somehow remembering all wrong, of her memory being distorted and coloured—perhaps by the endless things she had seen since her eyes had last rested upon that cave. This worried her sorely, far more than the fact that she should be remembering the cave at all, she who had never set foot on the island before that actual morning. Indeed, except for the sense of wrongness when she struggled to piece her memories together, she was steeped in a very profound contentment which surged over her spirit, wave upon wave.

'It's extremely odd,' pondered Miss Ogilvy. Then she laughed, so pleased did she feel with its oddness.

5

That night after supper she talked to her hostess who was only too glad, it seemed, to be questioned. She owned the whole island and was proud of the fact, as she very well might be, decided her boarder. Some curious things had been found on the island, according to comely Mrs Nanceskivel: bronze arrow-heads, pieces of ancient stone celts; and once they had dug up a man's skull and thigh-bone—this had happened while they were sinking a well. Would Miss Ogilvy care to have a look at the bones? They were kept in a cupboard in the scullery.

Miss Ogilvy nodded.

'Then I'll fetch him this moment,' said Mrs Nanceskivel, briskly.

In less than two minutes she was back with the box that contained those poor remnants of a man, and Miss Ogilvy, who had risen from her chair, was gazing down at those remnants. As she did so her mouth was sternly compressed, but her face and her neck flushed darkly.

Mrs Nanceskivel was pointing to the skull; 'Look, miss, he was killed,' she remarked rather proudly, 'and they tell me that the axe that killed him was bronze. He's thousands and thousands of years old, they tell me. Our local doctor knows a lot about such things and he wants me to send these bones to an expert: they ought to belong to the Nation, he says. But I know what would happen, they'd come digging up my island, and I won't have people digging up my island, I've got enough worry with the rabbits as it is.' But Miss Ogilvy could no longer hear the words for the pounding of the blood in her temples.

She was filled with a sudden, inexplicable fury against the innocent Mrs Nanceskivel: 'You . . . *you* . . .' she began, then checked herself, fearful of what she might say to the woman.

For her sense of outrage was overwhelming as she stared at those bones that were kept in the scullery; moreover, she knew how such men had been buried, which made the outrage seem all the more shameful. They had buried such men in deep, well-dug pits surmounted by four stout stones at their corners—four stout stones there had been and a covering stone. And all this Miss Ogilvy knew as by instinct, having no concrete knowledge on which to draw. But she knew it right down in the depths of her soul, and she hated Mrs Nanceskivel.

And now she was swept by another emotion that was even more strange and more devastating: such a grief as she had not conceived could exist; a terrible unassuageable grief, without hope, without respite, without palliation, so that with something akin to despair she touched the long gash in the skull. Then her eyes, that had never wept since her childhood, filled slowly with large, hot, difficult tears. She must blink very hard, then close her eyelids, turn away from the lamp and say rather loudly:

'Thanks, Mrs Nanceskivel. It's past eleven—I think I'll be going upstairs.'

6

Miss Ogilvy closed the door of her bedroom, after which she stood quite still to consider: 'Is it shell-shock?' she muttered incredulously. 'I wonder, can it be shell-shock?'

She began to pace slowly about the room, smoking a Caporal. As usual her hands were deep in her pockets; she could feel small, familiar things in those pockets and she gripped them, glad of their presence. Then all of a sudden she was terribly tired, so tired that she flung herself down on the bed, unable to stand any longer.

She thought that she lay there struggling to reason, that her eyes were closed in the painful effort, and that as she closed them she continued to puff the inevitable cigarette. At least that was what she thought at one moment—the next, she was out in a sunset evening, and a large red sun was sinking slowly to the rim of a distant sea.

Miss Ogilvy knew that she was herself, that is to say she was conscious of her being, and yet she was not Miss Ogilvy at all, nor had she a memory of her. All that she now saw was very familiar, all that she now did was what she should do, and all that she now was seemed perfectly natural. Indeed, she did not think of these things; there seemed no reason for thinking about them.

She was walking with bare feet on turf that felt springy and was greatly enjoying the sensation; she had always enjoyed it, ever since as an infant she had learned to crawl on this turf. On either hand stretched rolling green uplands, while at her back she knew that there were forests; but in front, far away, lay the gleam of the sea towards which the big sun was sinking. The air was cool and intensely still, with never so much as a ripple or bird-song. It was wonderfully pure—one might almost say young—but Miss Ogilvy thought of it merely as air. Having always breathed it she took it for granted, as she took the soft turf and the uplands.

She pictured herself as immensely tall; she was feeling immensely tall at that moment. As a matter of fact she was five feet eight which, however, was quite a considerable height when compared to that of her fellow-tribesmen. She was wearing a single garment of pelts which came to her knees and left her arms sleeveless. Her arms and her legs, which were closely tattoed with blue zig-zag lines, were extremely hairy. From a leathern thong twisted about her waist there hung a clumsily made stone weapon, a celt, which in spite of its clumsiness was strongly hafted and useful for killing.

Miss Ogilvy wanted to shout aloud from a glorious sense of physical well-being, but instead she picked up a heavy, round stone which she hurled with great force at some distant rocks.

'Good! Strong!' she exclaimed. 'See how far it goes!'

'Yes, strong. There is no one so strong as you. You are surely the strongest man in our tribe,' replied her little companion.

Miss Ogilvy glanced at this little companion and rejoiced that they two were alone together. The girl at her side had a smooth brownish skin, oblique black eyes and short, sturdy limbs. Miss Ogilvy marvelled because of her beauty. She also was wearing a single garment of pelts, new pelts, she had made it that morning. She had stitched at it diligently for hours with short lengths of gut and her best bone needle. A strand of black hair hung over her bosom, and this she was constantly stroking and fondling; then she lifted the strand and examined her hair.

'Pretty,' she remarked with childish complacence.

'Pretty,' echoed the young man at her side.

'For you,' she told him, 'all of me is for you and none other. For you this body has ripened.'

He shook back his own coarse hair from his eyes; he had sad brown eyes like those of a monkey. For the rest he was lean and steel-strong of loin, broad of chest, and with features not too uncomely. His prominent cheek-bones were set rather high, his nose was blunt, his jaw somewhat bestial; but his mouth, though full-lipped, contradicted his jaw, being very gentle and sweet in expression. And now he smiled, showing big, square, white teeth.

'You . . . woman,' he murmured contentedly, and the sound seemed to come from the depths of his being.

His speech was slow and lacking in words when it came to expressing a vital emotion, so one word must suffice and this he now spoke, and the word that he spoke had a number of meanings. It meant: 'Little spring of exceed-ingly pure water.' It meant: 'Hut of peace for a man after battle.' It meant: 'Ripe red berry sweet to the taste.' It meant: 'Happy small home of future generations.' All these things he must try to express by a word, and because of their loving she understood him.

They paused, and lifting her up he kissed her. Then he rubbed his large shaggy head on her shoulder; and when he released her she knelt at his feet.

'My master; blood of my body,' she whispered. For with her it was differ-ent, love had taught her love's speech, so that she might turn her heart into sounds that her primitive tongue could utter.

After she had pressed her lips to his hands, and her cheek to his hairy and powerful forearm, she stood up and they gazed at the setting sun, but with bowed heads, gazing under their lids, because this was very sacred.

A couple of mating bears padded towards them from a thicket, and the female rose to her haunches. But the man drew his celt and menaced the beast, so that she dropped down noiselessly and fled, and her mate also fled, for here was the power that few dared to withstand by day or by night, on the uplands or in the forests. And now from across to the left where a river would presently lose itself in the marshes, came a rhythmical thudding, as a herd of red deer with wide nostrils and starting eyes thundered past, dis-turbed in their drinking by the bears.

After this the evening returned to its silence, and the spell of its silence descended on the lovers, so that each felt very much alone, yet withal more closely united to the other. But the man became restless under that spell, and he suddenly laughed; then grasping the woman he tossed her above his head and caught her. This he did many times for his own amusement and because he knew that his strength gave her joy. In this manner they played together for a while, he with his strength and she with her weakness. And they cried out, and made many guttural sounds which were meaningless save only to themselves. And the tunic of pelts slipped down from her breasts, and her two little breasts were pear-shaped.

Presently, he grew tired of their playing, and he pointed towards a cluster of huts and earthworks that lay to the eastward. The smoke from these huts rose in thick straight lines, bending neither to right nor left in its rising, and the thought of sweet burning rushes and brushwood touched his consciousness, making him feel sentimental.

'Smoke,' he said.

And she answered: 'Blue smoke.'

He nodded: 'Yes, blue smoke—home.'

Then she said: 'I have ground much corn since the full moon. My stones are too smooth. You make me new stones.'

'All you have need of, I make,' he told her.

She stole close to him, taking his hand: 'My father is still a black cloud full of thunder. He thinks that you wish to be head of our tribe in his place, because he is now very old. He must not hear of these meetings of ours, if he did I think he would beat me!'

So he asked her: 'Are you unhappy, small berry?'

But at this she smiled: 'What is being unhappy? I do not know what that means any more.'

'I do not either,' he answered.

Then as though some invisible force had drawn him, his body swung round and he stared at the forests where they lay and darkened, fold upon fold; and his eyes dilated with wonder and terror, and he moved his head quickly from side to side as a wild thing will do that is held between bars and whose mind is pitifully bewildered.

'Water!' he cried hoarsely, 'great water—look, look! Over there. This land is surrounded by water!'

'What water?' she questioned.

He answered: 'The sea.' And he covered his face with his hands.

'Not so,' she consoled, 'big forests, good hunting. Big forests in which you hunt boar and aurochs. No sea over there but only the trees.'

He took his trembling hands from his face: 'You are right . . . only trees,' he said dully.

But now his face had grown heavy and brooding and he started to speak of a thing that oppressed him: 'The Roundheaded-ones, they are devils,' he growled, while his bushy black brows met over his eyes, and when this happened it changed his expression which became a little subhuman.

'No matter,' she protested, for she saw that he forgot her and she wished him to think and talk only of love. 'No matter. My father laughs at your fears. Are we not friends with the Roundheaded-ones? We are friends, so why should we fear them?'

'Our forts, very old, very weak,' he went on, 'and the Roundheaded-ones have terrible weapons. Their weapons are not made of good stone like ours, but of some dark, devilish substance.'

'What of that?' she said lightly. 'They would fight on our side, so why need we trouble about their weapons?'

But he looked away, not appearing to hear her. 'We must barter all, all for their celts and arrows and spears, and then we must learn their secret. They lust after our women, they lust after our lands. We must barter all, all for their sly brown celts.'

'Me . . . bartered?' she queried, very sure of his answer otherwise she had not dared to say this.

'The Roundheaded-ones may destroy my tribe and yet I will not part with you,' he told her. Then he spoke very gravely: 'But I think they desire to slay us, and me they will try to slay first because they well know how much I mistrust them—they have seen my eyes fixed many times on their camps.'

She cried: 'I will bite out the throats of these people if they so much as scratch your skin!'

And at this his mood changed and he roared with amusement: 'You . . . woman!' he roared. 'Little foolish white teeth. Your teeth were made for nibbling wild cherries, not for tearing the throats of the Roundheaded-ones!'

'Thoughts of war always make me afraid,' she whimpered, still wishing him to talk about love.

He turned his sorrowful eyes upon her, the eyes that were sad even when he was merry, and although his mind was often obtuse, yet he clearly perceived how it was with her then. And his blood caught fire from the flame in her blood, so that he strained her against his body.

'You . . . mine . . .' he stammered.

'Love,' she said, trembling, 'this is love.'

And he answered: 'Love.'

Then their faces grew melancholy for a moment, because dimly, very dimly in their dawning souls, they were conscious of a longing for something more vast than this earthly passion could compass.

Presently, he lifted her like a child and carried her quickly southward and westward till they came to a place where a gentle descent led down to a marshy valley. Far away, at the line where the marshes ended, they discerned the misty line of the sea; but the sea and the marshes were become as one substance, merging, blending, folding together; and since they were lovers they also would be one, even as the sea and the marshes.

And now they had reached the mouth of a cave that was set in the quiet hillside. There was bright green verdure beside the cave, and a number of small, pink, thick-stemmed flowers that when they were crushed smelt of spices. And within the cave there was bracken newly gathered and heaped together for a bed; while beyond, from some rocks, came a low liquid sound as a spring dripped out through a crevice. Abruptly, he set the girl on her feet, and she knew that the days of her innocence were over. And she thought of the anxious virgin soil that was rent and sown to bring forth fruit in season, and she gave a quick little gasp of fear:

'No . . . no . . .' she gasped. For, divining his need, she was weak with the longing to be possessed, yet the terror of love lay heavy upon her. 'No . . . no . . .' she gasped.

But he caught her wrist and she felt the great strength of his rough, gnarled fingers, the great strength of the urge that leapt in his loins, and again she must give that quick gasp of fear, the while she clung close to him lest he should spare her.

The twilight was engulfed and possessed by darkness, which in turn was transfigured by the moonrise, which in turn was fulfilled and consumed by dawn. A mighty eagle soared up from his eyrie, cleaving the air with his masterful wings, and beneath him from the rushes that harboured their nests, rose other great birds, crying loudly. Then the heavy-horned elks appeared on the uplands, bending their burdened heads to the sod; while beyond in the forests the fierce wild aurochs stamped as they bellowed their love songs.

But within the dim cave the lord of these creatures had put by his weapon and his instinct for slaying. And he lay there defenceless with tenderness, thinking no longer of death but of life as he murmured the word that had so many meanings. That meant: 'Little spring of exceedingly pure water.' That meant: 'Hut of peace for a man after battle.' That meant: 'Ripe red berry sweet to the taste.' That meant: 'Happy small home of future generations.'

7

They found Miss Ogilvy the next morning; the fisherman saw her and climbed to the ledge. She was sitting at the mouth of the cave. She was dead, with her hands thrust deep into her pockets.

Radclyffe Hall, 'Miss Ogilvy Finds Herself', in *Miss Ogilvy Finds Herself*
(London: Hammond, 1959), 7–31

Virginia Woolf
(1882–1941)

In both her fiction and her diaries Virginia Woolf explored the diverse ways in which the war was a catalyst and a landmark of change. 'The Shooting Party' was written at the beginning of 1932: like many of the novels which Woolf had written in the 1920s, it saw the war as bringing to an end a settled way of life. This story maintains a sardonic perspective which may derive from a reference in Woolf's Diary to a visit to Sir Henry Hall Caine and 'a caricature of Country house life, with the red-brown pheasants'.

68   THE SHOOTING PARTY

SHE got in and put her suit case in the rack, and the brace of pheasants on top of it. Then she sat down in the corner. The train was rattling through the midlands, and the fog, which came in when she opened the door, seemed to enlarge the carriage and set the four travellers apart. Obviously M.M.— those were the initials on the suit case—had been staying the week-end with a shooting party. Obviously, for she was telling over the story now, lying back in her corner. She did not shut her eyes. But clearly she did not see the man opposite, nor the coloured photograph of York Minster. She must have heard, too, what they had been saying. For as she gazed, her lips moved; now and then she smiled. And she was handsome; a cabbage rose; a russet apple; tawny; but scarred on the jaw—the scar lengthened when she smiled. Since she was telling over the story she must have been a guest there, and yet, dressed as she was out of fashion as women dressed, years ago, in pictures, in sporting newspapers, she did not seem exactly a guest, nor yet a maid. Had she had a basket with her she would have been the woman who breeds fox terriers; the owner of the Siamese cat; some one connected with hounds and horses. But she had only a suit case and the pheasants. Somehow, therefore, she must have wormed her way into the room that she was seeing through the stuffing of the carriage, and the man's bald head, and the picture of York Minster. And she must have listened to what they were saying, for now, like somebody imitating the noise that someone else makes, she made a little click at the back of her throat. 'Chk.' Then she smiled.

'Chk,' said Miss Antonia, pinching her glasses on her nose. The damp leaves fell across the long windows of the gallery; one or two stuck, fish shaped, and lay like inlaid brown wood upon the window panes. Then the trees in the Park shivered, and the leaves, flaunting down, seemed to make the shiver visible—the damp brown shiver.

'Chk,' Miss Antonia sniffed again, and pecked at the flimsy white stuff that she held in her hands, as a hen pecks nervously rapidly at a piece of white bread.

The wind sighed. The room was draughty. The doors did not fit, nor the windows. Now and then a ripple, like a reptile, ran under the carpet. On the carpet lay panels of green and yellow, where the sun rested, and then the sun moved and pointed a finger as if in mockery at a hole in the carpet and stopped. And then on it went, the sun's feeble but impartial finger, and lay upon the coat of arms over the fireplace—gently illumined—the shield, the pendant grapes, the mermaid, and the spears. Miss Antonia looked up as the light strengthened. Vast lands, so they said, the old people had owned— her forefathers—the Rashleighs. Over there. Up the Amazons. Freebooter. Voyagers. Sacks of emeralds. Nosing round the island. Taking captives. Maidens. There she was, all scales from the tail to the waist. Miss Antonia grinned. Down struck the finger of the sun and her eye went with it. Now it rested on a silver frame; on a photograph; on an egg-shaped baldish head, on a lip that stuck out under the moustache; and the name 'Edward' written with a flourish beneath.

'The King . . .' Miss Antonia muttered, turning the film of white upon her knee—'had the Blue Room,' she added with a toss of her head as the light faded.

Out in the King's Ride the pheasants were being driven across the noses of the guns. Up they spurted from the underwood like heavy rockets, red-dish purple rockets, and as they rose the guns cracked in order, eagerly, sharply, as if a line of dogs had suddenly barked. Tufts of white smoke held together for a moment; then gently solved themselves, faded, and dispersed.

In the deep cut road beneath the hanger, a cart stood, laid already with soft warm bodies, with limp claws, and still lustrous eyes. The birds seemed alive still, but swooning under their rich damp feathers. They looked relaxed and comfortable, stirring slightly, as if they slept upon a warm bank of soft feathers on the floor of the cart.

Then the Squire, with the hang-dog stained face, in the shabby gaiters, cursed and raised the gun.

Miss Antonia stitched on. Now and then a tongue of flame reached round the grey log that stretched from one bar to another across the grate, ate it greedily, then died out, leaving a white bracelet where the bark had been eaten off. Miss Antonia looked up for a moment, stared wide eyed, instinctively, as a dog stares at a flame. Then the flame sank and she stitched again.

Then, silently, the enormously high door opened. Two lean men came in, and drew a table over the hole in the carpet. They went out; they came in. They laid a cloth upon the table. They went out; they came in. They brought a green baize basket of knives and forks; and glasses; and sugar casters; and salt cellars; and bread; and a silver vase with three chrysanthemums in it. And the table was laid. Miss Antonia stitched on.

Again the door opened, pushed feebly this time. A little dog trotted in, a spaniel nosing nimbly; it paused. The door stood open. And then, leaning on her stick, heavily, old Miss Rashleigh entered. A white shawl, diamond fastened, clouded her baldness. She hobbled; crossed the room; hunched herself in the high-backed chair by the fireside. Miss Antonia went on stitching.

'Shooting,' she said at last.

Old Miss Rashleigh nodded. She gripped her stick. They sat waiting.

The shooters had moved now from the King's Ride to the Home Woods. They stood in the purple ploughed field outside. Now and then a twig snapped; leaves came whirling. But above the mist and the smoke was an island of blue—faint blue, pure blue—alone in the sky. And in the innocent air, as if straying alone like a cherub, a bell from a far hidden steeple frolicked, gambolled, then faded. Then again up shot the rockets, the reddish purple pheasants. Up and up they went. Again the guns barked; the smoke balls formed; loosened, dispersed. And the busy little dogs ran nosing nimbly over the fields; and the warm damp bodies, still languid and soft, as if in a swoon, were bunched together by the men in gaiters and flung into the cart.

'There!' grunted Milly Masters, the house-keeper, throwing down her glasses. She was stitching, too, in the small dark room that overlooked the stable yard. The jersey, the rough woollen jersey, for her son, the boy who cleaned the Church, was finished. 'The end'o that!' she muttered. Then she heard the cart. Wheels ground on the cobbles. Up she got. With her hands to her hair, her chestnut coloured hair, she stood in the yard, in the wind.

'Coming!' she laughed, and the scar on her cheek lengthened. She unbolted the door of the game room as Wing, the keeper, drove the cart over the cobbles. The birds were dead now, their claws gripped tight, though they gripped nothing. The leathery eyelids were creased greyly over their eyes. Mrs Masters the house-keeper, Wing the gamekeeper, took bunches of dead birds by the neck and flung them down on the slate floor of the game larder. The slate floor became smeared and spotted with blood. The pheasants looked smaller now, as if their bodies had shrunk together. Then Wing lifted the tail of the cart and drove in the pins which secured it. The sides of the cart were stuck about with little grey-blue feathers, and the floor was smeared and stained with blood. But it was empty.

'The last of the lot!' Milly Masters grinned as the cart drove off.

'Luncheon is served, ma'am,' said the butler. He pointed at the table; he directed the footman. The dish with the silver cover was placed precisely there where he pointed. They waited, the butler and the footman.

Miss Antonia laid her white film upon the basket; put away her silk; her thimble; stuck her needle through a piece of flannel; and hung her glasses on a hook upon her breast. Then she rose.

'Luncheon!' she barked in old Miss Rashleigh's ear. One second later old Miss Rashleigh stretched her leg out; gripped her stick; and rose too. Both old women advanced slowly to the table; and were tucked in by the butler and footman, one at this end, one at that. Off came the silver cover. And there was the pheasant, featherless, gleaming; the thighs tightly pressed to its side; and little mounds of breadcrumbs were heaped at either end.

Miss Antonia drew the carving knife across the pheasant's breast firmly. She cut two slices and laid them on a plate. Deftly the footman whipped it from her, and old Miss Rashleigh raised her knife. Shots rang out in the wood under the window.

'Coming?' said old Miss Rashleigh, suspending her fork.

The branches flung and flaunted on the trees in the Park.

She took a mouthful of pheasant. Falling leaves flicked the window pane; one or two stuck to the glass.

'The Home Woods, now,' said Miss Antonia. 'Hugh's lost that.' 'Shooting.' She drew her knife down the other side of the breast. She added potatoes and gravy, brussels sprouts and bread sauce methodically in a circle round the slices on her plate. The butler and the footman stood watching, like servers at a feast. The old ladies ate quietly; silently; nor did they hurry themselves; methodically they cleaned the bird. Bones only were left on their plates. Then the butler drew the decanter towards Miss Antonia, and paused for a moment with his head bent.

'Give it here, Griffiths,' said Miss Antonia, and took the carcase in her fingers and tossed it to the spaniel beneath the table. The butler and the footman bowed and went out.

'Coming closer,' said Miss Rashleigh, listening. The wind was rising. A brown shudder shook the air; leaves flew too fast to stick. The glass rattled in the windows.

'Birds wild,' Miss Antonia nodded, watching the helter-skelter.

Old Miss Rashleigh filled her glass. As they sipped their eyes became lustrous like half precious stones held to the light. Slate blue were Miss Rashleigh's; Miss Antonia's red, like port. And their laces and their flounces seemed to quiver, as if their bodies were warm and languid underneath their feathers as they drank.

'It was a day like this, d'you remember?' said old Miss Rashleigh, fingering her glass. 'They brought him home—a bullet through his heart. A bramble, so they said. Tripped. Caught his foot . . .' She chuckled as she sipped her wine.

'And John . . .' said Miss Antonia. 'The mare, they said, put her foot in a hole. Died in the field. The hunt rode over him. He came home, too, on a shutter . . .'

They sipped again.

'Remember Lily?' said old Miss Rashleigh. 'A bad 'un.' She shook her head. 'Riding with a scarlet tassel on her cane . . .'

'Rotten at the heart!' cried Miss Antonia.

'Remember the Colonel's letter. Your son rode as if he had twenty devils in him—charged at the head of his men. Then one white devil—ah hah!' She sipped again.

'The men of our house,' began Miss Rashleigh. She raised her glass. She held it high, as if she toasted the mermaid carved in plaster on the fireplace. She paused. The guns were barking. Something cracked in the woodwork. Or was it a rat running behind the plaster?

'Always women . . .' Miss Antonia nodded. 'The men of our house. Pink and white Lucy at the Mill—d'you remember?'

'Ellen's daughter at the Goat and Sickle,' Miss Rashleigh added.

'And the girl at the tailor's,' Miss Antonia murmured, 'where Hugh bought his riding breeches, the little dark shop on the right . . .'

'. . . that used to be flooded every winter. It's *his* boy,' Miss Antonia chuckled, leaning towards her sister, 'that cleans the Church.'

There was a crash. A slate had fallen down the chimney. The great log had snapped in two. Flakes of plaster fell from the shield above the fireplace.

'Falling,' old Miss Rashleigh chuckled. 'Falling.'

'And who,' said Miss Antonia, looking at the flakes on the carpet, 'who's to pay?'

Crowing like old babies, indifferent, reckless, they laughed; crossed to the fireplace, and sipped the sherry by the wood ashes and the plaster, until each glass held only one drop of wine, reddish purple, at the bottom. And this the old women did not wish to part with, so it seemed; for they fingered their glasses, as they sat side by side by the ashes; but they never raised them to their lips.

'Milly Masters in the still room,' began old Miss Rashleigh. 'She's our brother's . . .'

A shot barked beneath the window. It cut the string that held the rain. Down it poured, down, down, down, in straight rods whipping the windows. Light faded from the carpet. Light faded in their eyes, too, as they sat by the white ashes listening. Their eyes became like pebbles, taken from water; grey stones dulled and dried. And their hands gripped their hands like the claws of dead birds gripping nothing. And they shrivelled as if the bodies inside the clothes had shrunk.

Then Miss Antonia raised her glass to the mermaid. It was the last drop; she drank it off. 'Coming!' she croaked, and slapped the glass down. A door banged below. Then another. Then another. Feet could be heard trampling, yet shuffling, along the corridor towards the gallery.

'Closer! Closer!' grinned Miss Rashleigh, baring her three yellow teeth.

The immensely high door burst open. In rushed three great hounds and stood panting. Then there entered, slouching, the Squire himself in shabby gaiters. The dogs pressed round him, tossing their heads, snuffling at his pockets. Then they bounded forward. They smelt the meat. The floor of the gallery waved like a wind-lashed forest with the tails and backs of the great questing hounds. They snuffed the table. They pawed the cloth. Then, with a wild neighing whimper, they flung themselves upon the little yellow spaniel who was gnawing the carcase under the table.

'Curse you, curse you!' howled the Squire. But his voice was weak, as if he shouted against a wind. 'Curse you, curse you!' he shouted, now cursing his sisters.

Miss Antonia and Miss Rashleigh rose to their feet. The great dogs had seized the spaniel. They worried him, they mauled him with their great yellow teeth. The Squire swung a leather knotted tawse this way and that way, cursing the dogs, cursing his sisters, in the voice that sounded so loud yet so weak. With one lash he curled to the ground the vase of chrysanthemums. Another caught old Miss Rashleigh on the cheek. The old woman staggered backwards. She fell against the mantelpiece. Her stick striking wildly, struck the shield above the fireplace. She fell with a thud upon the ashes. The shield of the Rashleighs crashed from the wall. Under the mermaid, under the spears, she lay buried.

The wind lashed the panes of glass; shots volleyed in the Park and a tree fell. And then King Edward, in the silver frame, slid, toppled, and fell too.

The grey mist had thickened in the carriage. It hung down like a veil; it seemed to put the four travellers in the corners at a great distance from each other, though in fact they were as close as a third class railway carriage could bring them. The effect was strange. The handsome, if elderly, the well-dressed, if rather shabby woman, who had got into the train at some station in the midlands, seemed to have lost her shape. Her body had become all mist. Only her eyes gleamed, changed, lived all by themselves, it seemed; eyes without a body; eyes seeing something invisible. In the misty air they shone out, they moved, so that in the sepulchral atmosphere—the windows were blurred, the lamps haloed with fog—they were like lights dancing, will o' the wisps that move, people say, over the graves of unquiet sleepers in the churchyards. An absurd idea? Mere fancy? Yet after all, since there is nothing that does not leave some residue, and memory is a light that dances in the mind when the reality is buried, why should not the eyes there, gleaming, moving, be the ghost of a family, of an age, of a civilization dancing over the grave?

The train slowed down. Lamps stood up. They were felled. Up they stood again as the train slid into the station. The lights blazed. And the eyes in the corner? They were shut. Perhaps the light was too strong. And of course in the full blaze of the station lamps it was plain—she was quite an ordinary, rather elderly, woman, travelling to London on some ordinary piece of business—something connected with a cat, or a horse, or a dog. She reached for her suit case, rose, and took the pheasants from the rack. But did she, all the same, as she opened the carriage door and stepped out, murmur 'Chk., Chk.' as she passed?

Virginia Woolf, 'The Shooting Party', from A Haunted House
(London: Grafton, 1982), 60–9

Sylvia Townsend Warner
(1893–1978)

Sylvia Townsend Warner's earliest interest was in music: the war, however, denied her the opportunity of advanced study with Schoenberg. She worked briefly in a munitions factory and after the war she was drawn into the resistance movement against fascism in Europe. Warner pursued this commitment through her friendship and lifelong partnership with Valentine Ackland and through their shared work on behalf of the Spanish republic. Although Warner's first publications were poetry, her reputation rests on her novels and short stories many of which, like *Lolly Willowes* (1926), are feminist in their exploration of women's need to free themselves from ideological constraints. Warner's writing is also notable for the way it combines fantasy and realism, a combination revealed in a light-hearted way in this story: 'the great truth that my mother won the last war passed . . . into the larger rumour that the last war was won by somebody's mother. The fact that people get the mother wrong does not invalidate the archetypal truth.'

---

69   MY MOTHER WON THE WAR

I THINK it is pretty generally admitted that my mother won the last war. By generally admitted I do not mean officially recognized. Official recognition would have involved many difficulties. Admirals and Field-Marshals, for instance, who had spent their lives in the study of warfare, and panted into their sixties towards the happy day when those studies might be let loose in practice, might well have been piqued if the honours had been unpinned from them and fastened on a middle-aged civilian lady of the upper middle-classes. There were the Allied Nations to consider, too. And though my mother would have been quite prepared to become a second Helen of Troy, getting along with it in her spare time when she wasn't busy with her rock garden, her wardrobe, her housekeeping, and her water colours, it was thought best to leave things as they were.

It always seems to me a convincing testimony to my mother's part in the last war that the legend that the last war was won by somebody's mother is so widespread. I have met any amount of families with the same belief. They believe it about their mothers, not mine. But legend is like that. A truth is spread around, then it gets corrupted. And the great truth that my mother won the last war passed in this manner into the larger rumour that the last war was won by somebody's mother. The fact that people get the mother wrong does not invalidate the archetypal truth.

My mother won the last war in November, 1914. There was a British Red Cross depot in our town, where ladies met to scrape lint, roll bandages, pick over moss for stomach-wound dressings, and make shirts and pyjamas. The lady in charge was a Mrs Moss-Henry, and when my mother offered her services, Mrs Moss-Henry set her to cutting out pyjama trousers.

There was a pattern, supplied by the Red Cross authorities, and though it wasn't as good as my mother could have made it, still, it wasn't too bad and my mother followed it. Maybe she introduced a few improvements, but she didn't win the war on these, so I won't waste time over them.

The next time she went, my mother was surprised when the pyjama trousers she had cut out and handed over to the seamstresses were returned to her. She inquired the reason for this from a fellow-worker who was cutting out pyjama jackets.

'Mrs Moss-Henry asked me to ask you if you would mind marking where the button and buttonhole are to be.'

'Button?' exclaimed my mother. 'Buttonhole? Ridiculous! The woman's a fool!'

My mother has a decisive mind, a mind that goes straight to essentials. She realized at once that, as the pyjama trousers were made to be fastened by a cord passing through a slot, the addition of a button and buttonhole halfway down the opening was redundant. The other cutter, one of those dull, faithful souls who can only do as they are told, repeated, 'That's what Mrs Moss-Henry said.'

My mother brooded for a while, but not for long. Five minutes or so. Then, gathering up the pyjama trousers, she rushed from the room in search of Mrs Moss-Henry.

'I'm not going to mark these trousers for buttons,' she declared. 'It's totally unnecessary.'

Mrs Moss-Henry, in a very autocratic manner, said that she would be glad if my mother marked the trousers for buttons. It would enable the seamstresses, she said, to know where to sew them on.

My mother explained, clearly, why buttons were redundant. There were no buttons on the pattern which she had been supplied by the Red Cross, she said.

Mrs Moss-Henry said that it was a paper pattern, unsuited for supporting buttons under hard usage. But buttons had been specified, and must be affixed.

My mother again and categorically registered her protest, and was going on with some good reasons when Mrs Moss-Henry pretended to hear the telephone bell, and left the room. My mother remained a while with the moss-pickers, amplifying her position. Was it not an outrage, she asked, that our fighting men, who had gone so cheerfully and gallantly to the defence of their country, should, when they came all glorious with wounds into the Red Cross hospitals, be insulted by being buttoned into their pyjama trousers like little boys? Had they not suffered enough for their country and their dear ones left behind? Must they, weak and in pain, be teased with buttoning and unbuttoning themselves? Many of them, she added, would be too weak to do up buttons, anyway.

Some of the moss-pickers agreed with my mother, some sided with Mrs Moss-Henry. But none were indifferent; they realized that this was a crucial matter. My mother pursued Mrs Moss-Henry into the bandage-room, and again attacked her.

This time Mrs Moss-Henry was positively rude to my mother. She said, with a falsely sweet air, that perhaps my mother, as a civilian, was accustomed to civilian pyjamas. Mrs Moss-Henry's husband had been an Army man, and this enabled Mrs Moss-Henry to assure my mother that buttons were in order.

The blood of her uncle, who was a brigadier general in the Sudan, boiled in my mother's veins. It was one of those moments when deeds speak louder than words and tearing the pyjama trousers from Mrs Moss-Henry's grasp she flapped them to and fro in her face.

Mrs Moss-Henry again retreated. My mother stayed a while with the bandage-rollers, pointing out that even though Mrs Moss-Henry had passed so much of her life on a baggage wagon, that did not warrant her trying to boss everything and everybody. Some more arguments then occurred to her, and she went off after Mrs Moss-Henry.

This running battle continued through the morning. Finally Mrs Moss-Henry locked herself in the lavatory. My mother, careless of the ridicule to which the position exposed her, stood outside the lavatory haranguing Mrs Moss-Henry through the door, and the other Red Cross ladies stood around, some silently supporting my mother, some silently supporting Mrs Moss-Henry. At last the combatants dispersed for lunch.

On the morrow my mother, after a sleepless night, returned to the struggle. She found a new force to contend with. Mrs Moss-Henry, while refusing to give battle, had set up a peculiarly insidious propaganda, designed to belittle my mother's achievements, tarnish her laurels, and undermine any future advance. This propaganda took the form of suggesting that it was not really all that important whether the pyjama trousers had buttons or no; and a specious plea was made that the output of the workers would suffer if my mother continued to make such a fuss about nothing. During the previous morning, it was alleged, the Red Cross ladies had either done no work at all or worked less well than usual. Their attention had been distracted. Mrs Cory, for instance, had sewn sleeves into the necks of pyjama jackets instead of into the armholes; and the garments in question were produced, with striped-flannel factory chimneys extending where turn-down collars should have been, as an example of the sort of thing which might be looked for unless my mother gave up attacking Mrs Moss-Henry.

My mother instantly saw through these misrepresentations. Sleeves in the wrong place, she said, were no worse than buttons where no buttons need be. If output was so important, then time was important, too. Nothing wasted time more than embroidering needless buttonholes to corroborate buttons that were perfectly unnecessary. For her part, she would never grudge time devoted to our splendid soldiers; it was on their behalf, and for their comfort, that she had joined issue with Mrs Moss-Henry over the buttons, and she considered it time well spent.

When one of the Moss-Henry minions squirmingly alleged that, after all, the buttons need not incommode the wounded soldiers, for if they found it tiresome to button their pyjama trousers they could leave them unbuttoned, my mother demolished this in an instant. If the buttons were there, regulations to enforce buttoning would be there too. Everyone knew that military-hospital discipline was like that.

Mrs Moss-Henry entered the room.

'Not still talking about buttons, surely?'

Her tone was sarcastic. My mother replied with firmness, 'I am.'

Mrs Moss-Henry feigned a yawn.

'I really don't think we want to hear any more about them.'

'You will!' riposted my mother. 'This afternoon I am going to Devonshire House.'

Such words struck awe into every hearer. Devonshire House was the Ark of the Covenant, and the Lion's Jaws. It was the headquarters of the British Red Cross, it was in Piccadilly, and it had been lent to the Red Cross by a duke.

Naturally, my mother put on her best clothes. At the station she was surprised to see Mrs Moss-Henry, who had put on her best clothes also. Two other ladies—one apiece—completed the deputation. The suburban train took half an hour to get them into London. It was crowded and the four ladies were obliged to travel together, though in silence. Sometimes Mrs Moss-Henry consulted the papers which she carried in a large portfolio.

My mother had no papers to consult. Instead, she gazed at Mrs Moss-Henry's hat with an annoying air of unconcern.

The marble hall of Devonshire House was crowded with people waiting for interviews. There was a terrific air of splendour and organization. Secretaries darted to and fro. The two supporters of the deputation began, after a while, to stare about them and whisper, identifying among the waiting throng many stately profiles of England which they had seen in the society papers. Mrs Moss-Henry behaved as though the aristocracy were nothing to her. So did my mother.

After an hour or so, they were summoned into a large room with desks all round it. Behind each desk was a lady, and each lady was rustling papers. It was as though one stood on some majestic seashore. Their allotted lady gave them a gracious smile, and told them that they were from the Mutton Hill depot. They agreed to this.

As an act of courtesy to the Red Cross organization which had, however misguidedly, placed Mrs Moss-Henry at the head of the Mutton Hill depot, my mother allowed her to speak first. She spoke next.

The lady behind the desk looked grave; it was obvious that my mother's fearless eloquence had made an impression on her. She said she thought she had better fetch someone else who was more of a specialist. The lady she fetched told them they were from the Mutton Hill depot, and that it was a matter of pyjamas. They answered that it was so.

Mrs Moss-Henry and my mother restated their positions, exactly, circumstantially, and emphatically. They made it clear (my mother made it clearest) that this was something that must be settled at once, and settled for all time.

The lady who was more of a specialist kept her eyes fixed on the official trouser pattern, as though a button in invisible ink might be lurking there. At last she said, 'Thank you so much. We quite appreciate your difficulties, and we will write to you shortly.' And she gave them a little dismissing bow.

They were moving away when my mother, with a great surge of indignation and another argument, which had just occurred to her, turned back towards the desk. The lady saw her coming, and held up her hand.

'For the present perhaps you had better leave the buttons off,' she said.

That evening Mrs Moss-Henry resigned. No letter came from Devonshire House to the Mutton Hill Red Cross depot. After a while my mother resigned, too. There was no need to go on. She had won the war.

Sylvia Townsend Warner, 'My Mother Won the War', from
Scenes of Childhood (London: Chatto, 1981), 125–31

Bibliography

ABENSOUR, L., *Les Vaillantes: Héroïnes, martyres et remplaçantes* (Paris, 1917).

AUERBACH, N., *Communities of Women* (Cambridge, Mass., 1978).

BASSETT, J., 'Preserving the White Race: Some Australian Women's Literary Responses to the Great War', *Australian Literary Studies*, 12: 2 (1985), 223–33.

BAYLISS, G., *Bibliographic Guide to the Two World Wars* (London, 1977).

BEAUMAN, N., *A Very Great Profession: The Woman's Novel 1914–39* (London, 1983).

BENSTOCK, S., *Women of the Left Bank: Paris 1900–1940* (London, 1987).

BERGONZI, B., *Heroes' Twilight: A Study of the Literature of the Great War* (London, 1965).

BERKIN, C. R., and LOVETT, C. M. (eds.), *Women, War and Revolution* (New York, 1980).

BERKMAN, J. A., *The Healing Imagination of Olive Schreiner* (Amherst, 1990).

BRAYBON, G., *Women Workers of the First World War: The British Experience* (London, 1981).

BRIDGEWATER, P., *The German Poets of the First World War* (New York, 1988).

BRINKER-GABLER, G. (ed.), *Frauen gegen den Krieg* (Frankfurt-on-Main, 1980).

BUDGE, A., and DIDUR, P., 'Women and War: A Selected Bibliography', *Mosaic*, 23: 3 (1990), 151–73.

BUITENHUIS, P., 'Edith Wharton and the First World War', *American Quarterly*, 18: 2 (1966), 493–505.

—— *The Great War of Words: Literature as Propaganda, 1914–18 and After* (London, 1989).

CADOGAN, M., and CRAIG, P., *Women and Children First: The Fiction of Two World Wars* (London, 1978).

CARDINAL, A., 'Three First World War Plays by Women', in W. Görtschacher and H. Klein (eds.), *Modern War on Stage and Screen/Der moderne Krieg auf der Bühne* (Lampeter, 1997), 305–15.

CECIL, H., and LIDDLE, P. H. (eds.), *Facing Armageddon: The First World War Experienced* (London, 1996).

CONDELL, D., and LIDDIARD, J. (eds.), *Working for Victory? Images of Women in the First World War 1914–1918* (London, 1987).

COOPER, H. M., MUNICH, A. A., and SQUIER, S. M. (eds.), *Arms and the Woman: War, Gender and Literary Representation* (Chapel Hill, NC, and London, 1989).

CRUICKSHANK, J., *Variations on Catastrophe: Some French Responses to the Great War* (Oxford, 1982).

DAKERS, C., *The Countryside at War 1914–1918* (London, 1987).

DAWSON, L. I., and HUNTTING, M. D., *European War Fiction in English: A Bibliography* (Boston, 1921).

DICKINSON, A. T., *American Historical Fiction: A Bibliography* (Metuchen, NJ, 1971), 177–85.

EKSTEINS, M., *Rites of Spring: The Great War and the Birth of the Modern Age* (London, 1990).

ELSHTAIN, J. B., 'On Beautiful Souls, Just Warriors and Feminist Consciousness', *Women's International Forum*, 5 (1982), 341–8.

—— *Woman and War* (Brighton, 1987).

ENSER, A. G. S., *A Subject Bibliography of the First World War: Books in English 1914–1989* (London, 1979, repr. 1991).

FITCH, N. R., *Sylvia Beach and the Lost Generation* (London, 1984).

FREDERICK, P. G., *The Great Adventure: America in the First World War* (Indianapolis, 1961).

FUSSELL, P., *The Great War and Modern Memory* (New York and Oxford, 1975).

GEROULD, K. F., 'The War Novels', *Yale Review*, 8: 1 (1918), 159–81.

GILBERT, S. M., 'Soldier's Heart: Literary Men, Literary Women and the Great War', *Signs: Journal of Women in Culture and Society*, 8 (1983), 422–59.

—— and GUBAR, S., 'Sexchanges', *No Man's Land: The Place of the Woman Writer in the Twentieth Century*, ii (New Haven and London, 1989).

GLOVER, J., and SILKIN, J. (eds.), *The Penguin Book of First World War Prose* (Harmondsworth, 1989).

GOLDMAN, D. (ed.), *Women and World War I* (London, 1993).

—— GLEDHILL, J., and HATTAWAY, J., *Women Writers and the Great War* (New York, 1995).

GREENWALD, M. W., *Women, War and Work: The Impact of World War I on Women Workers in the United States* (Westport, Conn., 1980).

GREICUS, M. S., *Prose Writers of World War I* (London, 1973).

HAGER, P. E., and TAYLOR, D., *The Novels of World War I: An Annotated Bibliography* (New York and London, 1981).

HANLEY, L., *Writing War: Fiction, Gender and Memory* (Amherst, Mass., 1991).

HASTE, C., *Keep the Home Fires Burning: Propaganda of the First World War* (London, 1977).

HIGONNET, M. R., JENSON, J., MICHEL, S., and WEITZ, M. C. (eds.), *Behind the Lines: Gender and the Two World Wars* (New Haven and London, 1987).

ISTAS, H., 'French and German Attitudes to the First World War as reflected in Novels and Memoirs', Ph.D. thesis (Indiana, 1951).

JOHNSTONE, J. K., 'World War I and the Novels of Virginia Woolf', in G. A. Panichas (ed.), *Promise of Greatness* (London, 1968).

JONES, N., and WARD, L. (eds.), *The Forgotten Army: Women's Poetry of the First World War* (Beverley, 1991).

JONES, P. G., *War and the Novelist: Appraising the American War Novel* (Columbia and London, 1976).

KHAN, N., *Women's Poetry of the First World War* (Brighton, 1988).

KLEIN, H. (ed.), *The First World War in Fiction: A Collection of Critical Essays* (Basingstoke, 1976).

LIGHT, A., *Forever England: Femininity, Literature and Conservatism* (London, 1991).

MACDONALD, L., *The Roses of No Man's Land* (London, 1980).

—— *1914–1918: Voices and Images of the Great War* (London, 1988).

MACDONALD, S., HOLDEN, P., and ARDENER, S. (eds.), *Images of Women in Peace and War* (London, 1987).

MARLOW, J. (ed.), *The Virago Book of Women and the Great War* (London, 1998).

MARWICK, A., *The Deluge: British Society and the First World War* (London, 1965).

—— *Women at War 1914–1918* (London, 1977).

MURDOCH, B., ' "Hinter die Kulissen des Krieges sehen": Adrienne Thomas, Evadne Price—E. M. Remarque', *Forum for Modern Language Studies*, 28: 1 (1992), 56–74.

O'BRIEN, C., *Women's Fictional Responses to the First World War: A Comparative Study of Selected Texts by French and German Writers* (New York, 1997).

OLDFIELD, S., *Women Against the Iron Fist: Alternatives to Militarism 1900–1989* (Oxford, 1989).

O'NEILL, W., *Everyone was Brave: The Rise and Fall of Feminism in America* (Chicago, 1969).

OUDITT, S., *Fighting Forces, Writing Women: Identity and Ideology in the First World War* (London, 1994).

PARFITT, G., *Fiction of the First World War: A Study* (London and Boston, 1988).

PETERSON, H. D., *Opponents of War, 1917–1918* (Madison, Wis., 1957).

RAITT, S., and TATE, T. (eds.), *Women's Fiction and the Great War* (Oxford, 1997).

REILLY, C. (ed.), *Scars upon my Heart: Women's Poetry and Verse of the First World War* (London, 1981).

RIEGEL, L., *Guerre et littérature: Le Bouleversement des consciences dans la littérature romanesque inspirée par la Grande Guerre* (Nancy, 1978).

SHOVER, M. J., 'Roles and Images of Women in First World War Propaganda', *Politics and Society*, 5 (1975), 469–86.

STEINSON, B. J., *American Women's Activism in World War I* (New York, 1982).

STROMBERG, R. N., 'The Intellectuals and the Coming of War in 1914', *Journal of European Studies*, 3: 2 (1973), 109–22.

TANNER, J., *Women and War* (London, 1987).

TATE, T. (ed.), *Women, Men, and the Great War: An Anthology of Stories* (Manchester, 1995).

—— 'From Little Willie to Mother: The Tank and the First World War', *Women: A Cultural Review*, 8: 1 (1997), 48–64.

THÉBAUD, F., *La Femme au temps de la guerre de 14* (Paris, 1986).

THOMAS, G., *Life On All Fronts: Women in the First World War* (Cambridge, 1989).

TYLEE, C. M., 'Maleness Run Riot: The Great War and Women's Resistance to Militarism', *Women's Studies International Forum*, 2: 3 (1988), 199–210.

—— *The Great War and Women's Consciousness: Images of Militarism and Womanhood in Women's Writings, 1914–1964* (Basingstoke, 1990).

—— 'The Spectacle of War: Photographs of the Russian Front by Florence Farmborough', *Women: A Cultural Review*, 8: 1 (1997), 65–80.

—— 'Imagining Women at War: Feminist Strategies in Edith Wharton's War Writing', *Tulsa Studies*, 46: 2 (1997), 327–43.

WALL, R., and WINTER, J. (eds.), *The Upheaval of War* (Cambridge, 1988).

WILLIAMS, V., *Women Photographers: The Other Observers, 1900 to the Present* (London, 1986).

WILTSHER, A., *Most Dangerous Women: Feminist Peace Campaigners of the Great War* (London, 1985).

WOOLLACOTT, A., *On their Lives Depend: Munitions Workers in the Great War* (Berkeley, 1994).

WOODS, D., 'French Literature and Peace, 1919–1939', Ph.D. thesis (Illinois, 1957).

Index